SWEDEN
FINLAND
Helsinki
Stockholm
Talinn
ESTONIA
Riga
LATVIA
LITHU-
ANIA
Kaunas
Copenhagen
VOLGA R.
Moscow
U. S. S. R.
DNIEPER R.
DON R.
ODER R.
POLAND
Warsaw
Prague
ZECHOSLOVAKIA
Vienna
Budapest
HUNGARY
ROMANIA
Bucharest
YUGOSLAVIA
Belgrade
BULGARIA
Sofia
ALBANIA
Tirana
GREECE
Athens
TURKEY
Ankara

Mrs. Zubrow
Phila., Pa.

FIRE IN THE ASHES

FIRE

Europe

1 9 5 3

N E W Y O R K

IN THE ASHES

in Mid-Century

Theodore H. White *co-author of "Thunder out of China"*

WILLIAM SLOANE ASSOCIATES *Publishers*

Printed in the United States of America
by H. Wolff, New York

Published simultaneously in the Dominion of Canada
by J. McLeod Limited, Toronto
Library of Congress Catalog Number: 53-10166
Designed by Marshall Lee

To my mother

MARY WINKELLER WHITE

acknowledgment

I cannot possibly thank all the people who have helped in the making of this book, but among them are a few whose aid has been such as to make them almost a part of it. Mere mention of their names cannot in any way repay what they have done, nor does it mark the measure of my gratitude.

Thanks go first to my chief sources of information, fellow members of the Press Corps around the world; most especially Preston Grover of the Associated Press, Robert Kleiman of U. S. News and World Report, and David Schoenbrun of Columbia Broadcasting System. My thanks and warm affection go to Dr. Max Ascoli and the Reporter Magazine for assignments which have been the core of my work, and, more importantly, for the refinement they have brought to my thinking. I should like to thank several devoted officers of public information—among them chiefly Major General Charles T. Lanham, U.S.A., Sidney Fine, Benjamin Bradlee, Donald Mallet, Comte Pierre de Leusse and a few others whose anonymity serves them best.

Anna Wood, who has stuck by me from page one to page five hundred and one, has contributed to this book in more ways than I could list; and Nancy Bean, my wife, has been the indispensable editor and emotional sustenance from beginning to end.

All the mistakes, errors, and misjudgments are my responsibility alone and are in no sense attributable to the wise and gentle people above mentioned who have helped me.

T. H. W.

Le Lavandou, France, July, 1953

contents

PART

1

I

by way of introduction to Europe

The pilot who, all through the night, has flown his plane over the Atlantic, urged on from tail wind to tail wind by the invisible whirlpools of pressure in the air, has known for some time that he is approaching Europe. The green luminous circle that quivers on his radarscope has begun to grow a bud which soon will swell into a finger pointing toward the east. Long before the dark cliffs rise above the sea into the dawn, the pilot knows he is approaching the rim of another world.

As the plane reaches the coast, the rolling sea winds clash with the coastal breezes and the plane is carried imperceptibly higher and higher into the air as if to give it proper eminence to show Europe stretched out before the traveler from the west. From whatever angle of the compass the plane comes in off the Atlantic to home on Europe, the Continent unfurls in the same way. First, the coast, its high, rocky cliffs of chalk and stone falling everywhere to the long, sweeping sea. Next, the slotted indentations in the harsh coast out of which the rivers flow to the sea. Beyond the cliffs and harbors the land smooths out, carpeted by tiny meadows and farms which drape themselves over the low inner ridges. Then, finally, come the valleys and within them the rivers, like guidelines, that lead the voyager up their course to the great cities where history is made. However you approach Western Europe, this pattern repeats itself—the sharp coast, the rivers urging men out to the ocean, the inland fields, the cities. Down these rivers and through these cities, as down the rivers and through the off-shore islands of Britain, passed our fathers to make America.

Today it is only thirteen hours of flight to come home by air from America to Europe, and in our years almost as many men cross the great ocean by wings as travel it by boat. They leave

New York at dusk, arrive in Europe by morning and are abroad in its streets and strange languages, finding in the sound of each city some echo of the memories and myths they have brought with them. Few of them linger in the air to look down on the old Continent from above, to perceive that great natural unity of mute geography upon which, like flesh on a skeleton, the politics of the Continent have been shaped.

For the airman, the rocky heart of Europe is the Alps, a mountain mass higher than the highest mountains of the United States, crowded together in a single rugged outcropping on a patch of land no bigger than Louisiana. From these Alpine highlands the rivers of Europe fall off on every side, clasping people together in nation-families and separating the individual nations one from the other. These rivers clasp together France, Germany, the Low Countries and Italy, the four great communities which, with the people of England, an offshore island, and of Spain, a high bridge to Africa, give Europe its particular character.

From the air, each nation-family falls into a natural pattern.

The rivers that fall to the west–the clockwise spokes of the Rhône, Garonne, Loire and Seine–open an entry into the fairest and most fertile of European lands. This is France, the vast green mass that is the threshold of the old Continent, almost as large as Texas, so prodigiously rich in soil and climate that she alone of the old states can feed herself and spare food for her neighbors. In the days when muscle-power was the only source of energy and food bred muscle, France was automatically the first power of Europe and the world.

The rivers that fall off the northern shoulders of the Alps skein Germany–the Rhine, the Weser, the Elbe, the Oder tumble over Germany's southern highlands, then over its sandy flat northern moorlands to the North Sea. They course through serenely beautiful country all out of harmony with the violent history of its people. But this land is poor. The wealth of Germany, unlike France, lies not in the soil but under it—a wealth that came alive only a century ago when coal replaced food as the great source of energy, and Germany began that expansion which still rests uncontained.

Between the French and German watersheds lies another family of nations, the Low Countries. Here, the mouths of the Meuse, the Scheldt, the Rhine open like slits into deeper Europe to make the Low Countries inevitably portal countries. They are centers of commerce and industry dependent in doom and prosperity on the destiny of their more powerful neighbors.

Italy dangles off the southern edge of the Alpine mass, twice as long as Florida, sun-baked, ridged with bare mountains, overgrown with villages of quiet, honey-colored homes. One great river dominates Italy, the Po, flowing deep and sluggishly across Italy's northern plain, cradling Italy's strength and greatness. But as one flies south farther from the Alps and the Po, the cities thin out, the land grows drier, the shanties more scabrous until, below Rome, Italy is no longer Europe but some Levantine or Oriental appendix overcrowded with people and history. This is Italy's problem—simply that the burden of people and history are too much for her tired resources to support.

Finally, there is England, standing apart from these countries in geography as in spirit. It is an island pushed into commerce as the Low Countries were by its position, and veined like Germany with the energy of coal that made her the first giant of the modern world.

Down below on the ground, Europe dissolves quickly into headlines of clash and confusion, into the dates and frontiers of history books, into the jangling pattern of strife, politics and detail. This, too, is visible from the air. An hour out of Paris, flying toward Frankfurt, the airman's eye picks up beneath the soft green fuzz of winter wheat a crisscross of shaded sterile angles and lines, gray eyelets pocking those endless acres which, to the groundling, seem smooth, rolling and unruffled. These are the trenches of the First World War, hundreds of miles of them signaling each battle and every contested ridge with the clusters of shell craters that will always, for centuries, tell the airman that the soil beneath the wheat has been churned deep here.

But the airman sees other things just as sharply as strife—and these other things are invisible from the ground. He sees, for example, the kinship of civilization that has a hundred common faces. He sees, for example, the glow of electricity. Each city speaks for itself in light all through the night. Thus London, without boasting, proclaims its position as Europe's first capital by the throughways illuminated with green-blue arc lights that make it the most radiant city of the Continent in the dark. The street lights of Brussels are equally brilliant, but they cover a much smaller patch. Paris, by night and from the air, is, in contrast, conspicuously feebler—the main roads of the city and the expressway that circles Paris are bathed in a golden-yellow glow, softer and gentler to look at, but a sign that in Paris the city fathers must pinch their pennies. As one flies south in Europe, vitality falls off and the lights at night mark the degree—Italy is dim, so is Spain, the lights of Belgrade in Yugoslavia are the dimmest of all. Switzerland, however, is a-sparkle with lights as brilliant as the lights of Britain or Belgium. And Germany's Renaissance in the years since the war might have been traced from the darkness of defeat, through the convalescent era of dim strings of bulbs flickering in canyons of ruins, to the blaze of illumination and neon that lights its major cities today.

All these civilizations are kindred civilizations. The airman need only follow the one great east-flowing river of the Alpine watersheds, the Danube, to see how clearly it enters a contrasting civilization. Between Vienna and Budapest the Danube passes through the Iron Curtain to flow off toward Asia. Beyond that point, the lights of the cities are a dim and sickly yellow. Beyond that point, in the dark, the highways are long, pale slashes over the countryside. Only the rarest cone of radiance trails across them from the headlights of the automobiles which, all through the West, flicker and interweave and pass each other as the individual drives his automobile where, when and how he pleases.

The American traveler whom the airplane sets down so abruptly comes to a Europe which is more foreign to Americans today than it has ever been in all our history.

Americans before 1914, indeed, Americans almost down to 1938, knew Europe far better and with more instinctive understanding than they do now. Europe lived as we did, was housed as we were, worked as we did. Americans who crossed the ocean went not from one civilization to another but from one home to a second. Europeans and Americans read the same books, were taught the same sciences, saved, planned and lived on a level of material comfort much the same. Within the past thirty years, however, history has thrust Europeans and Americans both as individual human beings and as great communities further and further apart. There have been the revolutionary changes in the American way of life; the amazing growth of arts, cultures and material comforts; the choking off of the immigration which refreshed the European roots of American life with new arrivals for so long. On the other side of the Atlantic have come the wars, the social pounding and jostling that have followed them, the revolutions, the upheavals, most of all the inflations which have made Europeans today so different not only from Americans but from Europeans of yesterday.

The result has been to make Europe stranger to American understanding than ever before in our linked histories. No amount of individual touring in the greased and gilded grooves of European hotels-museums-festivals-casinos can replace the old understanding of yesterday, any more than the statistics of our economists and the war plans of our generals can substitute for it.

This separation of European and American civilizations happens, moreover, at a moment when America is finally more intimately involved in European affairs than ever before in our national history. This is not a theoretical involvement, either. A quarter of a million American soldiers, drafted from home in time of peace, are sprawled across Europe in bivouac and barrack. One hundred thousand of the finest men in America's army are strung out between the Rhine and the Thuringian ridges, on the alert day and night. They sleep with combat packs beside them, helmets by their pillows, rifles and ammunition stacked in company quarters, their tanks, guns, trucks, ammunition carriers ready to roll on an hour's notice. Each of them knows what he must do —what bridges his company must blow up over what strange foreign streams as he falls back, what roadblocks must go in where, what ridge of what strange German *kreis* will probably hold his foxhole. Even in sleep, his ear is cocked for the sound of the siren that tells him Europe's peace is disturbed and he must fight.

These men are the flesh of America's pledge that Europe's destiny is ours, the sacrament of the great structure of diplomacy that guards the peace of the world. If a Russian soldier moves to cross the border of Norway, if a Bulgarian fires a shot across the borders of Turkey, if an East German platoon raids a county in West Germany, then every one of these men is committed to battle. With them are committed not only those who dwell in Western Europe, but 150,000,000 Americans wherever they sleep, or work, or play between the Atlantic and the Pacific. A diplomatic revolution has twined them all together in indissoluble alliance.

This relationship seems as strange to Europeans as to Americans. Without American aid and support, Europeans five years ago would have starved, and most of their states crumbled to chaos; American involvement was inevitable. But few Europeans have made up their minds whether it is a happy thing or a bad thing, whether it must be permanent or should be transitional. While to Americans the relationship has seemed like an ugly burden, sucking taxes, demanding manpower endlessly, the dirty curse of greatness, most Europeans have seen it differently. They see the relationship as a major triumph of American diplomacy—which it is. They see it as a series of shrewdly calculated American mastermoves which have led them down a road they never chose, at a pace they never set, to an end they can only dimly discern. They are restive under the relationship, weighing at every season and every budget the comfort of American aid against the burden and strain American strategy imposes; they are unsure whether in the long run the one may not outweigh the other.

This restiveness of Europe will be, perhaps, the greatest problem of American diplomacy in the coming year. The victories of the Atlantic Alliance in Europe have been won under American leadership; they have been won, however, not alone but in a partnership to which the Europeans have contributed mightily. The numb, still years in which Europeans docilely submitted to American leadership have passed. Now, with the revival of energy, with their awakening from their postwar torpor, they are irritated and irritable with all the unhappiness of the convalescent. And, like the convalescent, they find most irritating of all their own weakness and helplessness in the strange new world which has changed so much in their absence.

For five hundred years, until the end of the Second World War, the nation-states of Europe enjoyed the luxury of rivalry or partnership, war or alliance, at their convenience. Until the twentieth century was a generation old, these rivalries and partnerships produced the history of the world. Alternating between long stretches of unbroken achievement and bursts of murderous explosion, each more prodigal and each more intense, the quarrels of the Europeans spread wider and wider around the globe until finally the whole world was blown apart every time the people of the Alpine watersheds and their offshore island set to quarreling.

In all this long period, Europe stood for two things in the minds of other men. She stood, first, for the act of creation—she made the music and the letters, generated the ideas and tools that armed the wars, equipped the science, laid down the factories and charged the revolutions that have touched every single man wherever he lives anywhere in the world. She stood, secondly, for power—brute force, the ability to kill efficiently, uncompromisingly, in well-disciplined, cohesive phalanxes of men at whatever point in the world this force might be needed.

Today, all this is over. The wars of this century have wasted and ruined Europe at a time when newer people all around the world were growing in power. Though Europe is still a prodigious body of energy—its 300,000,000 people produce almost as much coal as America, more ships, half as much steel, have twice as many spindles and looms—its primacy is over. Its engineering skills, its learning, its art, its creators are still elevated far above any comparison with the underprivileged half-barbarian civilizations across the seas. But the genius of creation that once belonged to Europe alone is now shared by other, new peoples. Europe stands caught between two descendent civilizations whose ideas, though borrowed from Europe, have come to strange fruit in strange soil. It stands not only between these two strange civilizations, but lives as a ward of one of them, its power of decision purely negative in the clash between the two.

It is not that Europeans seek to recapture again this solitary greatness and power. After the storms and passions of the thirties and the war years, Europe is still panting, hollowed out from exertion and spent emotion. The sound of drums in European ears, the shrill of bugles, the great flaming words with which East and West challenge each other, rather than exciting the Europeans, disturb them. This feeling, indeed, is one of the common qualities that sets Europeans apart from Americans and Russians. The United States and Russia constantly want to act, to do, to make history—and Europe has had a bellyful of history. Europe wants rest, quiet and forgetfulness. But even this it cannot have in the world of today, for it is helpless to calm the world.

This sense of powerlessness is the incubator of all European restlessness—this sense of being swung about by the actions of strange men in distant places. Where, to Americans a generation ago, it seemed grotesque that Americans should die because someone had flung a bomb at a prince in the Balkans, it seems grotesque to Europeans today that they might be summoned to die because an American lad swooped to blitz a power station on the Yalu.

The years since the war in which this sense of helplessness deepened and developed might well be called the Years of the Pause.

For two decades previously, one great man after another had made European history revolve about his comings and goings, his speeches, sins, ambitions. Since the war there has been nothing but the blurred image of faceless men, scurrying from conference to conference wherein nothing ever seemed to be settled. A common grayness suffused all the men elevated to power in postwar Europe—drab prime ministers, fussy foreign ministers, cold little police chiefs, pickle-faced economists with their dry statistics and bulging brief cases have mumbled where once great men thundered. No dramatic encounters have marked this period. Instead of Munich and Godesberg, Teheran and Yalta, the Europeans read each morning of some new conference in an interminable session of negotiations in which nothing ever changed within the drone. The dog races, the price of butter, the new tractor, the problem of where to go on vacation have all been more interesting and urgent to Europeans than what came out of the councils of state.

Thus it is that a long parade of nameless people wander through my memories of this period, people who somehow ring a truer echo of life in Europe out of trivia than any of the statesmen to whose speeches I have listened and whose deliberations I have reported.

I remember a midsummer afternoon at a café on Omaha beach when the miracle of D day was seven years past. Out from the shore about a mile and a half were the slashed and broken chunks of concrete breakwater, their gray stone mottled with green sea moss; half a dozen sunken ships; some antiaircraft guns still in place on the breakwater, rusting like broken pipestems in a junk yard. On the soft red sand of the beach a dozen-odd landing craft still remained, thrown high up by the tide, full of sand, weeds and faded poppies. It was lunchtime and the beach was utterly deserted, for even the fifteen workmen dismantling the wreckage for scrap had left. The owner of the café complained to me. She had invested all her savings in opening this café at Omaha beach because she was sure that neither Americans nor Frenchmen would ever forget D day and would come every summer to visit the beach and hence her café. But no one had come, no one, she said. She could not understand it, no one wanted to remember.

Two middle-aged ladies were sitting at the table behind me that day, the only other customers of the meal. They had come, they said, because when the Americans liberated Paris, a young American lieutenant had slept in their house. He had brought coffee, soap, food, butter when all Paris hungered at the mention of them. When he had moved off with his company they had asked him what they could do to repay him. He said there was nothing they could do for him, but if, someday, they ever got a chance to visit Omaha beach and the cemetery that was going to be built there, would they put some flowers on the graves of a few friends he had left behind. They said they would, and so, seven years later, they took a bus from Paris to put flowers on American graves, not because they remembered history and the Liberation, but because they remembered coffee, food and human kindness.

I remember one evening during the French elections of 1951 when I went to watch the meetings in the Third Sector of Paris, the grisly slums of Belleville and Montmartre where the Communists have ruled unchallenged since the war. I dropped in at a meeting of the Socialists, who, I had heard, were the stiffest opposition to the Communists in the sector. Their speaker was a stout, bald-headed little man, whose stiff cuffs, shiny cuff links, crisp bow tie and gleaming pate all glistened in the yellow lights of the school auditorium where the meeting was held. He launched into his speech with no ringing invocation of liberty or denunciation of communism. Instead, clearing his throat, he summoned his audience to remember that in the first government of Liberation, when prostitution was outlawed in Paris, he had been the only member of the Cabinet (he repeated the phrase several times before plunging to his climax) to vote against the outlawing of the fancy ladies. And now, he went on, look at what had happened—since the abolition of prostitution in legal houses, the whores had filtered into the streets to ply their trade unregulated, embarrassing all the neighborhood mothers who were trying to raise decent families. He made his point well, and the women who sat sternly in their faded housedresses nodded their approval. They could understand prostitution better than communism, and the speaker squeaked through to a seat in the National Assembly.

There are others, too many to list, who recur in memory, all of them trying to ignore or thrust out of mind the problems of an anguished world. There was the British physicist who had worked on the atomic bomb during the war, and who, after the war, in revulsion, had taken a post in a British school teaching mathematics to boys. His hobby was cybernetics, and he said to me, "Oh, I know you Americans are way ahead of us in cybernetics, but I've built a calculating machine that can do something yours won't do. When I feed data into our machine that it can't handle, it beeps a musical note. And we've learned how to feed data into our machine so that when things get really tough it plays 'God Save the King.' "

This feeling of being apart from politics, of standing outside of decision, has been general all over Europe, in every country. I remember going one evening with curiosity to a theater in Düsseldorf to see a hall of Germans watch *All Quiet on the Western Front;* Hitler had never let them see the picture fresh when it first came out. The audience sat silent all through the film until the company of troops on the screen sprawled resting under a tree after their bleeding at the front, and Kropp, the little corporal, suggested that the way to run a war was to sell tickets to a huge stadium in which everyone could watch the generals, the officers, the cabinet ministers and the statesmen who had made the war, fight it out in person. At this the audience broke into a storm of laughter and applause, and then was moodily silent as the film went back to the war itself.

And yet though Europeans try and have been trying for eight years to thrust out yesterday's memories and tomorrow's problems, they cannot. Fragments of yesterday's passion and sorrow come back to push and pull and draw them back to today's decisions. There is, for example, one of the great chiefs of the French Resistance who survived the Occupation to serve eminently and successfully in a key post of France's postwar government. From his Cabinet seat, he secretly helped the Zionists smuggle arms through France to Israel in the war between the Israelis and the Arabs. The man was a devout Catholic and, when the story became known to several people in Paris, a friend asked him why he ran such political risks. "I'll tell you," said the Cabinet Minister, "it goes back to the Resistance against the Germans. I came into Paris for instructions one day and my net gave me the address of a dirty little hotel on Montmartre where I could make my rendezvous safely. The clerk booked me in and then took me upstairs to a room with two beds. One was for me. In the other an old Jew was trying to go to sleep. I had just fallen asleep when the clerk rushed in and whispered to me. 'Pull the blanket over your head and pretend you're sleeping. The Gestapo are raiding here tonight, but don't worry, they're not after you, they're just raiding for Jews.' Then the Germans came into the room and dragged the old man from the bed. He screamed and howled; he clutched the sheets, the bedstead, the chairs. As they dragged him out, he was struggling, and he must have seen my leg sticking out from under the blanket. He grabbed it, trying to hold himself against the Germans. And I remember reaching with my other leg and pushing down on his hand to break his grip. I can't forget pushing that hand away from me; I'll never forget. I suppose that's why I let the Israelis bring arms through France."

The Years of the Pause are now ending. It is obvious that new leadership in both America and Russia is now wrenching the whole course of world affairs into new patterns and perspectives. What is less obvious is that in this wrenching process Europe, forgotten through the postwar years as a factor in power, must contribute as greatly as either of the two new titans. Having now recovered from their wounds of war, and having seen this recovery reach a plateau and stagnate, the Europeans, however much they wish to drowse and be quiet, are being forced once more, against their will, to consider great decisions.

Two events within Europe in these coming years rival events in America and Russia in their dimensions. Both these events, paradoxically, are events that were conceived, launched and nursed to their present pregnant power by American diplomacy. In the days when America's whim was Europe's imperative these twin movements seemed no more than the idle fancy of America's proconsuls in Europe. But now, rooted deep in European life, they have passed beyond the control of American diplomacy and challenge each other to see which shall shape the future of the old Continent.

These two events are the Birth of Europe and the Renaissance of Germany. Intertwined and locked together since their first stirring in conception, they move today in naked rivalry, each racing the other to realization; for whichever triumphs first will make of the other its servant.

The desire of Europe to be Europe, to become a union, is a vision that has haunted generals and priests, merchants and wanderers for all the hundreds of years since Rome ruled Europe and made it one. It is a vision of such grandeur and scope, and we have come so close and so swiftly to realizing it in the past few years, that it is impossible in our generation to tell what it may eventually mean for mankind. The vision has always been there; what has fleshed it out in the past few years has been the coming together of two great forces in the torn and tattered states of Western Europe. The first of these forces has been fear—sheer, brute, quivering fear of the Russian state which might at any moment strike and with its juggernaut weight crush any of the old West European states standing alone. This fear alone would not have been enough, even as the age-old idealism of the visionaries had never been enough, had it not been for the second force: American pressure. American diplomacy has insisted, year-in and year-out, in every capital of Europe from Oslo to Rome that the dream of union must clothe itself with flesh and institutions *now;* American diplomacy supplied the plastic of wealth and promise of arms to bind the European states together. It has been argued that American pressure on Europeans to unite has been too primitive, too impatient, too mechanical, too unfeeling in the single-minded insistence with which it has tried to force age-old enemies to forget their feuds and become brothers. It may well be that historians will read American pressure as too unrelenting and too swift, and will make it responsible if the dream of European Union fails. But there is no doubt that without American diplomatic pressure and insistence this dream would still be a paper nothing or the stuff of student debating contests. Instead, it is already a half-reality. It is a power which can already tax, dispose, order, create and regulate the greatest industries of Western Europe over and above any national frontier of law. Six nations have already signed a compact which may, tomorrow, clothe the men of half a dozen different states in one uniform, under one flag, and send them out to die under one command. And the elected political delegates of these six states have already drafted the constitution of a new community, called simply "Europe," in which supreme powers will be taken from the old national parliaments and lodged in one great new suprasovereign, subordinate to an assembly elected by all the people of Europe.

The Renaissance of Germany is something as profound and powerful in its movement of the coming years as the Birth of Europe. By the time this book is published, Germany will have enjoyed her first free, national elections in twenty years. Its government will enter the councils of Europe not as the object of other people's will, but as a proud and independent nation with a voice of its own. Here, too, in the Renaissance of Germany as in the Birth of Europe, the United States was the moving force. It was the United States that summoned Germany back to greatness, that fed and clothed her, equipped her with government and leadership, struck the chains from her will.

Were it not for the Germans, Western Europe would already be united—the fear of Russia, the pressure of America, the questing idealism of both religion and common sense would almost certainly, by now, have brought the scattered states of Europe together in an effort to regain their standing in the world. But the West Europeans looking east toward the Communist world see not only Russia, but Germany too. Germany is an unknown quantity. For fifty years this continent has revolved around the desperate urge of the Germans to make their neighbors conform to Germany's nightmare vision of what was right and just. More bitter than ever, half-healed from wounds they brought on themselves, the Germans are today being summoned to enter a new community in which, by the logic of power, they must be the prime movers. Which way will they move? What will they do with their new and ever-growing power? How deep is the tissue of decency in the new German Republic? How much vitality is left to the terrifying German ideas which have brought the Continent to its present broken and enfeebled state? Caught between the power giants of East and West, seeking to regain some grip over their own destiny, the European statesmen know that the new Europe, in order to become a power giant of rival size, must include the resources and energy of a freely consenting Germany. Germany, they know, cannot be left out of either the Atlantic Community or European Union, for to leave Germany entirely independent and free to her own devices is to invite her again to play East against West to inevitable disaster. Yet they know that if the Germans are swept again by one of those sea-tides of emotion which so violently seize them, then the new Union of Europe is useless; better it were that it had never been born.

Perhaps the single most important question of the new Europe is thus what the Germans have learned from their own history as they are invited to a new loyalty, and the future of Europe depends on whether the Germans choose to accept the new world struggling to be born or whether they choose to wreck it.

The approach of these new movements cuts the years that have passed from the years that come as sharply as if a page were turned and a new chapter opened. It is not that these movements and growths have been swelling in a vacuum. Through all these years the morning newspapers of the Europeans have dutifully recorded each dry morsel of negotiation and event in studious detail. But the Europeans, preoccupied with the daily tasks of feeding their families, sheltering themselves, putting together the roads, factories and bridges destroyed by war, have not been listening. The coming years are the years in which they must decide where they stand and what they are to do about the new world in which they live.

The decisions of the Europeans about these movements and the fate of these new movements affect not only their own lives but the lives of everyone else in the world, Americans most of all. Even in its present weakness, Europe speaks for enormous power, the power that hangs as a balance between the strength of America and Russia. With Europe's 300,000,000 people and their industries added in friendship, the American perspective is one of expansion. With Europe subtracted or hostile, the American perspective is one of contraction in a spiral of gloomy isolation.

Upon Europe's decision in the next few years rests the relationship of the Western world to the Russians. It is, after all, the Europeans, not the Americans, who live next to that huge Byzantine state which combines the most modern techniques with the oldest form of despotism. As if by instinct, without deep thought, Europe has rejected in every state of the West the gospel of communism without finding any other gospel to match it in vitality. Until now, Europe has given a brave "No" to the Russians, yet it is unsatisfied with the answer, for America has failed to draw from it an equally steadfast "Yes."

The decision of Europe will determine not only the clash of the West with communism, but also the clash of the West with the boiling civilizations of Asia and Africa. For Europe was not only the creator and power of the past five centuries. It was the hinge upon which the world turned. It was the pivot that linked the advanced civilizations of the Atlantic—America as well as its own member states—to the different civilizations of India, of the Orient, of Africa, of Southeast Asia. With the hinge rusty and broken, unable to bear the weight of these growing civilizations, they creak and grate one upon the other and upon ourselves.

There is no easy title for the period now beginning. It is altogether natural, however, that there should be none. The names of great centuries and epochs in human history are always given to them by their remote descendants. Few men realized while they lived it that the age of Augustus was the high point in a thousand years of history. When XX Legio Valeria Victrix left Britain in A.D. 403, none of its men realized that the golden eagles of Rome would never return to the island, or that they were part of the decline and fall of the Roman Empire. Certainly no Renaissance man knew he was living in a century that other men would call the "rebirth," just as his great-great-great-grandfather had no knowledge that he was part of the Middle Ages. Thus we do not know what to call our time, what label to give the remarkable and extraordinary events that we not only witness but live.

This book is written in the belief that whatever name is given to our age, the choice will be shaped by the events that take place or fail to take place in Europe in the next few years. It is a book, therefore, about many things:

—about the struggle of America and Russia for the loyalty of the hearts and the riches of the lands in all the countries of Europe.

—about what has been happening in the years between Germany's defeat and resurgence, and how that resurgence has come about.

—about Europe between the departure of the American troops in victory and their return five years later in peril, how we Americans have become involved and what we have won.

—about the struggle of the Europeans to refresh their enterprise and skills in the ebb tides of a contracting world that threatens to leave them stranded and dying far from free water.

But also, more than anything else, it is about Europeans and how they live today, what bothers them and preys on them in these years as they try to reach decisions that will affect us all.

11

the end of an alliance

Long before the war in Europe ended in May of 1945, it was clear there would be no peace.

The quarrels of the victors had begun almost as soon as it was obvious they would be victorious. To be sure, they had bickered all through the war, but that quarreling had been normal to any military coalition; it had blistered over supplies, deliveries, requirements, timings and where, how and when the West and Russia would apply the crippling blows to the Germans. The Allies had never diverged over ultimate goals—the destruction of the Fascist Powers.

By early 1945, however, as Germany visibly began to crumble under the combined weight of her enemies, it became obvious that the conquering alliance was showing strains and fissures that ran deeper than the military issues of the war itself. At first glance the strains seemed curiously similar to those that had split the victorious alliance of the First German War—they seemed to revolve fundamentally around the distribution of spoils. And again, as after the First World War, any objective approach to the discussion of spoils was complicated by the almost adolescent embarrassment of the United States, one of the three senior partners in victory, to discuss spoils as spoils.

The rules of American politics, cloyed with the sticky and persistent idealism which is at once America's strength and weakness, made it impossible to approach the subject as the two other grand partners, Britain and Russia, would have preferred. The Britons and the Russians had, indeed, made a modest attempt to accommodate each other as early as the fall of 1944 in the old-fashioned way. When Mr. Churchill and Mr. Eden had journeyed to Moscow in autumn of that year, they had found Messrs. Stalin and

Molotov in an uncommonly jovial mood. One night, late after dinner in the Kremlin, as the cups went around, a rare mood of hilarity settled over the great statesmen and their advisors. Juggling the map of Europe about, Stalin declared that Russia's interest in Rumania was at least "ninety per cent." To which Mr Churchill replied that, if so, Britain's interest in Greece was "one hundred per cent." Stalin then countered by saying that if Russia reduced her interest in Rumania to seventy-five per cent, it would be only fair if Britain reduced her interest in Greece to eighty per cent. The evening closed, as one Briton present said, on a note of good feeling and a sense of clean fun; it was not until the British delegation was homeward bound in flight that several of its members began to wonder whether the Russians had really been serious about the conversation.

Whether or not the Russians were serious, both Britain and Russia acted as if they had been—Rumania was to be for Russia and Greece for England. What upset the arrangement was the Americans. When Mr. Vyshinsky journeyed down to Bucharest the following February to take possession of the prize deeded to Russia in Moscow, and did so with all the ruthlessness and hypocrisy of which he is such a master, the Americans let it be clearly known, first, that it was naive to make any bargain behind America's back and, secondly, that Americans did not like such bargains.

This obscure incident must, almost certainly, have been one of the initial shocks to Russian diplomacy, if Russian policy in the outer world can be called diplomacy. Here, in their eyes, must have been undoubtedly the substance of a cold and logical deal. The Red Army had conquered Rumania, had paid for it with thousands of lives, was operating a massive military supply system across its communications net in the assault on Germany and had, furthermore, purchased a free hand there, by offering the Western Powers a free hand in an area similarly important to them. What must have been baffling were the grounds on which the United States refused to consider such a deal. The American attitude was based not on a bargaining position but on something else. The Americans seemed to object not so much to the deal itself as to the behavior of the Russians in Rumania, to what the Russians were doing inside Rumania. And their objections came wrapped with strange words like "liberty," "democracy," "freely chosen governments."

This strangulation of bargaining by words was to be the particular condition that set apart the peacemaking after World War II from any other settlement of modern times. Ultimately, this condition multiplied the titanic clash of real interests between the two partners into insolubility. Rumania itself was only the first detail in the clash, leaving little more residue than an initial abrasion of mutual trust which might be abraided that much more easily in the events that were to follow so swiftly. This trivial impasse might have been dismissed as a bit of Anglo-Russian clumsiness compounded by philology; what made it so grotesque was that the philology was more than the words. It was the echo of two systems, two bodies of ideas which, with the best will in the world, could not be measured in common terms. At Versailles, a generation earlier, the clash of the victors could have been described in words which all of them would have agreed as defining the substance, if not the justice, of the argument. It was impossible to find such words in 1945.

The Conference of Yalta, in February of that historic year, at which for the last time the great war masters met in person, was scarred with this grating of bargain and meaning. Where the great men could agree, they agreed on finite, measurable things: the Curzon line that separated Russia from Poland was a line on a map; the deal on Russia's strength in the United Nations could be pinned down in an agreed number of seats; the deal on the Pacific War could be pinned down with a fixed date for Russia's entry and a fixed, all-too-clear price in Manchurian bases.

But the other problems that were to cause such bitter dispute in the months to come were all left dangling in the air, suspended in ambiguities, because no words could bridge them. Poland was to be "reorganized" on a "democratic" basis with the "inclusion" of "democratic" leaders from Poland itself and from Poles abroad. No one defined "reorganized," "democratic," "inclusion." The key words for Germany were "disarmament," "demilitarization," "decentralization." No one could later agree what the words meant. Russia and the United States agreed that reparations should be paid, but neither could agree on how much or what kind, so the figure of twenty billion dollars—itself an abstraction—was taken as a "basis" of negotiation.

The great men had no sooner reached their capitals than the bargains of Yalta began to come unstuck, not only privately in the bitter cables of the leaders themselves, but loudly, publicly, and to the anger and excitement of millions of ordinary people. Poland was the first of the bargains to dissolve; it dissolved precisely over the definition of words and the meaning of the bargain of Yalta; within four months of the departure of the conferees, the new President of the United States had summoned Harry Hopkins from his deathbed, and sent him all the way across the world to try to explain, if possible, to Stalin in person exactly what the United States had meant in the Polish bargain.

Poland more than any other issue of dispute struck the tone of intercourse that was to paralyze understanding. The United States had finally, reluctantly, acquiesced in abandoning Rumania to the untender mercies of the Red Army because Rumania had been a willing partner in Nazi adventures and had enthusiastically helped ravage the Soviet Union. But Poland was something else. It was to preserve Polish independence that the West had originally gone to war, and the Poles had fought gallantly side by side with the Allies on every front. For six long sessions in the sanctums of the Kremlin, each of them stretching on to midnight or beyond, Stalin and Hopkins wrestled with each other. Poland, said Stalin, must be "friendly," "strong" and "democratic" because twice in one generation Poland had been the gate through which the Germans had marched to ravage Russian soil. Hopkins agreed on that. But when Hopkins and Stalin tried to pursue the agreement to understanding, their lips made words but no meaning came forth.

At their second session Stalin tried to explain what Russia meant by the Yalta agreement to "reorganize" Poland. This meant, said he, that the committee of Communist Poles the Red Army had formed at Lublin and brought along with it to help administer the Poland they were fighting in would be retained as the Polish government. It needed only to be molded or pulled about a bit by the inclusion of a few other Poles taken from the list submitted by Great Britain and the United States—perhaps four or five. Molotov, a man more experienced in dealing with the West, whispered in Stalin's ear and Stalin corrected himself to a more precise measurement—"four, not five," out of eighteen or twenty Cabinet members.

At their fourth meeting Hopkins tried to press home what was truly bothering the American people and to explain what "democratic" meant to Americans—a free press open to all parties, parties open to all people, all people entitled to vote, to speak freely, no man subject to arrest or imprisonment without trial. This was what America meant when she said she wanted a "democratic" Poland. Stalin nodded a yes, yes to that but obviously could not get the point, for, at the following session, Hopkins tried to boil the dispute down to a precise test of clarity. Fourteen Poles had been arrested without trial, said Hopkins, on the charge that they possessed illegal radio sets; they had been detained and had disappeared; this had enraged Americans; the United States wanted them released. Here at last was something both could understand and talk about, and understanding Hopkins at last, Stalin said, "No." Stalin did not expand on his "No," but it was not necessary. His Yalta bargain had given him Poland to be made "friendly" to the Soviet Union; this meant control; control meant police. Fourteen individual Poles were not an abstraction, they were of the essence in his political thinking. As it happened, these individual lives were of the essence in American thinking too.

Such clashes—whether over matters of deep substance like the disposition of Poland and Rumania, or the release and care of American prisoners of war liberated in Eastern Europe—had become commonplace between the Allies by the end of the war and had generated a bitterness that covered almost every point of their relations. But this bitterness, unavoidable in the clash of wills and the confusion of understanding, was amplified even further by the atavism of Russian suspicion so abnormally developed by the Communist state.

A morbid, almost hysterical suspicion of Western intent ran from top to bottom of the Soviet world. It had begun while Roosevelt was still alive. Roosevelt had returned from Yalta no more than a month when he received a cable from Stalin, signed personally, accusing him of bald treachery. The American Embassy in Moscow had informed Stalin that our secret service agents in Switzerland had learned that Field Marshal Kesselring, the German commander in Northern Italy, was willing to lay down his arms to the Allies on that front. The Soviets were invited to take part in negotiations with the Germans at a session to be arranged in Italy after preliminary secret contact with the enemy in Switzerland. Stalin reacted as if jabbed by a needle. He wired Roosevelt claiming that the English and Americans had already begun negotiating with Kesselring, had promised Germany easy peace terms, had permitted the Germans to transfer three divisions from the Italian to the Russian front—all of which was untrue. Roosevelt replied with a stiff and nasty note which cooled the Soviet dictator off. But the interchange was a laboratory specimen of Soviet reaction—to begin with a fact, rooted in truth, and then to coat the fact so thickly with lies as to infuriate anyone not bred in Soviet mythology.

Suspicion in the Soviet state is self-generating and self-accelerating. No one knows precisely by what mechanism the Soviet press is guided at home. That it is rigidly controlled is, of course, one of the common facts of knowledge; but how much it, in turn, controls the thinking of the men who control it no one can measure. A whisper of suspicion from on high, a gout of irritation seeping out of the Politburo to the Press Control must, in the Soviet world, be amplified, exaggerated and repeated by thousands of skilful and ambitious men until it reaches an echo that drums, deafens and freezes the thinking of the very men who started it. Already before the Yalta Conference, the American Embassy in Moscow had begun to report the alarming ugliness of suspicion of the Russian press. By the end of the war, six months later, Russians from end to end of the intercontinental war-fronts were soaked in this suspicion.

I remember years after the war telling an American Army officer of how swiftly and suddenly the tide of suspicion had come upon us in our posts in Asia. In the spring of 1945 I had been stationed in Chungking, and a group of friends—an American, a Chinese, a Briton, a Frenchman, a Russian—had taken to lunching together regularly once a week to exchange views. In the closing months of the war, our luncheons had been very gay with wine in celebration of the victories whose salvos came rumbling in from Europe. Our luncheon the week before Germany collapsed was the gayest of all until suddenly Fedorenko, the Russian, deep in his cups, burst into a tirade. "Gold! Gold!" he yelled from his corner of the table. "Gold! What do you Americans find in Germany? Gold! Gold! The Germans surrender to you and they leave you their gold but what do we find? War! They surrender to one side and they fight on the other. We know what you're trying to do, but it won't succeed, no one can take our victory from us." The incident shocked us, for Fedorenko was one of the friendliest officers of the Russian Embassy, a brilliant man with a flawless knowledge of Chinese and Oriental affairs, and we had always, hitherto, treated him as one of us.

When I told this story years later to my army friend who had finished his war all the way across the globe leading an American regiment to junction with the Russians along the Elbe, he said it had been the same way in Germany. After his troops had come to the river, my friend crossed to pay a courtesy call on the Russian divisional commander opposite him, a bull-necked, barrel-chested man, and had been invited to lunch at the Russian headquarters. There the Russian commander had launched his tirade: "Why are you digging in against us?" he snarled. "We know what you're doing, where you're putting your artillery and tanks. Why? Why are you preparing for war? We will not be frightened. We are not afraid." Ironically, from the window of the room, the American officer could look out and see Russian troops entrenching with pick and shovel on the river bank. He tried to explain that not even Dwight D. Eisenhower could persuade an American GI to pick up a trenching tool and dig in during that week of victory. But it was useless, the Russian was not convinced.

The real story of postwar Europe begins, thus, in this atmosphere of suspicion and confusion, at the Conference of Potsdam where, for the first time, the chiefs of state approached the root problem of Europe. What to do about Germany? Germany lay stretched all about them in a state of chaos that it had not known since the end of the Thirty Years' War three centuries before. Seventy million people were being pressed and pushed back into the confines of a country that had been shorn of almost twenty-five per cent of its territory and had seen the rest ravaged. The best of its manpower was in prison camps. Its cities were rubble heaps. Its bridges were broken, its roads torn, and the victims of the Germans were trudging homeward across these roads taking their human revenge as they went. Victorious troops were herding hundreds of thousands of dusty Wehrmacht veterans into barbed wire rings, while the generals and statesmen were staking out military zones.

Nothing had been settled before Potsdam—no decision had been taken on how to dismember or how to centralize Germany in order best to control it; no frontiers had been set for it; no form of government considered; no measures of punishment settled. The chiefs of state approached the great prize gingerly for none knew exactly what he wanted. They approved a control mechanism of four senior generals, one from each conqueror, to administer Germany while they made up their minds. And they marked out more clearly the zones roughly agreed on at Yalta. Where they sensed each other's deeper resistance, they retreated once again to bargains rendered meaningless by words, agreements carefully couched in ambiguous reservations that could be read either way in any translation. Thus the Russians were pleased that the borders of Germany and Poland were recognized as somewhere on the line of the Oder-Neisse Rivers, while the West carefully noted that there was to be no final settlement of the frontiers until the peace conference. The Russians noted that the accords guaranteed them ten billion dollars' worth of reparations, but the West noted that this was not to be pumped out of German production until Germany could support itself again. It was obvious that Germany was to be the subject of long and complicated negotiations. The heads of state were in a great hurry to get home—Stalin to deal with the reconstruction and convalescence of his sorely wounded country, Mr. Attlee to launch the cautious social revolution for which a generation of British Socialists had waited, Mr. Truman to the termination of the war against Japan. So, after fifteen days of almost fruitless talk, the conferees accepted the ingenious suggestion of the American Secretary of State that a Council of Foreign Ministers be set up to deal regularly with the recurring problems of a new world at other times and other places and home they all went.

It is difficult now, before all the pertinent documents and memoirs are publicly available, to judge the importance of the blunders of each of the powers from Potsdam on. The contemporary American citizen, who can be compelled to accept the huge obligations of power only by being kept in a constant state of nerves, sees the events of the postwar world as a long chain of blunders in American diplomacy. The future historian will probably record that the first, the outstanding, the overwhelmingly important blunders were made by the Russians. And that American diplomacy in Europe, despite some initial confusion and several minor fluffs, capitalized on these blunders, outwitted the Russians and won.

The initial Russian blunder began at Potsdam. There, without committing the Western Powers to any binding agreement on Germany, the Russians set out on a course of action which if it were emulated by the Western Powers, as it was certain to be, would give Russia the shabby end of the bargain. The real weight of Germany—the energy, drive, industrial skills and overwhelming portion of its peoples and resources—was as securely in the grip of Western military power as were the puppet lands of Eastern Europe in the grip of the Red Army. To seal the Western Powers out of Eastern Europe and Eastern Germany could only, inevitably, provoke the Western Powers to seal the Russians out of Western Germany, which was the real prize. In effect, the Russians thrust into the hands of the West that which they sought most to gain.

This blunder of real decision was multiplied by a blunder of manners. Exhausted by their own victory, unprepared to use force against their recent allies, the Russians persisted in a nastiness of tone and temper which was worse than useless if it was not to be backed by force. Unable to wring any major concession from the Allies in the next twelve months, they contented themselves with pinprick annoyances and suspicions on all the thoroughly minor matters which were in negotiation with the Allies. Slowly and aggravatingly, in conference after conference, at every fringe of contact with the West, the Russians rubbed the West raw, exhausting its patience and willingness to concede on each minor point of dispute, before ever approaching the main settlement on Germany where the West held every card in the deck except the trump of Berlin.

Russian tactics were as blundering as their manners. Though

their strategy has remained transparently simple throughout the postwar years—to wit, to split the Western Alliance—their tactics seemed fashioned for directly contrary ends. Their initial preoccupation with the exclusion of France from any say in the settlement of Europe failed, and failing, thrust the French into almost total diplomatic dependence on the United States. Their initial attempt to divide Britain and the United States failed by the grossest miscalculation. Imputing to the new Labour government all the mythological imperial sins of the Tory diplomacy of Mr. Churchill, they thrust it, too, into union with America in the first formative months, when its diplomacy might have entertained compromise. Having bullied the French and the British into closest partnership with America, they then frightened all other nations of the West into the association that later became the North Atlantic Treaty Organization. Instead of dividing the West, they unified it, creating by their own actions that which they feared most.

To judge what the Russians gained and lost in Europe in the first postwar year, one must pluck the long list of Russian demands out of the wild confusion of Russian propaganda. While Russian propaganda flailed away with rhetorical tom-toms, Russian demands were advanced in terms of hard things.

They wanted, first of all, a specific zone of influence on their borders and a share in the Mediterranean. They asked for control of the Dardanelles, they demanded control of Tripolitania, control of Eritrea; they requested that Turkey detach several vital slivers of her territory from her flag and give them to the Soviet. They wished to make Yugoslavia their Mediterranean bastion and demanded that the city of Trieste and the headlands of the Adriatic be given to Tito, as well as Austrian Carinthia. They wanted, in another area, most quietly but most insistently, a share in the oil of the Middle East and enough control in Northern Persia and around the Caspian to pad the security of their own Baku oil fields. They wanted, in Germany, huge reparations and physical control in the Ruhr. On a global scale, they wanted a large loan from the United States and a share in the control of Japan.

The Western victory stands out most clearly in the following summary of the bargaining: the Russians got neither the Dardanelles, nor Turkish territory, nor Middle Eastern oil, nor a buffer on the Caspian, nor Tripolitania, nor Eritrea, nor Trieste, nor Carinthia, nor West German reparations, nor the Ruhr, nor an American loan, nor a share in Japan. What they got, of the specific demands they advanced and the West could offer was: one-third of the captured German Navy, one hundred million dollars' worth of reparations from Italy, three votes and the right of veto in the United Nations.

The unhappy alliance of Potsdam, its members still bound in solemn oaths and contracts to each other, stumbled through the first year and a half of peace in a series of four great meetings of the Council of Foreign Ministers. These conferences had, as their rough outline, a general agreement that the lesser spoils and conquests of their common victory must be settled and organized before they could approach the central problem of Germany. They confirmed a settlement that might have been predicted by a neophyte and might have been closed in a week. Wherever the Red Armies stood, the Russians were permitted to organize and manipulate governments to their own taste; wherever the West had stationed its forces, it was allowed to organize and manipulate governments to its taste. The vast tier of East European states thus fell to Russia as spoils of war. American and Western influence was excluded from them as completely as Russian influence was excluded from Japan. By the end of 1946, the pattern of Europe as it exists today was sealed in an interlocking set of treaties —except for Germany and its appendage, Austria.

The victorious alliance had been late in coming to grips with the German problem, the intractable, irreducible centerpiece of European politics. Not until the summer of 1946, a year after Germany's defeat, did it become clear how violently divergent were their attitudes to the beaten enemy. The scene was Paris, the setting the Third Conference of Foreign Ministers, convened to discuss the peace treaties with the lesser enemies.

Mr. Molotov opened the debate with a carefully publicized statement in Paris on July 11, directed primarily at German public opinion but obliquely designed to bring the West to serious bargaining. Adopting an unusually conciliatory tone, Mr. Molotov declared that the Soviet Union did not want to destroy Germany but to make it work. Mr. Molotov called on everyone to admit that the levels of German industry (which the Soviets had previously insisted on restraining at impossibly low levels) were too restrictive and must be raised. He attacked those who wished to raze the Ruhr and insisted it be fostered and encouraged to work in peace. Then he got down to business. What he wanted was a thoroughly centralized Germany, rigidly controlled by the Four Power Commission set up at Potsdam, in which the Russians would sit with the right of veto. For the Ruhr, Germany's mighty industrial center, Mr. Molotov wanted an even stricter system of supervision to pump out reparations goods. Eventually, a German government would grow under this Four Power tutelage, and if it proved trustworthy, a peace treaty would be made in a number of years.

A few nights later, in private after-dinner conversation at the Russian Embassy with Mr. James Byrnes, the American Secretary of State, Molotov made things even clearer over a few drinks. All he wanted, said Mr. Molotov, was a share in the Ruhr and a guarantee of delivery on the ten billion dollars of reparations promised Russia. Later, much later, the Russians were to be willing to settle for much less. But then it was to be too late.

It took eight weeks for an official American reaction to develop to Molotov's position. When it came, it was delivered not in Paris at the forum of foreign ministers, but in Germany, directly to the German people, and was one of the turning points of postwar history. This was the famous Stuttgart speech of Mr. Byrnes. The flashy, yellow-kerchiefed troops of the American constabulary lined the streets at Stuttgart station when Byrnes arrived, and armored cars stood guard at every intersection. In the opera house of the town, a handful of the highest German dignitaries of the humiliated country sat tremblingly tense in the front rows when he rose to speak.

Mr. Byrnes' speech was, in tone, more minatory and less conciliatory to the Germans than Mr. Molotov's; it contained a more vivid evocation of the war just past, the sins of the Germans, the determination of the Americans never to let such crimes happen again, and their willingness to persist in sacrifice to preserve peace and victory. But, proceeded Mr. Byrnes, America too wanted the swiftest centralization of German economic life and government; she too was against any further reduction in the German standard of living. Moreover, America was adamantly set against any German reparations to be paid out of Germany's production so long as German production could not support Germans; and finally, America did not accept the Oder-Neisse line in the East as the final frontier amputating Silesia from the body of German politics.

The whole inner meaning of the Stuttgart speech was, however, summed up in one of its opening phrases: "It is not in the interest of the German people," said Mr. Byrnes, "or in the interest of world peace that Germany should become a pawn or partner in a military struggle for power between the East and the West." In that uncertain way history has of opening every great chapter with a negative, Mr. Byrnes had introduced the next chapter. Every intelligent German in the audience understood Mr. Byrnes instinctively. The speech was an invitation to every German to take precisely the attitude deplored, to become either pawn or partner in the struggle between East and West; they had been invited to participate in judgment at the dispute of the conquerors. German diplomacy had been given its perspective for the next decade.

The divergence of American and Russian positions on Germany was now clear. The Russians still thought of Germany as booty; having chopped away East Germany from West Germany, they now wanted to press for a further share in the riches of Western Germany which the Atlantic Powers held. The Americans thought of Germany as a burden; they wanted now to lessen the burden by making Germany operate; they wanted to increase German health, not in order to get more out of Germany, but to end the downward spiral and sickening disorganization of her economy, which was retarding all European recovery. On this note of divergence, having only just approached the German problem, Mr. Byrnes ended his stewardship of American diplomacy in December, 1946. Fifteen months before he had begun his report to the American people after the First Conference of Foreign Ministers with the melancholy words, "The First Conference of Foreign Ministers closed in a stalemate." He did not bother to make a report on the last of the meetings he attended in December. Instead, in his memoirs, he wryly recorded the quip of Georges Bidault, the witty history professor who had become France's Foreign Minister. By this time the Council had degenerated into a debate that dragged each argument around and around, inflexibly, caught in a groove from which there was no escape. M. Bidault observed that the Council was now a merry-go-round and asked his colleagues' indulgence since he "was now going to ride his own horse around and say something about coal."

It was General George Catlett Marshall who decided to get off the merry-go-round. Until Marshall succeeded Byrnes in the leadership of American diplomacy, all decisions had been made in the frame of the fictitious yet legal alliance that still bound the West to the Russians. From January of 1947 on, American decisions were made not only apart from the alliance, but in recognition of the open and increasing enmity between the two halves of the old alliance. Indeed, the entire strategy which has propelled the Western world ever since was conceived and drafted in the first fifteen months of Marshall's two-year incumbency of office.

Marshall, a man in whom the powers of logic are coupled with dignity and force to an extraordinary degree, found himself caught in a situation in which effective diplomacy was impossible. Effective diplomacy rests on power, and by the beginning of 1947, the United States and her Allies were powerless. In May of 1945, the Army of the United States had stood in Central Europe with a force of 3,500,000 men, organized into 68 veteran divisions, supported by 149 air groups of planes, supplied by one of the most elaborate logistical systems ever flung over the globe. Some 47 divisions of Allied power braced this force on the Western Front. By March of 1946, ten months later, the American forces had dwindled to 400,000 men, with homeland reserves insufficient to keep them at strength. The Air Force had disappeared. By June of 1946, while Mr. Byrnes and Mr. Molotov were negotiating the lesser peace treaties, redisposition of both American and Russian troops had taken place. The Russians had moved their divisions north to the critically sensitive German flatlands and so overmatched Allied strength that our intelligence reports gravely doubted whether, if a clash came, our troops would be capable of making an effective retreat to the North German ports where they might be evacuated without catastrophe.

By July of 1946, when Molotov and Byrnes entered on the first dispute over Germany, American strength had dwindled even further.

The United States Air Force homeland reserve of trained crews and squadrons that could be flown to Europe in an emergency was down to 90 bombers and 460 fighter planes. James Forrestal records in his diaries that only 175 pilots of these planes could be considered really first class. The illusion of American power rested almost entirely on the atomic bomb; yet this was the period when the exodus of American scientists from the nuclear energy projects had reached its high point and the assembly of atomic bombs at Los Alamos had come to a halt. Our Allies were similarly enfeebled. The British, burdened with war both in Greece and Palestine, had by 1947 cut their armed forces from 4,700,000 to 1,247,000 men, of whom only two divisions were stationed in Germany. The French had reduced their forces to two divisions in Germany and their Minister of National Defense was a Communist.

George Marshall, a soldier by training, was never for an instant unaware of the relationship between power and purpose. He entered on his term of diplomacy conscious, as were few other men in the Western world, that the Russians massed 40 divisions of combat troops in combat position in Central Europe with over 100 divisions behind them in reserve, while America's forces stood at two divisions and its homeland reserve counted no more than six ready battalions. The instinct of survival made the first order of the day the recapture of a balance.

Marshall had been in office no more than six weeks, however, when another fact was pressed home to him: that the balance to be recaptured was not only military but, even more urgently, social and political. On the morning of February 24, 1947, without warning, the British Ambassador in Washington, Lord Inverchapel, called on Under-Secretary of State Dean Acheson at the State Department to inform him that Great Britain was pulling out of Greece and Turkey. Great Britain at this moment was not only garrisoning Germany and feeding starving Germans with British money, but also holding down garrisons in North Africa, in always-restive Egypt, in turbulent Palestine, in Burma, Malaya and Hongkong. She was also caught in an economic crisis of crushing weight. The cost of British support of Greece and Turkey, said the British, would in the coming year be $250,000,000, which the British could not possibly afford. The customs of British political life bring the budget to its annual decision each April. America, thus, had only five weeks of thought before the British should announce to the world that they were shucking off the burden of Greece and Turkey, letting the Balkans and Eastern Mediterranean come unstuck.

More was involved in this British announcement than imminent danger in a distant flank zone. The basic assumption of American diplomacy had hitherto been that the United States, though the undisputed leader, was nevertheless a partner in a coalition of like-minded and powerful allies. This assumption was now about to be shown false. The British decision to abandon Greece was only the first in a series of sharp dramatic jolts that were to demonstrate that the strength of Western Europe as a community had been ebbing over a period of decades. The spasm of war had temporarily hidden this erosion by those same exertions which speeded and deepened it. But in early 1947, a year and a half after the war had ended, the erosion could no longer be concealed. The United States found itself not in a combination of power but in an association of decay that made no social or political balance with the Russians possible until it was corrected.

Nineteen forty-seven was the year that Europe almost disappeared from world affairs. One violent blizzard had gummed up the delicate mechanism of the overstrained British economy, paralyzed her business, made her people shiver in unheated homes like medieval peasants, set in motion the events that led to the end of her imperial pretensions. The drought of the following spring and summer months ushered in the dismal era on the Continent. There, blazing, rainless weeks produced the finest wines in a generation of memory and the worst food crops in a longer period. By the fall of 1947 Europe was as close to destitution as a modern civilization can get; she could not grow enough food and she could not find the money or goods to buy food elsewhere. That was the fall in which the Italian and French foreign offices found themselves quarreling over four shiploads of American relief wheat already on the high seas. Bread rations in both countries were down to 250 grains (half a pound) a day to meet their rationing commitments, and both insisted they needed all four ships.

With the judgment of Solomon, the Americans split the four ships, giving each two—but the margin was that thin.

Twice during his first year in office General Marshall sat down with the Russians to negotiate the problem of Germany, once at Moscow in the spring and once in London in December. Neither of these wordy bouts brought any conclusion or meeting of minds, but by then they had failed in importance as the alliance that had authorized them had faded and broken. By then, Marshall had set in motion those events and policies that were to separate the West from the East, perhaps forever.

The first of these policies, the Truman Doctrine, was an instinctive, almost reflex action. Three days after the delivery of the Inverchapel message to the State Department, the State Department and the White House had called in and persuaded the leaders of Congress (except for Mr. Taft) that the burden Britain was dropping must be caught by the United States. Demanding and eventually receiving $400,000,000 for the military and economic support of Greece and Turkey, the American government announced that its power was now, with a single bound, committed around the globe, one thousand miles beyond the Russian flank as far as the Black Sea and the Caucasus.

The Truman Doctrine was not, however, enough. Returning from his spring conference in Moscow, Marshall doggedly informed Washington of his conviction that Russia would not negotiate as long as we in negotiation could not win their respect for our force. It was impossible to discuss Europe with the Russians so long as Europe was quicksand. Europe had to be made firm before one could build on our side a bridge across to the Russians on the other. Europe had to be organized. In the busy spring weeks of 1947 while the technicians in Washington were translating the Truman Doctrine into the specifics of advisory groups, technical assistance, ships of supply, distribution mechanisms, the Marshall Plan was being slowly shaped in theory. On June 5, the idea, the policy, the techniques had matured enough in Marshall's mind to permit him to go to Harvard University and there at a commencement address to invite Europe, as a community of nations, to submit to the United States a program of community needs that might make them healthy again, which program the United States would then consider as a basis for vast and continued aid. Within this program of European revival, as certain as seed in the womb, the revival of German health and strength was implicit.

With the launching of the Marshall Plan in 1947, the Western world set forth on an entirely new course. By the end of 1947 the divergence of East and West had become so clear that further conversation was impossible. When next Marshall met Molotov in London at the Foreign Ministers' Conference of December of 1947, Molotov had recognized it. Molotov took off in flights of fantasy, mixed with fact and suspicion, in such language and with such vituperation that it was clear, as indeed it had been for several months, that no further basis of negotiation existed. At the last session of the London meeting Marshall unburdened himself:

"The United States hoped," said Marshall across the table to Molotov, "that there would emerge from this conference the beginnings of a united and self-respecting Germany. . . . The United States had even higher hopes for an Austrian settlement.

"We have failed to reach agreement on a treaty for Austria because the Soviet Union has demanded for itself properties and special privileges in Austria in an amount and to an extent which far exceed any rightful claim and which far exceed what a free Austria can afford.

"As regards Germany, we have been unable to agree on what we mean by Germany . . . Three of the delegations agree that boundary commissions be at once established to examine frontier questions. The Soviet Union rejects this proposal. So we neither agree on what Germany is to be, nor do we agree on establishing commissions to study these vital boundary problems.

"In examining the discussions on economic principles, we have progressed only agreeing to procedures without substance . . . The Soviet Union has refused to furnish vitally necessary information with respect to reparations removals. Thus we have been asked to reach agreement while information essential to such agreement is withheld by Soviet representatives. . . . The Soviet Union demands reparations for itself and Poland of ten billion dollars at 1938 values which is at least 15 billion dollars today. . . . It was accepted by all at Moscow that full agreement on economic principles was essential to the establishment of political unification. . . . We are unable to agree on what shall be the area of the German economy; we cannot agree how to make German resources available to Germany as a whole, a condition prerequisite to the revival of German economy. . . . The simple fact is that the present division of Germany has been caused by the policies and practices of the occupying powers themselves. Only the occupying powers can create German unity in the present circumstances. That is why the United States has consistently pressed for certain fundamental decisions by the occupying powers themselves as the absolutely essential first step for the achievement of a unified Germany. Three delegations at this conference have registered their willingness to take these decisions here and now. The Soviet Union alone refuses to agree. In view of these facts, it seems impossible at this time to make practical progress . . . and I suggest that the Council of Foreign Ministers might now consider adjournment of this session."

It adjourned. It met only once more seventeen months later in the late spring of 1949 at the pink stucco palace of Anna Gould in Paris. By then the Council was no longer a forum of discussion but a formality to settle the technicalities of the Berlin blockade. Marshall's statement had marked the end of the period of talk. Talk had been obsolete for almost a year anyway because great new events were under way in the Mediterranean, in Asia, above all in Germany and Western Europe. And the Russians, too, were shifting gears.

The initiative in Europe all through the great Year of Divergence, 1947, had been in American hands, leading first to the Truman Doctrine and next to the Marshall Plan, but this initiative had not been without Russian response.

None of us in the Western world will probably live to learn and understand precisely how policy is determined in the Soviet Union. In the absence of any certified information, every observer must therefore take the few available facts and fondle them like the shards of an antique civilization, trying to fit them into some general theory or doctrine that governs them. Russian policy in the great Year of Divergence must be examined in the same way, each fact fitted into the mythology of Marxism.

In the dogma of Marxism, certain laws are immutable. One is that the contradictions in the capitalist states must inevitably bring them to trade rivalry, friction, enmity and war. Another is that the end-phase of all capitalism is imperialism which, when it ripens to rot, falls before the revolt of colonial peoples and in its collapse brings down the society of the ruling country in chaos. These dogmas could be draped about the events of 1947 and stretched to fit.

Thus, the long decay of Western European states was expected and normal. In fact, it had been obvious to the Russians before it became obvious to the Western world. By Russian theology, this capitalist decay was foreordained by the laws of history, like Armageddon before salvation. Well before Britain cut Turkey and Greece adrift, the Russians had sat in anticipation of the crumbling of Britain's imperial influence. The Truman Doctrine snatched away the fruit of this collapse and also physically installed American air power so deep along the flank of the Russian land-mass as to be able, at some future date, to devastate Russia's vitals unless countered. Though the Truman Doctrine was probably a surprise, Marxist dogma could explain it. By dogma, the capitalist-imperialist states snatch prizes one from the other, and, further, capitalist-imperialist states are inescapably pledged to the destruction of worker-revolutionary states which, by definition, the Soviet Union is. The Truman Doctrine was thus a mortal threat, but understandable.

The Marshall Plan was more difficult to explain. By dogma, the leading capitalist-imperialist element, namely the United States, should proceed during the period of decay to gobble up and subjugate the lesser decaying states. But the Marshall Plan had curious qualities which did not quite fit into this dogma. Taken at face value, the Marshall Plan proposed that rather than ending their existence in a tangle of rivalries and contradictions culminating in chaos, the capitalist states should cooperate, which Marxist theory declared impossible. It was impossible for any Russian thinker, commentator or statesman to have accepted this notion at face value, simply because the very thought, in Marxist theology, was blasphemy, sacrilege or worse, punishable by disgrace or death.

Nevertheless it was very perplexing.

This perplexity showed itself at every level. It showed in the initial reaction of the tempered Communist leaders of the East

European satellites, who twitched irresistibly at the thought of American largesse to their shattered economies. It showed in the first clandestine reactions of Communists in Western Europe. One of them, in a rare burst of criticism of Russia, complained to me, "The trouble is that the West has learned so much from Marx that it doesn't act the way it used to before it learned from Marx. The Russians don't realize how much the Western states have changed since the days that Marx knew. Our enemies have read our books—what is Truman, after all, but a Prudhomme with an army?"

But the perplexity showed most of all, at the highest level, in Moscow and resulted in one of the most mysterious episodes of postwar history: Mr. Molotov's visit to Paris in June of 1947 to discuss the Marshall Plan. Within the Politburo, as in any group of men, there must be at least two or more ideas, two or more factions, two or more tactical approaches to any problem. And, since Russia's great problem is the United States, there must be at least two or more ideas of how to handle her, whether tough or soft, conciliatory or uncompromising, brutally frank or deceptively friendly. Discarding dogma, the facts could be read to satisfy either approach. Clearly, by the Truman Doctrine, America had proclaimed open enmity to Russia and communism; equally clearly, Marshall had offered American money and goods to the Russians as well as the other Europeans. (Marshall had defined his offer of aid to Europe privately as "everything up to the Urals.") Was America bent on enmity? Or was she holding out the olive branch?

Whatever the discussion in Moscow, its upshot was that Mr. Molotov arrived in Paris on June 27, 1947, with a delegation of some threescore Russian experts and economists, no mean token of interest, to join the Foreign Ministers of France and Britain in discussing the plan. Six days later he had left in bitter disagreement and the rupture of 1947 was complete. What happened in those six days is one of the muddiest episodes of the postwar period. Sources and statesmen of the highest authority, participants of the greatest integrity, tell directly contradictory stories. One Western statesman who visited Moscow in mid-June of 1947 saw both Mikoyan, the Soviet Minister of Foreign Trade, and Molotov, the Soviet Minister of Foreign Affairs. He found Mikoyan eager to participate and Molotov eager to stay out; whereupon, according to his account, Stalin with his peasant suspicion sent Molotov to implement Mikoyan's policy, and Molotov wrecked it. One American most deeply involved in the intricate negotiations insists that the American Embassy in London urged Ernest Bevin, Britain's Foreign Secretary, to force the Russians out, lest the American Congress repudiate any plan giving handouts to Russia. Other equally eminent participants say flatly no such pressure was applied. All agree, however, on one point: that Molotov's rupture of the conference was, from a Russian point of view, pure stupidity. Had he remained, no American Congress would ever have been persuaded to approve the Marshall Plan.

The story of the discussions as it is borne in the official records, however, reads thus: Molotov began the first day with unexpected enthusiasm, advancing the thesis that it was right and normal for war-ravaged countries to expect American aid. He then explained the Russian attitude: that each nation submit to America its individual shopping list and America meet the bill. It was on this technical issue, on the second day, that the other two Foreign Ministers broke. Mr. Bevin and M. Bidault clung to the original American proposal that Europeans first explore the meshing and common use of common resources before turning to America to meet their residual needs. Molotov would have none of this; he argued it was foreign interference in Russian affairs. Some observers present at the conference believe that in his insistence on the least possible degree of American supervision and coordination of aid, Molotov was inspired more than anything else by the restiveness of his satellites, by the possible intrusion of American agents and American diplomacy in such unsteady Communist Republics as Poland, Yugoslavia and Czechoslovakia. Moreover, as it became clear that European reconstruction could not be taken without Germany's revival, Molotov argued that the disposition of Western Germany was being lifted out of the frame of four power decision where it belonged. He was quite right, of course, but failed to admit that Russia had already removed Eastern Germany from just that same frame. In great anger, therefore, on Wednesday morning, Molotov departed from Paris, leaving the Western Powers to begin that task which, even without the Russians, was of staggering complexity.

Neither Molotov's report in Moscow nor the conclusions drawn from it will probably ever be known to us. What followed, however, was a rapid and definitive stiffening of Russian attitude, internally and externally, which seems, in retrospect, an entirely new policy.

The smiling face of the Russian dictator began to change. Down to 1947, a long procession of Americans had visited Stalin, all reporting the geniality and amiability of the little father of all Marxists. To Hopkins, to Byrnes, to Bedell Smith, to Elliott Roosevelt, to Harold Stassen, Stalin had turned the same jovial countenance. The last American visitor to receive the genial treatment was George Marshall. At Moscow, after the breakdown of the spring conference of 1947, Marshall had been invited to a final dinner and chat with Stalin, and the dictator had tried to cheer Marshall by telling him he must not be discouraged by these little skirmishes before reaching the main lines of settlement. But from mid-1947 on, Stalin no longer appeared, at least to Americans, in the old, familiar role. In fact Stalin received only two more Americans between 1947 and 1953: Ambassador Bedell Smith, who tried hopelessly to settle the Berlin blockade with the unyielding master of the Russians, and Ambassador Kirk, who was granted a perfunctory audience.

Soviet toughening was more clearly visible outside Russia than within. In September, the Russians organized the Cominform, which replaced the Comintern as the administrative arm of Russia in control of Eastern Europe and the Communist parties of the West. Simultaneously, a series of purges in Eastern Europe began to strip the dupes and the non-Communists from the governments of the satellites and to liquidate them. By early 1948, the process had climaxed in the Communist coup d'état in Prague. In Asia, too, a marked increase of Russian aid to the Chinese Communists, hitherto negligible, was noted.

The purges, the organization of the Cominform, the changed attitude to China were not the only areas where Russia suddenly stiffened. In their new sensitivity and harshness, the Russians could not ignore what was happening in Germany, the turntable of European power. For Western Germany, before their very eyes, was about to be transformed from a charred and miserable wilderness to be quarreled over as booty into something else entirely, a major ally of the West and, thus, potentially, a major menace to the Soviet Union.

The United States Army had begun to organize Western Germany long before the United States government had any clear idea of what should be done with it. While the State Department thought vaguely forward about such great problems as a centralized or dismembered Germany, about the borders and confines of Germany's territory, the proconsuls of the United States Army proceeded to govern Germany on their own, shaping a new society as they went. The Army's mission was to keep Germany pacified, hold it in submission, feed it, make it work, and do all these things at the least possible cost to the American taxpayer. While the civilian statesmen, for whom the uniformed proconsuls developed an easy contempt, talked theory and policy, the Army had to act, every single day.

It was not until the middle of 1947, when the Marshall Plan was conceived and General George Marshall had rehabilitated the State Department enough in Army eyes to merit attention, that broad diplomatic policy in Germany and Army policy in Germany began to mesh. The Army wanted to make Germany a going concern as quickly as possible in order to cut the burden of subsidy out of Army appropriations; the Marshall Plan wanted to revive all European industrial life to new historic highs, and this was impossible without Germany. Ugly, distorted, its streets full of homeless refugees, its currency a paper nonsense, Germany, once the anchor of Europe's economic life, had become its crazy, unbalanced vortex. A sweeping reorganization of Western Germany was necessary to cleanse and purify the madness.

Two things were clearly in order: first, to create some native German instrument of government to pull order out of anarchy; second, to purge its business life of inflation so that men could toil productively. In the spring of 1948, after the final breakdown of the Council of Foreign Ministers in London in December, the Western Powers proceeded to both tasks at once. A conference of the six Western Powers in London invited the Germans to elect delegates to a constitutional convention which would create a new popularly elected government for all West Germany. Simultaneously, they proceeded with the purging of German finances by a brutal repudiation of all paper money in circulation in Western Germany and the substitution of a new, hard, soundly controlled money.

These were the measures that provoked the famous Berlin blockade. The Russians, despite their own total exclusion of Western influence from every square yard of their dominance, could not bring themselves to believe that they were to be as totally excluded themselves from a share in the power and control of West Germany, the monster progenitor of their sorrows. To reopen discussion and provoke talk, the Russians knew only one method: force. This they invoked in the Berlin blockade, and when it failed, they had shot their bolt in Europe. By then, Europe and America were embarked on a new adventure of such magnitude and complexity that men scarcely noticed that the war had come to an end with no peace made.

III

a world we tried to build

The world we tried to build with the launching of the Marshall Plan in 1947 is one whose terrible problems, unquenchable yearnings and blinding aches would have been just as perplexing had communism never been invented or Russia never existed.

It is a world in which we sought and still seek that men live in political liberty with the hope each year and each decade of greater opportunity and greater comfort for themselves and their children.

If the excitement of this great American adventure has been hidden from the citizens who supported it, it is because its victories and defeats were measured only in the dusty ledgers of trade, its captains were economists, and its soldiers were dollars. Its history is written in millions of words and figures that concern themselves exclusively with the making, getting, buying, selling and payment of the world's goods.

Politics have always been shaped by the bitter struggle of ordinary men to get and have things. The difference is that in our decade all the great governments of Europe have convulsively seized huge areas of economic enterprise once left to individuals, and the tedious problems once settled by the myriad solitary decisions of calculating businessmen are now the stuff of public debate and government action. Governments are judged by their citizens today on the price of butter and fish, the rents on land and homes, the levels of wages and hours.

Not one government in Western Europe in the years since the war would have had the slightest hope of surviving this judgment of its citizens in freedom and without blood had it not been for the almost unimaginable sum of 27 billion dollars which the United States has given it in economic aid alone. The United

States did this for the simplest reasons: because it knew that if these governments fell, the defense and welfare of the United States would be in peril; and because it knew that if Europeans threw these governments out they would, quite likely, have thrown out liberty, too, and forever.

The United States had already given away over ten billion dollars to Europe by the time, in 1947, it decided that this aid should be linked to a plan with specific long-term objectives. Technically, in terms of finance, the first objective was to make Europe economically self-supporting and independent of American charity by 1952. Politically, it was to heal the European societies so that by 1952 the Russians would be forced to recognize them as healthy and stable, thus worthy of respect and negotiation.

Unfortunately, apart from these great objectives, the Marshall Plan lacked a logical series of clear and foreseen steps to arrive at its end-goals. There were many reasons for this, of course. There were the pettiness, weakness, jealousies and exhaustion of the European governments with whom it dealt; there were the human, uncontrollable prejudices of hundreds of millions of free men on both sides of the Atlantic who could not be disciplined but had to be persuaded; there was the burden on its actions of constant Congressional passion and suspicion. But, finally, most importantly, there was the simple inescapable ignorance of men addressing themselves to a job so new, complex and huge that no previous experience provided any education or clue to solution.

Western Europe in 1947 was mortally ill.

To the roving eye there was nothing that made this mortal illness apparent. It was hot. Rainless, golden, scorching days had followed one another from early spring until weeks and months beyond the wheat harvest, and this heat did, indeed, produce the impression of a high, debilitating fever. But the illness was more than a surface fever, and graver than the failure of the crops upon which Europe's wheat and bread depended. It was a condition of history.

Economists defined this condition as bankruptcy. Every government of Western Europe was pledged to provide its citizens with the minimum decencies of life. But these obligations could not be met, for Europe's resources were exhausted, or had failed, and they were dependent on a massive and continued flow of American food, fibers, fuel and goods for which they could no longer pay. A hemorrhage had opened in the central financial reserves of each European nation as governments attempted to meet their obligations, and gold and dollars were gushing out with no seeming possibility of stanching. The United States Army had pumped half a billion dollars into Germany for relief and it was gone. The French had received a billion and a quarter dollars in 1946 and it had vanished. UNRRA had distributed over a billion dollars' worth of aid and it had disappeared. The three and three-quarters billion dollars loaned to the British in 1946 was disappearing at a dizzy rate. Everywhere, each day, each month, gold and dollars drained away to pay for Europe's subsistence needs with the absolutely inevitable prospect that by the end of 1947 all would be gone. During one six-day period in August of 1947, the British Treasury saw no less than $237,000,000 of its reserves claimed by the inexorable bookkeeping of world trade.

Even the economists achieved eloquence in describing the situation: "Europe's dollar resources are running low," wrote the report of the European claimants for Marshall Plan aid. "If the flow of goods from the American continent to Europe should cease, the results would be calamitous. . . . If nothing is done, a catastrophe will develop as stocks become exhausted. . . . Life in Europe will become increasingly unstable and uncertain; industries will grind to a gradual halt for lack of materials and fuel, and the food supply of Europe will diminish and begin to disappear."

History was finally catching up with Europe; suddenly, she was exposed as a curiosity unique in all time. Here was a community of 300,000,000 men who had developed a civilization so unbalanced that they could not possibly survive as a civilization on their own resources. The vital margin of their food supply, almost all the fibers they used to clothe themselves, the tea at breakfast, the evening coffee, rubber sheathing and copper wires, liquid fuels—all of these products that Europeans not only enjoyed but could not live without came from overseas on the cycling tides of trade. The entire culture which seemed so completely European, from the coffee with *schlag* of Austria to the hot red tea of England, depended on the world being one. For a century the community had unthinkingly relied on invisible strands of trade which brought these necessities to the home ports in return for what Europe could ship out; these strands had seemed once as rugged and strong as bonds of iron. Now they were cut. With the strands cut, Europe threatened to sink, or rather to plummet, directly out of modern civilization.

The Marshall Planners had no blueprint for righting the situation, but they had something else—an image. This image was a set of habit patterns and customs, imperfectly remembered from another age which might best be called the Golden Yesterday. Europe had thrived in the Golden Yesterday, and though the Marshall Planners knew the Golden Yesterday could not be restored, somehow they felt they must recapture its vitality.

The Golden Yesterday, if it is to be given a precise date, began in the year 1815, at the moment the last string quivered with the last chord of the last minuet of the Congress of Vienna when the statesmen of Europe, having disposed of Napoleon, settled down to the longest period of peace that Europe had known since the days of the Romans. What followed thereafter has no parallel in all history. What followed was an expansive burst of conquest generated from four or five small nation-states on the rim of the European peninsula which ended a century later with all the great globe tributary to them.

Consider the globe at the beginning of that period. America was a wilderness which had been peeled back only as far as the Allegheny Mountains. Russia was a nation of serfs, ruled by a mystic, that stretched in various degrees of barbarism from the Pripet marshes to the boglands of the upper Amur and the Pacific Ocean. China and Japan were empires sealed from the world, each permitting the Western "savages" access to their shores at only one strictly regulated port on their respective seaboards. South America was a series of colonial outposts, indented in jungle, held in the grip of a decayed Empire. Africa was literally unknown. But by the end of that period, the whole world had been so linked together that the price of bread in England depended on the wheat yield in the Ukraine and the doom of the Amazon rubber trade was wedded to the plantation boom of the East Indies, all the way across the globe. Railroads laced every continent from end to end, and from every great port of the world a tight sailing schedule made every other port a regular partner in transport. For the first time the world was one; Europe had made it so and took a fee for her achievement.

The tides of trade that bathed this world coursed in channels as fixed and permanent, it seemed, as the circling of the moon. Men moved along these trade currents from country to country without passports, without visas, their wallets full of folding money that no currency regulation checked, and their minds crammed with ideas that no officialdom sought to investigate. All the fruits of Western civilization–science, law, medicine, learning –moved with these tides. Back and forth, from outer land to inner land, from backward land to advanced land, goods moved with such an ease, such an "automatic" simplicity dictated by need and supply that even now, half a century later, our imagination is compelled to imitate and revive it. For the Marshall Planners, the contrast of this globe of yesterday and the globe of this mid-century was mesmerizing. They wished to recapture its fluid, easy cycling health; the trouble was that the world had changed so much.

The heart of yesterday's globe was Europe and, more precisely, that northeastern corner of Europe where coal fields veined the ground with energy. The belt that starts in England's midlands, continues through the French and Belgian fields to the Ruhr and ends, with a jump, in Silesia, was the working heart not only for France and Britain, Germany and Belgium, but for Asia, Africa and America, too.

But if these coal fields were the heart of the world's sudden unity, the auricles and ventricles that pumped this heart were found in one country alone: England. The phrase "payable by draft on London" summed up the entire system. It meant that anywhere in the world a check on a London bank was a command of a standard measure of goods and services. The English were the first of the Europeans, and thus the first people of the world, to see the world as one; their banks and markets had become the clearinghouses of the globe. Their pre-eminence rested not only on the subtle skill of London's bankers and bill merchants in estimating the credit, the value, the good faith of any enterprise from Patagonia to Kamchatka, but also in the infinite skills of judgment and convenience that Englishmen offered throughout their island.

Liverpool, for example, seemed only a dirty city by the Mersey, but there men first learned to buy and sell cotton they might never see, grown in Georgia, Egypt or India and physically in transit at the moment of sale to Tokyo, Turin or Manchester. The traders of Liverpool fixed the grades and prices of all the world's cotton in one great market open to all the world's buyers. What the Liverpool brokers did for cotton, other Englishmen did for wool and bristles, copper and tin, peppercorns and sardines, insurance and shipping, investment and buccaneering. This dominance of world trade was enforced not so much by guns and ships—which were important—as by skill and wisdom. It lasted because it was convenient and useful. The pound was not only as good as gold, the pound decided what gold was worth.

In the Golden Yesterday, England was a captain both wise and strong. The wonderful value of the British pound nourished and was nourished in turn by the healthiness of nineteenth-century trade. England was both a market for and a seller of anything. England's customers never had to worry about getting pounds as America's customers worry today about finding dollars, because the English were constantly offering pounds to buy overseas more and more things that they needed—wheat, lumber, cotton, meat, wool. Countries abroad bought English tools, coal, cloth, engineering with the pounds they earned by their sales. As Englishmen first, and the rest of Europe later, developed their insatiable appetites, an upward rhythm of expansion developed and seemed without horizon. The plains were cleared in Argentina and America, the forests were felled around the globe, plantations rose where jungles had matted fruitlessly. As Europeans drew riches from the world, they expanded their production explosively to repay in manufactured goods. Between Napoleon's defeat and the mid-nineteenth century, production of iron in Europe quintupled; it doubled again between the mid-century and the Franco-Prussian War; tripled again between that war and the turn of the century; doubled again between the turn of the century and the outbreak of the First World War. All other production soared too: railroads doubled, tripled, quadrupled their mileage in single decades. The export of cotton cloth went up ten times, from England alone, between 1840 and the First World War; coal production in England multiplied by fourteen times in the course of the Golden Yesterday, so powerful was the demand of the world for the fruit of Europe's energy.

England began the century as Europe's prime industrial power and remained so for two generations. But in an age when the phrase "technical assistance" was unknown, she had taught her techniques to everyone else, unthinkingly, easily and to her own ultimate perplexity. Englishmen blew in the first blast furnaces of Belgium, of France, of Germany. English engineers traveled as far as Russia to open the first blast furnace there. The English engineered the first railways of France and Germany; their scientists discovered how to make useful the phosphoric iron ores of France's Lorraine and planned and directed the first penetration of the deep coal seams of Germany's Ruhr. All Europe learned the tricks which the magic English imagination had conceived. Sometime between the Franco-Prussian War and the turn of the century, England's place as the world's greatest industrial power faded; in the new world, America, and, in the old world, Germany, first overtook and then surpassed her in sheer industrial weight and efficiency.

But if other powers overtook the British in the making of things, none ever overtook, or even tried to overtake, the lead the British had in the trading of goods; nor, in Europe, did any power try to replace the British as the pointsman and middleman in Europe's relation with the great globe outside. The Germans in 1914 had four times the gold reserves of the British, and the French twice the gold reserves, but Germans and Frenchmen paid their bills and sold their goods around the globe "payable by draft on London." The pound remained the measure of value.

The key to Britain's dynamic relation with the outside world was in the British sense of investment. They did not call it "Point Four"; it was simply enterprise. Where they could not find what they needed for themselves and Europe, they created the resources or opened them by investment. English capital was risk capital, but capital risked with the wisdom and knowledge of the world. It opened packing houses in Argentina, tea plantations in India, rubber plantations in Malaya, mines everywhere, ranches on the pampas and prairies. It underbraced these investments with other investments to keep the world opening—waterworks, electricity plants, breweries, tramways, factories, shipyards all across the globe from the Whangpoo in Shanghai to the Charles in Boston. Other European nations–France, Germany, Belgium, Switzerland –followed in the footsteps of British capital, occupying and competing where the British had penetrated. And as British capital felt the hot breath of competition from others, it abandoned old areas and moved to new ones.

This great racing cycle of money chasing opportunity, opportunity meeting need, resources blossoming as need fostered them, reached its height in the decade before the accident of 1914. By then, England had invested 18 billion dollars around the world (about 50 billion dollars by present-day American prices), the French had invested 9 billion, the Germans 5.8 billion. As the French and Germans had followed the British, their investments were concentrated chiefly in the backward areas of Europe, in the Balkans and in Russia. Here, their investments were caught and wiped out by the First World War, an episode from which those countries have never recovered. The English, luckily, had been pushed out to investment beyond the seas; here they were safe for another generation.

The Golden Yesterday was no more than a memory in the days that followed the First World War. The circulation of trade was sorely wounded; Russia ripped herself and the resources of the Siberian wastes out of the old cycle entirely. Japan, under the incubating heat of war, grew an industry that pressed competitively on the most sensitive nerves of the European trading system. Most important of all, the United States burst in such an upwelling of energy that no nineteenth-century rules seemed to fit the titanic forces which gushed from the American continent.

Europe now seemed to fit into a pattern of trade that was bent into a triangle. At one corner of the triangle stood the United States, at the second Europe, at the third the backward and colonial regions of the world. The backward and colonial areas supplied the United States with what America lacked at home–coffee, rubber, tin, cocoa, tea, wool. The United States shipped out to Europe food, oil, cotton, sulfur and machines. Europe could not pay for what she got from the United States directly, but the third leg of the triangle took care of that; Europe would ship to the backward and colonial areas textiles, autos, chemicals, machines and government services. With what these earned Europe could partially meet her bill in America; the revenues on her old investments and her shipping services roughly closed the gap.

The great depression of the thirties closed in all too swiftly on this triangular pattern. Like men in a city about which a siege ring slowly tightens, the European communities began to grate on each other. The trade they did with each other, on which their internal efficiency and much of their wealth depended, began to beat sluggishly as quotas, tariffs, currency regulations threw up artificial barriers among them.

If the system worked at all, it worked only because the British still had the strength and skill to gear Europe into the outside world. Britain still bought huge quantities of goods from continental Europe; and the continental Europeans could change pounds they earned in London to dollars or gold and thus trade with the great globe beyond. The pound was the crutch on which Europe limped in its trade, and the British kept the pound a solid medium of exchange because they still controlled a world-girdling empire rich with rubber, tin, cocoa and wool, because British ships and services still earned dollars, because Britain's investments overseas still brought dividends.

The Second World War finished what the First had begun. Russia tore another chunk off the eastern side of Europe—the belly side that provided so much of its food. Asia, Africa and South America developed home appetites in war prosperity and began to consume many things they used to sell to Europe, or, simultaneously, they learned to manufacture things at home they once had bought in Europe. The United States quickened its industrial and technical development, producing at a price and a pace with which the Europeans could not possibly compete.

Europe still needed food, fuel and raw material from overseas to live. She had less of these at home than at any time in generations and needed more of them from aliens than ever in her long history. There were three ways for Europe to pay for what she needed. First, there was the commercial export of her traditional manufactures—but her goods were high priced, her customers had learned to make them at home or to buy them more easily in America. Secondly, there were her services—but her sunken and crippled merchant marines no longer dominated the world's sea lanes, and her skills in governing subject peoples had been repudiated by half a dozen distant revolts. Third, there was her income from generations of previous investment abroad—but these had been reduced or liquidated to pay for the war. Before the war Europe paid for twenty per cent of all she bought abroad with dividends on her investments. By 1949 these dividends paid only four per cent of what Europe needed to buy abroad.

And there was a final condition. Wars and revolutions all around the world, the great movements of colonial peoples with their new hungers, jostled the Europeans, crowded them in the market place, stealing from sources of supply that had once been exclusively theirs. All of them wanted more—more food, more paper, more clothing. They drove demand up so that the price of everything that Europe sought overseas was now rising almost by the day.

It took almost two years for Europeans and Americans to realize that Europe was not only incapable of resistance to the Russians, but that she was engaged in a desperate ordeal of survival that had nothing to do with the Soviet Union. The tides of trade in which Europe lived had vanished. Like a whale left gasping on the sand, Europe lay rotting in the sun.

Every event, big and little, seemed to conspire to force Europe to dependence on America. America had wheat and fodder, cotton and sugar, coal and copper, sulfur and zinc, ships and machinery, trucks and pipe. Europe could find some of these goods elsewhere—but not enough. America held the vital necessary extra margin of supply. Certain goods did not exist, in stark physical fact, anywhere else in the world but in America. And whether as the vital margin or the total supply, Europe needed dollars which she did not have to pay for the goods. The old captain of the Golden Yesterday, England, had always done business on a two-way basis. Her customers could always earn enough pounds to buy in England by selling to England. But the new captain, America, was so enormously rich and needed to buy so little abroad that her customers could never earn enough dollars to match their needs. The gap between what Europe could earn in dollars and what Europe needed to buy with dollars became known, immediately after the war, as the Dollar Gap.

The "Dollar Gap," with its companion phrase, "the Cold War," is probably the most ominous expression of postwar European history. The story of the Dollar Gap is one of the inner cords woven through all Atlantic diplomacy down to the present. It has been measured in specific terms as about $11,500,000,000 in a bad year like 1947 to $2,200,000,000 in a good year like 1950; here, between two billion and three billion dollars a year, the Dollar Gap still remains, closed only by American aid. The Dollar Gap is an economists' term, but it is a master phrase that covers the cost of baby's diapers, the amount of milk in children's diets, the absence or presence of oranges on the table. The story of the Marshall Plan, and of Europe's struggle to survive even today, is the story of the struggle with the Dollar Gap.

In the Golden Yesterday the Dollar Gap would have been a meaningless phrase.

In those days gold settled all problems. The "automatic" simplicity with which goods moved so wonderfully from supply to demand, from distant resource to distant consumer, was only matched by the "automatic" simplicity with which they did *not* move when the consumer could not find the gold to pay for them. When the sum of a nation's working citizens could not provide enough goods to pay for the sum of a nation's needs, some people simply went without. The "automatic" market simply squeezed down and out all those individuals whose earnings could not cover the price of what they wanted.

Thus, a century ago, if France and America had found themselves in the same position as they found themselves in 1947, France would simply have imported less cotton or no cotton. This would have reduced so sharply the amount of cotton goods in the country that rising prices would automatically have made it a luxury. There would have been no sheets on the beds except in the homes of the very rich, no diapers for babies, no aprons for women, and the price of a simple work shirt would have so skyrocketed as to limit a workingman to one a year. Several hundred thousand textile and clothing workers would have been unemployed. But the unemployment would have helped too, for the destitute would have consumed so much less cotton, coal, gasoline, meat, travel that France's need for dollars to buy cotton, wool, coal, petroleum would have begun to diminish. The spiral of unemployment and poverty would gradually have carried France's needs down to the point where trade balanced. The Dollar Gap would have disappeared, provided France could live peacefully with millions hungry, unemployed, barely clothed, while a lucky few still enjoyed the precious comforts from abroad. In England, Germany and Belgium, of course, the situation would be even worse, for Frenchmen do, after all, grow their own food while the others must import it or starve.

All these things would have happened again in 1947 and no Dollar Gap would ever have furrowed the brows of the Atlantic economists had not the morality of the world so changed. The Dollar Gap which still haunts Western Europe and America exists because people today will not sit by quietly as they are broken to misery. Today's Europe is a much better place to live in than it was a century ago, because consciences are so much quicker, because no modern government can easily deny a fair share of comfort to previously silent citizens.

No government freely elected in postwar Europe, with or without the challenge of communism, could have let the "automatic" adjustments of the Golden Yesterday settle their problems in hunger, violence, unemployment and sickness. They were elected by men and women intoxicated by dreams of tomorrow, anxious to vomit forth not only the deprivations of war but the memories of the prewar depression. The people had been told by radio, in the press, by their leaders so often during the grim years that tomorrow would be better, that no government could have permitted the "automatic" adjustment and survived.

Instead of "automatic" or "natural" adjustment to the movement of world commerce, therefore, almost all the European countries tried to plan their adjustment through a system of controls. These control mechanisms did not have to be invented after the war. The war had left a heritage of currency controls, rationing controls, exchange controls, export-import controls. The earlier depression years had provided a tradition of tariff controls, quota controls, allocation controls. The Dollar Gap simply arrived on the stage of politics and riveted them in place. Since Europe was dependent on America for both comfort and survival, the dollars that commanded these necessities had to be controlled in each country. Once dollars were controlled, dozens of other controls became necessary too. The flow of dollars had to be controlled not only between Europe and the United States but, in the scramble for them, between European nation and European nation. Finally, dollars had to be controlled down to each solitary citizen's purse and bank account so that every member of the community got his fair share of the cotton, the petroleum, the bread, the meat that dollars could buy.

To be fair, it must be recorded that the Dollar Gap was not solely responsible for the controls. Controls were buttressed in some countries—and notably in England, the key—by theories that had slowly gestated for a generation before the war. The general family of all these theories is socialism, which is the belief and hope that by proper use of government power men can be rescued from their helplessness in the wild cycling cruelty of depression and boom. No one can accurately judge how much of the glue that made controls stick came from the Dollar Gap and how much from socialism. But, in general, the emotional heat of Socialist faith gave the inevitable controls imposed by the Dollar Gap the strength that made them binding. For Europeans, and particularly for the English, socialism is as much a folk-reaction to a folk-dread as it is a reasoned program. Unemployment in Europe is second only to war as an emotional kinetic; for to the people who live in the wilderness of Europe's ancient cities, unemployment breeds terror and panic comparable only to the folk-terror of Asian peasants at famine. There are teen-age mill girls in Lancashire, whose parents were only teen-agers thirty years ago, who talk of the 1922 collapse of employment in the spinning mills the way Chinese peasants in Honan talk with ghostly fear of the famine of 1893 which their grandfathers knew.

Controls since the war have changed habit patterns down to the ground. The dollar shortage in England was such, and remains so today, that every Englishman who goes abroad, if he is honest with his controls, goes almost as a pauper. He must travel, if he wants to travel, only in those fixed channels dictated by the ledgers of British trade, not by sun, climate, memory or wistful yearning. The Englishman cannot visit America on pleasure at all, for dollars are hoarded for meat and wheat. But even if he elects to go across the channel to Europe he is tethered. For travel in Europe he receives only 40 pounds ($120) to cover all his spending. He may spend them if he chooses in one glorious burst of steak, wine and champagne on an Easter week end in Paris. Or he may bicycle down from the Channel to the Riviera, knapsack on back, sleeping in hostels, stretching it over a month. Subtly, imperceptibly, currency control has changed the image of the Englishman in continental eyes. The Englishman is no longer the aristocrat of voyagers and the Promenade des Anglais at Nice no longer murmurs with the sound of gentle Mayfair voices. The Englishman in Europe now is the clerk, the student, the schoolmarm, the penny-pinching person one meets on the shabby, raveled underside of tourist life. The Dollar Gap and its controls have made him so.

It was this kind of Europe, stiff and rigid with controls, bankrupt, helpless with hunger and confusion, that the first Americans found when they came to Europe to launch the Marshall Plan and summon her out into a new world.

The most common questions Americans ask in Europe are: Did the Marshall Plan succeed? Did the Marshall Plan fail? Where did the money go?

The answer to the question is subject to as many different variations as the answer to: Did we win the war? We certainly did not lose the war, yet we certainly won no peace. The war was a record of victories and blunders that gave us the world as it is today, a world much better than one in which we would have lived defeated. The Marshall Plan likewise did not fail, yet Europe has still not found out how to fit into the structure of the new world. If the Plan had failed, Europe today would be a continent in which liberty was extinguished except for a few fortunate enclaves, a continent living in an ugliness of spirit so different from today's as to make it another civilization. The Marshall Plan succeeded as the war succeeded in that we did not lose. It succeeded in the sense that a base was preserved from which men can try again. Its triumphs and conquests were prodigious, but no more so than its blunders and shortcomings. Only in another generation will the final balance be struck.

In April of 1948, seventeen European nations plus the Free State of Trieste gathered together in Paris to form the Organization of European Economic Cooperation, or OEEC, an international coordinating body that would represent all the European partners in the Plan. To these eighteen states, the Marshall Plan gave through the Economic Cooperation Administration, or ECA, between April 3, 1948, and January 1, 1952, the sum of $12,285,200,000. (Since then, under its successor agency, the Mutual Security Agency, or MSA, another two and a half billion dollars has been given, and more is on its way.) Three nations took over half this sum between them. England got two billion eight hundred million dollars, France, two billion six hundred million dollars and Germany, one billion three hundred million dollars. (Each of these nations, it should be remembered, had already received stupendous sums of aid from the American people, the British a loan of three and three-quarters billion, the French a loan of one and one-quarter billion, and the Germans almost one billion in United States Army relief.) Italy received over one billion dollars of aid, the Netherlands nearly that much, but the other states tapered off swiftly with lesser sums down to Trieste which received only 33 million dollars of American money in four years, and Iceland, low man on the totem pole, with 27 million dollars.

It was difficult to make so vast a quantity of money seem real. Those who wished to minimize it said it was far less than America spent on her liquor bill over the same period of time. Those who wished to demonstrate how large it was said it was more than the United States had spent to govern itself in the first fifteen years of this century. Some tried to chop it into measurable bits by saying that every day it lasted, the United States was spending ten million dollars every twenty-four hours to sustain Europe. But, finally and fundamentally, it could be understood only as ships bearing goods that Europe could no longer order with her own money.

In the winter of 1950, when Europe's pulse had revived from a flicker to a beat, and the Plan was in full flood, I checked the movement of ships to one country, France, alone. On that day, the S.S. *Godrun Maersk*, three weeks out of Baltimore, came butting through the heavy seas of the Channel to dock at Rouen and unload Marshall Plan tractors, chemicals, synthetic resin and cellulose acetate. Sixty miles down river from Rouen, at Le Havre, on the same day, the S.S. *Cape Race* also out of Baltimore checked in with another load of general cargo. And on that same day, five hundred miles to the south, the S.S. *Gibbes Lykes* pulled up the narrow twisting ship's channel of Marseille with 3,500 tons of Gulf Coast sulfur. In the next three days ten more American ships weighed in around the rim of France. Into their dirty holds the Marshall Plan had stuffed tires, borax, aircraft parts and drilling equipment on the S.S. *Samuel Stranger;* farm machines, chemicals, oil on the S.S. *Rhondda;* 2,500 more tons of sulfur on the S.S. *Shirley Lykes.* And, of course, cotton—on the S.S. *Geirulo*, S.S. *Delmundo*, S.S. *Lapland*, S.S. *Cotton States*, S.S. *Velma Lykes;* with such cotton one hundred and seventy thousand French textile workers held their jobs. By that date, in February of 1950, over one thousand ships had unloaded Marshall Plan cargo in France alone. To keep all Europe going, at any given moment of the day or night, there were an estimated 150 ships either bringing Marshall Plan cargo to Europe on the high seas or unloading it in her ports.

Another way of trying to trace the money was to follow not where it went but how it went. Of the $12,285,200,000, almost one billion (849 million) had gone simply to pay for hauling the cargo across the ocean. Another 360 million had been used for unfreezing Europe's trade by a device called the European Payments Union. Some of the rest could be tracked down in physical goods, ploughing, rotating, generating energy, like the tractors on European farms each bearing the red-white-and-blue shields that marked them as fruit of the ERP, or European Recovery Program; but most of the rest could not be traced except in yellowing vouchers in the General Accounting Office of the United States government.

The General Accounting Office broke its records down into two kinds of shipments, agricultural products and industrial products. They took equal sums, roughly more than five billion dollars each.

Of the five and one-quarter billion that went into buying American farm produce, about three billion dollars went for food. Most of the food was wheat in the form of grain or flour, but the food bill also covered the pantry requirements of every curious European taste right down to the last $20,000,000 budgeted for horsemeat. The other two billion dollars of farm produce was split, three-quarters for cotton and one-quarter for tobacco to keep nervous Europeans smoking.

Of the five and one-half billion that went into industrial products, $1,600,000,000 or about a third went into energy shipments, either coal or petroleum. Two billion went into raw materials which meant nonferrous metals like copper and zinc, plus pulp, timber, woods, chemicals. A final $1,900,000,000 went into machinery and vehicles.

A sum of money so huge ceases to be money. It becomes a force in its own right, that spends itself, that creates its own magnetic fields, that grows out of its own vitality the organs, tentacles, fibrils and limbs needed to match its growing responsibilities.

The Marshall Plan began its life in Europe in June of 1948 in a wing of two borrowed offices on the second floor of the American Embassy in Paris. Crammed into alcoves and under and over each other were dignitaries with hundreds of millions of dollars at their fingertips, whose immediate battle was to win a telephone, a wastebasket, a desk for one's private secretary. But as personnel poured in from America, it grew and expanded, flooding over from building to building, sprawling over downtown Paris, with its own buses, snack bars, house mothers and social life. With it a new American community developed. Professors of economics on leave from their universities came in with every plane; so did the bankers and businessmen drafted to save American civilization; so did publicity agents, animal husbandry men, malleable iron ore men, insecticide experts, guitar players, and finally a special osteopath to unkink the knots from the weary muscles of the master-men. It spread over Europe—in each country a regional outpost, called a Country Mission, was established with *its* finance, trade, agriculture and public relations specialists.

The superior direction of the vast operation, called the Office of the Special Representative of the President, or OSR, was soon installed in the Hotel Talleyrand. The Hotel Talleyrand, a labyrinthine maze of cubicles, pens, partitions and squeaking old corridors, was the home in which the great Talleyrand had once conducted his love affairs while simultaneously, as Victor Hugo said, luring the princes and statesmen of Europe thither, "as a spider into its web," and then destroying them one by one. Now, in 1948, it was to be the office of Mr. Averell Harriman, who arrived with the rank of Ambassador to take over command. Mr.

Harriman was the Special Representative, a man who as Chief of Lend Lease Operations had given away more money than any human being in world history and who was already a past master in the art of handling public billions. Here, in the gilt and green private sanctum of his office, beneath a bust of Benjamin Franklin, another American with a shrewd sense of the buck, Harriman made the great decisions. Downstairs in the technicians' offices and at the snack bar that served hot dogs and ice cream for Americans who had no time to luxuriate on French food, the lesser thinkers made their comment. And in the evening policy-makers large and small would wander out of the Hotel Talleyrand across the great Place de la Concorde, glistening with huge American automobiles, to the bar of the Hotel Crillon where Europe and the world were pulled apart, remolded, put back together again every evening in conversation by experts fresh out of Muncie, Indiana, and Knoxville, Tennessee.

Conversation at the Crillon Bar was like no other bar-talk. "They say they want to know how much wheat France is going to be able to export, so they ask how many tractors will France need to raise that much wheat. . . . Well, we get to work and produce a figure and we give it to the commercial boys and they say how many of these do you think France can make herself, then somebody else says well so many and somebody else says when? and there you are. . . . You take Turkey, that's really fouled up. I figure they could raise maybe a million tons of wheat there, but somebody else says there's no water. So we figure we could irrigate the land, and somebody else says how are you going to move that million tons of wheat out of there? By mule cart? Then after you get through figuring how to put in the machinery, the irrigation and the railways, you find out they've got 800,000 wooden ploughs there and if the wheat market goes down it'll squeeze those peasants out and they're liable to blow up the machinery and the railways. Every time you touch something it gets tangled up in something else and you have to spend all your time untangling it. I tell you this Europe is really a mess. Garçon, two more drys over here. . . ."

Men, caught up in the excitement, came and went so fast that it was difficult to keep track of them. In its first year the vital Program Review Division of the Plan, the watchtower division that was supposed to study all European requests for funds and tie them to one continental strategy of recovery, had had no less than three chiefs. The important Industry Division, supervising the reconquest of European efficiency, had three chiefs. So had the no-less-vital Trade and Payments Division, whose chief function was to watch the Dollar Gap. Within the first year the Chiefs of Mission in England, France, Germany, Holland, Austria, Greece and Norway had left their posts and returned or gone on to something else. The top-level command of the Plan, Averell Harriman and Milton Katz, stayed with it; so did the junior-level technicians who were caught up in its deep enthusiasm. But in the middle-command range seats changed like a game of musical chairs.

In those early days the personalities of the Plan stewed, bubbled and melted down to that curious amalgam of types that has been making American decisions overseas for fifteen years: enlightened businessmen, seeking a burst of adventure or impelled by patriotism and convinced that, by God, American business could put the world to rights; New Dealers who saw the Plan spreading America's New Deal all around the globe; college professors on summer leave, translating theory to practice and collecting material for future lectures and learned monographs in which all the mistakes would be illuminated by hindsight; and government officials, the permanent floating corps of civil servants searching for better job ratings to be found in Europe, from which they could return to Washington and prominence.

They came in all sizes, with many visions. Some stood on the mountaintop, surveying the world with lofty understanding and saw themselves touching it here and there with a wand to make it fruitful. I remember having lunch with one of the chiefs of the Program Division of the Plan during its days of high exuberance and asking him what we were going to do about India. He pulled his pipe out of his mouth and barely broke the stride of conversation to say, "Now if there's a big famine, we'll have to buck it through to Congress and let Congress handle it, but if it's a small famine we'll handle it out of our own funds without any trouble." Others were more perplexed by the dimensions of the task. I remember visiting one professor of economics who had had a three months' assignment as advisor to the Plan during summer leave from his university. I visited him to say good-by just as his leave was up and his desk, normally piled with reports, documents, surveys, papers and recommendations, was clear at last, and he was sitting with his feet on the desk.

"What are you doing?" I asked.

"I'm thinking," he said, "just thinking. You know, this is the first time I've had a chance to think about this thing since I came here, we've been so busy. We ought to have more time to think."

Underneath a frantic surface activity the Plan developed.

The basic idea was as simple as it was valid, as true in the Plan's beginning as it is now: Europe had to become productive.

The analysis behind this idea was shared by Europeans and Americans alike. To sell enough to earn her way in the world, Europe had to produce efficiently and cheaply enough to make the rest of the world eager to take her goods again. This analysis had been implicit in the Plan ever since that day in June, 1947, when George Marshall stood under the green elms of Harvard and explained that the problem was not the visible destruction of the war but the longer, slower, deeper obsolescence and deterioration of Europe's productive machinery. Europe's physical plant had to be overhauled, rebuilt, re-equipped and modernized from the ground up.

Certain contrasts between European performance were in 1947 and still are today so large as to be stupefying. Four hundred and fifty thousand American miners produce each year more coal than the 1,600,000 West European miners put together. The average American worker stands at his factory bench backed by seven horsepower of energy supplied him by machines, forklifts and mechanized hand tools; the average European worker is backed by only two and one-half horsepower. The most efficient automobile plant in France is the nationalized Renault works which, with 53,000 factory hands, produces 170,000 vehicles a year, 100,000 of which are the tiny four horsepower sedans that seem like toys to Americans. But General Motors with 320,000 productive workers produces 3,000,000 automobiles, the smallest of which is larger than the largest Renault product; these workers also produce refrigerators, locomotives, aircraft engines, arms, household appliances too numerous to mention. Or, to put it another way, a worker at General Motors gets out, in the course of the year, six or seven times as much automobile products as an equally skilled French worker; the average General Motors worker hence gets paid as much for an hour's work as most Renault workers get paid for the work of a day. When, in 1948, the Marshall Plan was launched, there was not one single continuous strip-steel mill in continental Europe, while there were over twenty such modern mills in the United States. Since cheap strip and sheet steel mean cheap refrigerators, cheap automobiles, cheap tinned foods, cheap washbasins and sinks, most Europeans lived and still live without these things.

Both the OEEC, the council of the European partners in the Plan, and the Americans therefore agreed that the great goal was to make Europe productive again, so that her manufactures could go out into the world in tremendous competitive quantities to earn Europe's keep once more. They likewise agreed on the emergency measures of the summer of 1948—the in-pumping of relief food, fuel and raw materials to meet the present chaos and to stabilize the peril long enough for long-range planning to begin. It was here, in the longer-range planning, that thinking became more difficult.

Certain measures were obviously necessary in everyone's eyes, Europeans and Americans alike. Americans and Europeans agreed that each individual country had to throttle inflation before fruitful activity could begin. They agreed that the Marshall Plan had to finance huge investments in new electricity generating plants, new coal mechanization, new oil refineries, new kinds of farming equipment. But these were not enough, either technically or politically, as a master strategy. Gradually, within the first year of the Plan's operation, this new master strategy came to clothe itself with the symbolism of a United Europe.

Thinking out of the sweeping continental glories of American geography, where the coal of the lower Lakes mixes with the iron ore of the upper Lakes without a single frustrating barrier, where the cotton of the South moves north without a single tariff interposed, Americans began to feel that only by getting such a circulation coursing through Europe could they make it healthy again. If the tariffs, quotas, currency restrictions, subsidies and import-export licenses that chopped up Europe's internal trade could be wiped out, then European industries would be led by each other's competition and cooperation to such efficiency as would match the world's best. It was ridiculous, thought Americans, that German life should be frozen for lack of freight cars while Belgian workers less than one hundred miles away should be idle in freight-car-making plants simply because Germany did not have the right kind of currency to order freight cars in Belgium.

For the Americans, the dynamic, exciting way to make Europe come alive was to force it to think in new, competitive terms in a Europe where old national barriers should be smashed. The Americans thus declared that they would not consider individual shopping lists from individual countries. Here are five billion dollars, said Mr. Harriman to the OEEC in its first year; this is the pie, you must cut it among yourselves. In the excitement of anticipation, the Europeans accepted the invitation as if it were entirely normal, instead of entirely new, and for the first time, in arguing and squabbling over the division of American aid, they bared, each of them, all their economic plans and secrets to all their neighbors in the first true step to European cooperation. Step by step, the Marshall Plan tried to force the Europeans together—much of America's aid to certain nations was made conditional on the promise of those nations to make an equivalent amount of aid available to their nearby neighbors in goods they lacked. Session by session, the European nations meeting at OEEC forced each other to lift quota restrictions on the movement of goods between them, first on fifty per cent of all trade within Europe, next on sixty per cent, ultimately on seventy-five per cent. By 1950 the Marshall Plan had subsidized a scheme of European trade payments called the European Payments Union which, in effect, linked all European currencies together in one new international currency. By then, too, the Marshall Plan had found a word for its goal: integration. Europe was being integrated.

Integration was vitally important for pure commercial and industrial efficiency, and among the great triumphs of the Marshall Plan has been its success in forcing Europe as far as it has come today on the road. But not all Europeans liked integration, and chief among these were the British. The British had an alternate point of view which challenged and still challenges the American.

The problem, said the British, lay not within Europe but in the outside world, and chiefly in America. The Europeans could not solve their problems by taking in each other's washing nor by setting up a free flow of trade within their own confines. Such a free flow, the British admitted, would greatly increase the industrial and commercial efficiency of the old powers, but it would also let their currencies leak and flow among each other so that the weakest and most anarchic in the European partnership could drain away the reserves of the strongest and best governed. The British were willing to be integrated, but only if the Americans also would let themselves be integrated. If the Americans were willing to reduce their tariff barriers and permit European goods to circulate freely in the Atlantic Basin, if the Americans were willing to reduce their immigration walls and let Italian, Dutch and Belgian unemployed seek work in America, then the British were willing to do all these things too. The problem, said the British, was not only one of a European deficit, but of an artificially preserved American surplus. This British reasoning has persisted ever since, until its final formulation under the Tory government of Mr. Churchill as a pursuit of "Trade Not Aid."

Such debate continued for the first year and a half of the Marshall Plan down to the spring of 1950, as Americans and Europeans groped their way toward the solution of Europe's problems. The spring of 1950 was a good time to look at the Marshall Plan. It is difficult now, looking back over the world through the emotional ache of the Korean War, to remember the image of Europe that spring. The Plan seemed at last to be working. Europe was not only at peace with the ending of the Berlin blockade, but seemed, finally, after a generation, to be working toward that upland plateau of sun and prosperity for which it so longed. Every production target of the Plan had been met and surpassed. Overall European production was forty-five per cent higher than in 1947 and twenty-five per cent higher than in the last prewar year. England's reserves of dollars and gold were showing their first healthy growth since the war, and moreover, the British were exporting fifty per cent more than ever before in their history. In France the sickening nausea of inflation was fading and prices were steadying, even falling. By 1950, five years before the most optimistic forecast, German production had reached the prosperous level of 1936. The relief shipments of the Plan's early years were giving way to the materials and equipment of industrial reconstruction. The OEEC had settled down to the unglamorous but fruitful spadework of industrial planning. The infamous Dollar Gap was being squeezed to its postwar low of two billion dollars. Happy days seemed close at hand, and the individual triumphs of the Plan stood out crisp and brilliant.

In every country in Europe there was some outstanding project to which a Congressman or visiting delegation of distinguished Americans could be taken and told, here is the Marshall Plan at work. In Sardinia, the Plan was draining the ageless malarial swamps that had withered its population with disease. Clean malaria from Sardinia, someone had said, and you have prepared an immigration outlet for two million Italians under their own flag. In the Netherlands, Marshall Plan financing was poldering off the Zuyder Zee with new dikes, preparing to raise 128,000 acres of fertile farmland from the sea. In Turkey, Marshall Plan ploughs, tractors, railways were changing an Asian way of life. Scores of geologists and explorers were chasing around the African empires of the European partners in the greatest treasure hunt in history, seeking new raw materials for a busy world. In France, Marshall Plan money was financing long-overdue mechanization of French coal mines and the giant task of electrification of a nation by hydropower; by 1950, four times as many tractors ploughed French farms as before the war. The muddy sockets of two huge steel mills, one north of Paris and the other in the blast-furnace country of Lorraine, were being hollowed out to hold American equipment being built across the Atlantic to give France the Continent's first continuous strip-steel mills.

Though a balmy, easy sense of euphoria and achievement now began to rise all across Western Europe and drench the public pronouncements and statements of all the captains of the Plan, within the Hotel Talleyrand, at the planning level, contentment was neither widespread nor solid. As the emergency seemed to dissolve, as the planners could relax for a longer, second look at Europe and savor their experience, they recognized that before them lay stubborn, persistent problems as yet unsolved.

The two chief problems fell very neatly into the two purposes the plan had originally set for itself in 1948. The first purpose had been to make Europe productively efficient so that it could support itself by selling to the world again; the second had been to earn, politically, enough loyalty to the democratic way of life so that the Europeans should turn a deaf ear to communism.

To make Europe productively efficient, the Marshall Planners had bet heavily on two tactics: integration and liberalization of trade. But by 1950 enough knowledge had been acquired by the Americans to realize that European business life was not going to be shaken up simply by opening its crisscrossing frontiers to trade. European business life and its productive efficiency were strangled in a jungle of intertwined cartels and habits that were even worse than the government regulations and barriers at which Americans had leveled their fire. They were protected in their ridiculously old-fashioned habits, not so much by government dictate as by the cartels, combines, and associations they had formed privately to fix prices, control competition, control supplies; these combines were built to shelter the most obsolete and inefficient eighty-year-old plants from the cost competition of the newest plants of European engineering, which were excellent.

No European government had an efficient antitrust law; in fact, most governments permitted industries to patrol and police their own cartel rules. In France the Marshall Planners learned sadly that the "groupements" or industrial advisory groups through which American aid was distributed by the French government, were no more than the official sharing agencies of the cartels themselves. The great new continuous strip-steel mill which the Marshall Plan had awarded to the French steel industry in Lorraine, it was learned, was to be controlled entirely by the French steel cartel. In Italy the Marshall Planners were trying to raise the standards of Italian farming by urging Italian farmers to use chemical fertilizers. But chemical fertilizer was too expensive for threadbare Italian peasants, because in Italy it was made by obsolete processes in obsolete plants. Yet new plants could not be built, for the great chemical cartel of Italy felt that new plants making cheap fertilizer would wipe out their investment in and profits from old, inefficient plants. The planners had thought that the lifting of government trade barriers alone would bring fruitful competition; they had never realized the depth, the extent, the frightful weight of European business combines opposed to competition. Now, in the spring of 1950, they pondered whether and how to bring American weight to bear against them.

The problem on the second, or "political," front was more important. The Americans at the Hotel Talleyrand, who felt that a new approach was needed, called the original approach of the Marshall Plan "logistical." The logistical approach had relied on technical figures—if so much new steel capacity was put in, then so many new tractors or automobiles might be built, so many more machines might be exported from so many more new factories which might, together, close the Dollar Gap. This logistical, or mathematical, victory would then become so apparent in physical well-being that Europeans would independently come to forswear communism, espouse democracy and all would be well.

Some of the opponents of the logistical approach called it the "trickle theory," or the theory which held that if enough is poured in at the top, something will trickle down to the bottom. The trickle theory had, thus far, resulted in a brilliant recovery of European production. But it had yielded no love for America and little diminution of Communist loyalty where it was entrenched in the misery of the continental workers. The rich and well-to-do rolled about once more in automobiles that were beginning to crowd the streets, they took their vacations in luxury, they ate well. But the workers had barely held their own; they lived in stinking, festering slums, dressed in shabby second-hand clothes. In Italy and France a working wage still averaged fifteen dollars a week. It was pointless to explain to the workers that without the Marshall Plan they would have been entirely unemployed, that they might have starved or died, that the Plan had saved them. The workers could see only that what had been saved was the status quo, that the recovery had preserved their discomfort and given its fruits to the privileged. In the slums the Communists held on to their voters even through the happiest days of the Plan.

By the spring and summer of 1950 the planners had come to recognize these great problems and were preparing a new attack. I called on one of the new chiefs that June and found him full of vigor, charged with enthusiasm. "The object of the exercise," he said, "is to win people over to democracy. Up to now the stuff has been helping only the people who've got to be with us anyway, the people who can't go over to the Russians even if they want. The loyalties we should be fighting for are those of the people who are in doubt, the poor and the workers, the slums of France and Italy that the Commies have captured and we've got to get back. That's who we're going after now."

The Plan did indeed make the beginning of an attempt, urging wage raises on the recipients of its industrial bounty, prodding lethargic governments to rebuild slum housing. But it was late. The five billion dollar appropriation of its first year had been spent, and the four billion dollar appropriation of its second year allotted. Congress had offered only two billion dollars for its third year appropriation, and the leverage of the Plan over European society was correspondingly reduced. Much might, however, have been done, for two billion dollars is a great deal of money; it might have built thousands of houses, thousands of new schools, pried open scores of cartels, forced up wages in thousands of European factories.

Indeed, all this might have happened, but for one great event—the Korean War. The Korean War changed everything, and all the Western world turned to one new objective—defense and rearmament. The original Marshall Plan had stipulated that not one penny of its largesse might be used by a European government for military purposes or to support such nonproductive enterprises as the war in Indo-China. Eight months after the Korean War broke out, the United States government informed the Europeans that every penny of Marshall Plain aid would be allotted on a basis of how much it contributed to the Western defense effort. Originally, American aid had had as its sole purpose the reshaping of Europe's peaceful life by making a more fruitful community of men. From 1950 its overriding purpose was to arm Europe. By 1952, eighty per cent of American aid was given in military weapons and the other twenty per cent in defense support.

Though the Marshall Plan continued in name down to the beginning of 1952, historically it came to its end the week the Communists attacked in Asia. It had lasted two years and had made a brave beginning; it had brought Europe to that point of convalescence where it might support the heavy charge of arms imposed by the new crisis. But when war came the Plan had only begun to understand and come to grips with the deeper persistent problems of European life. When the Plan was ended it left those problems, still unsolved, to Europeans, whose primary responsibility they still remain.

In 1952 the pretense that the Marshall Plan was engaged in reviving the society of Western Europe was finally dropped and the Plan was merged with its companion enterprise the Military Defense Aid Program, or MDAP, in the Mutual Security Agency, or MSA. The MSA continued to dwell in the old Hotel Talleyrand, but iron grills now barred its entrances, military guards watched its portals, and to enter one must have been carefully scrutinized and have shown a security pass. The summer of 1950 thus marked both the high point of the Plan and its departure from the page of history with its work unfinished. An anonymous bard at the Hotel Talleyrand penned its epitaph:

ERP in nineteen-fifty,
Is something spick and span and nifty,
Brightly polished, simonized, integrated, harmonized.
The Marshall Plan is obsolete,
Our 1950 model's neat.
New chrome plating strikes the eyes,
With the legend "Harmonize."
Nineteen nations lift their voices
In loving chant and splendid noises
"Bread and Guns to Harmonize."

Reconstruction, Integration,
Dollar Shortage, Liberalization,
Off with these old-fashioned ties!
Now's the time to harmonize.

PART

2

IV

dramatis personae

In Western Europe live approximately 300,000,000 people governed and separated by twenty-five different nation-states that range from the Vatican City (population: 940) to the United Kingdom (population: 50,368,455).

A tourist guide to the life of these people records with equal enthusiasm a wild array of interesting facts about them: the fact that French policemen have a mania for hustling and speeding the driver to whirl through traffic faster and faster; that the best herring and cream in Europe is served in the legislative dining halls of the Saar; that English epicures have invented a substitute for heavy sweet cream which requires only cream cheese, milk, sugar and a drop of kirsch; that one can buy a custom-tailored suit cheaper in Spain than anywhere else on the Continent; that the Roman arches, arenas and ancient temples of Southern France are more magnificent than any ruins in Rome itself.

What the tourist guide does not record is that although all these facts are distinctly related to the political process, there is one brutal and simple standard for deciding what facts in Europe count in current history and what do not. This standard is based solely on the name of the country involved, for in European politics there are only two kinds of country.

There are the Big Three—France, England and Germany. And there are the others.

Only France, England and Germany have, in themselves, the internal potential of decision which may alter the march of great events. The leaders of France, England and Germany are no more brilliant or able than the leaders of Holland, Belgium, Italy or Sweden. Indeed, when the chiefs of the lesser states sit in council with chiefs of the great states, they frequently by sheer personality overshadow the Frenchmen, Englishmen and Germans with whom they gather. But the leaders of these other states can only comment, whereas the leaders of the Big Three speak out of traditions that goad them to act, whether they will or not, as history-makers.

The others cannot be ignored. As industrial producers, as geographical buffers, as zones of dispute, as contributory influences, they bring enormous impact to bear on specific situations.

The Saarland, a state of a million people living on a patch of coal and woodland, set like a wart on France's northeastern shoulder, poisons the angry pride of both France and Germany and abscesses all the greater problems of those two countries.

Trieste, a city of broad clean streets and majestic Teutonic buildings at the headwaters of the Adriatic, is spotted on SHAPE's maps as one of the weakest links in Western defense, because here the conflicting emotions of Italian and Yugoslav peasants are locked in stalemate, and defense cannot be planned in the area until these emotions compromise.

Belgium with its 8,700,000 people, its powerful army, its muscular industry seems like no problem to anyone, but its very vitality drains and strains the economies of its neighbors so that any economic conference in Europe ultimately grapples with the Belgian problem.

The Vatican is a state no larger than a city park, but every foreign office in the world knows how potent and prodigious is its silent influence on the hearts of men.

Yugoslavia with its 17,000,000 people is far more important than its half-million-man army suggests because it is radiant with an heretic set of ideas which disturb the Russians more than guns.

What brackets all these lesser states together as chanters of the chorus is the prime political fact that they cannot of themselves offer a solution to any great problem, nor can they obstruct a solution once the great powers of the world have agreed. In Europe, only England, France and Germany can attempt to do this.

Except for Italy, these states are not necessarily sad because they are denied greatness. Most of them, by their very resignation from world decision, have been able to offer their citizens more happiness than the Big Three. The Saar, freed of both French and German burdens of arms, refugees, occupation costs, colonial war, is the most prosperous enclave in industrial Europe, offering its citizens more new homes per capita than any other state on the Continent. Some of the lesser states in Europe, like the Swiss and Swedes, are lucky—geography plus a century of tradition have permitted them to stand apart. The other lesser states cannot stand apart, because they know that in any convulsion of world politics they are inevitably embroiled. They can only watch, offer advice, ask or donate aid or support and sigh reluctantly once decisions are taken.

England, France and Germany are different. They are personalities of power. They cannot be controlled, choked or bribed without an upheaval that shakes world power. They are the states that can vote themselves out of the Atlantic Alliance and, by this single act, destroy it. If they quarrel with each other, all strategy crumbles. If they are healthy, then all their lesser neighbors will throb with good health too, and if they are caught with inflation or depression, the contagion likewise ultimately infects all their neighbors. If they can be brought together in common purpose they might make a force almost equal to the United States or the Soviet Union. Since the war it has been the cardinal aim of American foreign policy to bring and keep these three great states together and in harmony with our purposes against the Russians.

The men who speak for these countries, therefore, are those who make the story of Europe, not because they are greater men than the leaders of lesser countries, but because they speak with the resonance given them by peoples of greatness. The utterances and acts of most of these leaders—Churchill, Monnet, Attlee, Adenauer, de Gaulle, Eden, Ollenhauer, Schumacher, Schuman, Mayer, Pleven, Butler, Bidault—are the stuff of public record, as crisp as yesterday's headlines and as certain of memory as tomorrow's history books. But their power is not self-produced; their power rises from millions of their fellow citizens, all of them bearing a natural, hereditary responsibility that does not rest on a Monacan, a Luxembourger, an Austrian, a Frisian or an Italian.

If we can see what perplexes these people and what they seek, we can see how the struggle in Europe is shaped. And if Willi

Schlieker in the Ruhr, Pierre Bertaux in Paris, Joe Curry in Yorkshire, claim more attention in this book than de Gasperi, Spaak, van Zeeland, Tito or Franco, it is because they speak for Germany, for France and for England—they are membranes through which the forces of history filter and show themselves.

V

the mystery of France

Every country is a mystery composed of the lives of many men. Yet none is more sealed to the understanding than the mystery of France.

For a full generation the spectacle of French politics—fretful, whining, querulous—has become so commonplace, the hysterics with which French politics twist from turning point to turning point of decision without deciding anything has become, indeed, so normal that they have long since lost interest for anyone but a student of *psychopathia politica*. Frenchmen, like strangers, regard the politics of their country with the cynical detachment of total contempt.

The mystery of France is simple to describe. Here lies the richest and most beautiful land of Europe. Here live some of its most illuminating minds. Here are men of courage and great tradition, toilers of dogged diligence and consummate craftsmanship. Yet nothing comes of this human material, France wastes and abuses all the talents she possesses.

France, larger than England and Western Germany put together, is a jeweled country. Its fields roll in fragrant beauty from the English Channel to the Mediterranean, six hundred miles from north to south, six hundred miles from east to west. The great wheat plains of the Beauce that sprawl over the heart of the country about Paris, tender green in spring and golden dry in midsummer, are among the lushest in the world; many a wheat farm on the Aisne is more fruitful than the richest of America's midcontinent. The meadows of Normandy and the uplands of Gascony are speckled with fat cattle. Down the cleft in France's central mountain bulge runs the swift-flowing Rhône opening on a triangle of sun-washed, subtropical fruitland, vegetable land

and wineland. Beneath French soil lie some of the most formidable deposits of iron ore in the entire world, substantial coal—though not enough—enormous reserves of bauxite for aluminum, potential pools of oil and natural gas as yet untapped. Off the Alps, the Pyrenees, and the Massif Central plunge rivers with stupendous force to give France more natural hydropower potential than any other country in Europe. And what France lacks at home, she can find abroad, for her overseas empire, since the dwindling of the British, has come to be the largest colonial domain in the world. France is the envy of every nation in Europe, and the Germans, with that nostalgia of Germans for things which are not theirs, recite as a definition of happiness: "Fröhlich wie der liebe Gott in Frankreich"—"Happy as Dear God in France."

In this country, moreover, live forty-two million people of extraordinary skill, application and tradition. Second only to the British, they have provided the ideas and thinking of the modern world. The energy of the nucleus was first explored in France, the power of rushing water was first converted to electric energy in the French Alps, the medicine of the twentieth century descends from its beginning in French science. The genius of French art cramps the brush of every painter in the world today in imitation. French taste in clothes robes the women of all the world; French taste in food is the absolute definition of man's culinary achievement. Lastly, the individual courage of Frenchmen is unquestioned. Even now after the slaughters of the Second World War one cannot stand on the wild, torn slopes of Verdun before the great mausoleum of dead men's bones without imagination boggling at French bravery.

Yet all this adds up to nothing. Courage, brilliance, skill compounded with riches, land and sun come to fruit today in France, as for a generation, in bitterness, poverty and a paralysis of withering indecision.

This is the big mystery. But the mystery is a mosaic of lesser mysteries. Why, in a France that produces all its own foods, does butter cost twice as much as it does in a Britain that lives in a siege economy hauling butter from thousands of miles overseas? Why could the France of 1939 furnish 115 divisions to do battle whereas France today had such difficulty in furnishing an undermanned twelve? How have the Germans been able to erect out of defeat a solid, enduring government that has lasted four full years, while the victorious French have had so many changes of leadership in that period that not one Frenchman in a hundred can count the number of his Cabinets? Why should the resources of a nation so great provide an average working wage for her citizens of fifteen to twenty dollars a week, while a pound of meat costs 80 cents, a pair of baby's shoes four dollars, a black market apartment rental $150 a month? And why, finally, should the French, conscious of all these mysteries, after eight years of the most determined wrestling with them, have only succeeded in tangling things more than ever before?

The first quick impression at the surface of French politics is confusion.

But this confusion is only a many-faceted reflection of one central fact, the great and dominant fact of French life: that Frenchmen are divided against each other, distrust each other, execrate each other and are more cruel to each other than any other people in the democratic world. Other modern nations are divided too, but the others have been pressed, decade by decade, by the pounding of change and war into homogeneous groups. The Germans defeated twice, smashed twice, ruined by inflation twice, brutalized by barbarians of their own choice have been fused into, and remain, a community. The Russians have been whipped, cramped and drugged by a dictatorship into an even tighter community. Americans and Britons have arrived, out of their own history, at so peaceful a kinship that for the vast majority of citizens the divisions of politics are almost immaterial.

But France is different. Frenchmen are divided in so many ways, with so many cross sections of cleavage, lacerated by so many feuds new and old, that they cannot find any way to gather in groups large enough on issues clear enough to make decisions. All political alliances in France are formed against something, not for something, and they are impotent because they combine men who hate each other only a shade less than they hate their enemy of the moment. French life does not divide; it splinters. Frenchmen splinter on whether to revile the Church or to cherish it, on whether to socialize the country further or desocialize it. The rich hate the poor, the poor hate the rich; the rich are divided between Catholic and non-Catholic; the poor are divided between Communist and non-Communist; the city workers are divided against the country peasants; and in every village and neighborhood, fresh memory of wartime resistance and collaboration divides and subdivides these groups all over again.

These divisions breed paralysis and paradox. The only way so many disparate people can live together at all is to grant to each group an almost total liberty and thus liberty is more complete, the air freer, the individual human more unfettered in thought and expression—even if more perplexed—in France than anywhere else in the Atlantic Basin. This liberty has its counterface: a total social indifference to the hurts and aches of anyone outside one's own individual circle. There is less mercy between Frenchman and Frenchman than in any Christian country of the West. Organized charity, in the sense that it has developed in America and Britain, is all but unknown. What there is is a fig leaf of fancy balls and glittering receptions for the fashionable folk of Paris at which they can salve conscience and parade new clothes. The outstanding individual act of charity by a Frenchman since the war was the gift of five million dollars by a French merchant to found a new college—but not in France. The gift was given to Oxford, in England.

This suspicion, mistrust and indifference of Frenchman to Frenchman breeds a brilliant and dangerous courage in the individual man which, when compounded in a community, breeds weakness and cowardice. It breeds lastly a crowning paradox: all Frenchmen passionately love France and hate all other Frenchmen for bemeaning her.

All these divisions come to their natural political negation in Paris, in that great Roman temple called the Palais Bourbon which holds the French National Assembly.

The Palais Bourbon sits on the Seine, looking out over the gray space of the Place de la Concorde, as if brooding over the many memories of blood and wild excitement that have crowded across that most beautiful of city squares for almost two hundred years. Until two years ago, two signs—one of which is now gone—no more than twenty feet apart on its gray walls told more vividly than any essay of the attitude of the French to their sovereign Republic. One was a row of white marble plaques, incised with gold lettering, giving the names of four French youths who, at that point, in the glorious days of the August, 1944, insurrection against the Germans, had given their lives that France might be free again and her Republic flourish. Now and then, in devotion, Frenchmen still thrust spring flowers into the crevices of these marble plaques to honor their sacrifice. The other sign was a blue enameled plaque with white lettering which said simply: "Défence D'Uriner"—"Do not urinate against these walls," exhorting Frenchmen not to stain their sovereign's shelter with dishonor. Perhaps because the sign so amused strange visitors, or perhaps because it was no longer necessary, the French in the winter of 1952 removed the blue and white plaque and only the sockets of its studs are still visible. But the range of emotions the two signs spanned remains still as true as ever.

Within the National Assembly, 627 men make the laws of France, impose its taxes, conscript its soldiers and decide its role in the great world. The easiest way of understanding how the differences that bud in the villages harden into bitter fruit in this sovereign body is to sit in the gallery of its windowless chamber and look down at the deputies on their red plush benches spread in a half-moon about the speaker's rostrum. Only a long and dreary catalogue could list all the factions, splinters and purposes proclaimed in this hall. But if one disregards several dozen freewheelers in factional coteries, along with the Arab deputies in their tarbooshes and flowing robes, and the Negro deputies sent by the dark peoples of Africa, then one finds that the people of France have succeeded in packaging their differences in six different party-packages of deputies of nearly equal size, each holding a few more or a few less than one hundred seats. Within each of these groups, to be sure, there are further differences but—since anarchy must end somewhere—party discipline, the hope of spoils, the distaste or outright hatred for neighboring parties who sit nearby keep them bound together under the cautious control of their leaders.

The six parties should be read from right to left. Farthest right are the Peasant-Independents, the repository of all French reaction, swayed chiefly by two men: the stubborn, parsimonious ex-village mayor, Antoine Pinay, and the bobbing acid little ex-Premier Paul Reynaud. Next, comes the Rally of the French People, the party created by General de Gaulle and now abandoned by him, a collection at once of some of the finest and most despicable men in French life. Following them come the Radical-Socialists, a party supported by businessmen and peasant small-holders. The Radical-Socialist is the great republican party of France's yesterday; it is studded with able names, yet is unable to decide whether to go forward or backward. The MRP (Movement of Popular Republicans) which comes next, was born out of the wartime Resistance, is frankly Catholic in origin and inspiration, and is committed to a program of social reform at home and European Union abroad. Its two great leaders, Robert Schuman and Georges Bidault, have dominated French diplomacy and hence that of Europe since the war. The Socialist party to the left of it has become in France a middle class and white-collar worker party which, like its onetime rival, the Radicals, coasts on the memories of past greatness without a doctrine for the twentieth century; since the death of Léon Blum it has produced no great leader. Finally, there is the Communist party, a seamless phalanx of party hacks, rigid, inflexible, destructive, under a discipline that traces directly back to Moscow.

Since even the listing of these names and doctrines is confusing, most people who deal with the Assembly of France sort them out in a more convenient way. They draw a margin down each side of the Chamber and mark off the Gaullists (erroneously) as the extreme Right and the Communists as the extreme Left; these two parties have in common nothing but their kindred desire to destroy the present parliamentary system of France, though for different motives. The other four parties then divide up quite normally into two halves, a Right and a Left, like Republicans and Democrats or Labour and Tory, except that each of these halves is split. The splitting line in each case, in each half, is religion. The two conservative parties are the Radical-Socialists who boast that they destroyed the power of the Catholic Church in France, and the Peasant-Independents, devoutly wedded to Church and village curé. The parties of the mild Center-Left are the MRP and the Socialists, the MRP wishing to remarry social reform to the Christian-Catholic faith, and the Socialists coupling their social reform with unrelenting enmity to the Church.

This description of French politics becomes really complicated only when one lets the clutch in and tries to engage the gears.

It is immediately obvious that no possible majority of votes can be found in the all-powerful Assembly, unless at least three parties with profound differences among themselves get together; to make sure of a stable majority, four must get together. To make a marriage among four groups with such ancient and flaring hatreds requires an enormous, an incredible, standard of personal flexibility among the party leaders who sit together, quarrel, fall out, sit together again. It means a doling out of Cabinet portfolios to men of such divergent political credos that at times the French Cabinet seems like a horse with twelve heads, each head riding off in a different direction. When the Schuman Plan, the greatest event in French foreign policy since the war, was announced, it was proclaimed not only as the ending of the millennial feud between Frenchmen and Germans but also announced that it would open all of French Africa to German industry, too. Within a week after this historic announcement, the Minister of Overseas France, who controls French Africa and who had apparently been too busy to read the papers that week, held a press conference. He was asked what he thought of the suggestion and he said that the Schuman Plan did not include the opening of Africa to the Germans. Not only were the Minister of Foreign Affairs and the Minister of Overseas France members of the same Cabinet at the time, but they happened also to be members of the same party.

To produce any Cabinet at all in France, a majority can be formed in only one of two ways: either a national catastrophe must force divergent parties together, or their leaders must bargain out their various individual interests and claims to patronage until a weak compromise is reached, setting up a temporary partnership. Each new twist of events—a gust of inflation, the threat of war, the annual budget—wrecks the temporary compromise, destroys the voting partnership in the Assembly, and the Cabinet comes tumbling down. Since the Liberation of France in 1944, the National Assembly has chosen no less than twenty-two Cabinets from among its members, the longest-lived enduring for thirteen months, while several collapsed within a few days. As Cabinets come and go, as partners of yesterday become enemies of today and kiss and make up in the next Cabinet reshuffle, the images of public men become blurred and confused. They flicker on and off so quickly that Frenchmen get political eye-strain watching them. It is thus very natural that the two men who have had the greatest individual impact on French politics, domestic and foreign alike, since Liberation, were never elected to public office and have never been members of the National Assembly. They are, of course, General Charles de Gaulle and Jean Monnet.

No one in the entire world is more keenly aware of and sensitive to this formula of madness than the members of the National Assembly themselves. For no one can sit in the gallery of the French Assembly and listen to its speeches week after week without being astounded by the eloquence and vitality of its debate. The British House of Commons can, occasionally, when Winston Churchill and Aneurin Bevan are lacing each other with majestic fury, match it. But by the rules of the House of Commons, members may not clap, hiss or boo the speaker so that when Britons in Parliament are stirred, their emotions vent only in the deep rumble of "Hear, Hear" or "No, No"—a great angry roaring like a cage of chained lions. The French Chamber on any day of great debate offers something more like the sound of storm, with thunder cracking, lightning forking and catastrophe always imminent. Every major party will donate at least one speaker to a great debate and any number of free-lancers will follow them to the rostrum, each explaining his position in such pure and graceful language, turning aside barbs and darts from the floor with such precision and logic that the *Journal Officiel*, the Assembly's official record, is one of the most exciting continuing publications of European civilization. Nowhere else in any country in history have the words of men so illuminated the condition of their countrymen as in France's National Assembly. Yet it gives the members little pride. For each flight of eloquence is cancelled out by conflicting eloquence, and in the end France is left either leaderless or with a government that can lead only by doing nothing.

The itching, gnawing frustration of the deputies of the National

Assembly, condemned to live with each other, is aggravated by a particular historical condition that makes them perhaps the most sorrowful body of lawmakers in the world. It is a condition that springs from the war. The present crop of French deputies are not nimble graduates of the baby-kissing, wine-bibbing, hand-shaking escalator of politics, although they practice such customs with fervid good will, too. Most of the parliamentary leaders and at least half of all the deputies are men who challenged death as patriots of the Underground and Resistance, to drive the Germans from their country and make France great again. Georges Bidault, twice Prime Minister, eight times Foreign Minister, presided over the Council of National Resistance in Paris, dodging the Gestapo from lodging place to lodging place down to the last soul-scorching week of Insurrection. René Pleven, twice Prime Minister, four times Defense Minister, entered the Resistance immediately after the collapse of France in 1940, fled to Africa and there organized the uprisings of the Free French. Jules Moch, sometime Defense Minister, sometime Interior Minister, fought in the maquis of the Pyrenees, and his son, caught fighting in the maquis of Vercors, was murdered by the Gestapo. The Gaullists on the Right and the Communists on the Left count scores of heroes who survived the perils of Resistance and Insurrection; some members of the Assembly still carry on their arms the tattooing of German concentration camps. These are heroes who risked their lives to make France great again, and instead of bringing France to greatness they have brought her to paralysis, instead of giving France glory they have given her dust.

One must look back and trace the course of events from the moment of Liberation to see why these brave and brilliant men in the Assembly have failed.

When Liberation came to France in 1944, what emerged, it seemed, was a new kind of France. The shame and squalor of the French collapse in 1940, followed by reflection and suffering during the long German Occupation, had ended in a general contempt and loathing of every face and institution of the old France which had fallen so miserably to Hitler. The three great underground parties that towered over liberated France—the

MRP (or Catholic Left), the Communists and the Socialists—were all of them parties more revolutionary than reformist, sworn to take France apart and make her new again. Together, they commanded an immense popular majority of all French voters who cheered and urged them to action; in the early postwar Assemblies, they had so huge a margin of seats in their partnership that, for once, firm, clear majority leadership seemed possible. This majority of the Left in the French Parliament lasted only twenty months, but in its first sixteen months it pushed through a revolution which France has never since digested.

All three parties agreed that France was to be remade—a new system of social security would guarantee every man against sickness, baby subsidies would support each family budget, unemployment and accident would be covered by insurance, workers would participate in the control of all the plants they worked in. France had been crippled by an ancient, obsolete industry that failed every test of national usefulness before the war; therefore, declared the Liberation parties, they were to be nationalized. The coal mines, railways, gas companies, electricity companies, banks and insurance companies, airlines and steamship companies, most of the arms industry, and France's biggest automobile works were all nationalized between the summer of 1945 and the spring of 1946. Having in previous generations already nationalized all telephones and telegraphs, the potassium mines of Alsace, the tobacco and match industry, the French government became the biggest employer of labor in the nation. To mesh and coordinate these powerful socialist industries with the industries of private enterprise, a brilliant national plan, the Monnet Plan, was drafted to channel investment and reconstruction toward those targets which would make France the equal of any other Western nation and give her people the soft decencies of life. The old press had been corrupt and evil, said the parties of Liberation; it had been an institution of lying sheets bought by great moneyed interest or bribed by foreign powers. Thus, down with the old structure of the press. Most of the nation's printing presses were quickly nationalized and all newsprint came under control; every team of Resistance journalists emerging into freedom received the same grant of capital from the government, the same allotment of newsprint, the same right to print on government presses. Now France was to have a press of absolute freedom.

When they had finished their reforms, the Liberation parties had created a government which monopolized basic transport, all forms of power and energy, all the channels of credit, dominated every avenue of public information.

Such a revolution, it seems in retrospect, should have brought the alliance of the three Resistance parties to maturity as a solid, permanent governing body of free France. Quite the contrary happened, for almost at once a fissure opened between the parties of the Resistance. This fissure was caused by the Communist party.

The Communists had emerged from the Occupation as the most powerful organized force in France. Controlling its own shock troops, possessed of its own arms, in control of the great national labor unions, the party was led by hard and monomaniac men who knew exactly what they wanted. Moreover, it was adored by millions of Frenchmen, who might otherwise have been hostile to communism, for its courage and resolution in the dark days of the Underground. Even before the Germans were driven from France's cities, the Communists had begun to organize to take power. What frustrated them was that other men in France knew exactly what they wanted too, and though the Communists were the largest organized group in France, they were not the only organized group and the others, combined, outweighed them. In each village and city of France as Liberation crackled across the country like a chain of sputtering firecrackers, the armed men of the Resistance raced each other for the levers of power, the Communists winning in some areas but losing in most. Added together, the Communist minorities in every region made them, on a national scale, the largest single power unit in France. But, on a national scale, power could only be exercised by the Assembly in Paris and there the Communists were trapped. In Paris power was exercised, indirectly but fundamentally, by the huge conquering armies of America and Britain. As these armies flooded through and beyond Paris they left its control and government in the hands of that shrewd, brilliant and self-intoxicated soldier, Charles de Gaulle, whom the Communists could not remove except by a civil convulsion the Allies would not have tolerated.

Nothing could be done in France over the opposition of the

Communists, but the Communists could do nothing alone. Since all three parties of the Liberation agreed that France needed a revolution, the energies of the Communists could flow for a while in the same direction as the energies of its partners in the Liberation government without too much friction. But the Communists could not dominate their partners. For a year and a half the Cabinets of France included individual Communist ministers, as Vice Premier, as Minister of National Defense, as Minister of National Economy or as Minister of Arms Production. In some of these posts, such as that of National Economy, the Communists contributed remarkably to the swift and willing return of French workers to their mines, factories and farms; in others, as in Arms Production, they so colonized key offices with their party hacks, that even now no one can guess just how many covert and silent enemy agents remain embedded at key points. In the five rustling Cabinet reshuffles of that honeymoon period, one constant remained: the Ministry of the Interior, with its police control over French cities, and the Ministry of Foreign Affairs were always denied the Communists.

The revolutionary majority of the Left remained in power until May of 1947, long after it had ceased to become revolutionary and had bogged down in the technical and unexplored complexities of making socialism work. In May of 1947 the Communists were expelled—or quit—the government of France. The reason was simple. By 1947 the great Dollar Gap had caught up with the destiny of France and the bread failure of the spring months had forced France, like all of Europe, to turn to America for help. This situation held two mutually exclusive conditions. The United States would not give aid to any government which rested on Communist support. And the Communists would not support any government which also depended on American support and the influence that went with it. So they left, and as they left, the whole tone of government in France altered; the projects of reform and revolution lay half-finished on the statute books in illogical confusion, while all the dreams and promises of Liberation rested unfulfilled. The voters of France, perplexed and embittered, knew they had been cheated, but did not know precisely whom to blame.

The next five years, from 1947 to 1952, gave the special quality of confusion to the government of postwar France. Having lost the support of the Communists, the two remaining partners of the early revolutionary governments had to move across the center aisle of the Assembly to find new votes for a governing majority on the Right. These votes could be found only among the conservative Radical-Socialists and little clusters of Peasant-Independent deputies. But these deputies could be won only by bribing them with place, patronage and little privileges in the sharing out of sovereignty. The new coalition now no longer had common aspirations, for some wanted to continue the reforms of Liberation and the others wanted to undo them. They had only a common peril, the need of defending democratic liberties from the Communists on the Left and, they believed, from General de Gaulle's new counterparty on the Right.

Agreeing only on the peril, they could agree on nothing else. The mass of social reforms and nationalizations thrown together so swiftly in the first few months of revolution required the coolest and most logical thinking to make them work. But the new Center coalition government now placed the great enterprises of nationalized industry and nationalized finance and credit under the direction of their businessmen deputies of the conservative parties, who understood their mechanisms as little as the Marxists who had nationalized them. The nationalized industries became like orphans left with a surly and irascible uncle who could not make up his mind whether to choke or nourish them. The Center coalitions could not agree on the purpose, the financing or the burdens of the new system of social security; they could not agree on how new voting laws should be written, whether or not Catholic schools should get state subsidies or how people should be taxed. As they feuded and compromised among themselves, each party had constantly to yield at every reshuffle to some demand it had once categorized as pure evil, until finally its voters became confused, disgusted and apathetic. When no compromise could be reached on how the burdens or benefits of the state should be shared, the coalition parties simply took no decision, which meant that matters were automatically settled by another shot of monetary inflation, the most insidious and wicked of all taxes.

These governments continued in this paralysis until 1952, making only those decisions, such as rearmament and war in Indo-China, which were inescapably thrust on them by the outside world. By 1952 that indefinable change of political climate which was sweeping all Western democracies over the imaginary center line which separates Right from Left was operating in France too. In February of that year, a sickening gust of inflation, filling every French family with a sense of indefinable dread, coincided with the crumbling of the Gaullist party to give France for the first time in twelve years a government under Antoine Pinay which by its own choice was of the true Right. By the time M. Antoine Pinay—a short, frail man whose balding head, sharp pointed nose and little mustache make him look like the French version of Mr. Everyman—took the helm early in 1952, the entire climate of France had changed. The free press of Liberation whose journalists had survived and outfought the Gestapo had succumbed to the implacable logic of profit-and-loss accounting, and the major organs of the French press were now back in the hands of the same men who had run them before the war. M. Pinay was whooped into office with a clamor and a bang and hailed as the embodiment of all the sturdy, enduring virtues of the simple French villager which had survived the adventures of the mid-century. Though M. Pinay's government lasted only nine months, it was succeeded by another government of the Right, leaving France to contemplate her current paradox: though the overwhelming majority of Frenchmen vote for parties of the Left to protect their revolution or to push it further, technically the only possible governments in France's present divided Assembly are governments of the Center or Right, which repudiate that revolution.

It is impossible to make sense out of France by considering her parliamentary politics apart from those moods and attitudes which cannot be captured by dates, events or figures.

Some philosopher with an equally profound knowledge of human beings and economics may some day be able to describe adequately the disease of inflation, which is the creeping sickness of Western democracies. If he does, he will almost certainly choose France as his model of horror. Inflation has underlain every mood and change of French politics since the war, dissolving all decencies, all moralities, corrupting the noblest, obsessing the conversation of all French families with francs, with price numbers, with worry.

The peculiar characteristic of French inflation is that it has lasted for almost forty years, more than a full generation; it has been a pestilence that progresses in spurts of panic and slower lapses of seeming stability. Inflation as it has happened in Germany, twice in one generation, has come swiftly, like a quick ravaging plague, and been cured twice by savage repudiation. It is healthier when inflation comes like this, for all men are wiped out at once by a common disaster, and they are united in fear. When inflation happens slowly, as in France, over a generation, it slowly changes all habits and morals. Money is no longer money as it is in England or America, and all the patterns of thrift, planning, decency, good taste that go with solid money become stupidity. When people realize that money is meaningless they become vulgar or selfish or wicked and divide against each other. Old standards wither. ("They are such vulgar people," I have heard a French lady of good family say. "They never ask the price of anything they buy.")

The quick, foxlike men leap ahead as they ride inflation's crests; the sharpster, not the producer, succeeds. Those who do what is best for the community—who save, who plan, who put aside—are wiped out; those who grab, thrive. Inflation makes a life in which the grasshopper, not the ant, is the hero of the parable. The old people suffer most, for their savings and all their accumulations are reduced to nothing; no insurance policy more than ten years old in France is worth as much as a ten-year-old automobile. The widows of the soldiers killed in France's wars receive a pension of 85,000 francs a year, once sufficient to live on, but now worth only five dollars a week. Inflation eats the honor out of a career of honor; a French captain knows that if he dies in Indo-China his wife will get 117,000 francs a year, or eight dollars a week, and that in another five years these francs may not be enough to buy a loaf of bread a day. Ever since the Liberation the people of France have hoped that the process might be stopped, turned back, so they could make plans; each government—except for those that nursed at the Marshall Plan's breast in its boom years—has betrayed these hopes; the political appeal of men like M. Pinay and the French Right is that they promise to stop inflation, even if it means unemployment and the end of French growth.

The warping of a community by inflation is almost indescribable. Take housing: since somehow men must be protected against inflation and must be protected first in their homes, rent controls must be slapped on. Since rents fixed in terms of paper francs are soon reduced by inflation to nothing, landlords will not repair and will not build. No houses get built, and a growing population is crammed and stuffed into falling, disease-burdened slums. Since it is unwise to save to build a house four or five years hence, because by then inflation will have melted the money until it will not even lay a foundation, then buy an automobile and freeze the money. Since it is unwise to buy bonds or stocks which lose their value, buy gold—and thus three billion dollars' worth of gold is buried in French gardens, hidden under mattresses, stashed in socks. Since the best thing that can be done with money is to spend it quickly, then spend, spend in the high, luminous, grisly luxury of Deauville and Cannes, spend in the shops along the Rue St. Honoré and Rue de la Paix, build a summer bungalow along the Riviera because you will never build a home where you live. Spend fast because if you save you will end up like the old widows in black, or like those who have no money to spend anyway.

Inflation intertwines with another condition of French life. Since you cannot by diligence, application or planning acquire any security with your savings, you must acquire another base. If you are a Frenchman, you try to guarantee not your money but your status by a system of special privileges. More and more this status becomes as important as a property right in itself. If you have three children, you can get a special card as a "Père de Famille Nombreuse" which entitles you to half-fare in the subway, on the railway, at museums. If you work in the coal mines, your status as a coal miner entitles you to free coal. If you work in the electricity works, your status entitles you to cut-rate current. If you work in a factory with a well-run union, your status entitles you to send the children to the factory's summer camp; if the union that runs it is Communist and you are not, too bad; if the union that runs it is Catholic and you are not, too bad. Everyone has a special status which he tries to crystallize by law or custom in the production of wealth. The veteran has a special card which gives him special rights; a member of the Legion of Honor has special rights. Even the destitute have special rights. All those who are over sixty-five, all those who are incurably sick, all those whose income is less than $300 a year get a special card called the "Carte des Economiquement Faibles." Possessors of this card pay no taxes on houses or radios, they are given free medical care and free legal aid and may, once a year, make a trip anywhere in France at half-fare.

Those who denounce this system of special privileges and status are frequently those who benefit most, for to each man his status is justice and the other man's status is privilege. The businessmen of private enterprise spend hours denouncing the French nationalized railways for the manner in which the government's special cards allow millions of privileged Frenchmen reduced rates on the already-low passenger fares. But when it comes to a discussion of freight rates, they protest. The French government railways charge the same rate for hauling a ton of goods a mile, whether it be a low-cost, mass shipment, flat-valley haul or a winding, twisting, expensive, ill-frequented run into the mountains. This equalizes transportation costs all over France, making cheap haulage on the Paris-Lyons run more expensive than it should be, while old factories in the mountains, miserably placed for commercial efficiency, are subsidized by artificially low rates. Over and over again, the railways have sought permission to alter the rate structure so that freight charges will reflect freight costs. But this would, of course, make the low-cost rail hauls so competitive that private trucking would go out of business and make production in the mountains so expensive that mountain factories, too, would go out of business. At this, the business critics of the passenger-rail system protest that rate changes would be disruptive and wicked. The government, which reflects the votes of everyone and must run the railways to please everyone, therefore lets every individual sink the taproot of status into the railway system, and the system runs a chronic, constant deficit.

Yet a third major emotional mood suffuses French politics, a mood which flows from the treason of Occupation collaboration. All except the very pure in France live with a little yellow stain of treason somewhere within them. The pure were that handful who from the very moment of collapse in France refused to accept defeat, Vichy and Hitler. They were joined later, gradually, then more swiftly, finally in a rush, by more and more Frenchmen who came to revile Vichy, Pétain and Hitler. Somewhere between the ten per cent of the pure who fought from the very beginning, and the ten per cent of the vile who clung to fascism until the very end, is all the rest of France. The grades and distinctions of patriotism and treachery are blurred everywhere.

The great majority of Frenchmen cherished liberty even while they tasted defeat and turned against the traitors as soon as it was possible or safe to do so. But in the ebbing of memory it is difficult for any Frenchman to fix for himself or for another when he took the first act of Resistance, at what point and by what act in a country where ninety per cent first submitted and ninety per cent later resisted, an individual marked himself out permanently as a traitor. This blurring of standards has grown as memory has faded, and all through the after-war years it has permitted real traitors, both big and little, to creep back with greater and greater ease into French public life. Thus there was only a mild discomfort, an undefined malaise in French hearts when, as Premier, M. Pinay, once a Vichyite, later a Resistant, let himself be publicly photographed in vacation rendezvous with his old friend, M. Pierre-Étienne Flandin, a great enthusiast of Adolf Hitler, a hard-core Vichyite, deprived by law of all civic rights for collaboration under Occupation. Nor did they find it too strange that one of his closest economic advisors was a French industrialist, chief of a large American automobile producing company in France, who served a two-year jail sentence after Liberation because he had so completely put the services of his industry and France to the use of the Nazi war machine. It is not that Resistance had lost its glory nor that the Collaboration had taken over. Resistance is still the name of magic in French politics, and the purest of its heroes—men like René Pleven or Georges Bidault or Jean Monnet—are among the fixtures of French political life. It is only that in order to govern France in freedom they must call on the support of men who betrayed it.

It is unfortunate that Frenchmen and strangers alike are accustomed to judge France by what happens in the narrow arena of politics. It is unfortunate because if one's gaze is fixed on the forum of ants where French politicians debate their country's fate without ever coming to decision, the vitality and grandeur of all the unquenchable nonpolitical processes of France are ignored.

In their individual, everyday, working lives, the will of Frenchmen to live and flourish not only persists but pushes the nation forward, completely apart from politics. The politics of French agricultural subsidy and protection may be ugly and squalid, but six times as many tractors now plough the fields of France as before the war, and in some of the wheat counties around Paris where one family in ten had had a tractor before the war, now only one family in ten ploughs with a horse. The fields gleam neat and clean, shorn under the slick new combines, and in the meadows the cubes of mechanically baled hay dot the green like yellow dominoes. Politics ruined the French aviation industry for a year and a half after the war as the Communists colonized it with their agents, but individual French plane designers, who had been cut off from the development of world plane design for five years previous, survived both their isolation and the Communists to take off their drawing boards and put in cold production a new jet pursuit, the *Mystère*, which matches the best British and American engineering. French dressmakers who had thought that with the war the fashion center of the world had passed from Paris to Hollywood and New York found within three years after peace that they could again impose a New Look, an Old Look, a Wandering Waistline all around the world from Dallas to Delhi and Melbourne to Milwaukee.

There are other more human measures of vigor and revival too. One of the great and ignored facts about France is that the French are having babies again. After a forty-year period in which French population declined decade by decade, in which the tottering old man and the withered old crone had become the community silhouette, France has now achieved the largest birth rate of any major West European country, Italy included. Whether because of the social security's baby subsidy system or simply out of the individual determination of French couples to refresh the nation, the French birth rate is now twenty per cent higher than before the war, promising a regeneration of vigor in a country directed too long by old and tired men.

Even in that most maligned of all areas of enterprise, the nationalized industries, the French, outside of politics, have achieved much that borders on the spectacular. To hear the politicians in the National Assembly shriek with indignation as they discover that the budget of the nationalized railways provides for the purchase of meat for the cats of lonesome night watchmen at level grade crossings, one might think that the French transport system was covered with cobwebs and directed by fools. Yet by 1952 the French railways system which had been shredded to bits by Allied bombing was the finest in Europe. It had repaired and rebuilt 2,250 blasted bridges, installed the finest roadbeds of the Continent, was running on meticulous time schedules, offered the cheapest transport in Europe per ton-mile or passenger-mile. Moreover, it had increased its ton-mile capacity by fifteen per cent while decreasing its personnel by twenty per cent from prewar levels. By 1952, similarly, the French Nationalized Electricity Company had not only changed the face of the land with its dams and canals, but was producing twice as much power as at France's prewar peak, in an electric grid that forked power back and forth from the Mediterranean to the Channel, from the Alps to Paris at the flick of one master switch in one central control.

The talent, the devotion, the individual aspiration and courage of Frenchmen persist in the same measure as at any time in her history of greatness. And it is this that so tantalizes all men who deal with France or French affairs. If only the talent and the resources could be harnessed and directed to one end, then France would be in the Atlantic Alliance, as it was from 1914 to 1918, the cornerstone of all effective policy. If only the materials of greatness could be kindled, France might flame and warm all her citizens again with security and comfort.

So studying France, contrasting her frantic and ineffectual leadership with the promise of her people and resources, many foreigners have declared that France is suffering from nothing more serious than a case of nerves.

It is true that France is suffering from a case of nerves, but the truth ignores the fact that the nervous instability arises from certain cold, material situations which no magic wand or easy formula can erase. The explanation of France's parliamentary indecision, of her crippling inflation, of her dishonored promises is, very simply, that the governments of France have accepted for France burdens too great for her capacity to meet.

The burdens of France are enormous. Someone has quipped that most of France's troubles rise from her effort to pay for three kinds of war at once—yesterday's, today's and tomorrow's. She is paying for two wars of yesterday in pensions and annuities to veterans, widows, cripples, orphans, in the annual tax demands to rebuild the 1,500,000 homes either partially or completely destroyed by the Germans, in the physical effort to restore the public works blasted to bits as the liberating armies swept over French soil chasing Germans.

France is also paying for today's war in Indo-China. Indo-China has taken from France twice as much as the Marshall Plan gave her, more than has been spent to repair the last war's devastation. Indo-China costs not only money but men; it absorbs one out of two regular noncommissioned officers of her army, and two out of five of her commissioned officers. The war has continued for seven years. It has cost 35,000 men killed and missing, and 43,000 wounded; the number of officers killed or permanently disabled equals the number of graduates for the past four years from St. Cyr, the French West Point.

Finally, France is paying for tomorrow's war in her effort to brace the front in Europe. Alone among all the partners in the Atlantic Coalition, France has been singled out as the country spending more on arms—12.3 per cent of her national income—than NATO's economists thought wise.

These three burdens alone are enough to give France a task of titanic proportions. But there are two others equally as heavy. One of these is the effort to master the Dollar Gap by modernizing or replacing the archaic, unproductive, generations-old factories and obsolescent processes of her industry. This has required a tremendous disgorging of national funds for investment in dams, railways, coal mines, assembly production. Since French private capital has stopped investing, these funds must be raised by taxation or inflation. The last of the five great burdens is to wring out of industry or the budget the great sums of money necessary to keep solvent the new social security system of hospitals, medical care, summer camps, accident and unemployment insurance which the Liberation created.

All these five burdens—the payment of three wars, the investment in remaking French industry, the cost of social security—bear upon French resources with intolerable weight. It is estimated that forty per cent of all the national income of France is taken from its citizens by their government just to meet these burdens. Under a dictatorship like the Soviet Union, protests against such burdens are met simply by using secret police to muzzle the cries of misfortune and sacrifice, while the dictators, like surgeons, operate on the bound bodies without anesthesia. In a democracy, where liberty prevails, the sacrifices and burdens result in wailing and groaning which translate into votes that must be heeded.

Over and over such lucid men as Pierre Mendes-France rise in the French Assembly to tell their colleagues that France must make a choice; they tell her she must choose where and how she will be strong, for she cannot be strong at once in Asia, in Africa and in Europe. Over and over again Frenchmen tell each other that they must strip one or another of the many burdens of their country, or else must decide who will bear the weight of the burdens or who will be stripped of his privileges in the community. But Frenchmen in their division, in village as in Parliament, cannot decide which of the many claims to the greatness they have inherited around the world must be abandoned, or how to finance these claims except by inflation which corrupts the nation.

All the seeming instability of France rises, finally, from her inability to reconcile herself with reality. The French are as capable in the simpler arts of government today as they have been in the past. In twenty thousand villages and towns across the country village councils order their local affairs judiciously and wisely, putting in new water systems or new swimming pools or new roads. In any major branch of French national government in Paris, brilliant civil servants direct affairs, analyze events, draw blueprints with exquisite intelligence. Even in their restless, rustling Cabinet reshuffles, a certain common sense prevails so that year after year the same men—René Pleven, Georges Bidault, Robert Schuman, René Mayer and half a dozen others—shift their seats but preserve a common shared experience and knowledge of affairs.

Where France breaks down is at one point only: at the point where France must make new decisions. Each breakdown of a government, each new crisis inviting the formation of a new Cabinet is studied by foreign statesmen and Frenchmen alike in the hope that this is the moment when the French will decide how to organize their brilliance and resources and how to approach their burdens. Sometime, ultimately, everyone tells himself, the French must recapture their glories and importance, whether in the frame of a newer, greater Europe or in the frame of a smaller, nationalist France.

It might happen tomorrow or at the next crisis or in a few years. For eight years the world has been waiting for the French to make up their minds. And it still is.

VI

the story of Pierre Bertaux

Each man tells some essential part of the story of his country with the story of his life. A few, the great leaders, recite with their lives the story of command and decision that has shaped their fellow citizens' lot. Others tell how these distant decisions have pressed them unwillingly to do what they did, or endowed them, unconsciously, with good fortune. In between are the men who have both acted and been acted upon, who are the links between high politics and the impulses of their fellow citizens.

Pierre Bertaux is such a man. In his life is refracted all the story of France, that tortured country so rich in promise and human brilliance which so abuses its promise and wastes its talent.

I first met Pierre on a sunny morning while waiting for a riot that never happened.

The Communists were clotted on one side of the Church of Alesia, drifting and milling in the mob-herd, their mass color flecked with the flower patterns of women's dresses and the white of shirt-sleeved men. The Gaullists crowded on the other side of the church, more sedately dressed in dark business suits, their women more soberly tailored than the Communist women. Between them stood the troop columns—blue uniformed city police, brown uniformed army Gardes Mobiles, helmeted men of the black Security Companies. The occasion was the renaming of Paris' ancient Porte d'Orleans. It was now to be called Porte Leclerc in honor of General Leclerc, Paris' wartime liberator, and General Charles de Gaulle had been invited to preside at the rededication. The Communists had sworn they would not permit him to do so and called a counterdemonstration a mile away up the avenue. Between Communists and Gaullists the government had flung a barrier of armed men, proclaiming that both its enemies should enjoy the right to gather in the streets but that they must not fight and blood must not flow. It was all France in miniature there, straining with hating groups, knotted about the Church of Alesia.

My journalist's pass let me slip through the police cordon, and as I approached the radio command car at the base of the church, I noticed the presence of the Minister of Interior, Jules Moch. Moch, recognizing me, said something to the guards and they passed me into the command post.

Pierre was in the cluster of men about the Minister and we fell to talking. I did not catch his name but liked him. Tall for a Frenchman, wiry but not thin, his hair curly and black, his eyes brown and very youthful, he seemed to be one of the Minister's aides or secretaries, a type more at home in the cafés of St. Germain-des-Pres than here, at a command post, waiting for a riot to break.

What caught my attention, however, was not the exquisite precision of language in his talking, but the casual and coldly wise dictums he passed in comment on the mob. No, there would be no trouble or bloodshed today, he said. It's the women who usually make trouble in a riot and look, the Communist women have their children with them. No, the Gaullists aren't ready to fight either. Besides, we have more troops, more manpower than either of the two mobs, and we have guns, too. It was a huge show of force, so much power in such overpowering quantity and quality that no one would be tempted to test it. The government had 15,000 troops ready for this affair, with Security Companies summoned from as far off as Brest and Lorraine. Everyone in France was guaranteed his freedom of speech, and so much power had been gathered to back up this freedom today that no use of power would be necessary. (It turned out, of course, that Pierre was right—not a blow was struck, no blood was shed that day and never again did Gaullists and Communists try to face each other for a showdown in Paris' streets.)

Someone called Pierre away on an errand and before he took leave I said I'd like to talk to him again. He gave me his card and suggested I call at his office. I looked at it: "Pierre Bertaux" it said, "Directeur Général, Sûreté Nationale."

Bertaux. This was Bertaux, the cruel and brilliant Bertaux. Everyone in France knew the name, and most trembled at it. Men of the Left shuddered, for Bertaux was the man who had broken, in blood and violence, France's worst strikes since the war. Men of the Right froze. Bertaux, said the Right, was not malleable, you could not trust him, you could not deal with him. The card said it all—Pierre Bertaux, chief of the Sûreté Nationale, director of France's secret police and her internal security forces, the ruthless chieftain who had come out of the Resistance to break the back of the Communist party and reduce its once terrifying insurrectionary strength to the impotence revealed that day at the Porte Leclerc.

I called on Bertaux at Sûreté headquarters a few weeks later in the summer of 1949, but it was some years later before I was to know him well. By then the politicians had put the knife to him and he had been removed from command of the Sûreté and left functionless as a "prefet hors cadre"—a general without command. We used to talk then in his house in the Paris suburbs. In summer we sat in the rambling garden where he was trying to make Virginia dogwood flower in Northern France. In winter we would sit in his study, a large comfortable room with a huge fireplace, lined with bookcases from floor to ceiling, stuffed with literary curiosa. The works of Lenin flanked Diderot's encyclopedias, primary textbooks that French children used seventy years ago sat next to volumes of German poetry. The latest copies of the *Reader's Digest* were jumbled with the current effluvia of the French intellectual Left. In the garden and study Pierre told me the story of his life and France.

"I am peasant in origin," he said when he began his story.

"All of France is forever peasant at its base and the word you must start with is the Roman word for peasant: 'paganus.' 'Paganus' is the best word, for it means both pagan and peasant.

"In France there are only cavaliers and peasants. The cavalier rides across history on his horse and the peasant bows his head and is silent. He waits. The cavalier makes his ruins and rides away, but the peasant lives in the ruins and makes them grow again. He is always there, primitive, closed to himself, the most mysterious person in the world, French.

"We tell our children in school of the Gauls, men with blond hair and blue eyes, we teach them about the Romans and the Franks. But these were the conquerors and the conquerors were never more than a handful on top and the base of France never changed: the base is dark, anarchic, peasant, Iberian. Frenchmen do not know themselves or each other for there is always this crust, this rind on their lives. You have the impression of contact, you think you know the Frenchman, but when you press, the crust yields, it does not break. Every Frenchman has a little wall around him. He says, 'Nobody bosses me around,' or he says, 'Ni dieu, ni maitre'—'no god, no master.' The French dislike great men, they have known too many cavaliers, they like small people. You look at this government today and you say 'chaos' which is true. But it is what the French want, this anarchy.

"So. My people were peasants from Lorraine, on the border of Germany and the Low Countries. Wars always happen there, the archives are always burned and so my family has no history. History in our family begins with the rifle barrel my grandmother used to blow on the coals in the fireplace; the peasants had taken the rifle barrel from the Russians who had come chasing Napoleon back into France in 1815. My grandfather had history, too. He was captured by the Germans in the war of 1870 and they condemned him to death, just as I was captured in this war and condemned. It's always the Germans—for my grandfather, Les Prussiens, for my father, Les Boches, for us, Les Fritz.

"My father was the one who broke from the peasants. I remember him—he came directly out of the fields, a dark man, with brown eyes, dark hair, a Spanish complexion, a furious temper. My father grew up after the Franco-Prussian War and you must remember how the Church and the state were quarreling then over who should control the schools. When the state took the schools away from the Church and made public schools, they opened a new world to thousands of peasant boys, for the government wanted thousands of young men to train as teachers. For young peasants who wanted to learn, the schools opened a way out of the fields. This was the way my father went, but even after he became a professor he never forgot the fields—every summer in vacation he would go back to Lorraine and plough with the horses. Wherever he lived there was a garden where he worked with the earth himself.

"I was born in 1907 when he was teaching at Lyons, but I begin to remember things only later when he was teaching in Rouen and the war broke out. I was seven years old then so I can't remember much about that war. But I remember little things—do you know that Rouen was the first town ever bombed from the air? I was sleeping in my mother's room that night and suddenly I woke up because the house was shaking and my mother was holding me in her arms against her nightdress.

"I don't remember how the war ended except that there was not the slightest trace of joy or celebration when it was over. Only everyone saying, 'Enfin, c'est fini.' My cousins from Lorraine who had been staying with us because the Germans occupied Lorraine went back right away and my cousin, Marcel—he was just my age—was blown up a year later when his plough hit a shell in the field he was working."

From as early as Pierre Bertaux can remember, his parents had planned for him a life of scholarship. They did not know or care how a man enters any other profession; for them the key to all honor was admission to the École Normale Supérieure. All over France even today, thousands and thousands of families consecrate their children to the École Normale Supérieure in the same way, and each year in France two or three youngsters still die of overwork and overstrain as they prepare for the bitterly competitive examinations that give entrance into this school for greatness.

The École Normale Supérieure is one of France's two refineries of genius, the other being its twin, the École Polytechnique. Both were created by the great Revolution a century and a half ago, both have contributed to France's leadership over the past century and a half as powerfully as Eton and Harrow, Cambridge or Oxford have done to Britain's. Each year from thirty to thirty-five boys are admitted to the École Normale (about two hundred are admitted to the École Polytechnique), to be marked as men of distinction. For the rest of their lives, Normaliens and Polytechniciens are a fraternity, a blood brotherhood almost as close-knit as the brotherhood of West Point men in American life. From the moment the boys receive the magic admission to the École Normale they live in a club of fellow geniuses. All Paris' libraries are thrown open to them, all university lectures and research facilities are free to them, no academic discipline governs them. Mostly, the young men refine each other's spirits in long, windy sessions of evening talk, while each chooses the specialty that will be his life's work and investigates it on his own.

Pierre Bertaux was one of the lucky few. At the age of eighteen, in 1926, he was admitted to the École Normale as the youngest member of his class and decided to become a Germanist. The choice seemed normal to Pierre, for his father, a border country man, had been a Germanist, too. Pierre's father had dedicated himself to making Germans and Frenchmen understand each other after the First World War. Jakob Wassermann, Thomas Mann, Heinrich Mann and all the great men of German letters had stayed at the Bertaux home in Paris when Pierre was a boy. And Germany fascinated Pierre.

In 1927, when Pierre Bertaux was just nineteen, the École Normale sent him off to Germany to work on his thesis, and when Pierre arrived to enroll at Berlin University, he found he was the first French student at the University since the war. Berlin in the twenties, sitting at the gateway of Asia, with all the best of German life sparkling and tossing in its cold dry air, thrilled young Pierre. It is difficult now, he says, to look back at Germany across the Hitler years and remember the seductiveness of Berlin life in the late twenties, how like an island it sat in the middle of Europe, detached from the earth in a fever of brilliance.

An entire generation of Frenchmen fell thrall, as did Pierre, to this fascination. The number one student in Pierre's class at the École Normale was a young Frenchman who loved Germany so much that when he was captured by the Germans in the Maginot line, he not only became a collaborator but adopted German citizenship and died fighting for Germany at Stalingrad as a Wehrmacht officer. Germany ate its way through half of Pierre's class at the École Normale—Lautman was trapped by the Gestapo in the Underground and was murdered by Germans; Nizan was killed fighting the Germans at Dunkerque; and it was only luck that the Germans did not succeed in killing Pierre, too.

All that, however, was another Germany and far in the future. As a literary scholar, Pierre selected for his thesis the life of

Hölderlin, the purest of Germany's lyric poets, and back and forth, in the years that followed, Pierre traveled between Paris and Berlin. It was 1934 when Pierre made his last visit to Berlin to finish his thesis on Hölderlin, sneaking into the German capital without a visa, hiding in the nursery room of some friends, writing on a kitchen chair at the children's table beside the window. In the street below he could see the storm troopers marching by singing the "Horst Wessel Lied," and then he would turn back to the other Germany of Hölderlin, wondering whether that Germany would survive.

When Pierre returned to Paris in 1934, having finished his thesis, there were many openings for him, as there are for any young man who has finished his apprenticeship in ideas at the École Normale. H. was chief assistant to a friend running for election to the Assembly in the Ardennes, and thus experienced a grass-roots apprenticeship in politics. He was summoned to direct the news broadcast of the French Radio and served there for a year. Next the Under-Secretary of State for North Africa appointed him as his personal emissary in Tunisia, and Pierre learned about empire. When Jean Zay, later to be shot by the Germans, became Minister of Education, Pierre was chosen as his chief executive officer. These were interesting jobs, but always, as every sentient man in Europe, Pierre had the sense of things rotting, life withering, war gathering. Europe was about to explode and Pierre did not want to be in Paris when the cavaliers trampled France again. Thus, in 1938, he requested a university appointment in the provinces, and in the fall of that year he was named Professor of German at the University of Toulouse, the pleasant city which is the intellectual, industrial and political center of southwestern France.

"The war," says Pierre, "came as I always dreamed it would. The papers and politicians said it would be a short and brilliant war, but I remember when I was mobilized in September, marching to the station in Toulouse with my pack, a little fellow on the street called, 'Don't wear yourself out with this now—remember it will be a long war and you'll get tired before it's over.'

"I had the reserve commission of a lieutenant and since I was a professor of German they sent me to the intelligence section in Gamelin's great headquarters at La-Fertè-sous-Jouarre. Our section chief, an old major of the reserves, had been called back from civilian life and he had a completely infantile delight in wearing the uniform again. In the last war he had written the communiqués of Marshal Foch's headquarters and his first act in our new section was to tack up on the wall the last communiqué Foch had issued on Armistice Day in 1918.

"That was some headquarters we had at La-Fertè-sous-Jouarre. You know they say victory sterilizes the imagination—well, the French Army had been completely sterilized by the victory of 1918. Some of our agents got hold of the table of organization of a German panzer division and it came to me for analysis. You couldn't read it without realizing that the German panzers were not planned for infantry support but for deep break-throughs and penetrations of thirty or forty miles a day. But senior staff officers laughed at me. I was a reserve officer, they said, and naturally without the education of the War College in Paris. But if I had had the good fortune to have studied at the War College I would have learned there that no break-through can penetrate a front deeper in one day than half the width of the breach. This was an iron rule established in the 1914-1918 War and my theoretical analysis, they said, was nonsense. That was our headquarters.

"In April of 1940 they shifted me to Paris to direct the German broadcasts beamed at the enemy. So I was in Paris when the end came in June. There were thousands of Parisians who hoped, as I did, that the Army would stop and fight in Paris, for Paris is a wonderful place to fight. What if the Sainte Chapelle or Notre Dame were destroyed—*tant pis* for the ruins, but Paris would have been proud. By the night of June 11, the government had already left and my broadcasting section too. That night the city was full of movement, cars racing away loaded with baggage, smoke from burning papers, people drifting in the streets waiting for the Germans. Our German broadcast usually went out at midnight and when I came to the station the mechanics told me the radio net over France was fading. Radio Strasbourg was dead, Radio Lyons was dead, we were ordered to take Radio Paris off the air at midnight sharp. I asked them to give me fifteen minutes more; what difference does it make if Paris goes silent at midnight or midnight-fifteen, I asked. They agreed and so I sat down with the microphone in my hand and for fifteen minutes I talked to the

Germans in the night, in German, about France. I told them not to think that just because they were coming to Paris tomorrow they would win. We are leaving, that's true, I said, but we're coming back and you can't hold it because all you have is force and force isn't enough. Someday we'll have more force than you and we'll meet here again. Other people have taken Paris and lost France, and even if you get to the Pyrenees don't think you've taken France, because France will last and we'll be back.

"The next morning a friend and I got into our Citroën before the Germans came into the city and we left, driving, driving south and west to Bordeaux and Toulouse and home. In Toulouse they demobilized me, my post at the University was waiting for me, and in the fall I was teaching again."

By November of 1940 Pierre Bertaux had joined the Resistance. It was an entirely natural act. Pierre had been visiting in the town of Clermont-Ferrand and had joined an old friend for a drink on the terrace of a café. As they talked, Pierre asked his friend whether anybody still had contact left "over there," "over there" meaning London. His friend said, why yes, he had himself, and when Pierre journeyed back to Toulouse that night he, too, was in the Resistance. Pierre cannot remember now what made him do it; he supposes it was because of his children. He had one little year-old boy and there was soon to be another. No one knew how long the Occupation would last, but if it lasted long no man, he felt, could hope to shape his child's mind one way when all the power of the state would be shaping it another. The children would grow up little Fascists unless he did something. Therefore, if he could make France free again—good. But if he were killed that would not be too bad, for then it would be impossible for the children to love the state that had killed their father, and they would be committed from childhood.

The first net that Pierre organized in Toulouse was ridiculously amateurish. It included a local filling-station operator, an Italian refugee who kept a bookstore and several young boys. They wrote letters in invisible ink; they tried to map German coastal fortifications; when they finally secured a radio they ranged the directional antenna on London using a map from a schoolboy's geography book. Not until the spring of 1941 did they make any real link with General de Gaulle in London and not until September of 1941 could they arrange for their first parachute drop. That was an exciting moment, Pierre remembers, waiting in a clearing in the woods before dawn with flashlights hooked up to an old automobile battery to guide the plane in and then chasing out to see what the parachute had brought. It brought pistols, plastic explosives, incendiaries, but no machine guns, which was what the net wanted most. Pierre's wife wanted to use the parachute silk for the layette of the baby she was expecting, but for security's sake, regretfully, they decided to burn it. Yet someone must have talked about the drop—perhaps a boy who could not keep himself from boasting. And on December 11, 1941, before dawn, the police came to Pierre's house and arrested him.

Pierre was the first man of the Resistance arrested in Toulouse and in those days the Resistance carried no honor. It was only later, when the war was won, that everyone claimed a Resistance record and insisted that the Republic had never died in their hearts. But in that first year of defeat it was otherwise, for France was broken in spirit and good people thought of the first handful of Resistants as trouble-makers. Pétain and Vichy were France; to be against them was to be a traitor in time of trouble; to work for the Resistance was to be an English spy. The Minister of Education stopped Pierre's professorial salary seven days after his arrest and left Denise, his wife, expecting her baby in a few weeks, destitute. Not more than twenty people in Toulouse would speak to Denise after Pierre's arrest, for what he had done was not "chic"; and those who did befriend Denise refused to defend Pierre's action but simply called him mad.

A French military court tried Pierre as a British spy. Pierre's lawyer wanted to make a flaming defense, confessing all, invoking the glory and honor of France and the nobility of Resistance. But Pierre insisted that such a defense, though it would give the lawyer an attentive audience for his eloquence, could only result in Pierre's own death. For if he confessed to the act, the Germans would force the French military court to execute him, but if he lied and denied all, then the court might make believe it believed the denial and let him off with a lighter sentence. The Military Advocate-General demanded that Pierre be shot forthwith as an example to all other traitors, but the court decided that a three-year jail sentence would do. This pleased everyone except the Advocate-General, who was furious and still insisted on life imprisonment as a minimum. Later, when Pierre became governor of the Toulouse region on Liberation, the Advocate-General, still a colonel of the French Army, accused Pierre of persecuting him for "purely personal reasons."

Pierre was transferred from prison to prison and life proved more enjoyable than he might have imagined, for, when he could keep from worrying about his wife and babies, he found that here was life with no decisions to make, no responsibility, nothing but quiet and time to think. The most pleasant of the camps was the last, a huge jail in Dordogne where Pierre was penned with the common criminals and gypsies. Here, in the evenings, Pierre would recite to the gypsies tales of the *Iliad* and the *Odyssey*, for the crafty gypsies loved to hear about the crafty Ulysses. Here, too, Pierre learned about the world of the common criminal from the great jewel thief, Pierre-Paul Leca, never dreaming that this prison friendship would in later years cost him so dearly. Leca was a great patriot and had his own theory about France's defeat in 1940. "France was rotten," he used to say, "she never had a chance. The Army was rotten, the bourgeoisie was rotten, the people were rotten. It's only in the underworld that men know what true honor is; you in the legal world can sign papers and hold people to contracts. But we in the underworld can sign no papers. A man's word is his honor and I tell you even the underworld was rotten before the defeat. You couldn't even trust the word of a crook you trusted."

They sprung Pierre from jail at the end of 1943. By then the victory of the Allies was written clearly enough for all to see and the Resistance had become honorable. It was not too difficult, thus, for Denise to arrange with the officials of Vichy a commutation of sentence which let Pierre slip out of jail in December and be spirited away quickly to the southwest, back to the old Toulouse region, where all through the winter and spring months he hid in the foothills of the Pyrenees.

By early 1944 the life of the Resistance had changed too. Pierre's own net had grown and expanded. It was now no longer a band of amateurs; it had arms; its codes were developed; its call signal from London was "the leopard's claws are varnished." All through the Toulouse region were other Resistance nets, both larger and smaller, of every shade of patriotism, ambition and political aspiration. The Germans, it was obvious, soon must lose. But who would replace them? And even as the groups prepared for the final insurrection, they stalked warily one about the other, maneuvering for position of leadership on the final day of freedom. Communist nets, Gaullist nets, independent nets all cooperated, but cooperated with a sense of mistrust and rivalry that grew each day as Liberation drew near.

All the Resistance nets of France were, by this time, loosely coordinated from Paris where the National Council of Resistance sat in clandestine session, drawing up plans, appointing secret officials for Liberation government, balancing the claims of conflicting groups for authority and leadership in their regions of planned insurrection. It was Paris that decided that the insurrectionary Commissioner of the Republic for Toulouse would be Louis Finistere,[1] as the Communists demanded, but that the Deputy Commissioner should be Pierre Bertaux, a nonpolitical Resistant.

Even down to the middle of August, when the battle was about to be joined, when the Allies had already taken the beaches and were plunging to Paris, the Resistance still lived to total secrecy. On the night of the twenty-first, a courier brought word to Pierre in the mountains that all chiefs of the regional Resistance nets were to meet that night in town. Even then Pierre could recognize only two or three names and faces among the fifteen men whom he met at the rendezvous. Each had a secret assignment and only Finistere, the Commissioner-designate, knew them all; only he had been informed that Bertaux was to be second in command. The meeting dissolved without setting a date for the insurrection, although each man knew that it could now be only a matter of days.

The Germans triggered the action. By late afternoon of the twenty-second, the movement of the Wehrmacht out of Southern France had begun to pour troops through Toulouse on foot, by truck, by train. By evening one could hear the occasional crack of a pistol shot, then later the whine of a sniper's rifle and during

[1] This is not his real name. The man chosen on Communist demand has since broken with the Communist party and it does little good to publish his name now as a Communist ally.

the night machine guns began to splatter in the city. Pierre rose before dawn, pocketed his pistol and made his way on foot to the insurrectionary headquarters. No sooner had he arrived than a courier rushed in saying, "Finistere is dead . . . they shot him . . . they shot him." The report, as it turned out later, was untrue, for Finistere, though he had been shot by a German patrol in the night, was still alive. He had been gravely wounded, however, and on that morning of insurrection he lay in a coma in a Toulouse hospital. But for Pierre it was the same as if Finistere had been killed. No one but Finistere knew all the plans; no one but Finistere knew that Bertaux was Deputy Commissioner of the Republic. Yet now Finistere was in coma and speechless, Bertaux was the man upon whom the authority of the French Republic had been settled by order of Paris, and the sole instrument of his authority was the pistol heavy in his pocket.

For several hours Pierre wrestled with his problem, and then, finally, when it became clear that it was he alone who had to act, he set out to find two young men of his own net and do whatever had to be done.

"We set out on foot, all three of us," says Pierre, "to walk to the main square where the prefecture is. The prefecture is the seat of government; I was the authority of government. Across the street from the prefecture is the police headquarters, and there men crowded in the police courtyard, men in shirt sleeves, men without neckties, men unshaven, all in confusion. I walked into the courtyard very slowly. I was afraid. A man rushed over to me and I recognized him; he was one of the men I had met that other night at the meeting of insurrectionary leaders. He recognized me, too, and said his group was waiting for orders. What should they do?

" 'Finistere is shot. He's in the hospital. Unconscious,' I said. 'I am his deputy appointed by Paris. I am the Commissioner now.'

"He took it as simply as I said it.

" 'At your orders,' he replied, 'the police are with you. What do we do next?'

"I looked across the square at the prefecture and it seemed very logical so I said, 'Next, we take the prefecture.'

"The four of us walked across the square. Myself, with pistol in pocket, my two boys and Sirinelli—that was his name, I learned—the chief of the Resistance group in the police. I had never been in a prefecture before, but I walked in and went directly up the stairs. A pale little man was sitting behind the desk in a big chair, the Vichy prefect. 'Who are you?' he asked as I walked in.

" 'I am the Commissioner of the Republic,' I said. 'Who are you?'

"He told me he was the prefect of Toulouse, that he was glad to see someone with authority, and rushed around his desk to shake my hand. I refused it; I walked around him behind his desk and sat down in his chair. That chair was important, from the moment I sat down behind that desk, I was government. I questioned him: Waterworks operating? Electricity plant operating? How much food on hand in the city? How much gasoline? When I finished, I told him that he was a prisoner of the Republic, that he was to go home to his apartment and stay indoors until summoned. When he left it was 11:30 on Sunday morning, August 23, 1944, my two boys were standing guard outside my office, and I was the Commissioner of France in Toulouse.

"That morning! Outside my office, in my office, on the downstairs floors were the committees, the groups, the organizations, the leaders who came and went, everybody asking everybody else all day, 'Who are you?'

"The first person was a boy of twenty-three, his shirt open at the collar, handsome, excited, wearing the bars of a colonel on his shoulder. 'Who are you?' he said when he found me behind the desk. I told him and he stood back in surprise. 'Who are you?' I asked. He was Ravanel, I learned, the commander of the Force Française de l'Intérieur for the region; he had just made himself a colonel that morning and for him all the world was romance; he was young, excited, happy and here was insurrection. Another self-made colonel came, a third colonel, deputations came. Everyone was giving orders; German troops were still in the city, the Vichy Security Corps was still armed in their barracks, the FFI were racing around shooting, and the FTP, who had the most arms of all, were completely out of control. The FTP belonged to the Communists.

"From the countryside other Resistance groups were coming

in. From north of us in the district of Lot, the Communist Resistance groups, supposed to be the toughest of all France, were coming down. From the east of us, in the Tarn, the tough Gaullists were moving in. Everybody had guns to shoot each other, and the Germans had guns too. The newspaper plant was seized by two groups at once and each started to publish a newspaper that same day, one Communist, one Republican. Ravanel and I tried to take over the radio station that evening. But Communist FTP's had already seized it and they threw us out, firing as we drove away. I did not want to fight them at that time.

"We settled down that first night in Toulouse in chaos. I slept inside the prefect's office on the floor with my two boys. Eighty hostile Communist FTP's slept in the anteroom and corridors outside my office, bedded down on their mattresses and cots, supplied with their own food parcels for a long stay. I kept my pistol with me and before I locked the door I informed the people outside that if anybody tried to open the door that night, I would shoot.

"The next morning all the Resistance groups, big and little, FFI and FTP, Communist and non-Communist, gathered for a meeting in my office to decide what we should do. The Germans had left in the night, and the only enemy strength left was the Vichy Security Companies. It was a tense meeting. I had the title and authority from General de Gaulle, chief of the Provisional Government of France. But the FTP had most of the guns. They had expected Finistere, the Communists' choice, to be the Commissioner; now it was me.

"We argued; they insisted that the Vichy Companies be disarmed, I insisted I did not want to provoke bloodshed by fighting in the streets. There were many people in the room, knots of people waving hands at each other, yelling. One man in a corner caught my eye, a man with a hard face, broad nostrils; he looked tough but good; he smelled solid. I said to him quietly, 'Who are you?' He told me he was Colonel Georges of the Lot department. I knew Colonel Georges by name for he commanded the Communist FTP's up there, mostly coal miners, and tough. But I felt I could trust him. 'Will you bring your men down to the city to keep order at my command?' I asked. He said he would if

Ravanel's armed FFI would agree peacefully that Georges' FTP should come in with their guns. Then, and only then, I felt I could compromise. I agreed to use my authority as the Commissioner of the Republic to disarm and disband the Vichy Companies, if the Communists would place Colonel Georges and his Communist FTP's under my direct orders. To this they agreed.

"Neither Georges nor I gained any credit for this. Later when Paris was again the capital, the government criticized me for disarming Vichy's Security Troops without their permission. And the Communists threw Georges out of the party because he had cooperated with me in taking over. But we did it peacefully. Paris was far away and Toulouse was ripe for bloodletting; we had to make our own decisions. All over France that summer, men were making decisions by themselves, without Paris. There were eighteen regions of Liberation and everywhere, except in Marseille where the Communists got control, Frenchmen who knew nothing about politics took the government in their own hands and held it—a labor union leader here, a doctor there, a professional man somewhere else.

"For weeks, all through the summer of 1944, I was alone. Power is a terrible thing. When you have absolute power you are isolated. No one but police tell you anything. That's why a 'corps élu'—call it an assembly, a parliament, a congress—is so important. Even if it is only a consultative assembly it is important, for when its members talk you find out what goes on in people's minds. But the most terrible thing about power is not this, nor even the power to kill. The terrible thing is the power to pardon, to have to sit at night with the dossier of a man condemned to death and decide whether to let him be killed or not be killed. This power to pardon crushes a man.

"You ask when the Liberation and insurrection were over? It wasn't over on any one day. It's like a man falling sick—you fall sick and you remember that day. Then it takes weeks slowly to recover; one day you start eating solid food, another day you start sitting up in bed, another day you feel you can get up and walk, then finally you are well. The insurrection in Toulouse happened on August 20, 1944; it was weeks and months after that day before law came back."

It took almost two years before law and control from Paris returned to southwest France, creeping in as the people withdrew from the forum of action.

Pierre remembers the first step in the return of law as early as October, 1944, only two months after the insurrection. The Liberation Committee in the village of Lisle-en-Dodons had captured a French informer—a dirty, disgraceful, squalid traitor who had given away to the Gestapo dozens of French patriots to be shipped off to die in German prison camps. The village Liberation Committee thirsted for vengeance, insisting the informer be shot in the village square where they could savor his death. But since the traitor was held in the Toulouse prison where Pierre was Commissioner, this decision was his. There was not the slightest doubt of his guilt and Pierre, examining his dossier, knew the informer had to die. Yet he felt the man should die quietly at dawn, in the prison, not in a carnival in the village streets. This decision infuriated the villagers, and Pierre's police told him that if the prisoner were not handed over for village execution there would be a riot, perhaps bloodshed.

The night before the execution the village Committee of Liberation called on Pierre—a delegation of solid, middle-aged, family men. They had been thinking it over, they said, and had decided that after all it was not good to kill the traitor in the square, because it would be bad for the children to see a man bleeding and dying in the streets. As they talked, Pierre scratched notes on his pad and, when they were finished, slipped the paper across his desk to ask whether this really was how they felt. They said yes. Whereupon Pierre asked them to sign their names to it and they collapsed like pricked balloons. As fathers they did not want their children to witness a bloody execution, but as political leaders they did not want to deny the villagers their vengeance and had hoped that Pierre would take sole responsibility for the execution. At five in the morning the informer was shot in the Toulouse prison. The village boiled with anger when people found they had been cheated, but they could do nothing, for their leaders had consented to the return of law.

The law crept back gradually because people needed it. But Paris control returned more slowly. It was over a year later, in December, 1945, before Toulouse felt the first tug of Paris restraint. A sugar riot had taken place in Toulouse that month and a great warehouse of sugar had been stormed. Pierre, as Commissioner, had sent first one company of police and then a second to stop the riot, but none had come back to report. At four in the morning, therefore, Pierre drove to the warehouse to see what had happened and found all quiet. In the entry of the warehouse, however, he found a large basket full of parcels of sugar. There were fifty-four parcels and on each was marked the name of one of the policemen sent to keep order; the rioters had shared the sugar with the police and each policeman had marked a package with his name before going back to the barracks to sleep. That morning Pierre dismissed each of the fifty-four who had accepted sugar. And only two days later came the order from Paris: reinstate each of the fifty-four pending a full judicial investigation! Paris had begun to govern again; only on authority from Paris could a policeman five hundred miles away be fired.

Between the Liberation and the end of 1945, for a period of almost a year and a half, France had had no real national government—and France was governed better than for many a decade. For centuries before, Paris had drawn to itself all the brains, all the scholars, all the leadership of France until the beautiful capital city suffered from cerebral congestion, and the rest of France was a political desert. The design of a village schoolhouse, the opening of a new waterworks, the erection of a new bridge anywhere in France rested upon decision in Paris, hundreds of miles away, as it rests again today. But under the Occupation and during the Liberation, when Paris could not function as capital of the nation, the brains and talents of France were scattered all across the country and the great provincial cities—Lyons, Marseille, Bordeaux, Grenoble—became regional capitals in their own right, centers of proud men making their own decisions.

Toulouse, where Pierre Bertaux governed as Commissioner of southwest France, was no exception, and it was with unbelievable excitement and enthusiasm that the people whom Pierre led proceeded to rule themselves. Before the war local criticism of affairs had to wait for a national election to voice itself in a new selection of deputies to be sent to Paris. Now, Pierre found, a critic could be silenced by putting him on a regional committee and telling him to cure what was bothering him.

Such a system could not last long, for by the end of 1945 the men of political talent and ambition were gathering again in Paris. It was clear they could not govern France from Paris as before, if regional governments divided authority with central government everywhere beyond Paris' suburban borders. Prewar deputies in Paris had been accustomed to thinking of themselves as big men, the givers of favors and dispensers of patronage in each little department from which they came. The deputies could not now control the new officials in the Liberation regions, each of whom directed half a dozen or more little departments in an area as large as an American state. The ministers of government disliked the regional governments, the civil services disliked them, and the Communists disliked them most of all because it was the regional governments like that of Toulouse which had frustrated their bid for power in the hot days of insurrection and revolt. The Communists, in France as elsewhere, wanted a strong central government. In those days the Communists sat in the French Cabinet and their bitterness was unrelenting.

In the spring of 1946, therefore, on March 31, the national government in Paris announced the dissolution of all regional governments, and with that the war, for Pierre, had come to an end. He no longer had an apartment to live in; he was in debt; he was tired. With Denise and his children, Pierre rented a cottage in the Pyrenees and went off for a long summer of rest in the mountains until fall should come and he might return to Toulouse to teach German.

It was only a few weeks before the school session resumed when Pierre found that, after all, he was not to become a schoolteacher again. During the early days of the Resistance a stranger fleeing from the Germans had come south to the Toulouse region and fallen in with Pierre's net, where he worked on a plan for the sabotage of the electric power net in the Toulouse area. That man was Jules Moch, and now, in after-war politics, Moch was suddenly a Socialist chief of great importance. In September of 1946 Moch had just been named Minister of Public Works and Reconstruction and, casting about for an executive officer, he recalled Bertaux. A telephone call from Paris to the Pyrenees located Bertaux out hunting in the hills. Before Pierre realized what was happening, he found himself on a train to Paris, dressed in his country clothes, a hamper of food with him and a boxed cat as company.

The Ministry of Public Works was an exciting ministry in those days, for its job was the repair of all war devastation in France. So successfully did the Ministry go about its tasks that Jules Moch rose to be a power in national politics, and Pierre Bertaux, too, came to general attention. But 1947 was the year that the Communists were expelled from the French government and by late summer it was clear that there would be trouble in the streets of France. Recalling Pierre's clash with the Communists in Toulouse, it was suggested therefore that he be sent south to be the prefect, or chief authority, of the great hub city of Lyons.

"Lyons in 1947," says Pierre, "was wider open, better penetrated, more skilfully organized by the Communists than was Prague in the coup of 1948. The Communists controlled the city council, occupied the strategic buildings, dominated the streets and terrorized the police. When they wanted, they could throw 10,000 rioters in the city's streets. A few months before I came, in May of 1947, a housewives' demonstration had broken out, spontaneously, over bread rationing and the Communists had capped it. This was their standard technique. The party's orders everywhere in France were that party activists must move in on any riot lasting for more than two hours, take over leadership and channel it. If they were slow or missed their chance, local Communist leaders could be removed for the blunder. The Lyons riot in May was typical—the Communists shepherded the housewives to the prefecture, broke in, seized the prefect bodily and carried him to the radio station. Then, over the government radio, he was forced to declare that all outstanding bread tickets were cancelled and bread was free of the ration.

"I replaced that prefect in September and the Communists gave me my first riot two weeks after I arrived with Denise and the children. This one started at the Labor Exchange and they marched to storm the prefecture. We deployed the guards with machine guns and when the rioters charged us, gave them tear gas. When they had fled, I called in their leaders. They came to me with their eyes streaming tears and I told them how things would be run in Lyons:

" 'Here on my desk is a telephone,' I said. 'On your desk at the Labor Exchange there is a telephone too. You can see me any time you want just by lifting the telephone and asking. But you did not ask to see me, you came by force. I live in this house with my wife and children and you have no right to storm in. If I came with police troops to storm the Labor Exchange you would have the right to resist. So I resist when you try to force me. Next time, remember the telephone.'

"It took several months to reorganize the police, but by the time the Communists pulled the general strike in December of 1947 we were in control of the streets again. Lyons is the bottleneck for the rail and road traffic between North and South France; if the Communists could block it, they could cut France in two, which is what they tried to do. They pulled the switches on the railroads; they covered the highways with four-pronged spikes to puncture tires; they tried to seize the telephone exchange. But we survived. The trains were a bit slow, but they ran; the expresses never stopped; the roads were kept clear; they damaged the telephone exchange, but we repaired it very quickly; we held the radio station and twice a day I could broadcast to the people that all was well. We outlasted them.

"The last big strike was the coal strike in 1948—a bloody one. In our district the Communists tried to flood the mines by stopping the pumps, so our troops went down, 2,500 feet underground, to pull the Communists one by one away from the pumps and save the mines from flooding. We managed it without killing, and when the mines were cleared and the pumps going again, the strike was over.

"By this time, the situation had changed in Paris, too. Moch had become Minister of the Interior and responsible for all the internal security of France—he wanted me back in Paris, to be chief of the Sûreté Nationale.

"So there I was in 1949, police chief of all France. It amuses me even now to think of it—me, a professor, a man of the Left—police chief! My friends would say to me, 'You, you Pierre, a Normalien. . . . You, Pierre, on the side of the cops!'

"Yes, yes, it was a paradox. But I said, good, let's take it that way. If this is where history has brought me, so be it—Bertaux and the cops, me and the *flics*. For it's time to peel away the old legends and look at society as it really is. Society is like a body with needs of the spirit and needs of the flesh, and one isn't any more important than the other. It's more fashionable to be a psychiatrist and deal with the mind than to be a urologist and deal with filth, but someone must examine products of the body to be sure the toxins are efficiently carried away. It's more honorable to be the chef in the kitchen than to be the swill collector who empties the buckets, but the kitchen needs both. There's nothing more important for the world than that democracy should work. To work, it must understand its problems and learn how to dispose of the toxins in the system. Police are the men who deal with poisons, they are the sewer cleaners. They keep democracy healthy by cleaning out crooks and traffic violators, by catching thugs and arsonists, but also they must deal with totalitarians and terrorists. We talk so much about democracy being made of liberty and equality. But liberty and equality rest on two things we ignore—the police and the judges. The police must be efficient to preserve liberty; the judges must be incorruptible and honest.

"When I think about democracy, I come in through the back door, the garbage door, I come with the police. It is an old tradition of democracy to despise police, to laugh at them and hate them. The police know this. They have been despised so long, many of them have become despicable. Cops have a sense of inferiority that is enormous—it goes even to their highest commanders—all of them surly, suspicious, who feel life cheats them out of honor. They are recruited from average men, commanded by average men, and they lack pride. But—and this is a big but—if you handle them right, make them proud, then they become proud people, for cops are simple men. They can be more greedy, corrupt, more full of hate than any people I've ever known. Yet, under proud direction, I found they could be more devoted, more faithful and decent than anybody else I've ever worked with."

When Pierre arrived in Paris to take command of the French Sûreté Nationale at the beginning of 1949, the great strikes of 1947 and 1948 were fading into history, but the organized power of the Communists and their threat to the state remained almost as great as ever. The party's peak postwar membership of 1,000,000 had shrunk to 800,000, but it still controlled the greatest labor unions of the nation, its largest chain of daily newspapers, important arms caches and a band of zealots ready to kill and die for it. To oppose the party as chief of France's internal security, Pierre had the secret services of the Sûreté Nationale, a corps of 55,000 to 60,000 police and security guards, scattered over the country, plus certain convictions and ideas that had come to him first in Toulouse and later in the strikes in central France.

Bertaux's basic principle was a simple one: that if a government is prepared to act, to use the terrible force of state intelligently and skilfully, there is no reason why any democracy should be destroyed by such a coup as destroyed the Czech Republic in Prague in 1948. In Lyons, fighting the riots of 1947, Bertaux had learned certain tactics of civil strife and order which he now proceeded to generalize over France. Of these the most important was the rule never to permit police power to be dispersed. The tradition that each bridge, each powerhouse, each telephone exchange must be guarded was one, Bertaux felt, which could lead to disaster. For, if the government tried to defend only the hundred most important nerve centers in France against a Communist insurrection, it would pin down and immobilize 100,000 men. Moreover, with a Communist party as deeply infiltrated among the workers as was the French Communist party, external guards were almost useless, for, as Pierre had learned in Lyons, while guards watched buildings from the outside, saboteurs could cut wires and wreck equipment from within. In Lyons, Pierre had learned to keep his own forces concentrated and mobile, always at command and never to commit them against a mob unless they had absolute crushing superiority.

French security, today, is organized roughly on these Bertaux principles. The first line of defense is, of course, the civil police in any city; the ultimate reserve of defense is the Army. But between these two lines is the emergency reserve of the Companies of Republican Security, some 12,000 men organized in 60 companies of 200 each. These companies were organized by Bertaux to live, as they live now, in a state of constant mobilization Scattered over the nation, they are mobile, ready for instant concentration anywhere. Traveling in their own trucks with their own rolling kitchens, their own bedding and camping gear, they travel at a route-speed double that of the French Army on the move. They are trained to handle mobs in the street without killing; linked all across France by their own short-wave radio net, equipped with helicopters and ground-to-air communication for observation, they are so organized that if any local situation threatens to get beyond local police control, the Companies of Republican Security can be concentrated anywhere in overwhelming numbers within twenty-four hours—long before the Army could get out of bed. They are used only as a last resort, never committed until the last minute when the Communists have shown their hand. When they are used, with their radios, tear gas, helmets, riot guns and superior communications, they act with lightning speed and crushing force.

Force, however, is not enough in dealing with Communists, and here Pierre disagrees with the American approach to the problem. "You Americans are wrong," he says, "in trying to force your methods on our country. You believe in theology, in sorcery, in witchcraft. For you, communism is a sin, and the Communists are witches to be burned. The fact is they are very simple, ordinary people. For fifteen years the Communists have pulled to their ranks the finest young people of France. France is such an old country, so much is rotten in it, and the Communist argument is so simple—to make an omelet, they say, you must smash eggs. So year after year the generous, the noble, the bold, the brilliant youth of a full generation has been drawn to it and been led by it to the final abomination which is communism. For the error of original decision in joining the Communists is so slight and the final consequences are so terrible. They, the young men of communism, are the truest victims, and the job is not to persecute them but to liberate them."

To cope with Communists, says Bertaux, you need not only force but understanding. Communists can be stopped by force, but they can be wiped out only by understanding.

The first thing to be grasped about French communism, says Bertaux, is how rigid and mechanical the French party is. To begin with, its thinking is sterile. Since the death of Lenin, says he, communism has had no thinkers at all, for Lenin was a genius and, like a great tree, nothing has been able to grow in communism beneath his shade. If one reads Lenin carefully, one can always divine what the Communists plan next. On Pierre's bookshelf at the Sûreté the collected works of Lenin were always present.

Beyond that, one must understand Communist machinery of action. There are many parts to this machinery in France. There is the outer layer of fellow travelers and sympathizers, millions of non-Communists who listen to Communist propaganda and are caught. These are the voters. Within this husk lie the party members, hundreds of thousands of them who pay dues but who may or may not follow the toughs and the leaders at the moment of insurrection. Within these, in turn, lie the hard-core zealots—no more than 10,000 in all France, men who are ready to go down in the street and die for the party at any moment. They are not many, but in a state of governmental decomposition or paralysis they would be enough, for scores of thousands might follow them. Fifteen hundred Communist toughs could seize Paris if a government were unprepared to defend itself. And, finally, there are the most dangerous men, the crypto-Communists. The crypto-Communists are the agents of Russia, people who have no visible connection with the party; they may be businessmen, doctors, engineers, Russian nationals, mercenaries. Some are recruited through the party, but most have no apparent connection with it. In France many of Russia's most trusted agents are men who collaborated with the Germans.

All this machinery lies under the control of the Russians, but this control is never an easy one. Nothing could be more dangerous for the Russians, Bertaux believes, than a successful Communist revolution in France that might become its rival, like Tito's. A Communist party powerful enough to paralyze France and wrench her from the American alliance serves Russian purposes better than a Communist France which is strong enough to be independent. Between the two, therefore, between Russia and the French party there is always an element of doubt and suspicion, always a reluctance of the French party to tell its last secrets to Russia and always a Russian compulsion to penetrate every last cell, everywhere, with party spies and agents loyal to Russia first, not to French leadership. Even the highest functionaries of the French party live under this surveillance; they do not know which of their bodyguards is on the Russian payroll, reporting every movement to the international control organs.

For two busy years Pierre Bertaux sat in contemplation of the Communists from the chambers of the French secret service. During those years, as normal life returned, as the Marshall Plan began to revive French economy and industry, as the French police tightened their security measures, the Communist party began that long steady decline in organized power which continued until the end of 1952, when the French economy became stagnant and Communist influence revived. Year by year the circulation of their newspapers fell, their union membership dropped off, their party dues-payers declined until now they are estimated to be less than 400,000.

But he who deals in secrecy and suspicion cannot come away unhurt. Yet it was not the Communists who ultimately trapped Bertaux, but France's internal politics.

In France, the Ministry of the Interior is the police ministry, and in France, as in America, police are the easiest means of paying cheap political favors in government. The police must be ever pliable, accommodating, ready to fix tickets, drop charges, hush scandals. Within the Ministry, moreover, a senior bureaucracy of almost irremovable police officials has grown up with the years whose power lies in their fat dossiers of unpublished intelligence and investigation. For several generations French democracy has choked on such officials whose secret powers of blackmail have, in the past, terrified even their political superiors.

Into this swamp of ancient institutional intrigue, strode Bertaux with the harsh and biting standards of the new officials cast up by the Resistance, the men who had sworn to make France pure. While the peril of communism dominated French politics, Bertaux could act ruthlessly. In his first year as chief of French security, Bertaux could and did fire between 2,000 and 3,000 officers, high and low, for graft, incompetence and unreliability. But by 1950 the peril had abated and Jules Moch, Bertaux's political sponsor, had moved from the Ministry of the Interior to the Ministry of Defense.

Bertaux's enemies within and without the police bureaucracy were by this time numerous. In one of his earliest investigations, Bertaux had muckraked to light a scandal which revealed some of France's most eminent generals as the source of leakage of information to the Communist rebels in Indo-China. The scandal had been hushed but it had left an area of bitterness. Many men waited for Bertaux to expose a flank of weakness—or for a tool to present itself with which to strike at him.

They had not long to wait. Suddenly, on June 30, 1950, after Moch had left the Ministry of the Interior, an embittered ex-police official whom Bertaux had dismissed for incompetence and expense-account padding presented to the government a bizarre and fantastic set of documents. In them he charged that Pierre Bertaux, chief of the Sûreté Nationale, rather than being a paragon of virtue, not only was an intimate friend of gangsters, but had used his Resistance net in Toulouse to cover a vast enterprise of racketeering. Moreover, said the official, Bertaux had personally masterminded the fabulous theft of the jewels of the Aga Khan's wife, the Begum, on the Riviera in 1949. Only one shred of information supported all these charges: the great jewel robbery had been organized by none other than Pierre-Paul Leca, Bertaux's wartime prison mate in Dordogne, and in chasing Leca, the police had discovered in Leca's personal notebook the name and telephone number of Pierre Bertaux.

The new Minister of Interior pooh-poohed the charges. The highest court of France set up a judiciary investigation of the accusations. It was no surprise to anyone when a year and a half later the court returned its findings clearing Bertaux of all charges and allegations. Bertaux, in his term of office, had broken up more gangster bands of France's highly organized underworld than any previous Director of the Sûreté. But before then, in the spring of 1951, it had been suggested to Pierre that while the charges were being investigated it were best that he leave the Sûreté to other direction.

For two years, thereafter, Pierre lived in honored semiretirement as a "prefet hors cadre," the equivalent status of general without command, until the final explosion. Then, in the summer of 1953, when the jewel robbers were at last brought to trial in the sunny, peaceful little town of Aix-en-Provence, the blow was struck. The disgruntled police official whom Pierre had fired three years before was brought to the stand and startled the court with the old charges, amplified and embroidered with new detail. By the rules of French law, such court testimony is immune from libel action so long as the witness can claim that he sincerely believes his charges to be true.

Taking the stand in rebuttal, Bertaux swept the court with the eloquence and precision of his refutation. Then, closing his testimony, he described Leca in terms of a Corsican Robin Hood, explaining that Leca, though not an honest man, was, by the underworld code of the prison where he and Bertaux had been friends, a "man of honor." Never, since their days in jail, said Bertaux, had Leca sought a special favor or asked aught of Pierre as Chief of the Sûreté.

It was the phrase "man of honor" that brought Bertaux low. For, in the eyes of the current Minister of the Interior, the phrase "man of honor" implied inferential tolerance of underworld activities. No man of such high rank as Bertaux, said the Minister, could permit himself such words in public. Specifically repudiating the accusations made against Bertaux, the Minister suspended him in rank for use of the phrase and L'Affaire Bertaux became, as it is today, unfinished business in the politics of the French Republic.

For Pierre, the future is obscure as he considers whether the coming years should be spent in government, politics, journalism, or scholarship.

"I think mostly about politics these days," said Pierre recently, "for politics is where medicine was three hundred years ago—a science of guesswork and hope. Yet somehow there must be a way of making politics exact, of linking thought and action, of finding an analysis so that freedom remains healthy and works. For France cannot go on this way, it must change or it will perish. It would be silly to sit by idle, not ever trying to save freedom, nor even thinking about saving it."

VII

Germany: spring in the ruins

I had been driving down from the north all morning, and as I turned through the traffic toward the Rhine bridge, I noticed there, just as the bridge approach curled up, a tall, frail figure posed in the melancholy appeal of the hitchhiker. I slowed for him and when he scrambled in beside me I noticed that he was not frail but gaunt, a husky man fallen on evil days, and thin. He carried a knapsack on his back and clung to a battered brown suitcase over which he had folded an old oilskin raincoat.

"Where are you going?" I asked him in German.

He replied that he was going to Bad Godesberg and then, shifting easily to English, he said, "What is your language? English or French, I speak both."

I said I was an American and asked him how he came to speak two foreign languages. He replied that he was a schoolteacher who taught English, French and history. That is, he went on, I used to be a schoolteacher before the war and now, next week, I will be a schoolteacher again.

"Oh?" I asked, inviting him to go on.

"Yes," he said, "in Bad Godesberg there is a job waiting for me and next week I begin." He was looking forward to it, he said, because all during the war he had been an officer at the front and then, after the war, they had classed him as a Nazi. Because he was a Nazi he had been barred from teaching for three and a half years, and all that time he had worked as a farmhand near Dortmund, taking care of chickens, sleeping in the barn and tutoring the farmer's children in the evening. But now, finally, he had been denazified and cleared for teaching again. The school he was going to in Bad Godesberg was a school for teen-age boys, where he would teach history.

By the time he had told all this we were across the bridge and weaving through the traffic of Cologne, trying to find the autobahn that would take us south to Bonn and Bad Godesberg. We came out finally by the riverside just beneath the eminence on which sits Cologne's famous cathedral. It was the first time I had seen it and I commented on how lucky it was that the bomb damage all around and so close had left it almost unmarked.

"Would you like to go in?" he asked. "It's a long time since I have seen it and I will tell you about it if you want." We stopped, climbed the bank and entered the great nave. From inside, the cathedral was aglow with the sunlight streaming through the windows of colored glass, washing the hushed interior with blues and golds, reds and yellows, so light and airy and graceful that it seemed a fairyland. We wandered about in silence for a few minutes and I commented on how different it was from the French cathedrals of Notre Dame or Metz with their somber, heavy, almost Teutonic majesty. This cathedral was all motion and sunlight; I had not expected to find anything so graceful in Germany.

My traveler knew all about the cathedral. "Yes," he said, "if you wish to think of it that way, you can. For as everyone knows," he went on, "it was Frederick the Second who began the cathedral and some people said Frederick the Second was not really German, but Sicilian. I myself do not think so," continued the schoolteacher, "for though he was born in Sicily, his grandfather was Frederick Barbarossa which gives him half-German blood, and his mother was Constance of Sicily. Now Constance of Sicily was half-Norman herself, and the Normans are of blood which is entirely Aryan. So when you consider it, Frederick the Second had three-quarters Nordic blood, and is German too. This is German, part Gothic, a little 'romantisch.' "

When we took up our ride again, he seemed lost in thought. I tried to draw him out of his quiet.

"What will you teach your boys in history class about the last thirty years?" I asked.

"How frankly do you want me to talk?" he replied.

"Say what you want," I said, "you'll never see me again and I don't even know your name. Tell me how you'll teach your boys about Hitler."

He began his story haltingly, and then gradually as he forgot me he began not to talk but to recite, staring straight ahead through the windshield down the ribboning autobahn, as if he were master of an imaginary class of listening adolescents. It is only half an hour's drive from Cologne down the autobahn to Bonn and into that half-hour he compressed thirty years.

It had all begun after the First World War when the German people did not know they were defeated. The leaders of the German people did not understand their own nation, they did not know how much the people loved their country. Best of the leaders was Stresemann, but the Allies would not listen to him; Stresemann tried to explain that the German people needed dignity, but the Allies would not recognize Germany as a great nation and they gave him nothing. Stresemann had no force so the Allies would not listen to him.

Then came Hitler. He made Germans proud again. He ended unemployment, everyone had jobs. He built the great autobahns which will last forever. He had force and the Allies of the First World War gave him what he wanted because he was not, like Stresemann, a beggar. Hitler's greatest success came at Munich, when everything Germany wanted Hitler got for her peacefully.

The German people thought Hitler wanted peace down to the last week before the war, and when the war came they were a little bit frightened because they did not want it. But when Hitler broke through the Maginot line, then every German knew he was a genius.

After that came the mistakes.

"I would not hide these mistakes from the boys," said the teacher peering out the window into space. "I would make them learn carefully the three great mistakes of Hitler.

"First, Hitler should have been content with the great peaceful agreement of Munich.

"Second, Hitler made the mistake of fighting a two-front war. This every German schoolboy must learn, Germany must never, never fight a war on two fronts. In this big mistake Hitler made two littler mistakes: he underestimated the force of the Russians and overestimated the force of the Italians.

"But the third mistake is the one for which Germans can never forgive Hitler. This was to keep fighting the war for months after he knew he had lost. Thus, he let the armies of the enemy enter on the soil of Germany and they destroyed it; many thousands of Germans died in those last few months just because Hitler wished to preserve his power for only a few more months.

"From the peace, also, we have learned much," he continued to his class of imaginary disciples. "We see now that the conquerors who were supposed to teach Germany democracy do not mean democracy either. They show us now that in only one thing Hitler was right, that the world respects force. We find now the Russians are just as savage as Hitler, and the Americans and English are savage too, only they are savage in a gentlemanly way. They did not fight us to make democracy, but because they wanted to crush Germany forever. Germany must find a new way, only we do not yet know what the way is."

He had timed his story well, for we had come now to Bonn and there a turning separated my road from his. He got out, hitching his knapsack on his back, lifting the brown suitcase from the back seat. I stopped him as he got out, for I prickled with a desire to hear more.

"Tell me," I said, "won't you teach your boys about the concentration camps and what happened in them?"

He turned back to me. "Yes, I will teach them that too. I will teach them that the concentration camps were a shame to Germany. But you must remember that what is told about them is a great exaggeration. You Americans saw the camps at the end of the war and then, for several weeks, the food supply in Germany had broken down. The men in charge of the camps did not know where to find food for the prisoners, so naturally when you found them they said they were starving and the pictures you took of them made them look very thin.

"Auf Wiedersehen," he said, extending his hand to me in thanks for the ride, and then was gone.

It was February of 1949 when I bade good-by to my schoolteacher, and neither he nor I then knew that while we were talking Germany was passing the unnoticed midway mark between her total defeat and that volcanic Renaissance which is the hinge on which the story of after-war Europe turns. History moves too slowly to permit the daily news dispatches to capture the swift excitement of such a story as Germany's. Only scholars, generations hence, with their priceless gift of retrospect, will see in this story all its drama of rebirth and resurrection, the uncurling of life from the numb winter of defeat.

The day I met the schoolteacher was just three and one-half years from that week in 1945 when, having ravaged the continent of Europe from end to end, having murdered some ten million people in the helplessness of captivity, having by combat cost the lives of another ten million people in the summertime of their manhood, having sacked the thrift, enterprise and creation of generations, the German state disappeared from existence. Disappearing, it had left a people shorn not only of strength but of pride and will, out of whose windows there hung in limp submission bedsheets, tablecloths, white petticoats and shirts in individual admission that in every village and home along the conqueror's course defeat was personal and tight as skin.

For three and a half years, until the season in which I met my schoolteacher, winter hung over the land. It was a tiny land, as it remains today, for mighty Germany has been shrunk by disaster to a morsel smaller than half of France. In those Winter Years one-third of what was left was wrenched away by the Russians and riveted into another civilization. What remained of Germany was not even a land; it was a conglomerate of three separate zones stuffed with 48,000,000 people wedged together in a sliver of territory so narrow that a five-hour ride across its waist could take you from border to border. A businessman's drive from New York to Baltimore covers as much distance as separates the French frontier of Germany from the Red Army's advance posts on the Thuringian ridges.

Here and there in this Germany of 1945 lay little pockets of unscarred village and hamlet, bypassed by encircling armies or ignored by marauding bombers, their brown and gray church spires rising like accusing fingers to the sky from the sturdy, field-stone houses of the peasants. But the roads that ran from village to town, from town to city were torn and ruptured by the passage of war; tanks had disemboweled the roadbeds, artillery and planes had shattered the bridges. And the roads led to cities, one more appalling than the other–rubble heaps of stone and brick, rank with the smell of sewage and filth, dirty with the dust of destruction working its way into clothes, linen, skin and soul.

The forlorn people who lived in the ruins in those Winter Years could feel little beyond hunger. The clear German skin which glows so pink and ruddy in health shrunk sallow over shriveled bodies, or puffed over the unhealthy putty of children bloated by hunger edema. By April of 1947 even the conquerors' statisticians admitted that the daily German ration had fallen to 1,040 calories, or thirty-three per cent below the scientific calculation of the minimum necessary to sustain life. Allied health teams stopped Germans on street corners and weighed them bodily to confirm these figures, and found the nation decaying. White-faced men and women collapsed at their jobs for lack of food. Dignified people sought jobs as clerks or servants in the offices of the occupying armies because in the barracks of the conquerors they got one hot meal of stew a day, which kept them alive. The United States government appropriated money to give every German school child one hot meal a day in his classroom. When Germans could think of anything beyond food they thought of clothes; the leather jerkins of German workingmen and their black leather boots had frayed and cracked; the ugly woolen stockings of German women were thin and holed; children played in the streets in the cut-down Wehrmacht jackets and pants of their fathers. The search for shelter was a nightmare; for this country, forty per cent of whose homes had been smashed, was being forced to absorb and shelter eight million refugees thrust back into it. For a German the perspective of ambition was the search to find for his family two rooms with a toilet and running water, and, if this were found, he dreamed cautiously of a home where the toilet would not be in the kitchen where the food was cooked, but in a real toilet compartment of remembered privacy.

Values withered. Girls roamed the streets, sleeping with the conquering soldiers for a candy bar, a cake of soap, a tin of Quaker Oats, coming home to once-chaste beds dirty with disease. Money was meaningless, cigarettes were currency; two cartons of American cigarettes bought a set of Meissen china, three cartons bought a Leica camera, two cigarettes were a tip. Businessmen became pirates. Families dissolved.

By an enormous, instinctive act of national resolution Germans put thinking out of their minds and concentrated on simple things:

how to find a job, and how to work. For only by working could one find food, find clothes, find a roof. Even work was difficult; Germany could make only a strictly limited quantity of steel, of aluminum, of sulfur, of copper. She was forbidden to make again the vast range of intricate machinery in which lay her commercial strength; she could not build airplanes, could not fly airplanes, could not synthesize rubber or gasoline. One worked at what came to hand. In the Ruhr workmen stood in sullen silence and watched the dismantlers surveying for removal of generators, rolling mills and steel ovens. Krupp sat in his prison and British engineers carefully paced the jungle of his Essen works marking with white chalk the machine tools, the drop forges, the presses to be taken away. At the Bochumer Verein, which had made both submarine assemblies and the finest crucible steels, the newest and most efficient shops were dismantled. In what was left, Bochumer engineers explored new crafts with irrepressible ingenuity. They added two musicians to their technical staff and learned to cast enormous silvery bells of alloy steel—Protestant bells with one particular distinctive pitch of tone, Catholic bells with another distinctive tone. On the collar of the bells they molded the words: "God Is Love." But still there was not enough work for the hands available, and men drifted around the country seeking employment. Men accepted work no matter what the wages or hours, for if they did not there were millions more hungry, empty men waiting for the chance.

In this Germany of the Winter Years there were no politics. There was no time to think of politics, and all Germans had been numbed by politics anyway. Millions of them had filled out all the questions in the Allied "Fragebogen" and had been measured for the stain of Nazism, classified into Category I, II, III or IV of participation in crime. They were through with politics of any kind. There was only work and individual survival.

The Winter Years continued, leaden month dragging after leaden month, until the events of 1948 and 1949, when slowly, almost unnoticeably, things began to change. It was as if the silent addition of the effort of millions of hard-working, desperate toilers had come to fruit just in that moment when international politics split open to give Germany the opportunity which only a few months before seemed inconceivable. The Russians and the West tore their alliance irreparably apart and the Berlin blockade burst; simultaneously the Western Allies decided to return their Germany to German management. Spring broke through the frost in hundreds of thousands of little lives; ex-Nazi schoolteachers, like my hitchhiker, found themselves denazified and free to teach again; in the Ruhr workers struck and refused to dismantle the installations that were their promise of livelihood; Germans gathered in groups, protested Allied acts. Politics were about to begin.

Four years later, by the summer of 1953, Germany could look out into a world in which she was not only the strongest and healthiest of European states, but in which she was courted by her conquerors who competed for her favors. Four years later the greatest German problem was whether or not to accept the invitation of the Western world to sit in its councils in dignity and equality.

How had this come about?

The answer lies in the intertwining of two stories quite separate in impulse, and origin—the story of the Germans themselves, and the story of their conquerors. Both must be followed simultaneously.

The story of the Germans themselves is simple, for it springs from the biological urge of the Germans to thrive again, to become masters once more of their own destiny. It has been the most constant, deep and natural pressure in European politics. All the detailed complexities of German politics, party votes and Cabinet reshufflings are framed by this primordial urge. The differences among German parties and leaders have been differences of tactics and timings; there has been no divergence among them on the great goal of resurgence and recovery.

The story of the conquerors is as difficult to tell as the story of the Germans is simple. There were three conquerors, in fact, and a guest conqueror (France) to complicate matters. When these conquerors met in Germany in 1945, they totally expunged the sovereignty of the German state, its power over its individuals, and quartered that sovereignty among themselves.

The trouble was that none of these conquerors—except for the French, who were powerless—knew exactly what they wanted to do with this sovereignty. The two major victors, Russia and the

United States, were the most confused and, in their confusion, while they made up their minds, they left the direction of Germany to their respective armies, the Red Army and the United States Army. The Red Army, like any other organ of the Communist state, is a tightly controlled, highly disciplined expression of Communist policy. The United States Army is its very opposite—an expression of a people in arms, a body with its own leadership and rationale, intelligent and loyal, but politically uncontrolled and undirected. If the Red Army, in its frightening mechanical rigidity, was the constant, the United States Army was the dynamic, the moving, the creative element in postwar Germany. The story of Western Germany since the war, therefore, begins with its chief protagonist, the Merlin of the ruins, wearing the uniform of an officer of the United States Army.

When on March 30, 1945, Major-General Lucius D. Clay answered the telephone in his office in the old State Department building across the street from the White House, he had little premonition that its message would announce for him a role in modern German history outmatched only by that of Bismarck, the creator, and Hitler, the destroyer. The ringing phone that morning informed Clay that he was to proceed to Europe, at once, to become General Dwight D. Eisenhower's deputy for the military government of Germany.

The call came as a surprise to Clay. Until that morning Lucius Clay—a lean, dark-haired, gray-eyed officer of the United States Army whose extraordinary gift of clarity in expression and thought had only recently been noticed—had had no experience whatsoever with Germans, no wish for anything but a combat command and had heard not an echo of forewarning gossip. But Lucius Clay was one of those men like George Catlett Marshall, Omar Bradley or Dwight D. Eisenhower, who after a lifetime of obscurity in the peacetime Army (Clay had spent twenty-two years in rising from second lieutenant to captain) had, under the pressure of war emergency, shown such skills and talents as to rocket him to the eminence of statesmanship. A variety of wartime army assignments, all on the fringe where America's civilian life meshed with the needs of its demanding Army, had, by 1945, given Clay the reputation of being equal to the impossible. The governing of Germany, it was obvious in early spring of that year, was going to be a task of extraordinary complexity and difficulty. Therefore, it was to be Clay's.

Like a good soldier Clay accepted his assignment. He called on his proper army superiors and then on Mr. Byrnes, then the War Mobilizer and Deputy to the President of the United States. Mr. Byrnes accompanied Clay on a brief visit to President Roosevelt who, only a few months away from death, was too sick to tell him what America wanted in Germany even if he knew. He called on Mr. McCloy, Assistant Secretary of War, who was to be his ultimate successor in Germany, called on Secretary of War Stimson and on Army Chief of Staff, General George Marshall, and then he took off to govern Germany.

General Clay did not bother to call on the State Department, that branch of the United States government which is supposed to be steward of our relations with foreign powers, nor did the omission occur to him until several years later. "As I look back," Clay wrote after his retirement from the Army, "I find it amazing that I did not visit the State Department or talk to any of its officials." In retrospect the bald statement is not quite as startling as it sounds, for even if Clay had called, he would have learned nothing; the State Department had no program for Germany.

Years later I heard one of the State Department's wisest diplomats muse aloud about the problem. The United States, he said, has a corps of experts, a body of doctrine, a national tradition to fit every country that enters into our affairs except one—Germany, the nation with whom we have warred twice in this century. In the State Department, in all the great universities, in every big-city press corps there are men who have made a life-study of or who nurse a cherished interest in either England, France, China, Russia or Latin America. They have beaten out ideas which serve as the commonest coin of our schoolboy learning—the "Open Door" for China, the "Good Neighbor Policy" for Latin America, "Lafayette-we-are-here" for France, "Our British cousins" for England, and the phrases of deadly rivalry with the Soviet Union. But, although a few devoted scholars have excited some students in universities with an interest in Germany, though a few specialists in the State Department receive the German desk as an assignment of duty, though a few soldiers study its battle formations and a few businessmen trade with it, Germany had never fascinated Americans generally nor inspired them to explore it.

The State Department thus had neither the wisdom nor guidance to offer Clay even had he called. Its experts were, to be sure, working on a secret policy paper, too secret even to be shown to Clay, the man who was to direct policy. This was the paper later coded into the Joint Chiefs of Staff Order No. 1067, about which Clay was not to hear until after his arrival in Europe. Other State Department experts had been working in obscurity during the war years with subordinate French, British and Russian experts in London, in a committee called the European Advisory Commission, whose job it was to develop ideas for the occupation of Germany as soon as she should be defeated.

But neither JCS No. 1067 nor the memoranda of the London Committee had any real, valid relationship with the task that confronted the United States Army and Lucius Clay, when, at last, in May of 1945, Germany lay bloody and still before them. The thinking behind these policy papers started with a fundamental and erroneous assumption: that Germany would surrender to the Allies as a roaring, powerful, living state, the wheels of its industry humming with power and its ruthless administration still rigidly in control. The job, as foreseen during the war years, was how to slow those roaring wheels, how to trim the power out of German industrial might, how to remove and liquidate the evil men who directed its government.

The situation the United States Army found in Germany was so totally different as to make such policy directives irrelevant. Not only was there no government to dismantle and purify, there was nothing remotely resembling government; there was not even disorder; there was complete chaos and anarchy. Germany was a country without mail or telephone services; 754 sunken barges in the United States zone alone choked navigation on the Rhine; 885 railroad bridges dangled meaningless across spanless voids; no one could count the broken highway bridges; its fields, in midsummer, were deserted; its hospitals bursting with cripples lacked the most primitive drugs and anesthetics; in the American zone only 1,200 factories out of 12,000 still worked.

Policy, suggested by civilians far away, ordered the Army to reduce, dismantle and erase the threat of Germany forever. But to the Army's eyes the task seemed already accomplished. Far more difficult, indeed almost impossible, was the parallel task of keeping Germany alive and preventing it from lapsing into hopeless despair and disease. It was all very well for the State Department to agree with shivering French and Belgians that Germany's once-prosperous Ruhr mines should deliver 25,000,000 tons of coal in three months, to repay some tiny measure of Hitler's exactions from those invaded lands. But what if, as was the case, the once-fabled Ruhr mines were producing only 3,000,000 tons of coal each month in all? What then? No one in Washington had any answers, and the United States Army was on its own.

Most senior officers of the United States Army have been brought up to go by the rule book. Always, in their education and training, some rule book defines their authority and mission. But in Germany the given rule book simply did not make sense.

The rule book for Germany had several chapters. Chapter one was the Yalta agreement which had divided Germany into four geographical zones—for Russia, the agricultural east; for Britain, the industrial northwest; for America, the scenic south; for France, two Rhineland pockets. Yalta ordained that once the sovereignty of Germany should be expunged, it would be replaced by the authority of a Four Power Allied Control Commission sitting in Berlin. Chapter two of the rule book came from the Potsdam agreements. Beneath the Control Commission the Potsdam accords authorized a number of centralized German agencies—in no sense a government—which would operate the machinery of German affairs as the Control Commission ordered them. In each zone the military commanders would make sure that these orders were followed and implemented, either by their own troops or by local German authorities prodded by bayonets. So far, so good, but all this was abstraction.

What was not abstract was more difficult, and nothing was more difficult than the put-and-take of the German economy. There were three separate links to the put-and-take, and they did not fit. The first link was the definition of reparations. The Russians insisted that the Yalta agreement had not only clearly promised them ten million dollars' worth of reparations, but that the Potsdam agreements had defined the package. This package consisted of all the equipment and installations removed from the Eastern

Zone which Russia held, plus one-quarter of the much vaster equipment and installations to be removed from Western Germany which the Atlantic Powers held. The second link in the put-and-take said that all reparations and removals were to be calculated so as to leave Germany only enough productive power for industrial self-sufficiency and nothing that would make her militarily potent. But the third link seemed to say that no reparations at all should come out of *current* German production until the Germans should have earned enough by their exports to pay for their imports, because, clearly, if Germany could not support herself she would be a burden on the charity of others.

It did not take long to show that the Red Army interpreting the put-and-take one way and the United States Army interpreting it another could not possibly cooperate.

In the Eastern Zone the Communist Army measured with the first link of the Potsdam chain, savagely exacting reparations out of revenge for its own ravaged lands. With complete surliness of manner and suspicion of intent, the Russians slapped down on the 17,000,000 Germans of the Eastern Zone a wall of secrecy and terror while they performed the operation. This first spasm of Russian looting passed swiftly. By midwinter of 1945-1946 the looted entrails of German factories crowded the railway sidings and marshaling yards from Berlin all the way back to Moscow where they rusted uselessly in the open air. By spring of 1946 the Russians had decided that it was best to leave installations in place, make them work in Germany, with Germans, and take reparations out of production.

This change in Russian decision brought direct conflict with the United States Army which, in Western Germany, measured with the second and third of the Potsdam links. Potsdam, according to American reading, said that nothing was to be taken out of current German production so long as Germany could not support herself and was dependent on American charity. The United States Army had to wheedle $500,000,000 a year of relief supplies for Germany out of its reluctant Congress. Its job was not only to keep Germany quiet but get it off the back of the American taxpayer as quickly as possible. Thus, no reparations from current output. Russia should have only her promised share of the plant equipment rendered surplus in the Western Zone as German industry was stripped down to agreed levels.

Thus, one year to the week from the moment of Germany's surrender, reparations provided the immediate cause of the first open breach between the conquerors. Since Russia ran her Eastern Zone as a sealed enclave, since Russia pumped equipment and reparations out of it without informing other Allies of what was being stripped, since the Russians throttled off the normal food supplies of East German farms which feed West German cities, it was obvious that the early calculations of what industrial level all of Germany as a whole should be permitted were meaningless. Western Germany would have to have more, rather than less, industry if she were to earn enough to replace the loss of East German food. The British concurred in this American analysis because the Ruhr which the British occupied was the most heavily industrialized belt of Europe and needed food. It seemed silly for the British to waste their own slim hoard of dollars buying wheat and meat for their defeated enemy, while the enemy was forbidden to earn those dollars by his own exertions. On May 3 of 1946 General Lucius Clay announced that, except for advance plant, he was suspending all further delivery of promised reparations to the Russians so long as the Russians would not operate their zone, as promised, as part of a United Germany.

Self-sufficiency for the Germans had now become, for the United States Army, a goal in itself. While in Paris, London, Moscow and Washington, Messrs. Molotov, Byrnes, Bidault, Bevin and Marshall argued about what *should* be done with Germany, the United States Army did it. Each practical measure adopted for achieving self-sufficency generated its own momentum until, finally, the original purpose of dismantling and disarming Germany, along with the subsequent desire to get Germany off the back of the American taxpayer and abandon her, was lost in single-minded consecration to the task of making Germany self-sufficient in and for herself.

Step followed logical step. Obviously, a few basic measures were necessary to make Germany an operating concern: Germany had to be decompartmentalized and the zones abolished; Germans had to be invited back to the levers of control which they understood better than anyone else; they had to be given a sound currency so that business could revive; they had to have a government which could efficiently synchronize the myriad impulses and efforts of its individuals.

In May of 1946 General Clay suggested to Secretary Byrnes that he invite the other occupying powers to merge their zones with the American for greater efficiency. If they were unwilling, said Clay, let the British alone be invited into a bizonal merger. Byrnes assented and invitations were issued. Only the British accepted the invitation. General Clay's office worked out the organs of dual control and lo, the skeleton of a German state called Bizonia emerged by the end of 1946, complete with courts, judges, tax and regulatory powers over German economic life.

General Clay urged broader action. When General Marshall flew back from his spring conference at Moscow in 1947 where he had unsuccessfully pressed Stalin to raise the industrial levels of Germany, he was inclined to agree with Clay. New directives were issued, Clay and the military governors of the other Western Allies met, re-examined Germany's industrial potential and Germany's industrial ceilings rose.

When, in December of 1947, the Four Power Alliance of the war ruptured permanently at the meeting of Molotov and Marshall in London, Clay, who had attended the session, sat down once more to discuss the matter with General Marshall. During a long luncheon at Ambassador Douglas' residence, Clay reviewed for Marshall, Ernest Bevin and several other dignitaries the measures that might be taken to put Germany on the road to recovery. Two of them seemed inescapable. The first was currency reform. Since the Russians were using in their East Zone a set of plates for printing paper marks identical with those of Western Germany and no agreement with the Russians was possible, it seemed obvious that inflation could be purged only by repudiating the old currency and substituting a new one. The second measure was even more important: to get maximum efficiency out of West Germany, Germans had to be given broader control of their own affairs, more responsibility, more initiative—in short, a new national government. Clay flew back from this conference and, in the spring of 1948, took the first steps to achieve both measures.

Up until then Lucius Clay had been for the Russians only the American general who denied them reparations. The events of the spring of 1948—currency reform and discussion of a new West German government—convinced them that the issues were larger than reparations. What was at stake was the nature of the new Germany, the possibility that the new Germany might become not disputed quarry but the spearhead of a new and hostile alliance. The Russians retaliated in the only manner they knew—by the blockade of Berlin, an attempt to squeeze America to compliance by starving three million Germans.

Currency reform was merely the public pretext for the blockade. Ten days after the blockade was imposed, General Clay drove to visit his opposite number, the Russian Commander in Chief, General Sokolovsky.

"How long do you plan to keep it up?" he asked.

Sokolovsky replied, "Until you stop your plans for a West German government."

Europeans, criticizing American political attitudes, frequently claim that Americans are a people nursed on statistics, who believe that when they have measured any given situation or divided it by percentage points or classified it and enumerated the classifications, they understand it. This may be valid criticism, but if it is, then the technique of measurement applied to the Berlin blockade must be recorded as the most exceptional triumph of measurement over a political dilemma in modern times. Politically, there was no solution of the Berlin blockade short of war. But if one measured it, suddenly a way out developed. To supply the two and one-half million people of West Berlin, a minimum of 4,000 tons of food and fuel a day was necessary. With a slide rule one could divide this up into so-and-so many plane loads that must necessarily arrive every twenty-four hours at West Berlin's two airports, Tempelhof and Gatow. After that it was only a problem of getting the planes, filling them, flying them around the clock.

Something like one hundred American C47's with a total carrying capacity of 250 tons a day began the airlift into Berlin. By December a third airfield in the French sector at Tegel had been built; scores of C54's each carrying ten tons of payload had been rushed out from America; that month Berlin's airlift passed the 4,000 ton mark of minimum necessity. The fleet grew as British and American Air Forces poured in planes and personnel. It passed the 5,500 ton mark in January. By spring, when the Russians called it quits, the planes were winging in with as much as 13,000 tons a day, or sixty per cent more than the old ground-haulage figure of 8,000 tons a day for rail and water; by then West Berlin's food ration was not only higher than East Berlin but higher than before the blockade.

The planes made a beautiful sight all through the winter of 1948-1949, coasting down the long runways of West German fields between the golden glow of field lamps, their green and red winglights glinting, the plumes of their exhaust blue and white in the night. All through the day and night they droned, descending one a minute on the runways of Berlin, turning around, going back for more, their pilots briefly resting, tired, in the muddy alert shacks, smoking, playing Red Dog and poker, crabbing, talking of rotation—but very proud. Because the airlift involved so many human beings and was clothed in such vivid drama, it acted profoundly in the psychology of the Occupation as a turning point. It was not simply that the American pilots, as Americans everywhere, enjoyed the thought of dumping bags of candy for Berlin's children over the roofs as they came in to land. It was that in Berlin, Americans and Germans stood together, both beleaguered, both under attack, both facing a common enemy. Emotionally, they were allies. It was a change in attitude difficult to define. I remember arriving at Berlin during the airlift and noticing a curious change in phraseology. When, at a bar in the Ruhr or Frankfurt, one heard Americans use the pronoun "they," "they" almost invariably referred to the Germans, still the enemy to be watched and controlled. But at a bar or over dinner in Berlin when one heard "they," "they" almost invariably referred to the Russians. The Germans were included in "we."

Both the airlift and Clay's master plan for a West German government came to a climax in the month of his departure. On May 12, 1949, the first trucks and trains passed from the Western Zone through the Soviet Zone, to enter Berlin peacefully, and the blockade was over. On that same day General Clay flew down from Berlin to Frankfurt to receive the delegation of the German Constitutional Convention, bringing him for approval their final draft of the new German constitution.

This constitution was to be the title deed of the new German state and in its final draft it provided for a strong, centralized German government. Here was a question of enormous portent, a political question that could not be measured in tonnages. The approval of the constitution was General Clay's last act as proconsul. Dutifully, as a good Army officer, he tried to find out from the War Department whether the United States wanted a strong and centralized or weak and federalized Germany. It was a Platonic question, one for philosophers. The Army replied that it had no strong feelings one way or the other and that Clay should go ahead and do what he thought right. Dutifully again, Clay tried to find out what advice the State Department had to give him. State, still as perplexed by Germany as on the day of Clay's departure in 1945, had none. Judiciously, therefore, acting on his own as he always had, General Clay as chairman of the military governors, sat down with German representatives that busy afternoon and worked out a compromise. The compromise provided for a German government not too strong, not too weak, an efficient constitution that was to function better than any other in postwar Europe—a machine ready to be driven, although no one knew which way.

Thus, having finished his proconsulship, General Clay flew back to Washington, retired from the United States Army, entered American business and politics and waited for the verdict of history to judge whether he deserved well of the Republic or not.

The departure of General Clay, as he himself had long reported, was overdue. Only the blockade and threat of war had kept Germany under the stern control of a military occupation and an alien general. Already the forces Clay had set in motion had quickened and begun to throb with the strength of millions of Germans becoming once again aware of nationhood. They were ready and eager to resume their own story in their own way.

All through the winter of 1949, as the airlift had droned through the leaden skies to Berlin, a gathering of seventy elderly men had simultaneously droned on in seemingly endless talk in a quiet gray building commandeered from a girls' normal school by the banks of the Rhine in the suburbs of the little town of Bonn. These were the constitution-makers of the new Germany.

They were not an impressive assemblage. As they sat about the blondwood desks and tables which had once been school furniture, or as they strolled on the ragged lawn by the river's edge where several dirty yellow sheep baaed as they fitfully cropped the straggly grass, they seemed like the faculty of a provincial theological seminary. Of the seventy men, thirty-seven were entitled to the academic title of Herr Doktor, and seven were Herr Professor Doktor. Eighteen were government civil servants, and fourteen were municipal or local officials. The oldest was seventy-four, the youngest thirty-five. No one during the airlift winter paid much attention to them, but they were the most important men in Germany, for they were the end-fruit of American policy, the progenitors of the new German state. They had been chosen in local elections by forty-eight million West Germans to frame the Constitution of the Republic which the United States invited them to make. Their existence had provoked the Berlin blockade.

For eight months from September of 1948 to May of 1949, the seventy constitution-makers, lodging in the shabby overcrowded rooming houses or ill-lit hotels of Bonn, worried their task until they had arrived at a document of one hundred and forty-nine separate clauses as the skeleton of their new state. This document guaranteed to all Germans every form of individual liberty and personal freedom; it accepted the perspectives of defeat and outlawed future German national armies, forbade conscription, permitted any future German government to yield sovereignty to any future European union. It balanced state rights against federal government, giving the states an Upper House (or Bundesrat) with powers similar to the American Senate, and giving the Lower House (or Bundestag) broad powers of taxation and control of foreign affairs to make it a strong, efficient, centralizing body. Its most interesting feature was an invention of the scholars who wrote it. Reviewing Germany's sad earlier experience with unstable parliaments, they set out to cure parliamentary instability by a technical trick. By the new constitution, no German Chancellor can be overthrown by a parliamentary majority unless that same majority proposes and votes to power a new Chancellor it likes better. This constitution has since given Germany a more stable government than any other European country except England.

More important than anything the constitution wrote or did,

however, was the living spectacle of the constitution-makers discussing Germany as Germany. Here, finally, after the years of silence was a forum in which Germans could discuss their future, not as supplicants to enemy legates, but as Germans with each other. It brought the still feeble beat of German life to a rhythm, and its fragmentation to a focus. The German political parties, which had hitherto operated only on the level of individual states, came clear like crystals forming in a colloidal solution.

The Christian Democrats, who had sent twenty-eight delegates to the Constitutional Convention, were a party of religious and predominantly Catholic inspiration. Their party was one of compromise that ran from moderate Right to moderate Left. The Socialists, who had sent thirty delegates, were predominantly working class, predominantly Protestant, fiery, intemperate, anti-Communist but anti-Occupation too. The others were splinters: the Bavarian party, it was clear, was a sectional party, the Dixiecrats of South Germany. The German party, also sectional, was limited to the plains of northern Saxony. The Free Democrats were also a party of the North, nationalist, Protestant, whose ideas ran the entire gamut from McKinley to Taft. The Communists, spokesmen of Russia, were a negligible force. The Catholic Centrists had retained only a fraction of their prewar strength as spokesmen of the Catholic liberals.

Personalities emerged. There was Konrad Adenauer, a stiff old man, who walked as if his legs were hinged by rusting joints, an elder of seventy-three years dressed in starched collar, crisp pants, wearing an air of imperturbable, grave and unruffled dignity. No other personality could match him in the Constitutional Convention except Carlo Schmidt, the Socialist phrase-maker, a huge, burly, rumpled man of extraordinary wit and cleverness. But Schmidt, it was clear, was only the Bonn delegate of an even more extraordinary personality, Kurt Schumacher, who lived in Hanover and ran the Socialist party as if he were its Moses and its members his Children of Israel. Boss, High Priest, Theoretician, Tactician, Speech-maker, only Schumacher equaled Adenauer in impact on the nascent German state.

The new state came into being quickly, easily, with no confusion or fumbling, no grinding of the gears or any crisis. On August 14, 1949, three months after General Clay's departure, elections were held under the new constitution, returning a government dominated by a coalition of three parties—the Christian Democrats, the German party, the Free Democrats, all of them led by Konrad Adenauer. The opposition was the Socialist party. As a benison to the new Republic, military government was abolished and replaced by three High Commissioners, one each from America, Britain and France. To replace Lucius Clay, the United States government named as High Commissioner Mr. John J. McCloy, who was to conceive his task not only, as Clay had, to revive Germany but also to beseech her friendship.

Early in 1950, a few months after the new Federal Republic of West Germany had been established, I passed through Bonn, which I had not seen since the Constitutional Convention.

Bonn crackled and snapped with vitality. Blue and white signs pointed the way to Federal Ministries of Economics, of Refugees, of Justice, of Interior, scattered through half-wrecked buildings and still intact barracks of the old Wehrmacht. The old girls' normal school where the constitution-makers had once worked was bursting at the seams. A black-gold-red banner, Germany's national flag, snapped from its flagstaff. The old baaing yellow sheep were gone from the lawn and the lawn spread smooth and green to the river's edge. The trim gray building had shot out a long new office wing to the south that housed the German legislators. Between the old building and the new wing, German architects had designed a parliamentary chamber of stunning beauty. Its two protruding walls were sheer glass that opened on the grandeur of the Rhine; its furniture of green and black leather glistened; its lobbies were antiseptically clean and busy men rushed through them at a dogtrot, each carrying his bulging brief case. When Parliament was not in session, files of school children led by their teachers serpentined through the corridors, visiting the new capital of Germany.

The new government passed laws, imposed taxes—not very heavy by American or British standards—controlled its own police, staffed its own border guards, even had its own intelligence service —permitted for internal security. Its president welcomed the ministers of foreign powers, and its spokesmen traveled to Paris to join in the deliberations of the Marshall Plan's European Council. It sounded, thundered and made noises like a sovereign body.

But, as every German knew, it was not yet sovereign.

Every three weeks a symbolic act took place to demonstrate to the Germans how incomplete was this sovereignty. Bonn sits on the flatland of the Rhine's west bank, just as the Rhine opens out of the majesty of the Wagnerian hills. Across the river from the gray, rectilinear capital of the new German Republic rises a tall and forest-covered hill atop which a snow-white mansion looks out over the deep, beautiful valley. This snow-white mansion is the famous Petersberger Hof, where in bygone days, Adolf Hitler summoned Neville Chamberlain and Édouard Daladier to the craven capitulation that preceded Munich. The Petersberger Hof was now occupied by the three members of the Allied High Commission, charged with the supervision of the new Republic. The three High Commissioners possessed the power of veto over any law of the Bundestag, the power of decree, the power to suspend any act of any member state of the new Republic. Therefore, every three weeks, the aged Adenauer, now the new Chancellor of the Republic, flanked by three brief-case-carrying aides, would drive up the hill to the three Commissioners and be received by them. There he would explain the acts and bills of the Parliament, there he would listen to the Commissioners' complaints, exhortations and instructions. In other circumstances, the little act would have been humiliation and Adenauer himself was occasionally heard to mutter of "The Unholy Trinity" on the hill. But it was only four years after the bitterest of wars and a total defeat; the humiliation could not conceal the essential German triumph that now the conquerors were dealing with one man who spoke for Germany, planned for Germany, winced for Germany and resisted for Germany.

Down in the flatlands, at the Bundeshaus, politics revolved fundamentally about these symbolic visits. Just how should the spokesman of the new Germany deal with the conquering Allies? The two great parties, Socialists and Christian Democrats, split on the question. Both agreed that the ultimate goal to be won from the Allies was independence and equality, complete and untrammeled. But Adenauer's instinct was to go slowly, to take each grant of freedom as it was offered, ask for more, submit when refused, then wait, then ask for more again. The Socialists' instinct, perhaps only because they were the opposition party, was to press faster, to insist instantly on new and greater powers, to use the leverage of Germany's growing strength to bargain and demand that full equality which ultimately the High Commission promised to yield anyway. The Socialists, whose beating drums sounded frighteningly like rabid nationalism, were thus, automatically, one of Adenauer's greatest sources of strength in his diplomacy on the hill. If Adenauer refused or balked at Allied instructions, then down in the flatlands of German politics his political strength was enormously inflated because he had resisted in the name of Germany. But up on the hill it was all the easier for him to win his points from the High Commissioners by pointing to the vigor of the opposition and his need of holding Parliament in line under his own friendly leadership. Then he could return, and gravely—always gravely and without emotion—display to the Bundestag what he had won.

This curious charade continued for almost a year and then, again, politics made one of its sharp and dizzy turns.

On June 25, 1950, halfway around the globe, the North Koreans launched their attack against the South Koreans. Overnight the world was on the edge of war. At that moment the Allied Armies of Occupation in Western Germany counted seven slim and weak divisions. In Eastern Germany were some twenty-two Soviet divisions plus supporting units, or almost three times as many Red Army soldiers, better equipped, better trained. In Eastern Germany, moreover, the Communist counterpart of the Western German Republic had begun to recruit a small but menacing skeleton army corps of Germans in training, equipped with tanks and artillery. Backing them were satellite armies of ominous proportions. No Atlantic soldier reading the map of Germany could do else but shudder. The line had to be braced swiftly, galvanically, with power. The only pool of easily available manpower was in Western Germany, and it was superb soldierly material too, as sad experience had demonstrated. If Western Germany was to be held, if anything east of the Rhine was to be held, then German manpower, said the Western generals, had to be rushed into uniform. In December of 1950 the senior powers of the Atlantic world gathered in Brussels, nominated Dwight Eisenhower as their commander in chief and instructed the High Commissioners to raise, uniform and arm German soldiers once again.

Now, at last, the realities of politics had changed. One could not recruit German soldiers as mercenaries. They had to be furnished freely by the German people if they were to fight. There was a bargain to be struck. If the Allies wanted German troops, what would they give? The three High Commissioners returned from Brussels in late December of 1950 and summoned the old Chancellor to the Petersberger Hof to hear their invitation. It was the last time he was to be so summoned; he was to appear on the hilltop only once more in the next year and a half and then not as a supplicant but as a luncheon guest. A year later the empty offices of the Petersberger Hof had been reconverted into a tourist hotel.

Ever since the beginning of 1951 and the Western invitation to the Germans to bear arms, the Germans have written their own story. For Germany, although still legally bound by volumes of Occupation laws and treaties, is no longer the inanimate object of other men's diplomacy. The community of Germans is, as it always had been in Europe, a power made of men with their own genius, wills, aspirations, hopes and decisions. Nor is this power ever static. It flows and changes and grows so swiftly that each of yesterday's binding contracts, measured so meticulously to yesterday's relation of forces, is obsolete almost before its ink is dry.

The story of these contracts, and the impact of Germans on other peoples and other peoples on Germany is, from 1951 on, another story to be told in another chapter. Within Germany the story of the Germans is almost entirely their own.

No traveler making the seasonal circuit of Europe's political centers has failed to describe how swiftly the face of Germany has changed since the ending of the Winter Years. Once set on its upward course in 1949, Germany changed from month to month. People in the streets filled out visibly. Their clothes changed from rumpled rags to decent garments, to neat business suits, to silk stockings. Cigarettes disappeared as currency, then became available everywhere, then, finally, were sold from slot machines on every corner. Food returned, food as the Germans love it, with whipped cream beaten thick in the coffee, on cake, with fruit. The streets changed face as buildings rose, as neon signs festooned them, as their windows shone with goods. For a number of years I have visited Frankfurt twice a year, staying at the Park Hotel opposite the railway station. On my first visit I could look out of the window on a hot day and still smell the dust of rubble rising from the ruins up and down the street, ruins all down the curving Bahnhof square, ruins on every side of the railway station. At each visit thereafter, some patch of rubble was cleared, some new construction sprouted into the sky, some long stretch of broken cobblestone yielded to smooth asphalt until, finally, on my last spring visit I woke and heard the sound of hammers under my window and looked out to see the last red walls of the last red ruin on my street crumbling under the wrecker's sledge, to be cleared for what new hotel or new office building only the next visit will reveal.

The revival offered its most dramatic contrasts in Düsseldorf, the capital both of Ruhr industry and the British Occupation of that province. Down Koenigsallee, the beautiful main street of the city, luxury shops blossomed year by year to offer the steel barons and coal merchants the delights they have always enjoyed. Today, the cigar stores of Koenigsallee and Flingerstrasse offer the greatest collection of yellow, black, tan, brown, half-white stogies in Europe, gathered from Brazil, Manila, Havana, Hamburg. The Konditorei decorate their shop-fronts in midwinter with bananas and oranges, pineapples from the tropics, cheeses from Denmark, champagne and Burgundy from France, grapes from Italy, hams from Scandinavia. Gradually, as this happened, the British Occupiers of Düsseldorf began to wonder who had won and who had lost the war. The first season it became obvious that the German ration had passed the British ration, a group of British women, wives of Occupation officials, demonstrated in the main streets outside British military headquarters to protest that the Germans they had defeated were eating fatter than British soldiers' families, who themselves were eating better than Britons back home. But no housewifely protest could stop the surge. It was the next season that Americans, visiting Cologne and stopping at one of its larger hotels, noticed that its dining room was divided in two halves—one for the British Occupation officials, living on the dull, juiceless, meat-thin rations of the Ministry of Food; the other for German civilians, eating rich, heavy, stomach-filling German food. The American visitors preferred to sit on the German or conquered side of the dining room, rather than on the side of the victorious British.

Revival throbbed on all the roads and arteries of communications. Bridges went up and spans were sutured. On my first visit to Germany, in an early Winter Year, the smooth concrete paths of the autobahns were dominated by vehicles of the Occupation. The Army's olive-drab trucks purring in convoy formation, the American jeeps wasping in and out, the glittering, shimmering sedans of the American families with white Occupation plates made the wheezing old German sedans, the bumbling old German trucks—so frequently overturned, so frequently wrecked, so frequently waiting idly by the road in breakdown—seem like strangers on their own roads. But each succeeding visit has shown the roads reconquered by Germans, even though there are now three times as many Americans and troops in Germany than on my first visit. New Kapitans, Opels, Volkswagens, Porsches, Mercedes-Benzes whiz by, obscuring from sight American sedans in the procession of the autobahn; huge German double and triple trailers with their trailing black exhaust becloud the occasional American convoys. Rhine barges, furrowing the busy waters, are new again, spick and span in gleaming brass fittings, and red, white, green coats of paint. The railways run on time, efficiently, the dining cars proud with white stiff linen and solid plentiful food.

Germany is alive and vigorous again—to the sight, to the ear, to the touch. Nor is this only a matter of appearances, for statistically the profile of German effort now traces the outline of an industrial power again equal to England, and greater than any other in Western Europe.

Economists estimate that Germany's gross national product has increased by seventy per cent since the year 1948-1949; that her industrial production is two-thirds again higher than it was in 1936, Hitler's peak peacetime year; that her wage-earners are now numbered at an all-time high. Germany's exports have multiplied by seven times in the five years since currency reform; her Dollar Gap should vanish in 1953; her credits in the European Payments Union stand at almost half a billion dollars, higher than any other of the Marshall Plan countries.

Each set of statistics bears its own story, but none reflect the phenomenon of Germany's Renaissance better than the figures of her steel production. In 1946, the year after Germany's collapse, she poured 2,500,000 tons of steel; in 1947, 3,000,000 tons. Those were the years in which the Allies had sworn that Germany should never produce more than 5,600,000 tons again. At the end of 1947, when the Western Allies lifted Germany's limit to 11,100,000 tons, their experts assured them it would take at least five years for Germany to reach the distant level of 10,000,000 tons. By 1949, however, the Germans were pouring 9,000,000 tons of steel and had drawn abreast of the French. In the fall of 1950 the Western Allies tore up the 11,100,000 ton limit and urged Germany to go all out in producing steel for the Western defense effort. At that time Western engineers gave their solemn opinion that the old, outmoded plants of the Ruhr could not be overhauled to produce more than an outer technical maximum of 13,500,000 tons. By the end of 1951 Germany was producing 13,500,000 tons and was racing after Britain, the leading steel producer in Western Europe. In 1953 the Germans let another notch out of their belt and poured 14,500,000 tons, in some months equaling and surpassing British production. German engineers now figure that if business holds good they can pour 18,000,000 tons in the next twelve-month period, to make them the senior steel producer of Western Europe. At that point they will be pouring more than the Ruhr ever produced before, or just slightly more than three times as much as the Allies swore, seven years ago, she would ever produce again.

All other statistics crackle with the same energy. Coal production in Germany has jumped from 60,000,000 to 100,000,000 to 125,000,000 tons. The production of radios doubled Germany's prewar production by the spring of 1951, and by the beginning of 1953 Germany was producing almost twice as many automobiles as in 1936. Starting in the rubble and disaster of defeat, the Germans began to build houses. Slowly at first, as the cramped economy put itself together again, then more swiftly German craftsmen began to house their countrymen until, by 1951, Germany was building over 400,000 dwelling units a year, or more than the total number France had built in the eight years since Liberation. Germany's home-building rate per capita is, indeed, the only major European housing effort that can match America's.

Phenomena such as these beget questions: How do the Germans do it? Where does this strength and this drive come from?

There are a number of answers.

What has been done in Germany has been done in first instance by the Germans themselves. Now, looking backward, many truths are obvious that were unknown in the first days of German defeat. The dissolution of an entire nation is a social impossibility; the wreckage of Germany that so stupefied Germans and conquerors alike in 1945 was the wreckage of buildings and stone. But it was impossible to destroy the skills in the fingers of German workmen, the knowledge of German engineers, and the managerial know-how of German industrialists without the physical extermination of the German people, obviously a moral impossibility. The social capital inherent in the accumulation of years of human experience is, economically, a vaster asset than all installations of pits, turning wheels and rails. There is no nation whose physical equipment is so great that its people's skills are not an even greater part of its wealth. If all American industry were leveled to the ground, America would still be the greatest industrial power on earth because of her social capital. In Germany the social capital of skill and knowledge remained undamaged.

Almost as important, we know now, was the tremendous accretion of strength to German industry during the war years. The piles of broken brick in the factory yards, the twisted girders, the silent mines, the roofless manufactories appalled the eye in 1945. But in these rubble heaps were still rooted the enormous instruments of production which had powered Hitler almost to victory. Germany's inventory of machine tools had stood at 1,281,000 in 1938. But when she emerged from the war, deep in her ruins there were 2,216,000 machine tools or almost twice as many as prewar. During the worst year of bombardment—1944—only six per cent of German machine tools were put out of operation and most of these were repaired and put back to work almost at once. The Germany that emerged from the years of defeat was a Germany in rags, in cold and in hunger—but a Germany in which all the infinite skills of her greatness were only dormant, the tools of her craftsmanship only silent, waiting to be uncovered from rubble, oiled, greased and put to work.

To make this productive machine operate as Germans were sure it could, certain social obstructions had to be cleared, and this task the United States Army performed, more efficiently, more speedily, more wisely than any democratic German government could possibly have done with full authority of its own.

Now, in the years of Renaissance, when Allied interference irks German pride, it is commonplace for Germans to talk of how stupid, how unjust and how extortionate was the Allied Occupation of Germany. Quite the contrary can be argued—that an essential element in Germany's recovery was supplied by the guidance of the hated Occupation Armies and by the Americans, most of all.

Military government was cold and severe, completely removed from the political passions and influences that hobble all governments elected by their own people. The economists of the Military Occupation could decide what was right and logical, and order it done without having to win the consent of a debating parliament, torn and swept by the pressures of special interests and ordinary people. No native government could have preserved order and repaired ruins with its people starving on 1,000 calories a day, but the Occupation Armies held Germany still on starvation while necessary things were done first. No elected government could have wiped out and dispossessed millions of merchants by currency repudiation; the United States Army could and did, thereby giving Germany a new currency which is the soundest in Europe. The skilful and brilliant economists attached to the Occupation had an army at their disposal to impose their thinking; when they decided that the orgy of speculation and traffic in luxury materials threatened the new German mark, they could and did force the Germans to impose trade controls at the right moment, just in time to catch the post-Korea turn of world trade and give Germany the solidest trade balances in Europe. Though the Ruhr magnates howled that the breakup of their trusts was ruining German business, the Allied shake-up of the Ruhr cartels, without fundamentally destroying them, shook new and imaginative young German businessmen, more vigorous and capable than their stolid elders, to the top.

Other nations, being free and responsible, bore the burden of defense; Germany, being conquered, paid only Occupation costs. France, with an economic strength half that of Germany, pays four billion dollars a year to support the armies of the West. But Germany pays less than two billion dollars in Occupation costs, and, at that fee, is defended by alien troops who make no call on her young manpower. More than ten per cent of England's national product goes into her defense effort and most of this comes from the engineering industries which are Britain's chief export earners. But no German production goes into arms; all of it is shaped into civilian wares, which can be shipped overseas to customers who might otherwise buy British.

Detached, impersonal, logical, the Occupation Armies and their economic advisors pursued their objective: to make Germany self-sufficient. They pumped in some four billion dollars' worth of aid to start the process; then they cleared the way for the Germans to enterprise, and German businessmen did the rest.

These years of revival have done more than fill the trade channels with goods. For, as the revival has freed Germans from the daily drudgery of the ration lines, from the hollow sense of hunger, from the endless spirit-quenching hunt for a pair of shoes, for a job, for a hovel to sleep in, it has given Germans time to think. It has released them from individual preoccupation, each man with his own misery, to a contemplation of themselves as a people, which is the beginning of politics.

But, though revival has healed the flesh, it has healed the spirit more slowly. What has happened to the flesh can be measured in figures and made clear; what has happened to the spirit, in the darkness of the defeated mind, can be measured by no one, German or alien.

On the surface, at Bonn, where the legal parties gather to vote, German politics have a deceptive simplicity, almost comparable to that of British politics. But beneath this surface strange incalculable forces are at work in a peculiar, unfinished groping process which will not emerge clearly until its consummation. It is only natural that this should be so, for no nation has been more greatly disturbed in the past generation than Germany. Germans have been flung about between triumph and despair, rejected and wooed, their governments overturned and denounced; they have been pressed and urged physically by one compulsion after another, within elastic borders that expand and contract and expand and contract again, until it is difficult for anyone to say what is Germany and what is not.

Consider the many strange groups and new forces in Germany, rolling about like cargo unlashed on a ship's deck in a storm:

Eight million refugees form one-sixth of the population of West Germany. One of the greatest triumphs of West Germany since the war has been her ability to absorb this horde of human beings into her smashed dwellings, and keep unemployment down to one million and a half citizens. But these refugees are people who have lost all, and, though they are German by blood and tongue, they warm themselves with memories of Silesia or Pomerania or Sudetenland and the homes they have fled. They are people who have been forced down, down, down in an inexorable process of proletarization—the East German factory owner has become a plant manager, the factory manager a foreman, the farmer a farmhand, the merchant a clerk. Even in West Germany they are strangers and outcasts, unwanted and unloved. But they are citizens; they vote; they speak; they listen for voices that offer them hope and future. How will they vote on war and peace? On rollback or containment? On status quo or reconquest?

Consider four million German women, women without men because the men they did marry or the men they might have married were consumed in Hitler's wars. Consider each of them nursing in the solitude of a lonesome room her own neurotic longing and how, in the past, strange men have come to power on just such voting neuroses as this.

Consider, more ominously, the progeny of the Nazis. It is not the hundreds of thousands of fatherless children bred by the Nazis out of the broodmare bodies of concupiscent Hitler-Maidens—still in school, still learning that their only father was Hitler—who are most important. Beyond them, and more important, are the hundreds of thousands of young men who knew and tasted glory in officers' uniforms as the Wehrmacht carried the swastika all across Europe, and who are now excluded, totally, from any share in a society they once dominated. It is the hundreds of thousands of middle-aged men whose careers and ambitions first flourished under Hitler who cannot forget the banners, the youth-hikes, the solid substance of prosperity they first learned to enjoy under other and different standards.

Consider, then, the new influences at work on the great mass of Germans trying to learn, or decide, what to do with their strength.

Consider the Church, more powerful today in Germany than at any moment since Martin Luther nailed his thesis to the doors of the cathedral of Wittenberg. The Russians, in shearing off Eastern from Western Germany, have sheared away the ancient beds of German Protestantism and left a Germany in which the Catholics of the Rhineland and Bavaria for the first time in a century have the power to guide German destinies. Nor is this Catholic leadership in Germany a simple, solid force as embodied in the devout Konrad Adenauer. It is a force of many strains running from the most archaic to the most enlightened. It is not only political but intellectual, and in postwar Germany, modern Catholic thinkers provide the same film of ideas for German politics that American liberals provided for the New Deal and British Fabians for the Labour government. The Church belongs to the West, both liberal and archaic strains lead Germany to the West.

Consider, then, the uncharted influence of the Americans, not the America of baseball teams and PX's, youth clubs and women's clubs, but the more serious and lasting implantations of American spirit. American radios and broadcasts blanket the air of Germany so that, in the evening, the best picture of world affairs comes to German ears from American editing. Americans brought to Germany the doctrine of the free press. General Clay introduced German newspapermen to the technique of the press conference, and at first shyly, but then ever more seriously, German newspapermen have learned that the press conference is a device for the citizen to summon government to account. All Germany is dotted with little halls and buildings called Amerika Häuser, outposts of American culture, perhaps the most successful of our laboratory experiments in spreading America's message. In the evening, even now seven years after defeat, these halls are crowded with sweaty, tired, work-lined Germans who come to hear recordings of American music, witness American documentary films, study American technical magazines, read American books. How much of what they absorb do they carry home to create a German democracy?

It is impossible to judge precisely either these influences or the weight of the political groups at Bonn, the surface of German politics. In Bonn there gather 402 elected Bundestag members, ninety-five per cent of them chosen from parties who are, as far as we can tell, sincerely democratic in our sense. They are democratic today because we, in the early days of the Occupation, created these parties, purified their leadership and then presented them to the German people as the only alternates of choice. Considering the process by which the Germans came to choose these people, Bonn is a remarkably successful experiment. Bonn is far more democratic in instinct and procedure than we had any reason to hope after the savagery and acquired habits of the Nazi interlude. It is also vigorously and independently German enough to act as a true steward of German interests, erring neither on the side of slavish puppetry or demagogic nationalism.

But the rivalries of the parties at Bonn do not embrace all the alternate choices now open to the German people. Today they possess choices not only within Bonn, but beyond and outside it. By the time this book is in print, the world will have witnessed a German election to replace the present Bundestag at Bonn with another, empowered to act for a four-year term. In all likelihood the present parties gathered in Bonn will again harvest a vast majority of all the votes cast, but in all likelihood it will also show, for the first time, the true alternatives with which the Germans fumble in indecision.

A German newspaperman once explained these alternatives to me better than anyone else. "All that you see here in Bonn," he said to me, "is the good Germany, the democratic Germany. This is the best in Germany. But there is another Germany which is not democratic, which is now submerged. This is the Germany that voted for Hitler and voted for Hugenberg, the Germany that loved the Kaiser and fought for him. This you did not bring to Bonn. Not until that Germany is lined up on one side and all the men of Bonn are lined up on the other side will you see which is stronger. The trouble is, I can't tell you where to look for the other Germany because it is not located in one city or in one region or in one group. Germany is divided up into little bits in every German's heart; part of every heart belongs to this Germany, and part to old Germany, and a little bit to Hitler. You have to wait to see which wins."

Many men have tried to find a name for this other Germany

in the past few years. Those whose memories are still sensitive to suffering call it the Neo-Nazi Germany. Others call it Nationalist Germany. Many democratic Germans, among themselves, call it Restoration Germany. By Restoration Germany, they mean not Hitler Germany, nor the dead German Republic, but the Germany that goes back to the generation beyond—the Kaiser's Germany of order and established authority, the Germany of authority vested in Church, authority vested in parent, authority vested in trade-union bureaucrat, authority vested in schoolteacher and faculty. Yet even Restoration Germany fails to cover all the kinds of Germany with whom the men at Bonn must reckon someday, at the polls and within their own hearts.

The Germany that will oppose Bonn is the Germany that wishes, simply, to seek its own destiny in its own way, for its own interests, making believe that the war, and all its hideous crimes, had never happened, or if it happened, that it was an accident brought about by other people for whom they are not responsible. Nor does this other Germany believe its own or any other democratic liberties are serious values to be fought for if they tangle and obstruct power politics.

The years of revival have quickened this other Germany, too, along with the Germany of Bonn. It has been generally assumed that if Germans—or any other people for that matter—eat, dress and house themselves well, they become automatically peaceful and decent people. Yet the records offer no guarantee that simple prosperity can erase ambition and greed from men's souls. The Germany of Bismarck and Kaiser Wilhelm was entering upon a Golden Age of well-being before its adventures of 1914 ushered in the Age of Sorrow.

The naive and the cynical, reacting each in their own fashion, find it either frighteningly disconcerting or entirely natural that, in the years of the revival since 1949, the other Germany should have grown so swiftly and deeply in its appeal to the German spirit.

This other Germany cannot be traced by votes, for the laws and powers of the Bonn government forbid and dissolve parties and groups who summon Germans back to old tribal loyalties. It can be traced only by episodes and incidents, and each year the episodes and incidents come more frequently and seem to strike deeper. The episodes span the entire range from triviality to significance: the French will note that a border post of German customs guards is suddenly heard in the dark of night singing the "Horst Wessel Lied." Diplomats will note that as a new German Army is planned in the embryo German War Ministry, an office purge forces out the best young men of the old officer corps and that suddenly those German officers who tried to assassinate Hitler in July are stigmatized as traitors. The British will seine up through their intelligence a plot in the Ruhr that links both Nazis and respectable Germans together in a conspiracy to wipe out all the structure of Bonn.

The activity and power of this other Germany seems to come and go in shapeless waves. It was noticed first in 1949, coincident with the uncovering of the first clandestine organization of German Army officers, the Bruderschaft. It spurted suddenly in the election campaign of 1949, in the contest for the new Bundestag. When thoroughly democratic candidates began to vie with each other for the ultra-nationalist vote, they went so far that Konrad Adenauer and Kurt Schumacher squelched the rivalry by an unwritten agreement to hold their young men in check. It ebbed, so far as observers could tell, in the events of 1950, and then, in the spring months of 1951, took shape again, regionally, on the windswept moors of Lower Saxony, Hitler's old stamping ground. There, in provincial elections, the ranting, arrogant Socialist Reich Partei harvested ten per cent of all votes under the leadership of a roaring proto-Nazi, Ernst Otto Remer, whose chief claim to fame was that he had butchered off the finest of the German officers who had tried to assassinate Hitler in 1944. The government of Bonn, in the spring of 1952, outlawed the Socialist Reich Partei, driving it underground, and for a while, once more, there it was quiet. The quiet persisted until early in 1953, and then the urge showed itself once again, indestructible, natural to its roots, stronger than ever.

The current wave of episodes is broader in range than any that have preceded it, for they reach further to the Right, where the true Fascists coddle their hatreds, and further to the Center, where they nibble at the supporters of the legal parties, now represented in Bonn. A German Free Corps (Freikorps Deutschland), organized of ex-Army officers and ex-Nazis, has been revealed in operation and outlawed by Bonn. Its purpose was the outright overthrow of all democratic institutions and the implementation of the oaths of loyalty imposed by Hitler. Such crackpots as the German Free Corps can be handled by Bonn's police and laws. What worries the men of Bonn more are the personalities and planning involved in the plot exposed by the British in the beginning of 1953 in the Ruhr. Here for the first time real conspiratorial strategy was revealed—an effort to capture the Ruhr provincial organization of the Free Democratic party, one of the member parties of the governing coalition in Bonn. Here for the first time thoroughly respectable men, considered pillars of the Bonn government and its parties, leaped to the defense of conspirators proven to be in liaison with hard-core Nazis who had long since fled to refuge in Spain, Argentina, Scandinavia and other points of exile.

Up to now this other Germany has been formless and almost programless. It has had no leadership, no Hitler or Barbarossa. It does not seem to offer Nazism any more, for very few, even among the other Germans, would dare offer again to their citizens the idiot immorality of Nazism which proved so disastrous a failure. It still lacks the big money which financed Hitler to power; so far only one of the Ruhr industrialists, the younger Stinnes of the coal fortune, has backed the movement seriously. Most Ruhr industrialists are cautious, backing all the Bonn parties judiciously and impartially for political insurance.

What the other Germany wants is more tacit than explicit; it wants a Germany whose boundaries are determined by history and tradition. Immediately, it wants the Saar and reunification; beyond that it wants the lost provinces under the Polish flag; beyond that it murmurs of anschluss with Austria; beyond that, already, its journals and pamphlets talk of Africa and Germany's lost colonies. And it is prepared to use any methods to achieve these ends and to do business with anyone who can help, West or East. The cohorts and troops of the movement are as yet unshaped. No storm troopers in jackboots parade the streets; no assassins are yet organized for murder. Its support comes from a resonance in German memory. Its growth can be traced, crudely, in the samplings of public opinion which show month by month the growth in percentages of Germans who believe that there was more good than bad in Hitler. Until last year only a minority of Germans believed Hitler did more good than bad. The last official polls as of this writing show that now a majority of Germans so believe—and this majority is most pronounced among the young, in the age group between twenty and twenty-four.

It would be as great a folly to underestimate the forces of good, the inherent strength of the men marshaled at Bonn, as to overestimate the forces of evil, the men gathering against it. By the test of history, Nazism and Nationalism failed, and millions of Germans have been convinced by the evidence of their eyes and the scars on their bodies that they must find another way. These are the men who support Bonn. Thousands of Germans emerged from the purgatory of Hitler's concentration camps convinced that the shame and the wickedness of Germany could never be erased except by their own personal devotion and consecration to new ideals. Scores of such men sit in the Bonn Bundestag, knowing that if they fail, their lives and honor are at stake. They will fight the other Germany.

It is now, when this book is published, after their national elections that the two Germanys will begin to test each other. It may be that the Bonn parties will be strong enough to continue their rivalries in democratic frame; it may be they will be forced together in coalition to defend their positions and the new Germany against the old. It may be that the old Germany will creep into the skin of the new Germany, infiltrate Bonn and subvert it. Whatever happens, there, within Germany, lies the key to tomorrow's Europe.

VIII

the story of Willi Schlieker

Germany is energy.

Sitting on the flat plains between the great powers of the West and the Slav powers of the East, the Germans have learned always to respond to pressure on them with counterthrust. To preserve their lives, they know they must work harder and think quicker than most of their neighbors. The energy that the pressures of history generate in Germany, the talent and ability that guide these energies, have been Europe's greatest problems for a century —now fructifying Europe, now blasting her to bits.

Fundamentally, this unquenchable energy is human beings. One of these is Willi Schlieker, who, in his brief life, can tell almost as much of Germany as a history book. Nobody knows which way Willi is going, not even Willi. But wherever he is going, he is moving fast.

We crossed a half-ruined, tumble-down courtyard, picked our way over the puddled rain water on the cracked concrete and then tramped heavily up a flight of creaking, wooden stairs. My companion, a young and leanly-intelligent British political officer, muttered something in German to a blank-faced man at the door and off he went down the passageway. He came back, his face still blank, and told us to follow him—down the shabby, musty little corridor until we came to a door which opened on a room, even darker and mustier than the corridor. A man stood waiting for us there.

"Hello, Schlieker," said my companion, "here's someone who wants to talk to you." He made the introductions briefly and Willi Schlieker asked us to sit down. They chatted for several minutes together and while they talked I looked at Schlieker.

He was a man of medium height and stout dimensions. Once, it was obvious, this man must have been as solidly muscled as a tank, but now the chunkiness had softened to a pudding of flesh that bulged and rumpled his suit with odd stretchings and creases. It was not healthy flesh, for Schlieker was pale, almost saffron-colored. There was energy in him still, I could see, by the way he balanced his weight so gracefully from foot to foot, but it was nervous energy.

I listened to the conversation, not catching all the words but sensing an undercurrent of strain, the Briton's voice politely challenging, probing, and Schlieker's voice dryly parrying, on the defensive, vigorous but under restraint. The British officer finished quickly with Schlieker and then, in that crisp, sure voice of a Briton in command, said, "Well, Willi, I've got to go now. Mr. White has a lot of questions to ask. See if you can help him out."

It was not quite a command; in January of 1949 the days of commanding Germans in defeat were over. Yet it was the voice of Occupation. This was Düsseldorf, capital of British Occupation of the Ruhr; I was American; and Willi Schlieker was German. He was permitted to resent the voice of Occupation, but his resentment must be hushed.

The resentment was easy to understand. For three and a half years, ever since the collapse of Hitler's Germany, people had been questioning Schlieker. The Russians had arrested him, questioned him, then used him. The Americans had hunted him down and questioned him to exhaustion. The British had arrested him, questioned him, used him and cast him out. The French had arrested him, questioned him, released him. He was tired of questioners.

I wanted to ask Schlieker questions too, and for the same reasons. Willi Schlieker had been the boy-genius of Hitler's war machine, the young man who, at the age of twenty-eight, had been the boss of all the Ruhr's iron and steel production, the coordinator and master of the Third Reich's war arsenal. Willi knew more about the Ruhr than anyone else, and since the Ruhr was the very essence of German power, people came to him for answers. I, too, wanted to know about the Ruhr, for in that winter of 1948-1949 it was a land of mystery.

Under the fog and clouds of that dreary winter, the twisted and majestic symmetry of the Ruhr's industrial towers stretched away in the valley's wooded hills and gentle meadows, half-dead, half-alive, perplexing Germans and conquerors alike. The Ruhr is such a small place to have left so deep a scar on Europe's history. It is no larger than metropolitan New York; a three-hour drive along the curving autobahn from Düsseldorf to Dortmund embraces all of it. In that season the drive showed a Ruhr in all the tantalizing contrasts of ruin and revival. The gray mounds of rubble, the broken brick and dangling girders, the gutted homes and tenements with their rooms opening on cold air, like the slit cells of a beehive, cast a shadow as of death. But by night one could sense the Ruhr alive and see it glow with effort—far away somewhere a giant coke-wafer could be seen pushed blazing out of its oven to fall in a cascade of flame into some waiting car, to glow and then fade out. On and above the horizon the pink radiance of a cluster of blast furnaces illuminated a cloud patch, which brightened suddenly with the white flare of hot iron as the molten metal was tapped and ran from the hole. Elsewhere, in the distance, a caterpillar of bucket cars traced the contours of a steel mill as it crawled with molten white metal showering sparks in the night. By night it was clear the Ruhr was still alive. That was the year the Allied Occupation gratingly shifted its gears to stop strangling and begin encouraging the Ruhr. I wanted to find out how much of the Ruhr's old strength and magic was left.

Schlieker loved to talk about the Ruhr, as he still does, and as he began to talk, my questions stopped, for he knew more answers than I had questions to ask. He is one of those men enchanted by the making of things, by the organization of affairs, and the enchantment is drenched in a deeper, peculiarly German intoxication with the romance of steel-making. Just as some Frenchmen talk with magnetic force about the mystery of making and cooking foods, until the listener feels he is hearing of sacred rites, so do some Germans talk about the Vulcan's kitchen where steel is made, where it is cooked and poured and baked and sautéed, where it is patted and rolled and cut and quenched, where it is mixed with the spices and sauces of metallurgy, vanadium, molybdenum, manganese and tungsten to come out the master-metal of man's destiny, bars of silver-gray tensile strength and force. Schlieker was one of these men; he could talk about steel with more romance and love than any man I have ever heard.

For two hours he talked to me about the Ruhr. He told its history. He led me up to that imaginary mountaintop where the visionaries stand and described how the Ruhr is all one single piece. He fitted together with his words the fragments of the industry which I had seen in profile from the road—the stretching ridge of coal tipple following coke oven, following blast furnace, following steel mill, following fractionating column over and over for thirty miles against the sky. He explained how the kinked and twisting pipe mains and the interlacing wires bind it together in a single indivisible unit, coke oven feeding gas to mill, which feeds low caloric gas back to coke ovens, which feed other gases to drop forges; he described how the gases of the blast furnaces feed power stations which fork electricity back into steels mills which pour their own surplus current back into the one great power grid that binds the Ruhr together. He described the men who run the Ruhr, the managerial dominance of a tribe of slashed-cheek engineers and businessmen whose closed and primitive aristocracy and pride no upheaval yet had been able to erase. And Schlieker declared that the Ruhr was indestructible because heavy industry once founded can never be dismantled.

Every now and then I shook myself out of fascination to look around me, and returned to the conversation more fascinated by the contrast of setting and words. For if Schlieker stood on some distant mountaintop in imagination, talking of German industry with lofty command, he lived, physically, in squalor.

The room in which we sat was the shelter of a broken man, for it was half-office, half-living room. It was true, I knew by the records, that Schlieker had once bossed all the Ruhr for the Wehrmacht. But Schlieker's domain had now been reduced to a gray, damp flat where offices, bedroom, living room and presumably kitchen all radiated off the one short corridor on the second floor of 1 Breitestrasse, Düsseldorf. That living room was a curious place—a very dark, very crowded, yet essentially neat rectangle of space. The office side consisted of two desks back to back with one telephone teetering on a shuffled heap of papers. The other half was home—two shabby easy chairs and a shabbier old sofa. It was no more shabby than any other living room in broken Germany, but the shabbiness was punctuated and stressed by the refinement that Willi had tried to bring to it. In the half-light of the room two or three vases of flowers—crisp red and fresh—stabbed the dinginess with their purity of color. Above, on the wall, two rich paintings glowed with the medieval golds, browns and reds of madonnas and saints. The splotch of luxury added by flowers and paintings seemed only to accent the grayness. Yet when Schlieker spoke, the room fell away and there was only Willi in the room, deftly balancing his heavy frame, talking, oblivious of setting.

That meeting was almost five years ago. I asked Willi Schlieker many questions that day and have been asking him questions on every visit to Germany, year after year since then. Now, however, I no longer visit Willi in Breitestrasse. Today when I come to the Ruhr I must telephone through a chain of secretaries to reach him, and Willi has many other places to meet me. He may send his car—a shiny, compact Mercedes-Benz convertible—to find me, and occasionally, in the evening, we roar across the Rhine bridge up to Meererbusch. Meererbusch is the swank suburb of the Ruhr, where Germany's captains of industry nest at night much as Detroit's captains of industry do at Grosse Pointe. In Meererbusch, Willi's new home, Am Willer, shines like a jewel.

I always think of the old flat at 1 Breitestrasse when I visit Am Willer in Meererbusch. I think of the cooking smells of the old place, the telephone jangling in the living room, the flowers in the shabby dinginess. At Am Willer the living room is a long, exquisitely proportioned *L*-shaped room; one end of the *L* is paneled with bookcases crowded with the most recent serious best sellers of Germany, England and America. The other end is a huge double-paneled glass wall which should be a bookcase but is not; it is a wall of flowers in every glorious color. In the afternoon one can look out through the flowers of the glass wall to a huge garden, where flower beds burst in scarlet, blue and purple, all year around. Set in the green lawn is Willi's new swimming pool. In the evening Willi flicks a switch and the wall panels light up to flood the flowers like an imaginary greenhouse. We eat with fine silver, from shell-pink plates, of fine food. Willi has come a long way, as has Germany, in the past five years, and he has come all by himself.

Willi once more is a man of mark in Germany, and he is sought out by many men as a fountain of wisdom, which he is. It was not always so, for when I first met him Willi was a man of mystery, reported by British Political Intelligence in charge of Occupation as "possibly the most dangerous man in the Ruhr." In those days, if you were well-connected, one or two high American officials might let you glance fleetingly at the five-page, single-spaced report on Willi which the British had made available to them among other secret biographies of dangerous men in the Ruhr. Lately Willi has enjoyed himself in his new prominence by discomfiting both British and American intelligence agencies. When people ask about him, he occasionally hands them a copy of that old five-page secret report or briefs them on all the facts it contains. The first time this happened British and American security officers went into convulsions trying to find who had leaked such a report for publication; half a dozen careers hung in balance as security risks until they learned that Willi himself had handed out the document. No one knows how Willi put his hand on it, or what else he knows.

The intelligence report is a dull account of Willi's birth, family and employment record; it compresses his dazzling rise to eminence in Hitler's Third Reich into twenty lines, reports his turbulent postwar career, gives his Nazi party number and gives the pro and con of whether Willi was a true Nazi or a nominal Nazi. It discusses his postwar associations, his flirtations with the Socialists, his decision to make a business of his own.

Willi, however, is far from dull. His story, as I have heard him tell it and watched it happen, is Germany's story—of energy, ability and will, as irrepressible as the force of life.

The first man in Willi Schlieker's life was his father, a tall, burly, embittered Prussian from Altmark whom life had whirled around and brought to rest in the waterfront slums of Hamburg, where Willi was born. A locksmith by trade, the elder Schlieker had tramped all over Europe on foot as a journeyman, from Norway around to England before he came back to final employment at the shipyards of Hamburg.

Willi's father had been a Socialist. But disillusionment with socialism had made him bitter. When the Kaiser's Empire perished and the milky-thin social-democracy of the Weimar Republic replaced it, Willi's father first saw his Socialist dreams come true and then found them empty. The old Schlieker abandoned socialism, turned inward, grew more silent and when he retired on pension finally withdrew totally into himself, keeping bees in his yard and saying little.

Willi's mother, a Catholic, died when he was six years old, just when his father was growing bitter. On her deathbed she pleaded with his father that he let Willi be baptized in the Catholic faith and his father agreed that when the boy was twenty-one he might choose his own faith. Thus Willi was left to grow up almost by himself in the grim, dreary blocks of waterfront tenements of Hamburg in the topsy-turvy twenties. Only one man lifted Willi's imagination from the Hamburg slums—his schoolteacher, a man named Albrecht, a rare person who loved students. Albrecht was a doctor in Sanskrit, an amateur astronomer and anthropologist, a scholar of Goethe. In the summer time Albrecht would take his students tramping over the hills and forests of Germany. Willi reached high-school age in the late twenties, when the bronzed youth of the Wandervogel in their tawny shorts were wandering and camping all over Germany. Albrecht led Willi to South Germany, hiked with him across Bavaria and Thuringia, showed him the old masterworks of Catholic architecture, and Willi, who was a bright pupil, decided he would become an art historian, specializing in Catholic art and baroque architecture. Willi must have been a teacher's joy as he hungrily absorbed all the strange thinking of Germany in the twenties. Willi, who was to be Hitler's chief armorer, was a teen-age pacifist; he wrote one long essay on the sinking of the *Squalus* in America, furious that men should die in preparation for war. He wrote another longer schoolboy essay on the Kellogg Peace Pact, using everything he could find—especially the speeches of Senator Borah—to prove why war must be outlawed. Willi might have gone on to be a paunchy, beer-drinking, very gemütlich Herr Doktor Professor at some German university had it not been for the depression.

But in 1930, when Willi was only sixteen, his father lost his job and, because he had to live on unemployment relief, shipped Willi off to work as a farmer's helper. For six months Willi worked on a farm for food and board and no pay.

When Willi came back to Hamburg in 1931, he had left the

world of ideas far behind. In Hamburg, a bustling city of merchants, sailors and traders, commerce is the main thing. Here Willi found a job as apprentice to an export-import house at five dollars a week to learn how the world made and shipped, bought and sold goods. He was nineteen when that job ended, crumbling in the depression, and he, too, was on unemployment relief. It was then that Willi made contact with the Nazis. "I was hungry, I was nothing but hungry," he now explains. Unemployment relief gave him $2.50 a week to live on, and he had to pay $1.75 of that a week for his lodging. So it was quite natural, says Willi, that when a friend found him a job as a typist working for the Nazi S.S. in Hamburg, he took it.

Though Willi's life flowed imperceptibly but inevitably into the stream of Nazi change, it was, like most German lives, accompanied by the tiny halts and hesitations provoked by conscience and discretion. Willi lost his job with the S.S. within a year for voicing too freely his opinion about the Röhm purge. He found another as a clerk in the Nazi supreme court in Munich and lost that one too, under circumstances that were later to help him greatly. Willi purloined some papers in a case under consideration by the Nazi court because the principals involved were old Hamburg friends of his, and the major charge was that one of the members of the family had married a Jewess. For this Willi was fired, but the Hamburg merchant family was grateful and helped Willi find another job. This job carried him to Haiti as a salesman. Willi lived in the West Indies for three years, first selling German cement and machinery there, then working for a British firm and learning American and British business practice.

When Willi came back to Germany in 1938, he gaped at how much it had changed. Germany had been hungry when he left. The Hamburg he remembered was one where men sat in parks all day looking at nothing, or on street benches idly playing cards, where every open place, every square, every street was cluttered with shuffling, rotting unemployed. In the afternoons, any afternoon of those days, the idle would rustle together in demonstrations or parades, carrying banners, their hollow voices shouting slogans. By 1938, when Willi came home, Germany had a new face. No one loitered in streets or parks; Germany worked and nobody marched in the streets without orders. Across the countryside the new autobahns stretched in long ribbons of concrete; in the cities at night the factories gleamed working the night shift. Hamburg was thriving and Willi's friends, even the ones he remembered as most democratic and anti-Nazi, all said it was good, it was going well. So Willi stayed.

Willi had left Germany a boy, but came back a man, full of vigor and self-confidence. Without any difficulty he succeeded in snatching for himself the Eastern European Agency of a large Ruhr steel exporting house. Within less than a year he had capped this coup with another: he sold the Rumanian government an entire new bridge across the Danube. But Willi had little time to savor his triumph as a merchant-adventurer in the Balkans, for by then, back home, war had been declared and by 1940 the amount of steel that Germany could spare for commercial export had dwindled to nothing. So once again Willi came home.

By now even the big men of the Ruhr knew that Willi Schlieker was a hustler and he was hired by the biggest of all the Ruhr trusts, the Vereinigte Stahlwerke. His job in their raw materials department was to cut through the mad chaos of paper regulation and allocation quotas of the Hitler war effort and get them the raw ingredients they needed for steel-making.

Of all the major warring powers, the Germans, for the first three years of their war, were perhaps the most bizarrely inefficient in production control. During those years Hitler could afford to filter his dilettante commands down through echelon after echelon of ignorant Nazi zealots to the technicians of the Ruhr arsenal. By the end of 1941, however, as the cold terror of the Eastern Front suddenly made the war a mortal venture, the Nazi war machine began convulsively to tighten and men of talent began to move up. Among them was Willi Schlieker; by mid-1942 Willi had lone-wolfed raw materials for Vereinigte Stahlwerke so efficiently that the government drafted him as deputy coordinator of the tank production program. In Berlin, to which Willi now moved, he came to the attention of Albert Speer whom Hitler in the same year named boss of every phase of German industry and production. Speer, who now sits in the prison of Spandau serving a life sentence as a certified war criminal, was an architect, an amateur at war and a genius untrammeled by conscience. He recognized Willi, then only twenty-eight, as a fellow genius, and by the beginning of 1943 he had chosen him to be chief of all iron and steel production, direction, allocation and control, not only for Germany, but for all occupied Europe. By then, too, Willi had decided to take out a Nazi party card—No. 8,759,242.

The older industrialists, the stodgy civil servants, the veteran party members might laugh at "Speer's Kindergarten" as they called the fanatically efficient young men of the Arms Ministry. But Willi was too far above routine to worry about them. He was excited by the job. It was not money or comfort that made him happy, for his salary was only 20,000 marks a year ($7,500) and his home a one-room flat in Berlin. But Willi had power; every forge, every blast furnace, every rolling mill in continental Europe lay at his feet; under his offices on Friedrichstrasse, where he worked seven days a week, was a concrete bunker impenetrable by the heaviest bombs; in his bunker were teletype machines and long-distance lines that linked him to every headquarters of Nazi power and command; his eighty-odd staff members lived in barracks nearby to be close to him; the countries of Europe were provinces of his empire—Willi would fly to Italy once every fortnight just to currycomb the Italian steel industry and keep it on its toes.

The machine that Willi built, Allied investigators say, probably kept Germany in the war a full year after the date when she might otherwise have collapsed. The first two years of Hitler's domestic war effort had been nonsense, made tragic for the world only by the crumbling rot of will with which the Western Allies met it. Hitler launched his war in Europe when his arsenals were producing only thirty tanks a month, and got away with the gamble. Hitler flicked his war production about as the whim took him, ordering, canceling, guessing, exhorting without reference to fact, figure or statistic. In the summer of 1940 Hitler decided he had enough small-arms ammunition in stock and thus suspended small-arms ammunition production so that when Willi first came to Berlin in 1942 he found that the Wehrmacht was shooting off 400,000,000 rounds of bullets a month in Russia, and production, starting again from scratch, was only back to 115,000,000 rounds.

Germany's war production was a scramble of sharpsters, hustlers, bribers and special interests. Men bribed priority and control officials; factory plant managers ignored them to turn out commercial steel for commercial customers at fat war profits. The first day Willi sat at his desk in Berlin as boss, he found one neatly butchered rabbit and two cans of precious coffee delivered to him by a priority claimant to sweeten the claim. But worse than the corruption that infused the entire Nazi system was the confusion. The armed services of Germany would order irrelevantly and irrationally what they needed. Each producer might demand priorities on twenty different kinds of special steel to fill one order, although his total needs to fill the order might be less than ten tons in all.

Willi, with the simplicity of a bright young man, did the simplest of all things. He put German heavy industry on a punch-card basis. Each item ordered by the Army had to be ordered through Willi's office and each order had to be accompanied by punch cards breaking down the end-item requirement of 1,000 tanks, say, into so many tons of broad-gauge armor plate, so many tons of chain, so many tons of light-gauge steel, so many tons of tubing. All the rolling capacity of Europe's steel mills were similarly broken down into their monthly productive capacity of special categories of steel. Running a million punch cards a month through his filing machines, Willi made a balance sheet. On one side were the war's requirements listed in tonnages of each type of steel; on the other side, Europe's capacity that month to produce what tonnage of the needed kinds of steel.

The Speer Ministerium took over German production in early 1942 just as the bombings of the Ruhr began to hit hard. The measure of its success was that as the bombings grew, so did German production, until on the very eve of defeat when the rest of Germany had collapsed within, the Ruhr was producing more than ever before in the seven years of war. As the long Eastern Front stretched, widened and became a junkyard cemetery of German effort, production became the key to survival. Give me 600 tanks a month, shrieked Hitler to Speer, and we will abolish every enemy in the world. The Army General Staff echoed Hitler—600 tanks a month, 600 tanks was the magic figure. By the end of 1943 Germany was producing 1,000 tanks a month and it was not enough. By November, 1944, when the Western Allies had already made their first breach of German soil, Germany was producing 1,800 tanks a month and it was not enough. Production rose and soared, but each new high that the Speer Ministerium reached was overmatched by the multiplying effort of the factories of America and Britain. By mid-1944 airplane production had reached a peak of 3,750 aircraft a month; yet it was not enough.

Willi, looking backward, has told American bombing experts over and over again that they never succeeded in putting more than a minor dent in Germany's heavy steel production. What hurt were such blows as the bombing of gasoline plants, for by the time Germany was producing 3,750 aircraft a month she lacked the fuel to train pilots, or even keep her already trained pilots in the air. What hurt even more was the bombing of the railways. The Ruhr, says Willi, ultimately collapsed not because of the bombing of plants, mills and mines but because the railway exits were so clogged with blowouts, breaks and burned-out locomotives that they could not carry away the 30,000 tons of finished goods the Ruhr produced every day. The Ruhr strangled finally, in January and February, 1945, on its own production; it did not cave in under blast.

Willi knew early, as early as the fall of 1943, that the war was lost. He knew it, he says, by simple mathematics. Every month the steel mills of Europe produced 2,700,000 tons of rolled steel for his allocation. More than half of that had to be yielded to the ordinary every-day needs of human beings for tin cans and gadgets, for repair of railway bridges, for construction of new factories and bunkers, wires and communication. For his war Willi could take away each month only 1,150,000 tons of rolled steel, out of which he had to make at the end each month, 1,800 tanks, 1,200 field guns, 600 heavy guns, 25 submarines, 3,700 airplanes, plus ammunition and trucks. Everyone wanted more and more of these items, but they had to come out of a total steel quantity that stayed fixed, for Willi, under bombing, could not build new steel plants as America did. One day Willi got everyone in Army procurement around one table to try to settle their demands. When each man had boiled the demands for his service down to the minimum, Willi found that if he met their requests not even 350,000 tons of steel a month would be left to make shells, and by that time the Eastern Front alone was using more shells than that. In the winter of 1944, before the Second Front was opened, when Germany was making 450,000 shells a month, a group of young Wehrmacht officers arrived in Berlin from the Eastern Front to plead with Willi for more shells. Willi asked them just what they needed, and when they had figured it out, it came to 550,000 tons of shells a month to hold that front alone. By then Willi knew that Germany's total steel capacity had reached its ceiling, that the Second Front was about to break, and that defeat was inevitable.

Yet Willi stayed. He stayed to the end. In the twitching last days of his life, Hitler decided that he would fight to the end from the Redoubt of Bavaria and the Tyrol, and ordered Speer to draw up economic plans for resistance from the Redoubt. On April 21, Speer ordered Willi to fly south to organize arms production there. But Willi would not leave. He telephoned Hitler's Führer-Bunker to say that he, Schlieker, chose to remain in Berlin to the end.

That night Willi was very nervous, for the end was near, and he decided to drive out to the estate of some friends in the country. He drove through the darkness that night, April 21, without lights, for the British were bombing Berlin as he left. Thus, in the dark, Willi smashed directly into an army truck and was hurled to the side of the road with half his ribs broken. All that night and the next day Willi lay by the side of the road, half-senseless, dreaming, thinking, he now recalls, how curious it was to die by the side of the road at the age of thirty-one, being the biggest boss of labor in Europe and the largest steel producer in German history—a success story, ending in a gutter in defeat.

Some wayfarers found him the next day and delivered him to an army hospital. He was semiconscious when they carried him in and remembers through the haze that people examined his identity papers and an old doctor said, "This is Schlieker of the Speer Ministerium. Best let him die. Let's not make ourselves more guilty when the Russians come by having him here." But Willi is very tough and he would not die. Besides, one of the younger doctors did not agree with the older doctor and helped him to live. In eight days he was well enough so that his friends could come and carry him away to their country estate.

Willi's friends installed him in a large room on their first floor, on a clean white bed near a window that looked far out over the clear countryside. There Willi lay quietly until the next day when, precisely at noon, looking out through the window over the sunny fields toward the village beyond, he saw a huge black puff of smoke rise quietly from the village, then another, then another. He lay helplessly in bed and watched the Russians shell the village, and knew that for him the war was over.

Out of the disaster Willi emerged with his skin and a new wife. For the friend at whose house Willi was staying took fright as the Russians came and fled like a rabbit before their advance. But his wife, Marga, would not leave Willi there helpless, and she refused to go. She stayed with Willi through the next two weeks of madness, and now she is his wife.

It took hours for the Russians to cross the field from the village to the house, and Willi was dragged down to the cellar where all the peasants of the village crowded for shelter. It was 4:30 in the morning when the Russian troops came into the cellar. They were combat troops and even Willi admits they were good; they looked at the huddled people and one of them said, "We are not like Goebbels and Hitler; you are safe." Then they went away. But after the combat troops came the clean-up troops, and by mid-morning Russians, drunk and sober, European and Asian, were pouring through. They did not hurt Willi, or Marga, who sat on the bed beside him, because, says Willi, Russians are madmen, but to the sick and the children they are respectful. It was not safe to stay, however, so the next day Willi, hobbling on two sticks and helped by Marga, made his way into the forest. They lived in the forest, sleeping on the ground for seven days. When they came back from the forest to the big house they had left, they found it empty, stripped of its furniture, silver, beds, clothes, everything. On foot and homeless, therefore, Willi and Marga set out for Berlin, riding on a railway flatcar loaded with rails that the Russians had already begun to rip off the Hamburg-Berlin double-track system.

The Berlin they came to in May of 1945 was as quiet as death. People were hungry, says Willi, that was all, and they were dying of starvation. Through the streets, parents carried little wooden boxes they had made to encoffin their children. There was no cooking oil, no fat, no butter, no meat, only bread and the bread was always wet and soggy. Berlin lived a jungle life which reached its climax in the final days of June as the Russians stripped the city clean before the other Allied troops should enter and help occupy it. It was during these same days that the Russians arrested Willi and threw him into confinement along with several hundred other people, in a moist, stinking cellar where he would stay until they made up their minds what to do with him.

The Russians, it turned out, were like everyone else. Each of the conquering powers wanted to put its hands on Willi, to question him, to wring some punishment out of his body because he had made Hitler's machine tick and turn so efficiently. But as soon as people began to talk to Willi they found how useful he was, and instead of exacting vengeance they used him. The Russians made him, very shortly, director of what was left of the industrial empire of the Flick concerns in their Eastern Zone, and Willi had an office again.

The Americans found Willi working for the Russians in Berlin, and sought him for cross-questioning. Experts writing the U.S. Strategic Bombing Survey wanted to talk to Willi more than anyone else except Speer, for these were the two men who could best measure the effect and precision of United States bombardment of the Ruhr. They were fascinated by him, but the United States could not use Willi's services because the American Zone of Occupation had much scenery but little industry. So they introduced him to the British, who governed the Ruhr and did need him. In February, 1946, therefore, Willi was flown out of Berlin to advise the British Occupation Authorities on the operation of the Ruhr which he had directed so well against them during the war. Since Communist morality is so flexible a thing, the Communists of West Germany and of Britain could now attack the British Army for employing a notorious Nazi, which they did with great gusto, ignoring the fact that Willi had just quit the employ of the Communist Army.

Willi's job, said the cold employment description, was to "advise on production planning and office organization on the basis of his ministerial experience." Actually, as the British honestly declare, it was he who pulled the Ruhr together in 1946 as he had before in 1942 and 1943. Once again the Ruhr producers were milling around in simple, selfish greed, hoarding steel, black-marketing steel, producing special steels for high profit, ignoring demand for basic steels for reconstruction. The Ruhr in those days was leaderless, for all its top men had been arrested as Nazi collaborators. Soon, however, when the zeal of conquest slackened, they would all trickle back from denazification camps to look for plants to command once more, as they always had.

Willi had been a well-hated man in the Ruhr from the days of his first eminence when, as a young upstart, endowed with all the power of the Third Reich, he had pushed the proud barons of the German steel industry into the frame of priorities and controls that the Wehrmacht needed for production. He was even more hated by the Ruhr barons after he worked for the British, for he imposed on them a new set of statistical controls, directing their orders and allocations at British behest for reconstruction and repair. As the tight thongs of Occupation loosened, as the Ruhr slipped rapidly back to German leadership and German direction, Willi's days as boss were numbered.

By the beginning of 1947 Willi's many enemies had closed on him. A local German court which, Willi claims, was inspired by some of the oldest Nazis in the Ruhr, convicted him of being a Category III Nazi, a minor criminal offender. Therefore, by the rules of British Occupation, Willi had to be dropped from the employ of the occupying armies. For months he was a cause célèbre in the Ruhr as Germans and Britons discussed the precise shade of his guilt. There was no doubt that Willi was a Nazi, but his card number showed him as a latecomer to the movement. Certainly Willi had clung to the Nazi regime down to the very end and had made it function with incredible efficiency, but Willi claimed that he had served Germany out of patriotism not fanaticism. There was no doubt that the Speer Ministerium in which Willi had been so important was one of the most heinous and wicked employers of slave labor in the entire German Reich, but Willi insisted that he had always fought for better food for the laborers for "it was silly to let them die for lack of food." Though Allied courts sentenced Willi's captain, Speer, to life imprisonment for his part in the hideous camps, no one could prove that Willi had had any other interest during the war except to make things out of steel efficiently. Willi was neither pro or con slave labor; he was simply, in his own eyes, a producer.

It took almost two years for Willi to clear himself of the Nazi charge—lean months in which he and Marga lived on 250 marks ($80) a month, while he tried to earn his way as an industrial advisor and small-time trader. It was not until the spring of 1948 (he had been arrested and released by the French, too, during this period of wandering) that Willi was unblocked as a Nazi, oddly enough on the appeal and intervention of some German Socialist chiefs who recognized his talent for pushing the tycoons of the Ruhr about. In July of 1948, in the very week that he was cleared, Willi began a new career. With 2,000 marks as capital (which his wife Marga had raised) he bought an old trading name, Otto R. Krause & Co., the Düsseldorf outlet of a famous East German firm of the same name, and set up his business. On July 29, 1948, he opened the doors on the shabby office at 1 Breitestrasse, in the ruins just off Kasernestrasse, a stone's throw from the gloomy Gothic mansion which housed the old German Steel Trust. There he prepared to buy and sell steel in commercial quantities, to hustle on his own account.

That was when I first met Willi, in Breitestrasse, smarting, aching, itching to show the world. The businessmen laughed at him for, said they, "You're smart when you're working for Speer with the whole state behind you, and you're smart when you're working for the British with the Occupation behind you. But can you be smart by yourself, Schlieker, can you make money?" Willi wanted to show them; he wanted to show the men he had bossed that he could do as well as they, boss or no boss. "I'm thirty-eight years old now," Willi told me several years after I first met him. "I am going to stay at this until I am forty, then I will see whether it's worth doing something else."

By then, though Willi's office was still in Breitestrasse, he was well on his way to being a rich man. His postwar career was securely launched.

Willi brought to the art of the businessman the perspectives he had first seen from the height of German war production. All the infinitely complex tangle of Ruhr cokeries and rolling mills, feuds and jealousies, mines and blast furnaces, was a pattern that Willi had once seen from on high. Willi knew better than any man not only how the Ruhr fitted into the broader life of all German industry, but how it was linked and meshed with the huge, outer patterns of world trade. He understood what moves governments as they prod and push industry to compliance with the graphs of office economists and the concepts of political necessity. Willi could sniff a turning wind in business or in politics and swing with it quickly, before any of the older, stodgy businessmen of the Ruhr knew the turn was approaching. His career since the war has been a series of successes in catching these turns, riding with the spin, dropping off just in time to catch the next one, always increasing his wealth, power and importance.

Willi's decision to settle for a meager livelihood as industrial advisor and small-time trader of iron and steel goods after his expulsion from the Occupation was underlain with a shrewd gamble: that the worthless paper marks which were then the currency of Occupied Germany someday must be wiped out, and that the thing to clutch was not money but hard goods. So Willi tried to accumulate not marks but stocks of steel and iron. When the currency was wiped out and the early speculators of postwar Germany were ruined, Willi sat secure on his little pile of undevaluable steel and iron bars and was already a junior capitalist when he opened his new venture. There was nothing illegal in what he had done; it was simply shrewd. Later the Bonn government tried to raid Willi's house when he was off on a trip, to find ways of clipping him for an extra income tax or to turn up some special skulduggery. They found nothing; Willi had cheated no one, he had simply outfoxed everyone.

In his first year of business Willi did quite well, averaging about 250,000 marks a month of turnover in steel. The next year he caught another trend—sales to the Communist world. The large cartels and old established firms of the Ruhr were trying to freeze Willi out of major deals in West Germany, but the Russians and East German Communists were clamoring for steel, and Willi was ready to deal with anyone. In the summer of 1949, when the temporary downward slump of world trade forced Britain off sterling and made steel momentarily surplus in the Ruhr, Willi moved fast to fill contracts for the Russians and the East Zone. Within nine months he was the biggest "black trader" in Germany—from midsummer of 1949 to spring of 1950, he sold the

Russians 70 million marks' worth (18 million dollars) of steel and turned a personal profit of a million dollars. By the midsummer of 1949 Willi had a monopoly on steel sales to the Russians and did about half the business between the Communist world and the Ruhr. For this he was temporarily blacklisted by the American government, a charge from which he extricated himself by an unchallengeable answer: that every time he had made a shipment to the Russians he had informed the Americans, and they had not protested.

On the next turn, the outbreak of the Korean War, Willi was the fastest man in Europe off the start. The old-line Ruhr masters thought that now, at last, they had Willi because the war had made steel the scarcest commodity in the world. They would give him no steel to sell the Russians and no steel to sell anyone else. But for Willi the steel scarcity brought its own opportunity. Now everyone was clamoring for steel, steel at any price, and he quickly saw that steel was short in the Ruhr only because the Ruhr was short of coke without which steel cannot be made.

Therefore, Willi set out to get coke in order to get steel. His infinitely detailed knowledge of industry recalled to memory some of the most obsolescent coking ovens in Germany, idle for lack of the proper coal to make coke. But in the United States coking coal was surplus. No one had ever previously thought of going all the way to the United States to buy coking coal for the coal-rich Ruhr, but Willi thought of it now. He bought coking coal in America for ten dollars a ton and paid fifteen dollars a ton to ship it to the Ruhr. By midspring of 1951 the gamble paid off, for Willi was bringing 72,000 tons of American coal to the Ruhr each month, making 50,000 tons of coke, and with his 50,000 tons of coke he could demand an equivalent amount of steel in return. Now Willi was master again—free to sell steel at the peak of the gray market in New York, or at the peak of the scarcity in Germany itself. Everyone else tried to copy him in hauling coking coal from America, but, with his headstart, Willi had captured the market, and by 1952 he alone was responsible for forty per cent of the Ruhr's coking import from the United States. No one talked any longer of squeezing Willi out. Willi was in.

Willi's office is now sheltered in the handsome eight-story yellow-sandstone building he has built for himself just off Kasernestrasse. You come up by soundless elevator to the top story to wait in an anteroom, where huge bowers of lilacs and vases of potted plants flamboyantly recall the more modest flowers of other days. Willi's private office is lace-curtained and done in rich browns and greens. On his smooth flat-topped desk is a sampling of the world's opinion—the German papers, of course, along with *Le Monde* of Paris, the *Neue Züricher Zeitung* of Switzerland and the *New York Herald Tribune*. On the wall hangs a huge chart of the Atlantic Ocean, with three flags stuck in it. The three flags are his ships, which he bought in England, pennants of a new business, for Willi now owns his own shipping line: Reederei Willi Schlieker, with its own flag—a bisected field of black and white, initialed *W* on black and *S* on white.

Willi's excellent taste is, unlike his business practice, quite restrained, his preference in colors running to brown. His board room opens from a long alcove off his private office, and there a dark walnut table with sixteen dark brown walnut chairs about it rests on a dark green rug. Willi wears brown too. He has lost the fat of the defeated years and is now chunky, solid, relatively thin again. His brown suit is matched by a brown tie and soft brown suède shoes. A pearl stickpin glows softly on his tie.

Willi's enterprises now cover all Germany and are beginning to reach out around the world. From his handsome new office building he directs, in addition to his vast steel-trading firm, a recently launched housing development, a nationwide net of scrap iron collection, a new pipe and sheet steel mill he has built, plus another cold-rolled strip steel mill he has acquired. His new shipping line has interested him in Hamburg again, where he is, at this writing, preparing to open a shipbuilding concern.

A levelheaded businessman might be cautious after four years of such swift expansion, but Willi's excitement carries him from project to project as if each were a new adventure. His new pipe mill is Willi's answer to the monopoly on pipe and tubing in the Ruhr. When he decided to make pipe in 1951, he quietly acquired a tiny, run-down steel mill, so old as to be considered junk. Then, in the green meadows beside the old mill, Willi threw up a new plant, crammed it with new machinery so fast that no one knew what was happening, and five months from the day he broke ground he was turning out seamless steel tubing.

Only ten miles away in one of the gentle hollows of the Ruhr's rolling apron, Willi has another steel plant. There his workers turn out strips of shimmering steel one-tenth of a millimeter thick. These strips fill no primordial world shortage, as does the piping he makes at his tube plant, but they satisfy Willi quite as much, for his interests are as broad as German life. Willi covers these thin strips with a special coating to serve a growing German industry—the canning of whipped cream. Germany's citizens now like to purchase individual portions of *schlagsahne* for their everyday coffee, and Willi makes thin strip for canning their whipped cream just as efficiently as he made heavy strip for their tanks.

Willi works hard, very hard these days, for work is his delight and the source of his enthusiasm. Also he has to work hard, for all his many firms, by now doing very big business, depend on his one-man direction. In 1951 the iron and steel trading corporation alone did a business of $70,000,000. Willi is up early in the morning, into the office early, then quickly out inspecting or directing or conferring. He races his Mercedes-Benz through the Ruhr with a hard, desperate intensity and when he comes home tired and exhausted, he is ready to turn in early. After dinner at eight Willi is usually ready by ten to give way to the sleep that will power him the next day.

Willi is not yet forty, the age he set as quitting age. He has come a long way from the motherless boy of the Hamburg slums, but his memory of them is still fresh. When he walks through the new housing he has built near his plants he says, "Better than workers' housing in Hamburg where I lived." He has come a long way from the broken boy-genius of 1945, but he has not pushed the memory of the war and the war machine out of mind either. Now that he is rich he allots a small pension to the wife of his wartime boss, Speer, because Speer is still in jail as a war criminal.

In the evening Willi muses a great deal. What he wanted five years ago, he told me once, was "a base where I can stand and they can't hurt me"; he has the base now. What he does next he does not know; in business, of course, there is a new vista opening up now that Germany may soon be permitted to make arms again, for Willi knows how to make arms better than any man in Germany.

He has toyed with the idea; if opportunity comes he will probably move quickly. But beyond business Willi is unsure of what comes next. Perhaps music, perhaps politics. German music has been stilled for a long time, and occasionally the thought comes that he and Marga might be music patrons. Politics, of course, is interesting too. But Willi has not found any political party in new Germany he can join yet. "Everyone is waiting for a party," says Willi.

IX

England: no flags for the revolution

Any American who goes to England carries with him a baggage of memories that he has inherited from the centuries. Most of these memories are suffused with the soft green haze of country England from whence the ancestors of Americans came—that country England of moor and heather, of rose and garden whose images have been etched in our minds by every schoolbook from Shakespeare to Browning.

This England, to be sure, is still there. One can see its fields rippling and billowing like ocean swells, cut by hedges and walls into farms, pastures and parks almost too well-tended for rugged American taste. The city of London broods over this England, and beyond London are the stately country homes, the cottages of hewn stone, the villages of cobbled streets surrounded by fields of heavy wheat and pastures of fat sheep. This storybook impression of solid, nourishing roots in the earth is, however, entirely false and hides one of the most stubborn facts of Atlantic politics. England is a miracle of man's imagination, a daily denial of realities. No other country in the world is posed more delicately or perilously on the edge of perpetual disaster and collapse; no other country so completely unable to support its own weight supports so great a part of world politics and causes so many men to listen when she speaks.

The England that lives always ten paces from chaos and accepts this condition as normal is not the country England of our memory, but the city England of world politics. City England is not so much London, that monster agglomeration of 8,000,000 people in a jungle of brick, stone and paving, as the faceless towns that jostle one another across the central belt of the island. Of Great Britain's 50,000,000 people, eighty per cent live in cities and towns, and these cities and towns are crowded one on another so densely that within their country, smaller than Oregon, live more people than live in all of the United States west of the Mississippi. A century of industrial history has clotted these cities together in patterns: the steel cities—Sheffield, Rotherham, Birmingham and their suburbs—black, smoking, gray, sulfurous, hour after hour, sprawled about the Trent; the wool cities about Leeds, wet, dismal, chilly in the Yorkshire winds, so cramped, say the local chroniclers, that a squirrel can run for twenty miles out of Leeds without descending once from the rooftops; the cotton cities, on the western lip of the low hills of the Pennines—the red cities, of red brick, of red factories, of red cottages, that follow one another monotonously into the cotton capital of Manchester which dominates a larger urban agglomeration even than London.

All these cities were created by the world of yesterday, and today their citizens live in pawn to a world which tomorrow may leave them starving. Their island—the green fields and meadows to the contrary notwithstanding—cannot feed, clothe, fuel or make comfortable even half their number. All English politics start from this one fact. All Britain's movements in the world—diplomatic, military, economic, political—are magnetized by this fact.

The real England, city England, begins at the wharves. At the West India docks of London Port lies the S.S. *Triberg*, three weeks and ten thousand miles out of Vancouver in North America. Deep into her hold reach huge vacuum pipes sucking wheat endlessly aloft to the top of the ten-story red-brick granary. It takes four days for the roaring suction pipe to suck all the ten thousand tons of wheat out of the *Triberg*, letting it spill in cascades of red and gold grains to be cleaned, dusted and collected in the bins where it lies heavy and fragrant, waiting to be milled into London's bread. Every single week eight such ships must weigh into the ports that rim the island of Great Britain to deliver the yearly four million tons of wheat that England must bring from over the seas to feed her people. Without them there would be no bread. Along the wharves of the Thames are other ships and other warehouses—ships full of heavy, perfumed hogsheads of tobacco; of huge wine butts out of Bordeaux; of yellow, raw timber from Rumania, Russia and the Balkans. Surrounding them are the wares leaving England—scores and hundreds of shiny new automobiles, crates of intricate machinery, cases of Scotch whisky, textiles, refrigerators, radios, engines. What comes in and goes out must balance, for if it does not, English life will come stuttering to a dry, choking halt.

To feed the British, half of all Britain's food—12 million tons—must be unloaded at the wharves each year; to fuel her industry and move her trucks and automobiles, 28 million tons of oil must be piped out of the tankers; to clothe her people, 750,000 tons of wool and cotton must arrive. To pay for this food, oil and clothing, the British must export what the skill of their fingers can produce—coal, textiles, metallic goods, engineering equipment. To make these things, in turn, a further staggering tonnage of raw materials must arrive automatically and uninterruptedly every single week from overseas. Half of all Britain's iron ore, four-fifths of her timber and wool, nearly all her copper, lead, tin, zinc, aluminum, all her oil, rubber, cotton, sulfur, tobacco, tea and coffee must come from abroad. No nation in the world is balanced more precariously on the shifting tides of trade. In war the best of Britain's blood and courage, and in peace all her skills of diplomacy and persuasion are devoted to keeping the trade lanes open.

No great community in the world reacts more quickly and uncontrollably to the slightest ripple of events in the outer globe than does Britain, because on this island converge two great sets of uncertainties.

On the one hand is the uncertainty of the market, the old and well-known uncertainty of commercial chance. Uncertainty anywhere in the world makes the British wince. The cotton men of Lancashire know how to make dhotis for India, coolie cloth for China, sarongs for Batavia, organdies for Burma, white shirtings for fellaheen. But when there is trouble "up-country," as the Lancashire merchants say, trouble with Mossadegh in Iran, White Flag rebellion north of Rangoon, trouble with Indonesians revolting near Batavia, Egyptians rioting on the canal, then somewhere in Lancashire a mill closes down, covering the lint-fuzzed spindles with brown paper against the day when "up-country" reopens again. These little cycles of trade gather, too, in greater movements of decades and generations that bleach life out of entire cities. There was a time just before the First World War when the spinners and weavers of Lancashire made eight billion yards of cotton cloth a year and shipped seven billion of these yards around the world. Today they export less than a billion yards of cotton cloth, and for decades, one by one, the mills have been growing silent and closing down. When one stands on the Pennines with an oldtimer, looking down on such a spinning town as Oldham, his melancholy is understandable as he says, "I remember when from this hill the smokestacks down there looked just like a trayful of pencils." The uncertain market is not always cruel, of course. As the world's needs change and the British react to meet the need, new industries flourish and new, cleaner, fresher cities thrive. The market spreads the blight through Oldham, through Nelson, Strines, Wigan, Bolton and Blackburn where cotton once was king, but as the market calls for jet planes, for scientific instruments, for new research, little country towns like Cheltenham blossom a hundred miles away, fresh and sparkling in the green country. Yet no one who depends on the distant market is ever secure. Let Australia impose import restrictions—as she did in 1952—and, while the merchants try to find alternate outlets, 10,000 automobile workers in Birmingham and Coventry go on short time.

The uncertainty of the market is at least a century old. The other uncertainty is much younger—it is the uncertainty of supply. In the days when England alone had a modern industry and the pound sterling was the world's single measure of value, the resources of the freshly discovered globe were hers to pick and choose from. But in a world that is expanding its demands everywhere, supplies have begun to run short, or are sealed off by politics. England has built her sulfur plants to run on the pure sulfur of the American Gulf Coast; when the American government and American industry clamp down on the export of sulfur because of American need, the British chemical industry staggers. Food was cheap in the days when England was changing from country land to city land, and farmers everywhere poured their surpluses into her island. Food is scarce now and is eaten at home, as meat in Argentina, or as rice in the Orient. Everywhere the revolutions and changes of Asia, of Africa, of South America demand of the world more newsprint and pulp, more wheat and oil, more rubber and iron ore, reducing the amount Britain can claim as her own.

Britain lives at the meeting place of the world's uncertainties. Yet she wishes not only to survive, which is difficult enough, but to remain great, to prosper not only as a larger Belgium or a larger Switzerland, but to stand as one of the great powers with a surplus of energy large enough to shape the world and impose British policy on it.

To achieve this purpose the British have only three natural resources: the sea, coal and their genius. The sea is important. The great oceans and Britain's sharply dented coastline give her the enormous advantage of cheap water-borne transport from the far ends of the earth almost to the threshold of British factories; the sea evens up much of the advantage of the landlocked, continental giants with whom Britain competes. The coal resources of Britain, even though badly wasted by neglect and a generation of mismanagement, are still important. They are a prime, native source of energy which, if only they can be exploited efficiently once again, guarantee her forever the power to keep the wheels turning.

But most important of all is British genius.

The genius of the British is a difficult thing to transcribe in the cold accounting of power politics. Yet to ignore how greatly it multiplies the British is as impossible as to ignore how the perverse genius of the French divides and reduces them. For genius in England is not only the individual flowering of the human mind, but also the coming together of these minds and personalities in a kinship of community which no other free state can approach. This kinship is the source of Britain's fundamental political strength—the ability to hang together and respond to leadership in such a way that the whole effort of the nation may be devoted to one end, without terror, without police.

Continental Europeans know of this genius and respect it, but they have only very circumstantial explanations of why the British are different from other Europeans. In England, say some of the Continentals, men retain their dignity as men. Every country of the Continent (except Sweden and Switzerland) has been invaded by rude, physical turbulence—the shriek of the wounded, the furtiveness of the refugee, the tramp of the conqueror—which Englishmen have never known. Each country on the Continent (again, excepting Sweden and Switzerland) has known its government to be violently overthrown at least once, and some three or four times since the beginning of the century. The citizen has seen authority humiliated, despoiled, made squalid, replaced everywhere on the Continent; he has watched troops in alien uniforms come as conquerors, to occupy buildings and lay down rules. He has cringed against a wall as enemy police have passed and has winced at the real or imaginary feel of enemy fingers on his cheek. Each individual has been broken a bit in the process and his respect for authority has withered as his fear has increased. Englishmen have never known this. No policeman in England carries a gun; authority needs none. A French diplomat in Budapest once tried to explain to me how people who hate communism in Europe nevertheless grow to accept it: "Europe is different from England," he said. "Europe is part of the Land of Humiliation. The Land of Humiliation reaches from the Bay of Biscay all the way across Asia to China. Every man has been violated at least once and usually many times. Humiliation is no longer strange to Europe, but the British have never known it and they keep their dignity."

As intriguing as this explanation is, it is unsatisfying. For the political genius of the English does not result only from their miraculous escape from the disasters that have overtaken other people. It starts mysteriously far down in the roots of everyday life, and their attitude to politics is the ultimate fruit of a kinship that begins far below the level of politics. This kinship begins, I think, in the simple ability the British have to associate. They associate (despite their reputation for aloofness) more easily than any other people in the world, whether in London, village, mill town or suburb. They associate to bird-watch, to raise clothes for missionaries, to grow flowers, to play cricket, to trade, to put on plays long before they associate to defend individual political interest or that of the nation. Two sociologists recently decided to plot how much of British life is covered by simple neighborliness and clubbiness. They chose as the object of their survey the little industrial (furniture-making) town of High Wycombe, in a constituency of closely balanced politics. High Wycombe with about 35,000 people is thirty miles from London and has the same relationship to the great capital as New Rochelle, say, has to New York. The 35,000 people of High Wycombe, the two sociologists found, had managed to cluster together in the following groupings. There were some fifty-one general clubs—old folks clubs, legionnaire clubs, air force clubs, clubs for model-makers, chess players, amateur drama, amateur symphony orchestra, singers, masquers, camera faddists, clubs for radio, squash, billiards, badminton, ping-pong, politics, books. There were beyond that forty-odd football clubs and twenty cricket clubs, plus hockey, netball, tennis, bowling and swimming clubs. There were also nature-lovers, gardeners, beaglers, sailing, bicycling, motorcycling and fishing clubs. Beyond that there were thirty-five churches in High Wycombe, each with their diffuse penumbra of aid societies, choirs, Sunday schools, charity endeavors, Bible classes. There were in addition to all these the local unions and local factory sporting clubs. And since London is only about an hour's drive away, an even broader array of more specialized and distinguished clubs and associations await High Wycombians who want to combine yet further.

England is made of towns and people like this—men not so much herded together as woven together. Their differences with each other may be generations old, frozen on cleavages of class and status. But they know, almost instinctively, how to gather for common effort. When an enemy threatens, they gather sternly as home guards and fire-fighters. When a queen is crowned, they gather in rejoicing to roast oxen in the country, to decorate their neighborhood streets in the city, to put up commemorative benches for the old folks, to challenge the neighboring village to a tug of war, to build bonfires. They have somehow acquired a trust in each other that rises tier by tier to their trust in government and willingness to let it lead.

The ultimate expression of this attitude to politics is the House of Commons. Grave differences separate Government and Opposition by far more than the width of the green carpeting between their respective benches. But these are differences without hatred, differences that permit the men on one set of benches to laugh in a deep, rolling, healthy laughter at the quip of a speaker on the opposite benches that touches them to the quick; that permit a man to nod quiet assent to some particularly clever thrust of the opposition without being regarded as a traitor by his fellows. In the French Assembly, when far Left and far Right fire away at each other, one feels certain that M. Duclos in power would murder and garrote M. Reynaud and M. Barrachin, and M. Barrachin or M. Reynaud might do likewise to M. Duclos if they had the chance. But though men dispute in the British Parliament, they do not hate; they are gathered in a common cause, which is not to destroy but to provide leadership.

Leadership in England carries with it a special reverence, even when it is unimaginably dull or open to the most human criticism. In no other country could a failing giant present himself day after day before the eyes of an alert opposition and come out so unscathed in personal dignity. No one comments on how different is the Churchill who leads the Tories of today from the Churchill of 1940. Sir Winston of today is an old man, whose hearing is failing; dependent on and almost suffocated by cronies of other days, almost timid and sometimes hostile to new faces, his great brilliance is more and more obscured by the darkness of age and the forgetfulness of senility. Only rarely does a newspaper, public speech or gossip column in Britain fasten on these human frailties. Political debate still limits itself to the quality and purpose of leadership offered, attacking Churchill's deeds or applauding the rare greatness of his utterances.

It is these people, then, with these problems in an unstable world, under this kind of leadership, who have accomplished in the seven years since the war one of the most amazing and deep-flowing revolutions in the history of man.

The place where this revolution has come to focus is called Whitehall.

Whitehall is the name of a broad thoroughfare which runs flanking the Thames for little more than half a mile, from Trafalgar Square to Westminster Abbey. It is one of those curious place names which, like the Kremlin in Moscow or the Forbidden City in Peking, are supercharged by history with a symbolism that persists beyond episodes and centuries. Whitehall, in history, means the government of England, and if you walk briskly, you can traverse it from the black lions of Nelson's monument at one end to the green apron of park between the Abbey and Parliament at the other in just less than ten minutes.

You will see very little of the revolution as you walk, for the revolution has been almost invisible to the naked eye—it has borne no flags down its pavings, shed no blood, scorched no buildings. The commuters and clerks sitting on the upper decks of the bright red buses that roll through Whitehall pass daily before the window of the palace from which a king of England once stepped out on a specially built platform to have his head chopped off. This revolution has chopped off no heads. The blackened five-story buildings that follow one another down the northern side of the avenue are black not with flame but with the peaceful soot of old age. Admiralty, Treasury, Board of Trade, Colonial Office, Home Office, Foreign Office and War Office follow one another in the same order they did half a century ago, halting before the same smooth and verdant lawn of grass that separates them from those abiding twin witnesses of change, the Houses of Parliament and the Abbey where the sovereigns of Britain are crowned. It still requires no more than two blue-coated bobbies to keep the peace on Whitehall's famous little appendix, Downing Street, where, at Number 10, the Queen's First Minister lives.

It is as difficult to detect the change inside the buildings of Whitehall as from outside; Gladstone and Disraeli would feel quite at home in the offices and easy chairs within. Gaslights, it is true, have given way to electricity, but the halls are just as dim. Elevators now rise through the wells of marble stairs, but they are slower than a quick-footed man can climb. The same coal fires burn in the same coal grates of the offices of Her Majesty's more distinguished servants, the same passageways twist in and out to bewilder strange visitors.

Little, indeed, has changed at Whitehall except its meaning and function. In the past fifteen years Whitehall has gathered in its thousands of dingy cubicles, in tighter space, more power over the lives of ordinary human beings than has the government of any other free country. Whitehall controls not only the safety, the politics, the education of the nation as all governments do, but nearly the sum totality of the citizen's life—almost everything, indeed, but his thoughts. Whitehall decides how much meat, how much butter, how much sugar, how much cheese every English family shall eat each week. Whitehall insures against unemployment and sickness, provides orange juice for babies, wigs for bald pates. Whitehall can dictate to any owner of real estate in England how he shall use his land or deprive him of his land; Whitehall sits in judgment on every farmer as he farms his acres, fixes the price of his produce and, if it chooses, can turn the farmer off his acres for farming them badly. Whitehall controls and channels all investment in England and says where and how it shall be made. Whitehall owns and controls all the mines, all the railways, the total power system of the island nation; it buys most of its foods and much of its metals abroad; it sets its credit, determines or allots its scarce materials, effectively decides how many new homes shall be built each year. Whitehall determines whether or not Englishmen may go abroad for vacation, and how much they may spend when they go.

No other capital in the tradition of democracy has ever held so much power over the lives of so many individuals; no other nation has ever voted into one single dot on the map of one city such immense control and stayed free. Yet the English have, and it is all concentrated here in the ten minute walk between the Lions of Nelson and the bell towers of Parliament.

The measure of any revolution's power is how quickly and deeply it is accepted by the people whom it has disturbed. By this measure the revolution in Britain has passed its tests, for in the past two years it has been reluctantly confirmed and accepted by the party that fought it, tooth and nail, for the fifty years of this half-century. Two years of Tory government, after six years of Labour adventure, have proven that no power now exists in the island nation which can undo or reverse what has been accomplished by the quiet revolutionaries of the postwar years.

Since the men who brought this revolution to England are the men of the Labour party, England's story since the war has been mostly theirs.

The British Labour party is the newest and youngest great governing party in the free world. It was born on February 27, 1900, at Memorial Hall on Farringdon Street, London, where several score men and women gathered together to "devise ways and means of securing an increased number of Labour members in the next Parliament." They were men of various strains of faith: Christian Socialists whose conscience would not let them rest; Marxist Socialists, infected by doctrines from overseas; Fabian Socialists irritated by the intellectual untidiness and disorder of the system in which they lived; trade-union leaders spurred by the hunger of their men. What bound them together was a sense of revolt at British life and a consciousness of rot within the Empire which, at that time, still stretched around the globe as the greatest constellation of power in world politics.

The rot and decay out of which the Labour party was to grow in the next fifty years had already, at the moment of its founding, been festering for a century. It did not show itself as true misery of life, as Europeans and Asians understood it, for at the turn of the century Englishmen had a much higher standard of life than any other Europeans, a standard not even remotely comparable with the subhuman standards of southern Italy. It was a moral decay, a comparative rot, that could be translated into political force only by a close-knit, highly civilized people whose conscience was unable to accept the vivid contrasts of wealth and poverty which a century of world dominance had brought to their island.

Though Englishmen did not quite understand the uncertainties of the trade cycle, the mechanism by which those uncertainties were evened out had already become abhorrent to the founders of the Labour party. The mechanism was the simple flexibility of old-fashioned business life. When a market collapsed or when a slump hit, adjustment was made simply by cutting down production and sacking men and women. You hired when times were good, paid as little as you could, fired when times were bad, re-employed when the world called on Britain for more goods again. The system depended on millions of marginal floating workers who could subsist under the poundings of up-and-down, who were content with tea and bread and jam when things were good, and just tea when things were bad. What the fathers of the Labour party proposed was to iron out the cycles, press out the uncertainties, give voice to millions of English men and women ready to demand a better life for themselves.

It was twenty years before the new-founded Labour party could make the British people give ear to their story. It was then, after the First World War, that the rot developed from the obscenity of comparative standards into a grisly, stinking visible thing in the streets of England, so vivid that not only the working class but England's middle class began to listen to Labour's story.

Mostly it was unemployment that made the British listen, for unemployment came and settled over England like a blight. During the twenty interwar years, fourteen per cent of all British workers were permanently unemployed; in the bad years twenty to twenty-five per cent were jobless. The figures were bad enough, but their persistence made them terrible. For if one out of four people was out of a job, then no one was safe and the fear of individual rejection crept into every home, nagging every breadwinner and every young man looking at the future. Unemployment was not the short, sharp, spasmodic terror it was in the United States and Germany in the pit of the depression years; it was permanent, an illness with no turning, a pestilence that could make entire regions like South Wales (coal) or Jarrow (shipbuilding, eighty per cent unemployment, 1930) names that bespoke a new kind of death.

The roots of the curse lay, of course, in the great outer world. British industry which had led the world all through Victoria's reign had been outstripped. The industries of other powers had borrowed the techniques Britain had lavishly offered them, had chosen only the best, and gone on to perfect and elaborate them beyond Britain's power to compete. By the time the Second World War broke out large and vital stretches of British industry had fossilized. Almost all the skills of spinning and weaving are developments of old British craft and invention. But by the beginning of the Second World War the British textile industry was a house of antiquities, ninety per cent of whose power looms were hand-operated. (In the United States more than ninety per cent are machine-operated.) The individual genius and astounding fertility of the solitary British mind still persisted. Englishmen conceived radar, the jet plane, brilliantly explored the atom, discovered the first antibiotic. But it was, by and large, other peoples who benefited from British discovery. The British still made the finest textile machinery in the world, but they exported it to such countries as India which used the machinery with cheap labor to compete with the work of Lancashire weavers.

If one had the eyes to see, the rot could be and still can be seen in the flesh of human beings walking the streets. One comes off the Yorkshire moors down the low, humid slope of the Pennines into Lancashire, into the slums of red-brick cottages, each cottage built edge to edge as if laid out with a child's ruler, the rectangular boxlike image of its neighbor. Here, in these towns, the cotton industry was born almost two hundred years ago. In two hundred years that industry has made of the millworkers, physically, almost a race apart. The men in the streets are thin-faced, long-nosed, pigeon-chested males; the beshawled women are short, pygmy-like, starch-stuffed feminine goblins who stand only chest-high to a full-grown American. Bred out of a century of dampness, beer and suppers of bread and jam, they are almost as distinct ethnically as a separate tribe.

From the unemployment and decay of the interwar years the British went directly to the war against Hitler. The war was not only a time of action, but of the simmering of ideas. For millions of young Britons in camp, aboard ship, overseas, in the desert, in the jungle, it was a time when there was nothing to do but talk, think or read books. Out of their thinking, talking and inner speculation came a decision as clear-cut as any given by a democratic election in this century. It was the mandate of the general election of 1945 to the Labour party to socialize Britain.

The men who received this mandate were perhaps the most lackluster crew of leaders to captain a revolution since revolution captured the imagination of men. Only yesterday, as outcasts, visionaries, street radicals, they had seemed to threaten bloodshed and riot. Ernest Bevin, a hard, solid, hefty man, had first become famous for crippling Mr. Churchill's intervention in the Russian Civil War by leading his London dockworkers to strike against the shipment of arms; he now in 1945 became Labour's Foreign Minister. His successor and bitter rival, Herbert Morrison, had been a belligerent pacifist in the First World War, but in Labour's long growth to power had become a solid, powerful executive of great administrative talent. Sir Stafford Cripps had once been so wild a radical that the Labour party at one time expelled him from its ranks as too Red for its tastes. But now, in office, a common drabness settled over all of them, a drabness that seemed perfectly to reflect their leader and Prime Minister, Major Clement Attlee—a slightly built little man with a balding pate and precise dry voice who still looks like the social-service worker he once was, but who conceals beneath this rabbit-like exterior a determination of iron and an inflexible power of decision. Only one of Labour's senior ministers preserved any of the fire with which Labour spokesmen had won Englishmen to their support. That was Aneurin Bevan, a silver-haired, ruddy-faced, burly ex-miner from South Wales, a man of dancing wit, silvery voice, remarkable eloquence and unrestrained exuberance. Beneath these men was a solid phalanx of new parliamentarians; mostly trade-union leaders, but sprinkled with intellectual junior ministers and several brilliant scholars and journalists who seemed more fit for a university faculty or for the pulpit than for the clash and battle of partisan politics. It is difficult to imagine these men as insurrectionaries, staying up until two or three in the morning over a bottle of brandy in a smoke-filled room plotting conspiracy or attack, or lying on the cold floor of the Smolny waiting for the agitators to storm the Winter Palace and report insurrection had swept the crest. Yet they changed history.

The chief instrument by which the Socialists changed Britain was their morality. Socialist morality started off with the single principle that in a modern state it was wrong, indeed sinful, to allow unemployment, hunger, sickness and cold to weigh upon millions of ordinary citizens while the few should be cushioned through thick and thin in wealth, opportunity and comfort. Their chief legacy was the decision that the state is responsible for the security and welfare of every member of society, and that the state, similarly, is responsible for seeing that its wealth as well as its burdens is shared fairly among all its citizens. What the Socialists changed was the social climate of England; they failed to change the underlying reality of industry and enterprise or solve Britain's dilemma in the disturbing world.

The morality acts of the British Socialists were the quickest, easiest and perhaps the most successful of all their bold ventures. Every British citizen now found himself insured by the new National Health Service against every form of sickness and disease insofar as medical science could meet the guarantee. The rupture and flat foot, the pregnancy, the infected tooth, the strained eye, the accident or disaster were all woes which the state now shared with the individual family. Children in their cradles and later in the schoolyards became the special wards of the state; for them there was orange juice at a time when fine hotels had none to serve their richest customer; there was milk, fairly rationed, when strawberries with cream were just a memory; special stores sold special baby foods against special ration books, guaranteeing the same scientific dietetic selection for the poor as for the rich.

This morality, however, was expensive. To pay for the new schools, new houses, national health, baby grants and the subsidies to keep food cheap required huge sums of money. To be specific it has cost the British government about one-third of its annual income or upwards of four billion dollars a year. To pay for this the welfare state thus presupposes a sweeping transfer of wealth from those who have to those who have not, by a taxation so merciless as to make American taxation negligible by comparison. The normal British tax rate on a $5,000 yearly income is $1,470 and goes up from there. It goes up so sharply and steeply that by now even the most hard-shell Socialists know that it can go no further. Where before the war Britain could count some seven thousand people who kept incomes of 6,000 pounds (then worth approximately $24,000) or over after taxes, the Britain of today counts only sixty people who still retain 6,000 pounds (now worth $16,800). And if the British government should decide to cream off every cent that these sixty individuals earn over $16,800 a year, the net result of the confiscation would bring the British Treasury less than $1,500,000 to add to its revenue. This taxation has been, in its effect, as revolutionary as the social climate it was created to support. There are, perhaps, no more than 500 families left in all England today who can send two sons to a good university at the same time without drawing on their capital. Nor, after two years of Tory government, is there any prospect of lightening this tax burden to any appreciable extent.

All these are abstractions. But the abstractions translate down into the flesh and blood of men and women who have lived through the change and thrived, or been broken by it. There comes to mind a long series of British individuals reacting to the change with varying degrees of dignity, delight, horror or cowardice.

On one of my trips to London I called on an old friend whom I had last known as one of the more important servants of the Empire in Malaya in 1940. He had lived then in a great mansion in Singapore, with servants softly padding about opening doors, serving whiskies, passing cigars and brandy. The years since have brought him promotion, advancement and respect, and he has reached the peak of his career in a position which in Washington is equivalent to that of Assistant Secretary of State. In his office in Whitehall he makes decisions on which the life and future of Britain depend. But in the evening he comes home to an old house he has rented in a London suburb with half an acre of garden behind it. There I found him with abounding energy and in astonishing good humor, bringing the same drive and intellect to bear on the problems of kitchen socialism that, officially, he shed on the decisions of war and peace. The revolution had come upon him as a challenge and he had met it so. In his garden he raised all the potatoes and greens the family used through the summer; before egg rationing was abolished he had put up a chicken run, installed chickens, given up his official egg ration, gambled on feeding his chickens enough from kitchen scraps to get four or five times the eggs his family was entitled to purchase by ration—and won. He put in two beehives in his first year and took out 71 pounds of honey to supplement the sugar ration. We ate well at his home and his teen-age daughter served the table.

There are others who react differently. One Tory M.P. with a distinguished record and illustrious parliamentary career ahead of him was swept out of office by the 1945 vote. He decided then simply to quit; packing his bags, leaving his home with his wife and family, he gave up his British citizenship and went off to live in America, a country where he could enjoy the fortune left him by his American grandmother. But most men of his class, even the very wealthy, have no American grandmothers with American fortunes. They stand and watch the change with somber detachment, like the moody man who drove with me down the long row of noble clubs on Pall Mall. "Waiting lists still on good clubs," he jerked out, "not so long as they used to be though. Too expensive. Seventy-five pounds for a good club. Who can afford it? Not much point anyway. Food's no better than any place else. All rationed. Fifty years from now they'll all be gone. Best part of London life, you know. Don't see how they can keep up. Suppose the first step will be closing the dining rooms. Probably put in 'snack bars.' " He dropped the last word into the conversation as if he were lifting a bug between thumb and forefinger and dropping it into the gutter.

I remember spending an evening in 1949, during the height of

Socialist austerity, with a friend who was trying to convince me that visitors to London saw only what was fashionable and unimportant and missed what was coarse and critically important. We were sitting in the bar of a Mayfair Hotel, in that corner of stylish London where most Americans naturally congregate. The bar was almost empty; at the other end of it sat a tall Briton in dinner jacket nursing his whisky; sitting beside him was his lady. We watched them in the bright-lit silence for a full ten minutes; now and then the polished leather of their stools creaked as they shifted, but they said nothing.

"I can't explain it to you here," said my friend, "these people got hurt. Come and I'll show you something else." After a long half-hour in the subway we came up again into a long, still street between a row of silent warehouses, through which we passed before coming to a housing development.

"This is Wapping," he said. "The local Labour government built these houses. Not bad?"

They weren't. The windows were larger than usual in an American public housing project, the courtyards had more grass and more playground space. Under a light two teen-age girls were giggling loudly to attract the attention of two teen-age boys who were reading a large poster which said, *London County Council—Technical Colleges, Schools of Art, College of Commerce, Evening Institute.*

"Night schools—all free," said my friend. "Let's go down to the pub." The pub was in the center of the Council and we heard singing before we got there. One man with a concertina, laughing as he played, sat near the bar while a teen-age boy sang in a high-pitched tenor voice. Several old women with very bad teeth, quite fat and dumpy, sat in chairs about the wall and in the middle young people danced and sang, their arms locked. "Ten cents will buy you half a pint of beer and a whole evening of this," said my friend. "They like what's happened." The noise carried quite far and dropped warm over the acres of slumbering flats.

What finally laid the Socialists of Britain low in the year 1951, and wrenched the government from their hands, was that they ran out of ideas—or, at least, out of ideas vigorous enough and clear enough to show the people how Britain could recapture greatness in a changing world.

The British had bought the fundamental Socialist idea: that never again would the converging uncertainties of a cycling world be adjusted by the automatic cruelty of unemployment, hunger and rejection. They had accepted the discipline of Socialist regulation in the belief that sometime, at the end of the adventure, Britain would become strong and powerful enough to rise above the uncertainties. But after six years of hard work, devotion, good order and red tape, here was Britain still cycling from trade crisis to trade crisis.

The theories of British socialism had been worked out by intellectuals over a period of fifty years before the Socialists came to power, and they had all been worked out as if Britain, an island power, was a vast and self-contained continent. If morality was the mother of British socialism, then planning was its father. But somewhere along the way the idea of "planning" had become confused with the clichés of nationalization, a confusion which persists in every European Socialist party. By the old dogmas of Socialism, if an industry is nationalized, then the workers working for themselves ignite with enthusiasm, and productivity soars. By the corollary of the dogma, a government that controls the basic industries directs them to operate on lines drawn by a long-term plan, so that they move ahead by direction and control ever onward and upward, immune from the swings of boom and depression.

With this sheaf of operating ideas, the British Socialists moved in their first five years to control British industry. They swiftly proceeded to nationalize the Bank of England (the archenemy of Socialist mythology and an institution that had proven its obsolescence some twenty years before). Next, they nationalized the coal mines, the basic resource of England and its sickest industry; they then proceeded to take over all railways and road trucking companies, all the cable and wireless system, all the airlines, the gas industry, the electricity system, and wound up in 1949 by nationalizing the British steel industry. Simultaneously they slapped on the most rigid control of all land use and land values in Britain and equally rigid control of all investment, public and private.

There was no doubt that the new system worked; it worked

very well indeed. Recovery in England started more quickly and, until 1950, hit higher goals than in any other country of Western Europe, except for one or two Scandinavian countries which, like Britain, were also governed by Socialist parties. But it did not work as the fathers of socialism had dreamed socialism would work; nor did it work well enough to guarantee Britain against the buffeting and beating of an unstable world.

What had happened was that the simple credos of Britain's turn-of-the-century socialism, a compound of hunger-Christianity-and-Marxism, had never measured the complexity of the human soul, the modern state or the massive needs of a true revolution.

Nationalization could be ordained, for example, by law, but not the rosy dream of worker-ignition that was supposed to follow on nationalization. The Union Jack rose over steel mills, gasworks, railways, electricity plants. And afterward everything was as it was before. Productivity in Britain increased, but it increased no more rapidly than in that archcapitalist state, America. The workers called no bloody, nationwide strikes in mines, steel mills or gasworks as they did in the nationalized industries of France, but neither did they invest their benches and pits with the enthusiasm and devotion which Socialists had thought would follow automatically on the magic of nationalization. The workers looking up to pit boss, mine engineer, plant manager, found his face exactly the same the day after Vesting Day as the day before. The plants belonged to the people, but the people operated them through the same managerial bureaucracy as private capitalism had. Where labor relations were good in private industry, as in the steel industry, they remained good under Labour, and the nationalized steel firms did not even bother to change their letterheads or boards of directors. Where labor relations had been bad, as in the coal industry, they remained bad after nationalization and no amount of extra rations, extra soap, extra meat or extra pay could wipe away the human suspicion that festered in the dark pits. In was the spirit of the worker that counted; if his spirit could be quickened and British production spurt then all the uncertainties of Britain in an outside world would be solved by his superior fertility and effort. But if his spirit remained fundamentally unchanged—as it did—then crisis, too, would persist unchanged.

Nor did a series of nationalizations automatically add up to a plan, as the Socialists once had hoped. The Socialists tacked one nationalization upon another, one new guarantee of security upon another in their first explosive efforts to reorganize Britain. But not until the summer of 1947, when the dollars and gold gushed out of Britain's reserves so crazily that it seemed only a matter of months before the island would be unable to buy its food and raw materials abroad, did the Socialists get around to planning. It was then that Sir Stafford Cripps was given control of all Britain's economic life and ordered a survey from his civil service which showed that, beaten back to live on its own resources, Britain could provide her citizens only with a starvation daily diet of 1,600 calories. And it was then, finally, that a central Planning Board was set up.

A planning board, so conceived and so organized, inevitably had two characteristics. First, since it had been created under the pressure of the Dollar Gap, most of its planning was geared not to domestic British life, but to the recurring trade crises overseas. It was a planning whose chief targets were the moving, vague, fluctuating figures of foreign trade. Secondly, it was set up as a Board of Civil Servants, out of that tradition which makes the magnificently efficient permanent British civil service the first instrument of command of any British government. As a government might tell the General Staff of an army, "Plan us national defense," so Labour instructed its civil servants to "Plan the national economy." But civil servants are, in essence, men who make regulations and apply rules, not men who draw policies and inspire revolutions. Thus, instead of a plan, the Socialists got controls and regulations—very efficient, but not the stuff of inspiration.

The failure of the civil servants to give Britain a plan was not, in any sense, their fault. By the code of British politics, civil servants must hold themselves as ready to regulate socialism for a Labour government when the people demand it by a Labour vote as to deregulate it when people demand it by a Tory vote. The real creative work of any society must be done not by its paid civil servants but by its elected political spokesmen. The men who came to power to act for Labour had entered with an accumulated capital of ideas; when they had spent these, they were too busy in administration to create new ideas to meet the new problems they had found.

Labour had come to power to effect a social revolution, unaware of the complex industrial and political revolution needed to support that social revolution. The political instrument it found at hand was the British House of Commons, but the House of Commons had never been designed for the kind of changes Labour tried to make. The tradition of the Commons is that of a gentlemanly meeting place where men of wisdom debate policy, but it is not a working assembly and provides neither its majority nor minority party members with the working tools for complex study. A member has no office or secretarial staff of his own, as an American Congressman has; morning after morning, night after night, one can see the younger members in the open corners of public alcoves of Parliament's basement laboriously scrawling long-hand answers to their constituents' letters. Parliament has no elaborate permanent committees with trained staffs to hammer out problems to working conclusions as the American Congress has. Moreover, the members of Britain's House of Commons are grossly underpaid. An M.P. is paid a salary of less than $60 a week (from which taxes are deducted) which is insufficient to buy him bed and board in London during the sessions and still support his family at home in the provinces. Most parliamentarians without private incomes are frantically engaged in outside activity to make a little extra money. They have little time for thinking, less time for the leisurely contemplation of great and intricate problems and are moved mostly by morality and common sense which is highly commendable but in the twentieth century not enough.

Labour had overwhelming control of Parliament during its first five years of power, yet it made no effort at all to reorganize Parliament into a new and effective tool of the revolution it was trying to consummate. Nor did it attempt to create any forum, academy or clearing place of ideas where it could examine its own program and the new problems that arose. Labour, for example, had come to power determined to give India its freedom and so, in an act of historic statesmanship, it did. But it had never previously dispassionately examined the fermenting problems of the Moslem Middle East and thus, during the five years in which it might have altered completely the course of events in the explosive crescent, it did nothing. Labour theorists had devoted remarkably little attention to the problems of education and schools in their long preparation for power. When they came to power they attempted with a touch here and a touch there to reshape what they found, but they had no basic ideas, and at the end they left almost intact that cruel system of public education which separates English children at the age of eleven into those few who shall go on to higher education and become leaders and those whose education shall be terminated at fourteen and who shall, thenceforth, become hewers of wood and drawers of water.

By 1950 these shortfalls and shortcomings of socialism were evident to no one more than to the humanitarian leaders of the British Socialist party. But it was not until their last year in office that they invited any true re-examination of ideas and policies, and by then there was little time left to furnish forth a complete new, workable doctrine for the British people. The great trading crisis of 1951 was soon to be upon them. When it came, Labour, divided in itself, raised a confused voice, and the British turned Labour out and summoned the Tory government of Mr. Churchill to power.

The clearest reading of British politics and of the Tory government which directs England today comes from the civil servants of Whitehall. The civil servants of England are men of far greater importance and continuing power than any servants of the American government except the Chiefs of the Pentagon and the Justices of the Supreme Court. They sit in everlasting judgment and attendance on the ministers chosen by a political parliament to guide them in the administration of England.

One could summarize a dozen conversations with them by this analysis which they all share: in a modern government, they say, policy is set by forces beyond the control of politicians. Politicians come to office fresh from their election rounds, bearing with them the phrases for which they were cheered and the promises they belled from the platform. The Tories campaigned across England promising Englishmen good red meat again, promising houses to be built out of the wellspring of private initiatives, offering the taste of greatness. Although the Tories earned less votes than

Labour at the polls, they won the government—and then the facts were explained to them.

On the Friday after election Mr. Churchill, the new Prime Minister, named Robert Austen Butler Chancellor of the Exchequer and thus Britain's virtual industrial dictator. On the next day Mr. Butler lunched with the two senior civil servants of the Treasury who had, during the election weeks, wrung out of their lesser staff two basic twenty-page memoranda on Britain's recurring emergency. The two civil service papers explained just how grave was the situation in that fall of 1951, and just what the few possible courses of action were. On Monday, having been briefed in reality by his civil servants, Mr. Butler lunched with Mr. Churchill and explained reality to the Prime Minister, and that week the government of Mr. Churchill brought all steel sales under strict licensing control, slapped on the most rigid import control since the war. It took, in short, the action the Civil Service said it had to take and which, on civil service instruction, the Labour government would have taken too.

No red meat followed the Tory victory, because the entire world is short of meat, except for those who can pay in dollars, and England is short of dollars.

No sudden liquidation of the vast National Health Service followed Tory accession to power because Mr. Butler, who holds the purse strings, is as passionately devoted to the social services as the Labour M.P.'s themselves and knows that the nation is too.

For years the Tory opposition had attacked Labour foreign policy for Britain's failure to urge and lead the European states to unity, but only a political micrometer could distinguish any difference between the new Tory foreign policy and the old Labour foreign policy, not only in Europe, but in the Middle East, Far East and Commonwealth, too.

The Tories came to power bearing the tradition of strong national defense with them. But within four months of their electoral victory, the Tory spokesmen at the great Lisbon Conference of the NATO powers told their Allies that whatever their wishes they could afford no greater arms effort, because of England's financial troubles, and thereafter proceeded to cut England's arms and defense program more swiftly and deeply than the previous

Labour government had dared, even under the pressure of its vociferous Left.

The intricate structure of control and direction of industry that the Conservatives promised to sweep away persists in all its basic branches; all capital investment is still controlled and regulated by the same committee of Treasury specialists. Every British housewife still carries in her ration purse the same brown ration book that has been doling out her butter, cheese, margarine, meat and sugar for fourteen long years. Coal is still rationed. The state still does most of England's major overseas shopping, buying the nation's wheat, meat, butter, sundry foods, cotton and nonferrous metals. Allocation by license and end-use control still channels the flow of materials through industry as the state wishes.

The urge to rip British life out from under this cross-lacing of control still throbs in thousands of clubs across England where true-blue, old-fashioned Tories congregate. But the urge spends itself and dies within the Conservative party itself, without affecting policy. Those who must direct the Conservative government know that any changes they can make will not affect the substance of decision forced on them by the same world that perplexed Labour's leaders; they know that the only changes permitted them are on the margin of procedure. In trying to apportion Britain's over-all resources differently from Labour, they have found they can advance one project only at the expense of another. Thus, in the Tories' first year of government, enough materials were shaken out of the licensing system to build approximately fifteen per cent more homes than in Labour's last year, but factory-building, consequently, dropped by about seventeen per cent. Their attack on food subsidies has brought the government's contribution to each family's grocer's bill down from 410 billion pounds to 109 million pounds for the coming year, but at this point food costs begin to rise in Labour and Tory families alike, and farmers' subsidies are shaved where it hurts Tory votes most.

This cautious approach of the Tories to the changed England they have inherited is sometimes described as a policy of "fiddling with the fringes." Yet to the surprise of most Tories and to the even greater surprise of Labour politicians, "fiddling with the fringes" has proven popular, and two years after their elevation to power by the thin margin of sixteen parliamentary votes, the

Tories, at this writing, seem stronger than when they entered.

This popularity has been won not by a crusade to undo the work of socialism, or re-establish the England of private enterprise. Indeed, at this writing, almost two years after the Tory victory, the Tories have succeeded in repealing only one major measure of socialism, the nationalization of iron and steel; and no one is yet sure whether private industry can or wants to reabsorb the vast properties offered back to them. More importantly, the long debate on repeal has left the country unstirred, arousing neither violent opposition from the workers, nor violent enthusiasm from the masters. I visited Birmingham, a dark and smoking city in England's steel country, during the debate on steel. Unions and management alike were unmoved by the controversy. The local chief of the iron and steel workers union said, "I don't give a damn who owns the thing so long as they treat us fairly. There's a hell of a lot of fuss in London, but it's not up here in the trade. I deal with the same people under nationalization as I did before, and as far as labor relations are concerned, the position hasn't changed in any way, shape or form. Frankly, the union would rather the industry stay nationalized because it's easier to get a nationwide policy that way. But we won't strike if they denationalize it. All we want is for them to stop making steel a shuttlecock of politics in London." In almost the same words the old industry managers in town say the same thing. "No," said one of them, "we're not hot under the collar about denationalization. Things haven't changed much really, you know. The same people sit on the boards of directors. Stewart and Lloyds' and United Steel even use their old letterheads and stationery. We did a good job before nationalization, we did a good job after nationalization. It's a political scrap, you know, it doesn't affect us much."

The popularity has been won chiefly because the Tories, in accepting, as the people have, most of Labour's changes, have tried above all to make the changes more comfortable. Held rigidly in place by the pressures and strains of the outer world, the English are grateful when a thong in the necessary discipline is loosened here and a lacet there. They were grateful when, six months after the Tory election, they were told they need no longer carry personal identity cards around with them wherever they go. They were grateful to the party in power when tea was derationed, even though Labour's leaders tried to explain that they, too, would have derationed tea under similar circumstances. They were grateful when the ministers decided that eggs might come off the ration although it meant less eggs for some and more eggs for others. Even though food costs creep up monthly, the same housewife who complains, "It's two bob more a head for everybody in the family every week," hastens to add, "but you see more in the shops now." As the Tories attempt to ease control by a loosening here and a loosening there, someone, to be sure, pays a price; there is only so much to go around in England, and if some get more, some must get less. This, indeed, has happened and many British families can now no longer claim the meager meat ration of 33 cents a week allowed them by the book, because their purse has already been emptied for more costly, more essential things. But in the broad millions of British life, these families are still a small minority and no one in the Tory government contemplates letting Britain adjust to her limited resources in the old way, dividing again into the many poor and the few comfortable.

The careful, exploratory way in which the Tories have tried to modify the revolution they inherited is, when seen in the proper perspective, only a continuing demonstration of the ancient pattern of British politics. Two great parties compete, as they always have, for the loyalty of Englishmen. One is the party of experiment which changes its name from generation to generation as it recruits the power of new social groups and carries new ideas over into deed. It has been called, from age to age, the Barons, the Roundheads, the Whigs, the Liberals, and today it is called the Labour party. The other party changes its name less frequently and for over a century has been known simply as the Tories. But though its name seems changeless, the party of the conservatives changes just as much as the party of experiment; English conservatives are always the residuary legatees of all once-radical ideas now become respectable, of all once-revolutionary changes become normal.

When the party of experiment runs dry of ideas, the party of the conservatives always returns to administer its reforms, consolidate its changes, tidy up the scene, which is what is happening now. England's chief problems lie, for the moment, outside of

England, not within England. It may be that no one can solve England's problems in the outside world, but no Englishman can bring himself to believe it. If a settlement of world affairs solves England's problems in a greater world prosperity, the conservatives may continue to manage English affairs until all the changes now so fresh have become old-fashioned. If the world spirals down in disaster either economic or military, they will continue only until the party of experiment, under whatever name, comes up with fresh ideas and a fresh solution.

x

the story of Joe Curry

The British are quiet people.

The roads of history are strewn with the wreckage of great states and empires which have underestimated the British by trying to read Britain's strength and purpose from the surface pomp, the mumbled eloquence, the archaic glitter. Underneath are millions of sturdy, determined, undemonstrative men and women like Joe Curry, solid as rock and just as enduring.

Joe Curry does not look like a revolutionary. Certainly, he does not think of himself as such. But he and millions of men like him in mill, mine and factory have pushed England along through these living decades to the transformation that has made her a land more changed from her past, yet more true to that past, than any other in Europe.

When Joe Curry came back to Doncaster in the fall of 1952, a large sunlit office awaited him in the gray, ivy-covered mansion of the National Coal Board. As he walked down its corridors people said, "Good morning, sir," and drew back shyly, in deference and respect.

This Doncaster had quite a different feel from the Doncaster that Joe Curry had first seen twenty-five years ago when he stepped out of the dark station, tired, hungry, threadbare and with but two coins jingling in his pocket. Not that the face of the town had changed—the same buildings turned the same soot-smeared, greasy faces out on High Street, under the same gray skies. Tuesdays and Saturdays the market still boiled and bubbled in town-hall square. The Danum, the big hotel for commercial travelers, was still as cold and drafty as ever. Even the people looked the same—solid, stocky men with the stamp of the worker's life in their bearing; round, stout women with kerchiefed heads, busy at their shopping.

The change that had come to Doncaster was invisible, and Joe, himself, was somehow at the center of it. The car, the office, the waiting secretaries were only part of it; the deputies and administrative assistants attendant on Joe's instructions were only a detail in the change. The change, if it could be traced, was somewhere in the hearts and lives of 140,000 coal miners in the pits and villages of England's largest coal field, who were watching, waiting, to see what Joe Curry, the new chief of labor relations, was going to do. Some there were, but only a few, who could remember Joe in the pits with them, stripped to the waist, sweating, hacking coal off the face. In nearby Bentley, Joe was sure that he could walk down the streets and someone would say, "Why, Joe, how's it going with thee, Joe?" "Pretty well," Joe might answer. "How's it going with thee?" And the answer would come back, "All right, but not as bloody well as thee." But there were others who would not call Joe Curry "thee." They were the young men who knew Joe Curry only by reputation—as the new man sent up from London to take over labor relations in England's richest and most turbulent coal field. "Poacher turned gamekeeper" they called him, thinking back to Joe's old days as a labor leader, summing up the suspicions and dreams that mingle in the gathering places where British workers talk about the revolution they have won.

Joe Curry knows both the suspicion and the dream, for he grew up with the suspicion and he bled and fought for the dream.

It had all seemed much simpler that cold December day twenty-five years ago when Joe and his brother, drifting, black-listed miners, climbed off the coach from the North Country with three shillings and sixpence each in their pockets to look for work in the Yorkshire coal field. Behind him Joe had left father, mother, two brothers, three sisters and a girl eager to marry him, all waiting to see if Joe could find a job in the mines of the mid-country. Behind, also, Joe had left the memory of the General Strike, with its blood and hunger, and all the bitterness of the ancient exhausted mines of Durham. In those days the hate and the dream went hand in hand. The hate was generations old in every miner's heart and included all the masters and all their ways; the masters were the men who let you work only when they wanted to, who paid you as little as they could when you did work, and then dumped you when they didn't need you longer. The dream was fresher and simpler: to take the mines away from the masters, nationalize them, socialize them.

The dream has been won now, for the mines are nationalized. But the suspicion remains. And the dream can only work when the suspicion goes. It is Joe Curry's job to see what he can do about the suspicion. He knows it well.

The suspicion was already old in the home of every miner when Joe Curry was a boy, growing up in the village of High Spen fifty years ago. High Spen is too small to appear on any map, but lies just three and a half miles south of Rowlands Gill, which in turn is fifteen miles off from Durham City. Men like to say that when Joe Curry was a boy, just after the turn of the century, such villages were flush and prosperous, as English miners dug 250,000,000 tons of coal each year and shipped nearly 100,000,000 tons out of that to a world that had not yet learned how to use oil.

Joe remembers High Spen differently. One gaunt, black skeleton of a colliery rose in the heart of the village, another rose on the village fringe, and everyone worked at coal. One muddy street ran down the center of High Spen, flanked by rows of two-roomed, hewn-stone cottages where the miners lived. When Joe was born into a family of four children, two rooms housed them all; not until much later, when the family had grown to fifteen, including nine children, a brother-in-law, a cousin and two orphan boarders, did it expand into the luxury of four rooms. In Joe's early youth such houses had no water; across the street and down its length ran a cold-water pipe, with one tap for every five houses, and the mothers drew the family water in buckets. Such houses had no toilets either. Families, in groups of four, shared common outdoor privies, where each family had its own seat in the bench of holes that opened on the ash midden.

Englishmen had been digging at the coals of Durham almost two hundred years when, in 1903, Joe Curry was born, for Durham coal, the first coal dug in England in the early days of industry, is good coal, perhaps the finest gas coal in the world. Those two hundred years had already given the miners of the North

Country bodies different from those of other Englishmen—short, enormously powerful, heavily muscled men they were, like Joe's father whom Joe describes as "not tall, but tall across." Joe's father worked in the mines, as *his* father had before him, and his father's father before that. Joe's father, like all the miners, was a man's man, which meant that he met the standards of High Spen—he worked hard, drank hard, gambled hard and was master in his own house. "They were strong men," says Joe remembering now. "Many of them worked all day and boozed at night, sometimes coming home in the morning with little or no rest, just in time to get into their clothes to work it off in the pits, and then came home at night to work it on again."

Joe's mother was a miner's woman with a miner's family of nine children to wash, cook and care for. When the boys were growing up and started to work in the pits, Joe's mother was up at two in the morning to send the first shift off to work, up at five to send the next ones out, up again to send the children off to school, after which she had to prepare for the men off the first shift, and cook and feed them. Men were hard on women in mining towns, and when a boy went down to the pits he was a man and he, too, could be hard on his women. Joe was only a boy when he first went down the pit, but when he came home at night, he felt like a man sitting in his chair saying, "Mother, get me a glass of water." It was only when Joe, at sixteen, had had pneumonia and spent long days at home recovering, watching his mother work, that he realized how hard it was for her, caring for the swarming family. Joe, reformed by this experience, made less demands on his mother and would often help with some of the household tasks, though other miners thought that softish for a man.

"She wasn't an educated woman," Joe says of his mother, "but she was the finest woman in the world. A beautiful woman she was, dark, strong, attractive and well made. She had an understanding—she knew something was wrong and she knew something had to be done for improvement. She never went beyond being a worker in any cause, but she was always reading, she was the first woman in High Spen to join the Woman Labour Party's Co-operative Society. 'Twas her sounded the tune of socialism in our family."

Joe went down the pit at the age of fourteen, as nearly every boy in High Spen did. A draper in the village offered him a job at ten shillings a week in his shop, a mighty good wage, but the pit was in Joe's blood.

He learned mining the way every miner did in those days. He went down with his father that first morning, very frightened but anxious to hide it. The overman looked him over for a minute and then called another boy who had been down the pit for all of three months. "You take Joe," said the overman to the second boy, "and show him what to do." That was all there was to instruction in mining.

Pony-driving was boy's work in those days and in fifteen minutes Joe was a pony-driver in the mine, with strange echoes and rustling sounds settling all around him. Now, with all his years of knowledge, Joe says that every sound in a mine has its meaning, and a mine that is totally still is dangerous. A good working mine breathes and murmurs underground, but that first day, there in the darkness, Joe was frightened. There would be the groaning of a roof movement, the sound of a stone jumping, the dry scratching of a rat as it rattled along the roadway. Alone with the pony Joe shivered.

The way up from pony boy to collier followed the flow of the coal. The colliers dug and dumped the coal into tubs; the tub-putters, burly men who manhandled the loaded wagons, pushed the tubs out to narrow passages where little Shetland ponies could get in to haul. The pony boys led them to larger tunnels, where larger ponies could pull the tubs. The big ponies drew the coal on to the rope haulage which carried it up the drift whence it rose into sunlight and commerce. A boy might work on the pony-line for months; then, in a quiet moment he would help the tub-putter push the empty tubs back to the face; he would linger at the face and watch the colliers hacking coal from the seam. When he wasn't busy, he would sneak up to the face alone and say to them, "Let me try." The men would look around and say, "Where's the deputy?" If the deputy was far enough away, the older men would let the boy heft a pick to help them hack the coal. Without knowing it a man graduated into a miner, his muscles hardening to iron, his body cramping into the cut, his back twisting in the Durham seams, often no more than 18 inches thick, cutting, hewing, taking the coal.

Coal-cutting was work. But in High Spen, the union was religion. From the time a lad went down as pit boy, he was expected to pay his sixpence a week to the union, and he did. Weeks when there wasn't any food in a miner's house, a miner paid his dues. The years when Joe was growing from boy to man, from pony-driver to face-worker, were the years after World War I when the unions of England were first feeling their strength and flexing their muscles. The men were coming home from France, spent with four years of trench war, full of new questions, wanting new things—more pay, better working conditions, more respect. And what they wanted of the coal industry, the coal industry could not give. The coal mines of England were aging, as were all of England's old industries. They were unable to meet the harsher competition of the continental mines, unable to find an outlet for the millions of tons of coal once shipped overseas to a world that now dug its own coal or used oil.

The Curry brothers, like hundreds and thousands of miners all over England, felt change whispering in them. Even when they were youngsters, kicking tin boxes around in the street, Joe and his older brothers would walk miles in the evening to hear Socialist speakers at miners' meetings. Sometimes Joe and his brothers hadn't the slightest idea of what the men were saying, but they knew it was important. Hour after hour they sat at union meetings, listening to reports and discussions; other nights they went to the Club and Institute Union whose hall offered a library of books for workers. Long before they could vote Joe and his brothers were in politics, tramping from village to village, canvassing votes for Labour candidates for local or national office.

Joe's first strike came soon after the war. The pit Joe worked in belonged to the Priestman family and had never had a strike before. The Priestmans were fairly decent among the hard masters of the North Country; they took a good profit but gave their men consideration. Joe and the men went out in the summer of 1921, not in anger, but because striking was in the air. Joe cannot even remember now what the strike was about.

The strike lasted thirteen weeks and a "bloody, glorious time" it was, with nothing to do but look at the sun and the open sky.

By the time the strike was settled, Joe had another interest. He had met a girl named Ruby on a merry-go-round at a village fair. Ruby was the only daughter of a miner's family and she knew what a miner's life offered, but she loved Joe and was willing to wait until he could afford a home. "Don't get married, Joe," said some of the older union men. "It'll be a trap and you should get on with the union work." But Joe thought differently, and for the next five years he was quiet. He paid his dues and loyally attended the meetings, but his extra time went into courting Ruby, until the year of the General Strike.

No whistle blew the workers of High Spen awake on that May morning in 1926 when the General Strike began. No whistle blew in any coal town of the North, for there was no one at work even to blow the whistle. Everyone had known for weeks the strike was coming and that it was to be big, the biggest thing a generation of English workers had ever tried to do.

The long slump of English effort had finally, in 1926, brought England's mining industry face to face with ruin. The seams that had powered the world's first industry were old and hollowed out with generations of digging; their costs were high; overseas, men dug coal more efficiently. According to the masters there was only one way out: to cut the wages of the men and make them work longer hours. For months masters and unions had talked about the matter with no agreement and both sides hardened. Backing the masters was the Tory government. Backing the miners were other workers, millions of them. As the miners' unions stiffened against the wage cuts, the other unions of England, in their massive Trades-Union Congress, lined up in support, promising that if the miners had to go out, every other union in the country would back them up. If the miners went out, all England would go out—spinners, weavers, printers, steelmen, dockmen, craftsmen, railwaymen, busmen—everyone who worked for a living. General strike it would be, the long-awaited master stroke of organized labor.

In High Spen, as in every other working village and working district of the land, Councils of Action were set up—"Soviets" the Tories called them. These Councils of Action were, in fact, shadow governments with their own police forces organized in flying picket squads that patrolled the country's life and movement. Only those trucks which received Council of Action permits because they carried food and emergency supplies could pass the patrol picket squads on the North Country highways.

No strike in England had ever been so well prepared before as the General Strike of 1926. But the leaders, unaware of what they were doing, did not prepare for a revolution, and so they were doomed to lose. Looking back on the General Strike a quarter of a century later, the men who led it, now sober, middle-aged officials or parliamentarians, still do not know whether it was naive or brilliant. For a general strike that closes an entire country down must be centrally organized and centrally directed. Whoever directs it successfully dominates the country and is, in effect, its government. If a general strike is victorious it is, therefore, a revolution. The General Strike of 1926 was called out over a wage dispute and the revolution was far from the minds of its leaders. It failed because its leaders did not understand the implications of their own deeds. It was the last great strike that England has ever had.

There were two parts to the General Strike, first the violence and then the hunger.

The violence came everywhere as it did to the Currys in High Spen—swiftly, with short-lived sharpness. For Joe it was no more than a brutal clubbing over the head in a moment caught off guard. It happened this way: two of Joe's brothers had been assigned by the Council of Action to patrol the highways; they clashed with a potato truck cruising the road without a Council of Action pass. Joe's two brothers, along with a number of others, including Will Lawther, now Sir William Lawther, the President of the Miners' Union, were caught by police and swiftly brought to trial at the town of Gateshead. On the day of the trial miners from all the neighboring villages, Joe among them, gathered, marching with lodge banners flying, their bands playing, their women and youngsters tailing along in the procession of protest. They invaded Gateshead, flooded its streets and courthouse square, demonstrated, and having made their protest, started away. Joe was at the head of his column on the way home when down at the rear he heard the sound of women screaming. He had just turned to run back when suddenly in front of him there was a policeman and before Joe could dodge, a club was swinging down on his head, and then blackout.

Joe came to on the couch of some people he never saw before or since. They were friendly to the strikers, as were all the North Country people. They had dragged him unconscious from the road. They bathed his head, bandaged him, warned him that the police were out over all the roads looking for rioters, that he must stay with them until dark. When dark came, the young man of the family took him out the back way, over the back fields, around the police blocks on the road. Other people put Joe on a bus back to Rowlands Gill; there he crouched on his hands and knees under the seat as police stopped and searched the bus for rioters. Finally in the darkness before dawn Joe made his way to Chopwell, to Ruby's house and safety.

That was the end of strike violence in the High Spen area, as it was almost everywhere in England. Once the government called force into being, the unions were bound to lose, for they had only two choices—either to seize the country by force or to crumble when the government struck back.

In High Spen the miners could protect themselves. One of their chaps, who had been a bugler during the war in France, was appointed signalman. When the patrol wagons of the police approached High Spen, the bugler blew his call. Then the miners poured into the streets, their pickshafts stacked neatly against the wall like rifles and they lolled about talking as if they were discussing the races, or the weather, or women, while the police lorries rolled through. Very peaceful they looked, but the pickshafts meant that they were ready to fight to defend their own. Defense, however, wins neither wars nor strikes, and men knew they were beaten.

The General Strike was over in ten days, as union after union all over England went back to work, the labor leaders nursing their wounds and pondering the lessons they had learned. They had lost on the picket lines. But they had learned that government is an instrument of power that can be used either way. This learning was to flower only much later, after the Second World War, when Labour won the government and made its own peaceful revolution.

For the miners the hunger began when the violence ended; other unions went back to work when the General Strike collapsed, but the miners stayed out. In High Spen they stayed out six full months and would have stayed out for twenty years, says Joe, if it had been only a question of spirits. But it was a question of hunger. The local government fed High Spen's children a hot meal each day at school; it set up a special kitchen for pregnant women where, if they came, they might get hot soup; it continued public assistance to families with many children, and there, if the father stood around while the children ate their scraps, he might find a bite of their leaving. But for most of the men there was nothing to eat all day, every day, except an occasional bowl of soup at the union's soup kitchen. When the children's shoes wore out, the miners opened a cobbler's shop and learned how to repair shoes. First for the children, then for expectant mothers, then for other women, then for themselves. Sometimes they gave singing concerts, charging a penny or two admission to raise funds to keep going. But, finally, when winter came and it was cold, there was no other way but to admit the strike was over and they were beaten.

The morning the strike was over the men of the Curry family trooped to the pit with the other miners. At the entrance the manager met them. "No work for you here—today or forever," he said to every man in the Curry family. Joe, his brothers and his father waited for weeks in High Spen, not knowing what to do, and then they realized, as did thousands of other black-listed miners all over England during those months, that now they were men without jobs, or homes, or futures—they were to be wanderers. Week after week they walked from mining village to mining village, crossing England from coast to coast. Once, in the winter of 1927, Joe and his brother found jobs in the Eccles pit, in Northumberland. But no sooner had they brought the family after them in an old truck than the black list caught up with them and they were wanderers again.

It was then that the Currys gave up the North Country altogether and came down to Yorkshire. The coal beds of south Yorkshire about Doncaster were new beds and in the nineteen-twenties they alone would hire new men. From Wales, from Scotland, from the North Country, hard men, black-listed men, desperate last-ditch strikers drifted down to Yorkshire to seek work there.

Joe and his brother arrived in Doncaster late in 1927 and found a Welsh lady who took them into her home, feeding them out of charity until they found work. For three weeks they trudged about the pits in Doncaster's suburbs looking for work and then they did it the rough way. One morning they cornered the undermanager of the Bentley pit in his office and closed the door firmly behind them. "Now you know there's no work here, lads," said the undermanager, "you'd best go quietly." But the Curry brothers explained that there was no use their going quietly, for they were hungry, and the family in the North was hungry, and neither they nor anyone else would leave that office until they got work or were overpowered and ejected. "Is it that bad, lads?" asked the undermanager. They explained again that all they wanted was a chance to work. The same day, at two in the afternoon, the Currys were underground cutting coal again.

Yorkshire was good to the Currys and, their passion spent in the General Strike, they settled down quietly. In a few months Joe's mother and father and the other children followed them down. A year later Joe's five-year courtship of Ruby ended in marriage, and he began a different kind of life.

From the General Strike until the war in 1939, solid, placid years followed one on another. Doncaster was not a coal-patch town like High Spen, but a vigorous, healthy Yorkshire working town with quick, alert politics. It was years before Joe was able to become part of it, busy as he was with his work, his family and his union meetings. But by 1937 the Labour party had put Joe up for the Sprotborough Parish Council, and a year later he had become its chairman. By this time, too, Joe had gone ahead in the union; most days he was down in the pit cutting coal; in addition he negotiated on the Union District Committee with the colliery managers or other employers' representatives. Labour elected him to various public authorities, and by 1941 he sat on the West Riding Magistrates Court.

Joe Curry was thus a man of solid local substance, if not of fame, when the war came to England. War did not come to Doncaster as it came to London, Coventry, Birmingham and the burning, bleeding towns of the Midlands. Only occasionally did a night-raiding plane, aiming for Hull or Sheffield, disturb the peace of Doncaster, summoning air-raid wardens like Joe to rush to their posts. War came to Doncaster through the change in the pits around it. There it found Joe and took him out, and changed his life forever.

For the miners of England the war was an escape. As the nation's factories expanded and all England called for manpower, the men bound to miners' wages and miners' sunless jobs began one by one, and then in scores and thousands, to desert to the clean above-ground jobs that were offered everywhere. By 1942 the drift from the mines had become so serious that Mr. Churchill's government established a Ministry of Fuel to control all the mines of England and the men who worked in them, lest the fiery core of Britain's industry grow gray for lack of fuel. Men were forbidden to leave the pits without permission; young men were drafted into them; the industry across the country was divided into regions, and in each region a panel of three men—one for labor, one for the masters, one for the mining engineers—controlled the pits. In Yorkshire the labor director was the secretary of the Yorkshire Miners' Union, W. E. Jones, and Jones in turn insisted that his deputy be young Joe Curry. One day Joe was in the pit, his hands grained with coal dust and his finger muscles cramped about a pickshaft, and the next he was in an office, with a telephone, a typewriter and a secretary. It was the secretary that scared Joe most. "I learned later," said Joe, "that she was terrified of me. But I was scared to death of her, more scared that first day in the office than the first day in the pit."

The mines looked different from above ground, and Joe had to learn about mining in a new way, considering the men in their thousands, studying how many worked in one pit and how many in another. The problem was not only to keep the men from moving out, but also how to move them around so as to get the most out of those who stayed. The coal faces screamed for more men, and Joe's job was to gather men scattered in old, poor pits and bring them to work in richer, more bountiful pits. But miners are stubborn people who do not like to be moved, and though a war was going on in Europe, they felt their old private war with the masters had never ended. Stronger than ever now, while England screamed for coal, they settled old grudges with lightning strikes and quick stoppages. The Ministry needed men like Joe

Curry to talk to the miners, men who had called for strike at pit-head meetings of their own, men who knew that now was not the time to strike and knew how to say it in the words of miners. Joe did well, and in South Yorkshire the men began to listen to him.

By 1944, when Jones left the Ministry of Fuel, Joe Curry was ready to take his place as regional labor advisor; two years later, in October of 1946, Joe was ready to leave Yorkshire and go to London when summoned. In London, Labour was now the government, socialism was being made and the King had proclaimed in the ancient words "Le Roy Le Veult" that on New Year's Day of 1947, the mines would no longer belong to the masters but to the nation.

Generations of dreams had gone into socializing the mines of England, but the new Labour government that proclaimed the dream to be reality had neither plan nor program. Seven hundred thousand miners, one thousand pits, more than one billion dollars of invested capital had accumulated over the years in England's greatest industry, but no one had explored how they should be put together under socialism.

In May of 1946 the Labour government had set up an organizing committee of nine men, later to become Britain's National Coal Board, to plan the reorganization of the resources on which all England's welfare rests. But the Labour government was busy with many things and many great adventures at the moment. "Here are the mines," it said in effect to the committee. "Do what you want, tell us what you need, we'll finance your schemes, off you go."

Off they went, nine men and two secretaries in frantic travel by coach and plane around England to survey their domain, while in London, almost overnight, staff and experts and secretaries began to gather. In the heart of fashionable Mayfair the government had cleared one of London's more stylish apartment buildings, Lansdowne House, to make office space. Filing cabinets forested the bathrooms, typists pounded away in kitchens, Lord Hyndley, chief of the Coal Board, installed himself in what was formerly the apartment of Snake-Hips Johnson, the jazz band leader.

Joe Curry arrived in the midst of this hubbub in London, in the fall of 1946, to learn his job as everyone in socialism was learning theirs. His office was a cubbyhole in the first floor of Lansdowne House, overlooking a tiny triangle of grass and garden. His title had great ring—deputy to the chief of the Coal Board's labor relations, who was Ebby Edwards, the grizzled old union chief. But, in fact, it was different. In all the vast, rambling confusion of the Coal Board, few people noticed that only two men in the whole new Socialist apparatus had ever been working miners down in the pits themselves—Ebby Edwards and Joe Curry. The mines, everyone assumed, belonged to the nation and that was enough to satisfy the miners. There were other more important problems on the Coal Board's mind than labor relations.

These other problems were indeed imposing and difficult; they had been generations in reaching their ugly complexity. For thirty years coal owners had let their mines run downhill. The best and easiest coal had been taken out; the workings were ancient, obsolete, inefficient; mechanization was twenty years behind time; haulage was antique; the pits were too many, too costly, too small. It would be a fifteen- or twenty-year task, estimated the engineers, to reorganize and modernize the mines of England, but meanwhile coal had to be taken out at any cost and so, on with the work. First nationalization, then reorganization. Thus, on January 1, 1947, the miners who had gone down in private pits on the night shift at ten o'clock came up at six in the morning to check out of nationalized mines. In South Wales the new shift sang hymns as they marched to work; in other districts they sang the Red Flag.

Within three weeks of Vesting Day the Coal Board learned where its real problem lay. Nature provided the occasion—a vast low-pressure area in the mid-Atlantic came swinging down over Scotland and England on January 23 of 1947, to lacerate England with her worst blizzard in living memory. As the snow piled up, life stilled. Trains stopped, factories stopped, electric power ran down. England had no reserves of coal for power; trains could not haul coal to the cities; miners could not even get through the snowdrifts from home to pit head. The thin margin on which English life had run for decades was worn through. There was no reserve coal, no energy. And there was no reserve coal because men did not want to dig it.

Mining depended on men, and surveying their enterprise, the directors of the Coal Board learned that there were less men mining coal in England than for over half a century. To get coal the Coal Board would have to find men; it would have to win them away from the clean, well-paying above-ground jobs of Socialist full-employment and make them want to dig.

From 1947 to this season and as far in the future as one can see, the problem of England's mines will be to find enough men, and once having found them, to do something to their spirit to make them want to stay and dig. Ten per cent more coal, say the economists of England, and England's basic trading problem would be solved, and that ten per cent could easily be taken out of the mines, without any new engineering, if only the miners wanted to take it. But something lingers in the miners' minds, bred out of generations of bitterness and cruelty that no edict of socialism can cure. Miners' pay packets are fat these days. Around Doncaster many of the white-collar workers are so envious of miners who earn twelve and fifteen pounds a week that they vote Tory out of jealousy. The pits offer clean showers, milk, good food, fresh opportunity. Houses are better; the rations of the miners have been the best in England for seven years. Yet the spark has not come. The miners work, to be sure, better than they did under the old system, but miners come to work when they want and are absent when they want. Lightning strikes still come and go, costing England more than a million tons of coal a year. For England to be great and solid again, the mines must work not as the old masters worked them but as the Socialists claimed they could and would work once they belonged to the nation.

For six years Joe Curry wrestled with the problem from his desk in London, a pit-head oracle for the white-collared engineers, technicians, administrators, economists and scientists of the Coal Board. "Joe," they would say, "what does a miner do with his dirty laundry?" or "Joe, can we put this kind of appeal in their pay packet?" or "Joe, what would the lads in the pit say to this?" Joe answered questions for six years before the Coal Board decided that he was needed more in Doncaster than anywhere else. Doncaster is the center of the Northeastern Division of England's Coal

Board; here in this region more and better coal is dug than anywhere else in England; here in this region the men are tougher and harder than other miners. Absenteeism is higher than in any other region in England—one out of every five face-workers in the northeast region was absent every day in 1952. Here suspicion has lasted longest, for here in the Yorkshire beds thousands of men beaten and black-listed by the General Strike, the hottest and most fiery of the coal workers of other regions, drifted to find employment in the twenties. They still remember. Joe Curry knows, for he is one of the men that came that way.

As director of labor relations for the Northeastern Division of the Coal Board, Joe Curry is responsible for more big pits (114 in all) and more miners (140,000) than fall under the direction of any other division of the National Coal Board. He has come a long way from the days when he learned about socialism in his mother's kitchen at High Spen and since his head was cracked by the police of Gateshead. Dressed now in a neat, gray business suit, his sandy hair now less thick and bushy, his ridged eyebrows vigorously protruding over green-blue eyes, Joe is still cast in the miner's mold. He is short, chunky, possessed of the enormously powerful shoulders of a pit worker, walks with their sturdy, heavy-footed gait. Only Joe's ideas have changed; he has seen socialism made; now he wants to make it work. His problem now is not the masters, it is the men, his mates, and how to ignite them.

"You can't ignite them overnight," Joe says. "All you can do is plant the spark and fan it and let it smolder; it will smolder a long time before it burns up into a good, strong fire.

"It's true the men aren't working like they used to. God grant, they'll never have to do it again. Those days when you had to count every penny in the packet and when you lost a penny it was sorrow, those days are gone. Ah yes, in those days the miners were disciplined. They were disciplined by fear and hunger and economic compulsion; a manager who took a man's job away destroyed him. When I was growing up, you saw grown men who couldn't find work waiting for little brothers and sisters to give them food. It broke them. The young fellows of twenty-four or twenty-five in the pits now don't remember those days, and the older ones can live like men for the first time in their lives.

"I look around me here in Doncaster. It's not so long since I saw people ill-nourished, ill-clad, their homes sparsely furnished. Now you see them well-dressed, well-fed. You go into their homes and they have decorations, pianos, carpets, radios, some of them are getting TV sets. It's all changed.

"We worry about absenteeism; I know it's bad. But think of the lads. Everything is OK, and they're lying in bed snug and warm next to the wife in the dark, when the alarm tinkles and it's four o'clock, time for the shift. What's the thing you want to buy most in the world that hour of the day? Another hour of sleep. And they ask who are they hurting if they take another hour's sleep, or stay in bed that day? It isn't as if they were paid by the week and they'd be cheating someone if they came late; they get paid by what they take in coal and if they don't cut coal that day, it's their own time. What they need is a new loyalty, something to belong to.

"They call this work of mine personnel management. I hate the bloody term. That's one the efficiency experts brought in, it's not a human term. What's got to be done is not big things but a lot of little things. The average pit manager thinks of his problem as work attendance. But you've got to think of this thing as men. Nationalization is just a soulless machine to the men up to now. If only the average pit manager could see how you have to go through the mass to the individual, to make the men feel that the Coal Board is in the pit there with them. If the manager only thought the men were as important as the engineering, as the firedamp, the drainage, the haulage, the ventilation. When a man's out you don't just dock his pay. You've got to talk to him when he comes back, not scold him like a child, but ask him was he sick? was the wife sick? did something happen to him? If the manager knows of a family with a bright young lad growing up in it, he ought to go around and talk to the lad's family. He ought to tell them about the opportunity for the boy in the industry, the schools we have now, the place in management waiting for him.

"It's not the intentions that count with the men, it's their seeing that the Board thinks of them as human beings, their seeing that the industry listens to their ideas, that the Board offers redress for anything that goes wrong, and if there's a doubt, the benefit of the doubt goes to them. But you can't do it by appeals. For ten years England's been appealing to the miners—for Dunkirk, for the Middle East, for Italy, for the Invasion of France, for the Dollar Drive. They're tired of appeals and they say, 'Let t'buggers come down t'pit themselves and see how it is.'

"What they've got to do is feel that they're part of the mines, and they've got to be loyal to the mines. I speak, whether I like it or not, with a mind that's been broadened. I won't go back on anything I thought or said when I was twenty-four. There's been no change in my principles or intentions. I've just been forced to see things differently."

XI

through three looking glasses

If no simple story can be traced through the complicated years that followed the breach between the Atlantic world and Russia in 1947, it is because classic diplomacy has decayed and all but disappeared.

Classic diplomacy was an art of a world that is dead, a profession practiced by a handful of men who were specialists in esoteric matters that ordinary citizens could not understand or were not greatly interested in. It was a routine of measured notes, conversations and formal calls, a charade of receptions, dinners and entertainment in which gentlemen, secure in their knowledge of what their governments sought, could bargain intelligently and secretly with other gentlemen equally secure in *their* knowledge of what *their* governments sought. The passions and pressures of furious domestic politics rarely annoyed them, either at home or abroad. Before the people entered the scene, in that long yesterday from Talleyrand and Metternich down to Bismarck, Gray and Izvolski, a modest intelligence and a strong army were enough to give a man a reputation as a successful diplomat. When, after many years, his dispatches and memoirs were published, it was possible to reconstruct a simple account of how events had been shaped.

Today, all this has changed. Foreign affairs are the central problem of politics for every country in the world. They touch into every home by the blood tax of war, or the money tax of peace. In every country of the West, therefore, foreign affairs are now fundamentally directed by Congress and Parliament, Assembly and Bundestag. Diplomats still draft notes, press the seals of red wax on treaties, advise their chiefs in what order and rank important guests should be seated at table. But essentially most diplomats are now clerks and their secrets are clerks' secrets.

Moreover, the frame of diplomacy has changed. Nations no longer deal with each other, except on the most trivial matters, as individual with individual. They deal with each other in great groups and associations, in agglomerations of force, in communities that collide and grate and bump. As much diplomatic effort must be spent within, holding these communities together—whether Atlantic, or Communist, or Moslem, or Latin-American—as is spent outside them, as their leaders try to deal with hostile or rival communities.

Both changes have erased the old mysteries in which diplomacy once shrouded itself. All that is important in the years since the war is public knowledge—so public, so overwhelming in detail, that instead of the obscurity of secrecy ordinary citizens are now blinded by the obscurity of total detail. No excitement can, therefore, be distilled from stripping the facts out of the secrets that diplomats whisper to each other over the green-baize tables of negotiation. The major facts have been worn bone-smooth in the many meetings at which men have met and wrangled since the war.

What excitement is left comes from guessing how the domestic political prejudices in each country will collide with the political prejudices of every other country, when they interlock in the new communities of association abroad. The excitement comes in watching negotiators trying to write a sound proposal that will please their voters at home without sounding too outrageous to foreign negotiators who, like them, are burdened and wince under contrary pressures in their homes.

Great events and crises sometimes sweep around the world like tidal waves, urging the new communities to common effort and common creation. But ultimately each country is moved by its own impulses, generated from the grass roots, conditioned by different nursery rhymes and remembered traditions, based on unspoken assumptions never formalized in documents of state. The tidal wave may momentarily jostle these impulses together or submerge them, but when it recedes these impulses rise again, true to their own sources deep in their own peoples.

The Western world has experienced three such tidal waves of

decision since the war—the first in 1947 when it decided to break with the Russians; the second in 1950 when it decided to rebuild its defenses; the third in 1953 when it pauses to ponder whether it should accept the overtures of the Russians who seek to resume the conversation interrupted six years before.

During these six years the Western world has been forced into two new kinds of association, one within the other. The larger is the Atlantic Community of NATO, the smaller is the Union of Europe within NATO. Each has been shaped by overmastering world tides. Now, as the tides change or recede, the permanent, persistent impulses of the peoples forced into these communities reassert themselves. The future both of NATO and European Union depends to a large extent on the contending magnetisms and purposes of the United States and Russia. But they depend just as much on the impulses that rise naturally in Englishmen, Frenchmen and Germans as they look out on the world and its changing tides.

* * *

The sentinels of British foreign policy keep their guard post in the ugly, ornate, grime-frosted building just across the street from the Prime Minister's residence in Whitehall. Across their desks, red-ribboned packages of dispatches bring them daily tidings of menace and turmoil. Yet even as they open these dispatches, the professional diplomats of Britain know they will enjoy, in replying to them, an advantage which is the envy of all foreign diplomats. This is their knowledge that behind them stands a united country, whose major impulses are so clear that they have never once needed expression in a formal document since the war. In England, partisan dispute festers only on details of foreign policy, not on its major purpose.

This major purpose, under Tory leadership as under Labour leadership, is Britain's desire to retain complete independence, not to be hammered into the status of satellite in any association of any kind, and to go on from there to recapture her old freedom of decision in the world. The British cannot adjust themselves to a world in which there are only two magnetic fields of power, the United States and the Soviet Union. There must be a third of equal magnitude, and in their Commonwealth they hope to create it. They propose, no matter what, to remain great and remain Britain.

The pursuit of this purpose is complicated by two grim problems.

The first of these is physical security. Physical security is no abstraction for the British, no distant menace from across the oceans. Many of us in the United States are already obsessed with worry about the defense of our continent from the thrust of bombers raiding over the pole or from oceans half the world away. Our radar pickets sweep the sky thousands of miles north and hours of jet-flight away from Detroit and Toledo. But Britain's radar pickets have no such range. From the time radar on the East Anglian or Kentish coasts picks up the first pip of an enemy jet until the time that jet is over London is no more than twenty minutes—twenty minutes in which the operator must make identification of plane and course, then telephone Air Control, Air Control telephone the alert fields, the alert fields scramble the fighters into the air, the fighters hurtle to 30,000 feet, search out the enemy and bring him down. Twenty minutes is the maximum possible margin of British safety. Each night millions of British women, children and men sleep with only this thin film of warning against death, and they know it.

For the British, trying to meet this danger, the only possible logic is to wed themselves to the strength of America and join an Atlantic Alliance which pushes the picket line of radar as far into the heart of Europe as possible.

But there the complication begins. Britain's second problem is economic survival. The British know they can starve in peace just as surely as under wartime blockade. They live in a world that challenges them with two kinds of danger at once. And though the Atlantic Alliance may be necessary for military security, it may be the crippling last-straw burden in their struggle for economic survival. Without the Atlantic Alliance, Britain stands naked and alone in an angry world. But with the Atlantic Alliance, the British are forced to accept the trading rules and patterns set by America, which, over and over again, force her to near chaos and disaster.

Britain's long-range strategic goal is therefore relatively simple: to retain the military alliance with America as its base of strength, but to struggle out of its implications toward political and economic independence. But this imposes on Britain tactical problems that are immensely difficult. She must keep the American partnership intact, yet without submitting to American strategy when she feels it unwise; she must applaud America's drive to European Union without letting herself be trapped in that Union; she must restrain or disagree with America without being left to face the Russians alone in a divided Europe. Last year the British Broadcasting Company scheduled a series of five weekly talks on the nature of British foreign policy in the world today. The eminent speakers were scholars and parliamentarians, both Labour and Tory. None wasted kind words or praise on America except to say that she was strong and she was necessary.

These basic British impulses have been refined into an unexpressed but conscious policy by all the events of the postwar world. Every two years since the war—in 1947, in 1949, in 1951—the British have experienced a monotonous but terrible trading crisis, bringing them to the edge of bankruptcy. These would be merely dreary ridges in international bookkeeping were it not for the way they have influenced British thinking about the world and their strategy in it.

The convertibility crisis of 1947 confirmed the suspicion the British have always had of America's best intentions. On loaning the British $3,750,000,000 in 1946, the United States insisted that the British make their pound sterling freely convertible into gold or dollars a year later at anyone's demand. The British declared this was unwise, but, intoxicated with the aroma of the huge loan, they finally submitted. Came the day when they had to meet this promise, in July of 1947. First slowly, then in a rush, traders and merchants all over the world who held English pounds demanded that the pounds be cashed for gold and dollars. From August 7 to 14, England cashed $115,000,000 to redeem its pounds; in the next six days she bled $237,000,000 more. At which point Britain broke its promise and made sterling inconvertible again to avoid bankruptcy. They had been right in their predictions, America wrong. The jaundiced examination the British have given every American proposal since then springs from the convertibility crisis.

The devaluation crisis of 1949 taught Britain other lessons and further refined her attitude. This crisis was born in the spring of

1949 when a slight downturn in American business dried up the markets of tin, cocoa, rubber, wool, which are the chief dollar earners of the sterling area, and simultaneously choked England's own dollar earnings from automobiles, textiles and whiskies. Again a run on sterling began, and Britain's reserves were drawn low. This time the run could be stopped only by devaluing the pound and offering it so cheaply that the world's traders would be lured to seek it for its very cheapness.

Devaluation left two residues in British foreign policy. The first was the morbid realization that Britain, like the rest of the Western world, hung like a cork at the end of a fishing line, to be swung about every time American business snapped; it left the British with an almost hysterical fear of their dependence on an economy whose liability to slumps automatically carried Britain with it.

The second residue was more important. It was this same devaluation crisis that finally shook the British out of Europe and made them from that time on turn their back on all projects of European Union however importunate the Europeans and demanding the Americans. The final devaluation of sterling in 1949 had been forced on the British against their will; all through Europe merchants who held pounds in the summer of 1949 had begun to offer these pounds unofficially to any buyer at any price and had, in effect, cut the value out from under the pound before the British did so officially. Now this was strictly illegal. At the tables of the Organization for European Economic Cooperation in Paris where the Marshall Plan powers met, all the European Ministers of Finance and Foreign Affairs held up their hands in horror at the black-marketeering of their merchants. But these European governments lacked the mechanism or courage to suppress black-marketeering; nor did they really want to; nor did the United States insist that they abide by the rules of controlled trade. When the British devalued the pound with abrupt brusqueness, they did so convinced that any understanding with Europe which involved common controls was impossible. And their island's survival depended on the efficiency of controls. Ever since, the British have stood sympathetically aloof; they have blessed all projects of European Union—but for Europeans only, not for Britons. Britain will go it alone.

The third and last of the trading crises, in 1951, finished the refinement of British attitude to the world. But that came after the war in Korea in 1950, and its story falls later in the chapter. By 1950, Britain's attitude to Europe and America was already clear.

England is the senior ally of America in Europe for the often-repeated reason that the English, if they are attacked, are the only people who will certainly fight to defend their liberties whether they stand alone, or with America behind them. England has done so before and will do so again.

But France is the second ally of the Atlantic Basin because although in a war much could be held, nothing could be won without her. Nothing could be won militarily without France because France holds the most valuable real estate in Western Europe. If France, as a rear zone of military maneuver and support, were neutral or hostile, no possible military line of resistance short of the English Channel could be drawn to meet an attack from the East. Equally, nothing can be won in peace without France. Such is the magic of France's name and culture, so vigorous are the intellects that flower in France that everywhere in the world France casts an absentee vote of the spirit.

This France, however, cannot be held in the Atlantic world as other countries are by troops of occupation, by bribery or ballot-stuffing. It can be held there only by the French themselves, freely assenting to the sacrifices in blood, money or sovereignty required of them.

In retrospect, the most brilliant and most imaginative foreign policy of the European states has come out of France. This has been the drive to European Union, born in Paris, shaped in Paris and sealed in Paris. If France has not received the honor and credit due her for leadership in this bold adventure, it is only because no serious observer can tell whether this same drive to European Union may not die in Paris, where it was born, and no one can measure how deeply the French people themselves support their leaders who have given Europe new banners to follow.

France offers the world a picture the very opposite of England. The words of English diplomacy are fuzzy, confusing and, all too often, meaningless; the vigor of English diplomacy springs from the way Englishmen understand each other and stand united in purpose without need of wordy persuasion. French diplomacy speaks in lucid, clear analysis, but it speaks for a people divided from village roots to sovereign assembly. Even France's diplomats are divided; it is doubtful whether ten out of a hundred of the professionals at the Quai d'Orsay are wholeheartedly agreed that their government's support of European Union makes sense.

Deep down inside France many contrary impulses stir its citizens as they look at the outside world.

There are those Frenchmen, almost a quarter of the population, who, stirred by the mythology of communism, have infected millions more to regard America as the evil in the world; automatically, they detest and denounce anything America praises or proposes.

There are millions of others, crossing all party lines, for whom foreign affairs begin and end with the Germans. They are the men who have seen the Germans come into their villages to kill their friends, who have grown up in towns where the public square, in which they have played as children and courted their girls, is dominated by one lone monument of sorrow to the dead in the German wars. They have learned on the knees of their grandfathers and from their history books that all France's strength has been wasted by a century of German aggression.

Then there are those who remember the heroes of French glory, from Du Guesclin and Joan of Arc through Napoleon to Clemenceau, whose throats choke when the tricolor passes, whose hearts skip when a frontier post in Indo-China is isolated, who wish only that France stand great and alone in her own immemorial tradition.

There are, finally, those who believe that France must merge herself in a greater union and greater loyalty called Europe. Some have been forced to this conclusion by fear and the conviction that French liberties cannot be defended unless France multiplies her power by association. Others have been led to the belief by religion and the mystic vision of Christian brotherhood. Still others believe that neither France nor any other country in Western Europe can offer her citizens a decent livelihood cramped in the frame of small, economically obsolete nation-states.

What is remarkable is that the French people, with all these conflicting and clashing emotions, have held still for so long and permitted men with but one policy—that of European Union—to persist in offering France as the first state in the greater union. The French have not yet given their final assent to the proposals of their own leaders, but they have let themselves be led.

Partly, the French have done so out of apathy, because they can see no solution for the political chaos of their own divided state. But more importantly, because year by year since the war events have led them to realize that the only other alternatives open to them are internal decay or frank submission as satellites to Russia or America. Events more than deep conviction have refined and shaped French policy since the war.

The French did not re-enter the great world in 1946 as a nation bearing arms and power. They were invited back. One of the brilliant triumphs of Western diplomacy over Soviet stupidity was Anglo-American insistence, in the face of violent Soviet opposition, on the participation of France as an equal in the deliberation of the victors. Had the Russians chosen, they might have altered the story of postwar Europe by cultivating France. In those early postwar days when France was governed by an overwhelming Left-Wing majority, when the Communists sat in the government and were the most powerful single force in disorganized France, the interests of France and Russia were identical. The French, like the Russians, had suffered bitterly from the German armies. Their instincts were the same as the Russians: to sack, strip and dismantle Germany in order to pay for the reconstruction and reform of their country. But the Russians, instead of earning French gratitude by supporting them on issues where their interests meshed—reparations, Ruhr control, dismemberment of Germany—sought instead each opportunity to humiliate the French and, by treating them as puppets of Britain and America, forced them, in practice, to behave so.

Being thus driven into the Atlantic world, the French realized, as did the British, that in this new world the dominant voice would be that of the United States. Unlike the British who instinctively looked forward to the day when they might face America in equality, as friends and partners, the French—all broken from the war—felt that a partnership of France and America would be a union of the horse and the sparrow, a package of clay pot and iron pot. France thus sought to expand her power by association, and obviously there was but one power with which to associate in Europe—the English.

There is something almost feminine in any French approach to London. The French in 1946 knew themselves to be weak, emotional, but desirable. The British were strong, true victors, not nominal victors, yet incomplete. Both France and Britain had undertaken great new planned economies. These economies seemed to dovetail: the French had food, the British fuel and the greatest needs of each might be filled by the other. Around the world their interests were parallel—in the Middle East, in Southeast Asia, in attitudes to America and Russia.

But the marriage of France and Britain was not to be. One of the French ministers most intimately associated with the negotiations of the early postwar months said, "It's little things that hold up big things—take the personality of de Gaulle, for example. De Gaulle had spent four years in England saying yes to Winston Churchill when the man's nature shrieked to say no. When he became Premier of France he didn't want to say yes to the British any longer, he just had to say no." Despite de Gaulle, their Premier, French politicians persisted in their wooing of the British. Had there been any serious response, de Gaulle might have been overcome in his own Cabinet. But the British, though cordial and polite, though they went on signing treaties of alliance and unimportant protocols of commercial exchange, would have none of marriage. They were British; they could not link their destiny with that of a defeated land. It is idle now to speculate what might have happened had the United States tried to force this marriage on Britain and France as vigorously and sternly as later we tried to force the marriage of France and Germany. All Europe might have changed.

Being thus rejected by the Russians and snubbed by the British, the French spent the next three years, from 1947 to 1950, in total dependence on American will. Each major event around the globe seemed to force France to dependence on the one positive outgoing diplomatic force in the world of freedom. The Dollar Gap crushed France and made her a supplicant, as all other West European countries, on Congressional favor. Unrest in Africa and violent war in Indo-China seemed insoluble without American understanding and support. Until the spring of 1950, France's confused impulses cancelled each other out and French diplomacy expressed itself only as marginal comment on American action.

It was not until May of 1950 that a French Cabinet could offer a French program to the world: that of European Union. The idea, as we shall see in another chapter, had long been electric in the air, but not until then did a French government, the first among European governments, take the idea and clothe it with authority and program. Since then it has magnetized all European politics about it, summoned to its support all the resources of American power and persuasion, lain at the root of every negotiation and every gathering among the Atlantic Powers and between the Atlantic Powers and the Russians.

It is commonly argued, criticizing the French, that for them European Union is a method of solving domestic problems which they cannot solve themselves, that it thrives on French apathy and is supported not by the conviction of Frenchmen but by their despair. All this is quite true, but it subtracts nothing from the courage or wisdom of the French statesmen who proposed the idea, for in history a policy of desperation is quite as valid as a policy of confidence. If it is true that no nation-state in Western Europe can thrive in its old compartment and offer its people the hope and comfort of the greater power states of the world, then French wisdom must get credit for having first recognized the situation and offered a solution.

For the Germans, foreign policy began late, but it began at home. It began with two sharp facts that still ulcerate the pride and dignity of Germans every day of the week: Germany is occupied and Germany is divided.

German foreign policy has sought to end first the Occupation and then the Division. This foreign policy is quite as simple and clear to every German as British foreign policy is clear to every Englishman. But the Germans differ bitterly among themselves on the method of reaching the goals.

All through the Winter Years down to the establishment of the Bonn government in 1949, Occupation took precedence over Division as the chief weight in German policy. No individual German could ever, at any moment, escape the Occupation. Germans drove on their own highways under traffic regulations fixed by alien armies; when they turned the tap in their homes, the water tasted of chlorine dictated by the hygiene field manuals of Occupation armies; their children studied from textbooks written, published and approved by alien conquerors. No impulse existed in Germany greater than to conduct their own lives as they wished.

From 1949 on, as the Occupation atrophied and the German Renaissance began to flush the country with health, Division and Unity superseded Occupation as an emotional pressure in the German mind.

From 1949 on the Occupation became increasingly a symbolic rather than a real grievance. As the Bonn government grasped ever more competently the tools of control that slipped from Allied administration, the Occupation became not so much a political as a technical problem of foreign affairs. For most Germans, living as close as skin to the Russian armies, do not yet want the troops of the Atlantic Powers physically removed from their frontier posts. Politically, it is German purpose to keep the defense troops of America, Britain, France and Belgium in place and in posture for the time being, and to deal with them as the French or the British deal with American troops stationed in their countries. Germans do not want to see American soldiers pack up and go. But they want to make sure that Americans in Germany live by German rules—that their Coca-Cola, as was suggested, be taxed as German beverages are taxed, that their hunting trophies be weighed and checked by German game wardens, that their railway fares be paid as Germans pay their railway fares, that their PX coffee be prohibited from dodging German taxes through black-market channels. Lastly, they would like to see that portion of the Occupation cost of these armies which Germany still bears removed and assumed entirely by the governments which command the troops.

Division, as an ulceration in German pride, has, however, never ceased to fester and suppurate. This desire of the Germans to be reunited is, today, the most explosive, unpredictable political emotion in Central Europe. In the partition of Germany by Russian and Atlantic troops more than in any other single European condition, lies the threat of turbulence, the possible wrecking of every project, alliance or plan Atlantic diplomacy has conceived.

This is so because no German, of any strain of political faith from purest democrat to most evil Nazi, can accept the partition of his country as permanent. He cannot accept it out of pride, out of conscience, out of logic. Seventeen million Germans live under the puppet tyranny of a Communist government. Each year between 200,000 and 500,000 of them slip across the frontiers from East Germany to West Germany as refugees to tell their hideous tales of pillage, barbarism and desolation. It is as if all England north of the Trent, or all France west of the Garonne, were under the iron occupation of an alien power. It is as if all Americans living beyond the Alleghenies knew that New England, New York, Virginia and the Carolinas were policed by men of strange tongues and obscene morals, who day and night continued to arrest their cousins and brothers, friends and families. Such a people have no greater objective in foreign policy than their territorial wholeness and integrity. No morality, no treaty, no understanding is binding that stands in the way of the purpose.

Nor, it should be noted, do Germans think only of East Germany under the Russians when they yearn for German Unity. They think also of the Saar which is held by France, and the fact that the Saar, relatively peaceful, is one of the most prosperous enclaves in all Europe and has flourished under paternal French administration does not abate German passion even a tiny bit, for in the Saar live Germans like themselves.

One other major impulse moves the Germans as they look out on the world. This is the impulse to draw a line across that past which has brought Germany so much sorrow by a new act of association with other nations in a European Union. This impulse probably awakes more genuine enthusiasm among young Germans than among the people of any other European state except Holland and Italy. It moves some Germans because they wish to make an end of the wars that have ravaged their country; it moves others because they fear, as do Germany's neighbors, the still-throbbing subterranean barbarism of many of their compatriots and want to manacle it forever in a larger union where it will be suppressed.

But where the impulse to European Union clashes with Germany's single-minded pursuit of Unity, the impulse flickers and fails. If European Union is to be fruitful, meaningful and lasting for Germans, it must have as one of its major purposes the reuniting of their country. If to reunite their country, the Germans must abandon European Union, they will choose to abandon European Union.

When the Communist armies of the Orient invaded South Korea in 1950, a tidal wave of panic swept the whole world and momentarily submerged the separate impulses of England, France and Germany. In that moment of peril nothing seemed more important to any of them than that their lives be defended. Thus, between 1950 and 1953, mighty achievements were written in Europe as NATO took up arms and as the organs of European Unity were fashioned to protect one and all. Yet, as year by year, the peril receded or changed in character, as the strain of the great rivalry began to tell first in the West then later, but more profoundly, in the Communist world, the old national impulses reasserted themselves. Each nation began to examine the world again in its own dissimilar interests.

The British, after the Americans, were the quickest power to add hard military strength to the Atlantic Alliance after the Korean War. The North Atlantic Treaty had been as much theirs in concept as America's, and it was thus that they consented in 1950 to place their troops, in peace, under the command of an alien American general. Within this frame they burdened their budget with new arms and moved their best forces onto the Continent until, by 1953, they had more armored strength in Central Europe than anyone else except the Russians and substantially more than the Americans.

But no sooner had the British made this effort to guarantee their physical security than they realized that in so doing they had exposed themselves to the cycle of trade and imperiled their economic survival. By 1951 Britain was in the strangling clutch of another of her biennial trade crises. The post-Korean boom in raw materials, the dizzy acceleration and consumption of American industry suddenly rocketed the price of everything Britain had to purchase in the world to impossible heights. Again her financial reserves went into that familiar, sickening downward spiral which is always arrested just this side of disaster by stricter controls, greater deprivations, Spartan throttling of imports from overseas.

By the time the economic crises of 1951 had been mastered by the new Tory government, two new refinements had been added to British thinking.

The first was economic and is shared by Tory and Labour leaders alike. It is the conviction that economic partnership with America under present terms is impossibly difficult, for both in boom (as in 1951) and in slump (as in 1949) American industry squeezes the juice out of British economic life. This conviction rests on the thesis that the source of British troubles is the permanent scarcities in a world of growing demand. Britain's effort must, therefore, be focused on the expansion of basic resources. This means, at home, an effort to dig more coal and to raise more grain and meat on her moorlands and highlands. But more importantly, it means that abroad Britain's efforts must be devoted to expanding and developing the resources of the Commonwealth. Only the globe-girdling belt of British colonies and communities with their 600,000,000 people and measureless undeveloped raw materials can offer Britain that base for future independence and greatness which she instinctively seeks.

The second refinement of policy rising from the crisis of 1951 was the practical conclusion that, under American leadership, the Atlantic Alliance might become an inflexible suffocating burden. It took no more than four months of power for the new Tory government to inform the Atlantic Council gathered at Lisbon in February of 1952 that, henceforth, Britain would do less rather than more than she had committed in the panic year of 1950. Balancing, as they always have, their problem of security against their problem of survival, the British are now convinced that the first is closer to solution than the second. For the British the tidal panic of 1950 had run out by the summer of 1952; it has been their influence in the Atlantic Community and in Europe that has chiefly prepared the way for the relaxation of 1953.

The French like the British reacted to the panic of 1950 with a galvanic military effort which, in the next three years, more than doubled their effective force of arms and nearly destroyed their economy in so doing.

But the French, unlike the British, were faced not only with a trading crisis as the boom brought by Korea swept over the world;

they were faced with two other complications even graver and more portentous.

The first of these was Indo-China. Until the end of 1949 the French had fought a relatively casual action in Indo-China, bloody and expensive, yet considered more as a colonial police sweep than as a major war in which the prestige of France was at stake. But the same Communist triumph in China that made Korea a bloody trap for Americans made Indo-China, in 1950, a bloody trap for the French. In the fall of 1950 the Annamite revolutionaries of Indo-China, now supplied by freshly-victorious communism in China, succeeded in wiping out the entire border chain of fortresses and frontier defenses that the French had erected to keep the Chinese and the native rebels apart. In a stroke the guerrilla forces of rebellion were transformed into a frontal army which has grown year by year in size and skill, drawing each year more and more strength in men and money from the French homeland. Thus, each year as the Atlantic Allies have needled France to do more on the Central European front of communism, France's strength and capacity have been drained inexorably out to Asia until now the French know they must either resign from their effort in Europe or resign from their effort in Asia, because they cannot maintain both.

The second complication was Germany. In the French impulse to European Union before the Korean War, the Schuman Plan had been an act of forgiveness to their old enemy. The French saw European Union as a community growing under their leadership by slow and gentle progress toward a goal decades away. The Korean War did two things. It flushed the German Renaissance along at a pace of such vigor and power that it became obvious, as men negotiated European Union, that Germany, not France, would swing the greater weight in this Union. The Korean War also thrust European Union forward at a faster pace than the French ever intended. Since rearmament was necessary and since German soldiers were necessary, the French found themselves, at the end of 1950, the reluctant sponsors of a European Union which required both Germans and Frenchmen to serve under the same command, same flag, in the same uniform.

It was all very well to launch European Union with the Schuman Plan, to pool the iron and coal resources of the Continent.

This could be explained to French voters as generosity coupled with shrewdness, for by the Schuman Plan they would gain as much as they yielded. But generosity has its limits. Frenchmen could not forget that Germany had paid back in reparations to all the Western Powers for all the damage done by German armies only some $500,000,000 or less than one per cent of the ruins they had caused, and the Germans had received four billion dollars of Western aid over the same period. The Germans had killed in cold blood tens of thousands of Frenchmen, yet less than 300 Germans had been executed by the West as war criminals and less than 800 were still imprisoned for all the crimes of Hitlerism. The Germans had stripped 80,000 machine tools from French factories during the war, and had restored less than 8,000.

Each month that negotiations over Union dragged out, French enthusiasm cooled. German strength and power were rising. But if Indo-China were constantly to drain the best French officers and the best French noncoms to Asia, and if the British were to withdraw (as they were doing) from all participation in new organs of European control, then inevitably the Germans would be the dominant power, both staff and line, in the new European Army. The European Army, indeed, seemed something which a French phrasemaker would entitle "Alone in Europe with the Germans." And at this point, by 1953, the French have stalled in a complex of contrary indecisions.

For the Germans alone, the Korean War brought quick, complete and unconditional profit. Within three months of its outbreak, the most onerous restriction on German industry—its steel limits—had been swept away, to be followed by the annulling of practically every other. The post-Korea boom drew German industry back into the world markets at such prices that it was able to re-equip huge sectors of its run-down plant. Most of all, it restored to Germany her bargaining power. From the moment in December of 1950 when the Western Allies decided they needed German soldiers, the Bonn government was effectively free to pursue a true foreign policy—the insistence on a quid for every quo, an insistence on satisfaction of its essential needs in return for German troops.

The first impulse of the Germans in this bargaining was to seek the formal ending of the Occupation. The negotiation of the formulas necessary to end the Occupation (called "contractual relations," not "peace treaties") was completed by May of 1952. These, though not yet ratified and still without the force of binding agreement, have already in substance returned German government completely to German hands.

The second German impulse—for the reunification of their land—gave the West relatively little trouble all through the period from 1950 to 1953. This was due to neither German indifference nor Allied shrewdness, but chiefly to the intransigence of Russian diplomacy. The Western Allies had only to say—as they did over and over again—that they favored the reunification of Germany, provided free elections were held in both East and West Germany as a precondition, to provoke the Russian refusal that was certain. There is no doubt that any free election in East Germany would repudiate communism; the Russians know this too. Therefore, up to now, the Russians have consistently refused such elections, preferring to hold on to their conquests in East Germany and let Western statesmen make what they will of West Germany.

The foreign policy of Western Germany has been shaped by this Russian attitude.

Until the summer of 1953, the best way out of their dilemma has appeared, to most West Germans, the way which Atlantic diplomacy offered them. If truncated West Germany were to speak with the force that could persuade the Russians to yield back Eastern Germany, she needed a new and greater base of power and the only base offered was the Union of Europe associated with the Atlantic Community.

The summer of 1953 has, however, changed this West German attitude, for the Russians, since the death of Stalin, have displayed an indecision of purpose in Germany so great and so apparent as to tantalize even the most devout German supporters of Western diplomacy. Shifting their proconsular staff in East Germany three times since the death of Stalin, alternately savaging the Communist economy of East Germany with Stygian demands and then relenting with completely unprecedented softness of manner, the Russians have provoked not only the startling uprising of Berlin and East German workers, but also the vastest confusion and anticipation in Bonn leadership.

Until the spring of 1953, the diplomacy of Konrad Adenauer had the solid backing of the majority of West German citizens, and upon this diplomacy rested all Allied planning. No shrewder record of statesmanship has been written in Europe than the policy pursued by the aging Chancellor of Germany, emerging at the age of sixty-nine from years of disgrace under Hitler, with no more imposing previous experience than that of Burgomeister of Cologne. Adenauer has acted with such dignity that none of Germany's bitterest enemies can accuse him of duplicity. Yet, at the same time, he has prepared a platform from which any, even the most disturbingly dangerous, German ambition can, in the future, be pursued with ease.

The diplomacy of Adenauer and the West has appealed, essentially, to two strains of Germans who together, up to now, have made a majority. These two strains can be roughly summarized as the Germans who saw European Union as a means and the Germans who saw it as both a means and an end. Neither Adenauer nor his majority have ever regarded Eastern Germany as lost; they accepted only the fact that Germany was powerless to free her eastern marches without enormously powerful allies in the West. But one large school of Adenauer supporters saw the policy of European Union only as a device to gain those allies who might be useful in reconquering the East and defending what was already free. The other saw his policy not only as a means of amplifying German strength but also as an end in itself—a new community which might mollify the ugly harshness of German history in a larger social, cultural and religious union with gentler and more humane standards.

Whether the policies of Konrad Adenauer can carry Germany forward through the elections of 1953 on to the consummation of the European state depends, more than anything else, on the reading the Russians finally make of the German problem. Up to now Adenauer has been flanked by enemies—from the Socialist Left to the Nationalist Right—who have held that he underestimates German strength. Where Adenauer has insisted that Germany is not strong enough to go forward alone, they have held that Germany is. Adenauer's enemies have insisted that only by bargaining on her own can Germany swing her weight back and forth between East and West, and peel the Russians back from the eastern provinces of the nation. To which Adenauer has always been able to reply that there was not the slightest trace of Russian willingness to bargain, or even to consider the acid test of free elections throughout Germany. This answer has always been sufficient to hold Germany in place in the Western scheme of things because the Russians have been up to now so adamant. Should the Russians suddenly decide it serves their purpose to soften on German Unity, to trade back Eastern Germany in return for a guaranteed neutral, but whole, Germany, they may be able to split the Adenauer majority in two and reduce him and his wretched coalition to a minority.

It is impossible to believe that the Russians with their network of agents and Communist party zealots have been, or are, unaware of all these contrary impulses playing back and forth within the Western world. Yet, by the time Joseph Stalin died, it must have been obvious that despite these contrary impulses, something was happening to force them together in two great associations of hostile power—the organs of European Union and the organs of the Atlantic Community. It must have been equally obvious that Russian intransigence and the stubbornness of the supreme dictator had provided the glue and the force to make such new groupings stick. For six years, the Western world had been permitted to move forward, uninterrupted, organizing that complex of power and politics which brought the Russian advance in Europe to a halt. No conversations with Moscow, no serious negotiations had impeded the work; indeed, each new clash of arms or words had speeded it.

Nineteen fifty-three is thus a cut-off year. Now, at last, fresher intelligence in Moscow, shrewder minds, since they are uncommitted by past blunders, are permitted to re-examine the European scene. There they find, as before, the old contrary impulses, the old diversities and the old hatreds. Yet they find them capped, or almost so, by new institutions which, if they become permanent, may forever deny Russia the opportunity she so casually let slip six years ago. To disrupt them Russia must act fast and with new tactics. Let us look at these institutions and see how much vitality they have, within and without, to face whatever the Russians may do next.

PART

3

XII

the making of Europe

The dream of Europe is so old that no one knows who first dreamed it.

The dream begins somewhere in the days of the Romans. For the Romans, when they disappeared from history, left not only those gaunt and sun-bleached ruins which stretch like giant skeletons casting shadows over little mortals from Scotland to Timgad, but also an afterthought of unity which glowed all through the centuries of darkness that followed their passing.

This memory of Europe-as-one has haunted Europeans ever since. From Charlemagne through Napoleon to Hitler, soldiers and madmen have tried to hammer Europe together, in Caesar's image, slave to their single will. Scholars and statesmen, men of good will, wild idealists and scheming intriguers alike have found their thoughts shaped by this memory. Philosophers and financiers, poets and wanderers have been unable to rid themselves of it.

But Rome left more than a memory. It bequeathed to Europe the same sounds for the same meanings, the same tincture of law, the same code of honor and *respublica.* This common culture and thought persisted all through the dark ages in an interchange of art and learning across all national boundaries down almost to our own days. For centuries, Englishmen, Frenchmen, Flemings, Germans, Italians, Spaniards found it natural to pay their dues and give obeisance to a distant church in Rome whose Pope might be an Englishman, Frenchman, German, Spaniard or Italian. Until yesterday few Europeans thought it strange that Leonardo da Vinci, born in Italy, should come to die as a retainer of the French king and be buried by the banks of the Loire. Nor did anyone find it strange that Handel, born in Lower Saxony, should come to live in England and refashion the island's music. Not until this decade, looking back, has anyone marveled that during the wars of Napoleon and England, the greatest scientist of England, Sir Humphry Davy, should be invited by the French to Paris, be given his passport by the English government, and cross the channel to lecture on his scientific findings in an enemy country, and then return home, no less honored and respected than before.

The dream and the common culture have always been there. But never until our time has the compulsion to union been great enough to force action. Until our time, the nations of Europe rose so powerfully above the barbarian lands that neighbored them or lay across the oceans that neither prosperity nor security required Europeans to bow to common laws and leadership. In our time, in a world of rival, emergent giants none of the little states of Europe (except possibly England) can hope to win a livelihood out of the world by itself, and not even England can guarantee alone the safety of its citizens. This simple thought, occurring to thousands of Europeans at the same time, has brought Europe for the first time to sober consideration of Union. The dream is not new—only the effort to achieve it is new.

The Union of Europe, as an active force in the power politics of today, was begun with two distinct projects launched in the pivotal year of 1950. (A third was to be added later, but that was not until 1953.) The first project was born out of hope, before the Korean War, the hope that Europe might be united economically for the welfare of its citizens; it was called the Schuman Plan. The second was born out of fear, after the Korean War; its purpose was to unite Europe in a community of defense, with its own European Army, to guarantee the safety of its citizens from Russian attack. These two separate projects have interlocked ever since and in their interlocking they have now strengthened, now weakened one another. But they were as distinct in origin as hope and fear, and they have separate histories.

Long before 1950, to be sure, the scenery of Europe had been crowded with schemes, organs, councils, committees and treaties which, all of them, paid lip service to the ideal of United Europe. Professors in universities lectured to their students; students burned their passports at frontier boundaries; thyroidal women lobbied their legislators; people of every class and faith demanded their governments hasten to make European Union. In 1949 twelve European governments set up a nonsensical body called the Council of Europe in the town of Strasbourg in France. But the Council of Europe was an advisory gathering that could talk, yet do nothing; it was the sounding board of men without jobs, political figures outcast in their own countries who could recapture the illusion of their own importance by making bold statements to other distinguished out-of-office statesmen in a foreign forum. It was a boneyard of great names—out-of-office Spaak of Belgium, out-of-office Churchill of England, out-of-office Reynaud of France. Each charmed the others with his wisdom, but they bore no responsibility. The Council of Europe had the same relation to the real mechanics of European politics as the Good Government League used to have to the politics of Boston, Massachusetts.

The men who did hold office and who bore responsibility moved very much more carefully when European cooperation was urged on them. In 1948 they signed the Brussels Pact, the little defense coalition that preceded NATO, but the Brussels Pact invited little more than old-fashioned staff conversations between generals. In 1948, similarly, they had been forced by American pressure to gather together in the Organization for European Economic Cooperation in Paris, where they had to divide the billions of Marshall Plan aid.

But when the governments tried to go beyond such limited organs, when they tried to satisfy American insistence that European Union was essential for regeneration, they ran into trouble. Strange and wonderful names and projects stuttered from the pens of bureaucrats turned dreamers. The most illuminating of all these was something called Fritalux. Fritalux was to be a great economic union of France, Italy and the Benelux countries. Someone suggested that the name Fritalux sounded like a Mexican potato chip so the name was changed to Finebel, to cover the same country initials. But whether as Fritalux or Finebel, the scheme would not work. It would not work because the economic life of the participating countries was wedged about Germany as a centerpiece and without Germany the fragments fell apart. Germany dwelt, still, in the outer purdah of rejection and the old enemies could not yet bring themselves to forgiveness or reconciliation. Thus, in the winter of 1949–1950, without any announcement, at a quiet dinner at the French Foreign Office at the Quai d'Orsay the foreign ministers decided to let Finebel die.

"Europe," as a concept like "peace," had thus been heavy on Europe's mind for a long time before the moment of the decisive act. The moment, to be precise, was the last week end of April in the year 1950. The place was a thatched-roof cottage in the village of Houjarray, twenty-seven miles outside of Paris. The man was a short, dumpy individual whose balding head, solid face and sharp nose expressed untold generations of French peasant descent. His name was Jean Monnet, and that Sunday afternoon he had invited four young aides to come to his cottage to talk about an idea he had been quietly nursing for some time. This idea, which was to be known in a few days as the Schuman Plan, had several striking novelties: first, that European Union could be achieved only by creating a supersovereign Authority to which its member states would yield totally federal powers of action in whatever matters required common action; secondly, that this European Union must include Germany, and that France, as Germany's most ancient enemy, should make the first gestures of reconciliation; thirdly, that the Union should begin by striking at the roots of the suspicion where they dug deepest into Franco-German hatred—in the Ruhr. The Plan would lift Germany's Ruhr and France's rival Lorraine out of the supervision of national governments to be subordinate to a new supranational High Authority which should have the power to govern, tax, order, condemn or create all enterprises of coal, iron and steel in France, in Germany and in any other European country that cared to join the new pool. Monnet's young men thought it was a fine idea.

If a United Europe is created in our time, then Jean Monnet will probably be revered centuries hence as its patron saint. This majestic little man, tart of tongue, brusque of manner, never elected by any vote to any public office, has remained the most mysterious major public figure of modern times because of the peculiar nature of his art. His art is the brokerage of ideas, in which he is certainly Europe's, and quite possibly the world's, greatest dealer. This art is far more difficult than that of the intellectual who spins the ideas. Monnet's skill lies in recognizing a valid idea, knowing the men to whom it can be sold, sensing the time when they need it, and then locating the technicians to make the ideas work. Monnet has been practicing this craft for some forty years; he has sold ideas in turn to Clemenceau and Lloyd George, Chiang Kai-shek and T. V. Soong, Churchill, Roosevelt and de Gaulle. In his time he had been, by turn, one of the shrewdest cognac salesmen of the world, the boy-wonder of France's World War I war effort, a powerful international civil servant, a banking wizard, a brilliant World War II industrial mobilizer and a great patriot before he settled into peaceful eminence as chief of France's postwar national plan, which bears his name.

It was Monnet's position as the Chief National Planner of France that gave him the base from which he could insert his new idea into European politics. Housed in a gray four-story building on the Left Bank of Paris, divorced from the turbulence and shrieks of everyday French politics, Monnet with a devoted staff of thirty brain trusters sat in constant, thoughtful analysis of inflation, taxation, defense, foreign policy and the future. Governments came and went in France. But Monnet remained at the Rue Martignac permanently, explaining to each new set of ministers exactly what had to be done, as a schoolmaster instructs each new set of bright and aspiring students. His prestige and influence on the Cabinets of France rested on his personality, his mind and the knowledge that he alone, divorced from partisan politics, was thinking about France as France.

Europe might have been created anyway, for too many minds and too many forces were all pushing Europeans in the same direction. The accident of French politics, however, made it happen that Monnet's idea should germinate at just that moment when it should find the most support in the crew of perplexed men who made France's Cabinet. At that moment the Foreign Minister of France was Robert Schuman, its Premier, Georges Bidault, its Defense Minister, René Pleven. Each of these three key men had a peculiar vested interest either in Franco-German friendship, in European Union or in Jean Monnet.

Robert Schuman, the Foreign Minister, was the most important. This benign and grandfatherly old man is as curious a political specimen as the history of Europe can throw up. A bachelor, with an oval, gnomelike face, he is devoutly Catholic, the most religious man in all his religious party, the MRP. Moreover, he was born in the border country of French Lorraine, in the days when French

Lorraine was German territory under the Kaiser's flag. He was brought up to speak German, had studied in German universities and did not become French until the Treaty of Versailles restored the tricolor to Lorraine. Then, as a local Lorraine politician, he was elected to the French National Assembly and served through the interwar years as one of its most inconspicuous members. The surge of Catholic revival in postwar France made the party that Schuman joined in 1945—the MRP—the only permanent participant in all postwar French governments and elevated Schuman successively to Finance Minister, Premier and Foreign Minister, a post he held from 1948 to the end of 1952. As Foreign Minister, Schuman had one passionate dream: to end the timeless feud of France and Germany, to blend the two cultures and societies in which he had been nursed in Lorraine.

When, therefore, on Monday, May the first, after driving into town from his Sunday discussion at Houjarray, Jean Monnet visited the Foreign Minister to explain his scheme for a Franco-German coal-steel pool, he found Schuman an attentive listener. Schuman had just returned from a visit to Bonn, the capital of the new German Republic, where, as the representative of punitive France, he had met a frigid reception. A sensitive man, Schuman was seeking some token to offer Germany as an earnest of his good will. Schuman liked Monnet's project, accepted it, offered to give it his name and bring it before the Cabinet. Thus was christened the Schuman Plan.

The Premier of France at that moment was Georges Bidault. Bidault, a dapper, brilliant, witty little man who had been a history professor before the war had done more to shape the doctrines of liberal Catholicism that generated the MRP than any other thinker. Of these doctrines none is more important than European Union. But Bidault had served during the German Occupation with exquisite daring and utterly reckless courage as chief of the underground Council of National Resistance and he had emerged from the war with two emotional residues. The first was the memory he bore of comrades tortured and killed by the Germans during the Occupation. "Many things change with time—Germany is something that never changes," Bidault had publicly observed in 1946 when he was Foreign Minister. The second residue was his religious conviction, shared by his whole party, that Europe must be reunited under the high arch of Christendom. Bidault's bitterness against the Germans had faded somewhat with the years; his belief in European Union had grown. When Schuman brought Monnet's proposal to the Premier, the Premier was ready to accept it and let it become France's official policy.

There was only one other hurdle in the Cabinet to be cleared—the Army and the Defense Ministry, bearers of a tradition of battle with Germany that went back three hundred years. But the Defense Ministry at that moment was headed by René Pleven, a burly, practical businessman from Brittany whose personal devotion to Jean Monnet was complete. Pleven, in his youth, had once held a job in one of Monnet's business enterprises. Now, in his maturity, he still remembered Jean Monnet as the master. Whenever Pleven, in the various reshuffles of French politics, fell from the Cabinet, Monnet cleared office and desk space in the National Plan Building to house the displaced Minister. If Monnet thought the coal-steel pool was a good idea, then Pleven did too, and the Defense Ministry would go along.

Thus, eight days later, on May 9, 1950, Foreign Minister Schuman summoned the press of the world to the gilt and cream Salon de l'Horloge in the Foreign Office to hear his announcement that France would launch Europe now. France invited Germany and all European states to join in freely electing men to a supranational High Authority which would have sovereign power over their most basic industries.

One must see European business life as it is to understand how revolutionary the Schuman Plan sounded in May of 1950.

All of Western Europe can fit into less than a quarter of the United States, snuggling comfortably, with room to spare, in the states bounded on the south by the Ohio River and on the west by the Mississippi. But this quarter-size continent has been cut up by so many artificial national barriers of tariffs, quotas, licenses and currencies that normal commercial and industrial exchange has been an obstacle race. For a century each nation has tricked its freight rates to cheat the traffic of its neighbors; for a generation national regulations and discrimination have throttled enterprising producers and deprived them of the continental markets and competition that might have made them efficient. Behind these national barriers have grown up the feudal autonomies of cartels and trusts, sharing among each other a fixed portion of this national market, their production only remotely urged to competitive efficiency, their customers forced to accept dictatorial prices and terms.

The Schuman Plan proposed to drive a breach through these walls. Of all the offending industries—textiles, automobiles, food, industrial equipment, machinery—none was more offensive to common sense than the coal and steel industry, and it was the coal and steel industry the Schuman Plan proposed to tackle. Coal and steel in Europe mock by their very distribution the artificial barriers of nation and flag. The largest iron ore reserves of Europe lie in French Lorraine. Only one hundred and fifty miles north lie the finest beds of coking coal in Europe—in Germany's Ruhr. Industrially, they fit together like nut and bolt, like the coal of Pennsylvania and the iron ore of the Upper Mesabi. But the bitter hatred of Frenchmen and Germans had divided them by invisible walls: by cartel rules, by customs, by double pricing so that one price was charged within the possessing country and a penalty price was charged outside, by quota allocations, and by pure national jealousy and orneriness.

The Schuman Plan now declared that in the jungle of European commercial life it would clear channels for iron and coal to flow free of all customs, free of all discrimination, simply as efficiency required and supply and demand dictated. Within the Plan, to be sure, were buried the elements of a cold-blooded bargain. French heavy industry has always, historically, been starved for coking coal, and Hitler, in the days of his hegemony, turned France's supply of German coking coal on and off like a faucet, starving or feeding French Lorraine as he chose. Since the war, as a victor, France had wrung coking coal out of Germany by main force and had joined with the other victors in shackling Germany's steel production at a limit of 11,100,000 tons a year. The businessman's bargain in the Schuman Plan was simple: Germany would make her coal available to all Europeans, including Frenchmen, on terms of commercial equality. France, in turn, in an act of unprecedented generosity, would intercede with the Allies to lift all controls from German steel and heavy industry so that she would be free to compete once more as a free nation.

But the structure built to seal this simple bargain was much more elaborate than required for the mechanics of iron and steel alone. The Schuman Plan, as it unfolded in negotiation, envisioned the creation of a new, germinal community that would grow to shelter much more than coal and steel. Sovereignty, the fundamental power of regulation and control over heavy industry, would be removed forever from each national parliament or government. It would be transferred to a High Authority of nine men nominated by their governments, but, once nominated by their governments, these nine men would be responsible to an Assembly chosen by all the contracting powers jointly. Together, the Authority and Assembly would be suprasovereign. It would hold true power over men wherever they dug coal out of mines, wherever they tapped the furnace to channel hot iron gushing from the tap, wherever they spun the rollers and squeezed the steel, white-hot and glimmering, into given shapes. It would be able to tax these activities, wipe away any national tariff or quota on their product, police their prices and rates, require governments to eliminate any freight rate it thought discriminatory. It could underwrite investment, build housing for the workers, be able to open the books of any businessman dealing in steel and coal, prevent, with powers modeled on those of the American anti-trust laws, any combination of producers or merchants persisting in their ancient restraint of trade.

Moreover, whenever it acted in any of these functions, no national government could interfere with it. In itself, the High Authority of the Plan was sovereign above the powers of the states, as the American government is sovereign in its constitutional limits above the individual American states. In the minds of Monnet and Schuman, as in the minds of the Belgians, Dutchmen, Italians, Luxembourgers and Germans who worked out the details of the compact, this High Authority was only the beginning. Coal and steel were only the first step. The perspective drawn then, and the perspective that remains today, is for an Authority which constantly widens its powers until all economic life in Europe is regulated, not by individual states, but by the supranational Authority. Only then will Europeans have the opportunity to think in the giant, expanding terms of modern technology which is the base of human welfare and comfort.

Today in Europe the High Authority of the Community of Coal and Steel is already a reality.

Much nonsense has been written about the making of the common market in Europe, as if it alone were the guarantee of human welfare. At Luxembourg today, where the Schuman Plan is directed, its leaders insist on underlining that it is not a guarantee. It is the opportunity; it is up to Europeans to seize and make the most of it.

The second shove to European Union was given six months later in October of 1950, when France proposed to the world that Europe pool not only its coal and iron but its flesh and blood in an enterprise called the Community of Defense which should have an army of its own, a European Army.

The European Defense Community, or EDC, began with Korea. In the military panic that followed the outbreak of war, the State Department of the United States became convinced of the soundness of a view which the generals of the Pentagon had long argued without success. It was that if the Russians were to be fought in Europe, the most useful people to organize in arms were the Germans who had once almost destroyed the Russians singlehanded. By late summer of 1950 both French and British statesmen learned, to their consternation, that the United States government proposed to arm the Germans at once in order to bolster the handful of Western troops in Central Germany. The British wavered on the proposition, now against, now for. But when Robert Schuman arrived in New York in September of 1950, he found that after some indecision Ernest Bevin, the Foreign Minister of Britain, had finally decided that the Americans, in the cold calculation of military arithmetic, were right. Faced with a solid Anglo-American determination to arm the Germans once more, the Foreign Minister of France was in quandary. Under pressure, he agreed at once to strike the limits off Germany's steel production and let her produce all the furnaces could pour, provided it went to Western defense. But to agree to the arming of a nation which had thrice ravaged France in the memory of living men, was something else again. Schuman, with his great compassion for the Germans, had led the French to the unprecedented generosity of the Schuman Plan, an offer which had struck the manacles from German muscles and implicitly forsworn the reparations which were France's due for the destruction Germany had done to her. The Schuman Plan could be explained to Frenchmen as an act of common sense, for one could bring the delinquent back to decency only by giving him a decent opportunity to earn a decent living. But it was something else to give a delinquent Germany arms again so swiftly after she had so shockingly abused them. Schuman insisted that the proposal for arming Germany had to be brought back for consideration by the French Cabinet and the whole French Parliament.

The dilemma that faced both Americans and Frenchmen in the next six weeks was one of those poignant and terrible problems in which right and logic are so evenly divided that protagonists starting from sound but differing premises can reach equally sound but contradictory conclusions.

The American case was simply that the French had appealed over and over for American troops to come and fight in defense of Western Europe. Congress had just promised to send four more American divisions to help those defenses. But our generals, the men responsible for the lives of our troops, insisted that these alone were not enough to resist the Russians or protect their own lives. In those days it was impossible to foresee the Russian response in Germany, or to envisage the elaborate machinery which SHAPE and NATO would build up to give us armed superiority in Central Europe, without the Germans. If the generals' gift of foresight was weak, their logic was implacable. If the French would not put up another twelve divisions of troops to brace the line against the Russians—which physically they could not do—how could they deny the Americans the right to recruit from Germany the necessary dozen divisions to brace that line?

The French answer, swelling out of honest emotion, clothed itself in sound logic. No French minister raised the memory of evil that Germans had done in the past, nor did the new French Minister of National Defense, Jules Moch, cite the memory of his son who had been captured and murdered as an underground resistant during the German Occupation. They were perfectly willing, said the French, to have Germans fight Russians and die in defense of France—after all, Germans had always made the best mercenaries in the Foreign Legion. But what the Americans proposed was something else again, something unheard of in history—a one-way army, a German legion built to march only East, never West. Given Germany's history, it was unlikely that any new German Army would be a docile tool of Western policy. From Bismarck through Rapallo to the Pact of 1939, Germany had grown powerful by swinging its weight back and forth between Russia and Western Europe. Who could guarantee that in five years Germany would not stand as arbiter, the balance wheel between two world blocs, playing one against the other for its own advantage? Who could guarantee that even if Germany remained loyal to the West, she would not send her National Army plunging across the dividing line between West and East Germany to recover her lost territories, thus dragging all the rest of the Atlantic Alliance with her in that war against Russia the West was trying so desperately to avoid?

The French could not say "No" and could not say "Yes." Therefore they said "Europe."

Rising to the rostrum of the crowded National Assembly in the late afternoon of October 24, 1950, speaking in his usual high-pitched, strong but melancholy voice, René Pleven—by now Premier of France—presented the Pleven Plan. By the Pleven Plan, Germans would be brought to arms again, but there would be no *German* Army, *German* General Staff, *German* divisions; neither would there be *French*, *Belgian*, *Italian* or any other kind of divisions and armies in Europe. Instead there would be a great new *European* Army in which all the troops of all the European powers would be scrambled, this army subordinate to one supranational Authority, controlled by one great European parliament, chosen as the Assembly of the Schuman Plan was, by all the states of Europe. Where the Schuman Plan had proposed to submit only coal, iron and steel to an international sovereign, the Pleven Plan proposed to submit every man in Western Europe to a new international loyalty. The new sovereign would write the defense budget of every country in Europe, train youths in international schools as brother officers, organize them in the "smallest possible unit of command" so as to get the widest mixing of tongues and nations, and when necessary, summon them to die in defense of their common brotherhood. It was the first time in history that any nation had offered to give up control of its own army, its own lives, its essential power to act and tax, its flag and its glories to a new master, as yet unborn.

When René Pleven stepped down from the rostrum to the mixed reception of his thunderstruck fellow colleagues, he had changed the politics of Europe. He had scrambled all its elements together in a tangle which has ensnared the intercourse of nations ever since. He had scrambled the strategy and logistics of the generals with the idealism and dreams of its visionaries; he had altered Germany's position in the world, wrenching her not only out of the frame of East-West negotiation but also out of every context in which the Western Allies had discussed Germany among themselves. Most of all, he had taken two crystalline and separate problems—one military, the other political—and fused them together.

It was eight months before the final fusion—or confusion, as some would have it—took the form in which it has ever since presented itself.

A month after the Pleven proposal, the United States, unsure whether it wanted European Union or German troops most, consented at the Brussels meeting of the NATO powers to an exploration of the Pleven proposal. But at the same time, through NATO, it insisted that Konrad Adenauer be invited to explore with Allied generals how to raise German troops at once in Germany. These explorations began simultaneously in two parallel sets of discussions, one in Paris, one at the Petersburger Hof in Germany. From January to July of the next year, these discussions went their separate ways, like a two-ring circus, with spectators bobbing their heads back and forth to find out what was going on.

The discussions in Paris pleased the French, for these were framed by the political principles of the Pleven Plan. A delegation of nondescript Germans arrived in Paris early in February, 1951, to be installed in a shabby four-room suite at the Hotel d'Orsay, where entrance to their offices were made through a toilet. The delegation, headed by a tired old sexagenarian named Dr. Roediger, was faced with a French delegation captained by such a man of skill as Hervé Alphand, the Foreign Office's slickest negotiator. The French dominated the Paris discussions. They outlined their image of the European Army—German regimental units of 3,000 or 4,000 men each would be recruited under international officers and trained under an international flag. As these Germans became combat-worthy, the French and other European powers would convert regiments and divisions into international units too. Finally, when the Germans filled their quota, all the French Army in Europe would enter the European Army too. Then the new flag would be raised, and the new army would be entirely subordinate to the sovereign international defense community.

The Germans would hear nothing of such a proposal. They felt that regimental combat units were only bits and pieces of strength, in no sense an army. As a proud and resurgent people, asked to bear arms, conscious of their bargaining power, they declared it monstrous that Germans should be recruited as Foreign Legionnaires, internationally commanded from the word go, while the French clung to their army until the day when it should be incorporated as a compact mass to become the crowning striking force of a European Army already dominated by a French staff.

The Germans preferred the proposals of the Petersburger Hof conferences, which focused on the military nature of Germany's contribution. These discussions pleased the United States Army too. The United States Army wanted German troops, flesh and blood soldiers, quickly, not a long philosophical discussion about the creation of a new superstate. Philosophers might talk at Paris, but soldiers talked at the Petersburger Hof. From the dustbin of history, Konrad Adenauer retrieved two Wehrmacht generals, Speidel and Heusinger, to speak for him. These generals-in-mufti arrived promptly on the morning of January 9 at the Petersburger Hof with their scheme of Western defense and Germany's contribution to it. After four months of talking at the Petersburger Hof, it turned out that what Germany wanted was some 250,000 troops as a starter, to be recruited over four years, complete with a German General Staff and a German war industry, responsible to a German War Minister who would associate them with other European troops in a coalition whose type was familiar from wars gone by. The force the Germans envisioned was twelve heavily armored divisions, the equipment to be contributed and paid for by the United States, of course, until the Ruhr could once more resume the manufacture of arms.

By early summer of 1951 the scenery of Europe was so tangled with contradictions that no man could describe precisely what was happening. The talks at the Petersburger Hof offered a neatly packaged symbol of the confusion. The French delegate to the military discussions was General Jean Ganneval, but General Ganneval was also the senior French general on the Military Security Board set up some years before to make sure that Germany did not rearm surreptitiously. Mornings, General Ganneval would cross the Rhine and sweep up the mountaintop to the Petersburger Hof to discuss with the Americans, the British and the Generals Speidel and Heusinger how Germany should be rearmed. Afternoons, he would drive down to Coblenz to the Military Security Board where he met with another set of generals to discuss with them how Germany should be kept disarmed.

By mid-July of 1951, a full year after the American government had decided that German rearmament was essential to American defense, it surveyed a Europe in which tables were piled high with documents and memoranda, estimates and constitutions, but in which nothing remotely resembling a European Union or a German Army seemed to be forming. It was at this point that a single individual took a lone decision, and by this decision shaped all American policy in Europe. He affirmed that European Union and German rearmament were, as the French suggested, equally and inseparably interwoven in the need of American security. He was then the most eminent soldier in the United States Army and his name was Dwight D. Eisenhower.

The intervention of General Eisenhower in the making of Europe was the climax of an American attitude which had been slowly forming since the war.

Americans had, for many years, been loftily instructing Europeans in the virtues of their own great Union of States, and chiding Europe on the stupidities of its rivalries and separatisms. During the war several American brain trusters had even toyed with the idea that, come Liberation, it would be best to sweep away all the currencies of the Liberation countries and replace them with one new common European currency issued by the United States Army. But these attitudes did not add up to policy, and as late as 1948 the enabling act of the Marshall Plan contained not a single pre-echo of the demands for European Union which later were tacked on every proposal made in Washington for export to Europe.

It was the Marshall Plan that hardened American conviction that Europeans must unite. The Marshall Planners faced a problem. To deal with eighteen-odd European nations gathered in the OEEC, each with its contradictory problems, was baffling, wasteful and inefficient. To deal with them individually was impossible. Italy could not solve her unemployment problem unless other European countries let her citizens migrate. Belgians complained that their azalea and lace merchants were going bankrupt because England forbade the import of azaleas and lace. Dutch artichoke farmers wailed that German restrictions choked their traditional market in the Ruhr. Everyone complained that French inflation was infecting all European trade. The Marshall Planners had no desire to arbitrate these petty and obscure European disputes. They wanted to speak to a leadership to whom they might say, "This is what America will do. Now, what will Europe do?" Over and over, the Americans prodded the Europeans to give the OEEC more power, more authority and a single, vigorous, executive head. When visiting Congressmen asked the Marshall Planners what they were trying to do, they would answer, "We're trying to pull them together, we're trying to integrate them." "Integration" was a convenient word and each successive delegation asked sternly, "How far have you got with integration now?" as if expecting the Marshall Plan to pull out of its desk drawer a draft constitution for Europe and a design for a European flag.

By 1949, in the second appropriation of the Marshall Plan, Congress, without debate, set the unification of Europe as one of the major purposes of the Plan. The Schuman Plan, when announced in 1950, soon became the favorite foster child of American influence in Europe.

But the Korean War injected a second purpose into American policy in Europe. This was the rearmament of the Germans. The perilous military imbalance of forces in Central Europe made German troops appear, momentarily, as the quickest and easiest increment to Western strength. This correspondent has tried since 1950 to find out how, when and where the American government decided to rearm the Germans. The decision is certainly one of the most important in history; yet it has never been the subject of public debate or analysis, although, like most American foreign policy decisions, it will probably be a subject of long post-mortems. By September of 1950, however, it *was* American policy to arm the Germans, and by December of 1950 the Germans had been officially invited to the muster.

The first half of 1951 thus found American purpose in Europe utterly schizophrenic. It wanted European Union. And it wanted German troops. There seemed to be much talk, little progress, and Washington's patience frayed. Early in July of 1951, therefore, Secretary of State Dean Acheson cabled the American legates in Paris that, in effect, he had had it. He had been in consultation with Mr. Jessup and the two suggested that, to please the French, conversation about the constitutional structure of the European Defense Community should continue uninterrupted. But that while the talk went on, so should the recruiting of German troops, which should be begun at once.

To American diplomats in Europe, zealously nursing the Schuman Plan through its weary round of ratifications, the suggestion seemed most unfortunately timed. The Germans had already seen the limits on their steel industry struck away as soon as the Korean War broke out. If now they were to be given in addition national armed force immediately, they might think twice before ratifying the Schuman Plan.

The proposal from Washington seemed to strike a blow at the very heart of the theories of European Union that had developed among Americans in Europe and particularly in the Paris embassy. For, though European Union was explained to Congressmen and others sometimes as a noble and altruistic venture, sometimes as a practical economic solution to European business difficulties, there was much harder-headed American thinking involved than that. European Union was a way to control Germany. For Germany had been even more dangerous to America than Russia has been in this century and might become so again. European Union was a diplomatic device to make use of the enormous energies of the German people, yet so harness them politically that they might not turn on us. The Germans understood this, but they liked the Schuman Plan, for it had been presented to them as an act of generosity (which it was), releasing them from the servile state of vanquished enemy to honorable equality in democratic union. Now, if the Germans were to be given troops and released anyway, it might be better in their eyes to have honorable independence untrammeled by any union.

At this point General Eisenhower intervened. Eisenhower had come under various influences as Commander in Chief of SHAPE, where he served twelve Allied governments. He had found his job, as he put it, "a can of worms." He had learned, as had the Marshall Planners, how exhausting it is to deal with a dozen different governments each with its own traditional area of sensitivity. Like the Marshall Planners he yearned for the beautiful simplicity of dealing with a package of nations called Europe. Moreover, he had come under the influence of two extraordinarily persuasive personalities. The first of these was Jean Monnet, who had been introduced to Eisenhower by a mutual friend, John McCloy, the American High Commissioner in Germany, a staunch supporter of the Schuman Plan and strong European Union man. The second was David K. E. Bruce, the most accomplished American Ambassador to air his talents in Paris since Benjamin Franklin. Bruce, an experienced diplomat, politician, soldier and businessman, was also an amateur historian and art-lover, a man of exquisite civilization and firm courage, who possessed as clearly and vividly the convictions of United Europe as did Jean Monnet.

Under the influence of Bruce and Monnet and under the pressure of his job at SHAPE, Eisenhower had become by early July, 1951, what the cynics call a "hot-gospel" European Union man. Speaking now with the heavy responsibility of commander of American and Allied forces in Europe, Eisenhower flatly rejected Acheson's proposal that Germans be recruited forthwith. Eisenhower pointed out that if it was true that Europe could not be victoriously defended without the Germans, it was equally true that the Germans could not be invited to bear arms over French objections. For strategically and geographically the French were even more necessary than the Germans for defense of the Continent. If the Germans were to be armed, they must be armed, said Eisenhower, in a way that would strengthen rather than weaken the association of powers in the Atlantic Alliance. This meant a European Army, or it meant nothing.

From then on European Union was Eisenhower's baby. A twist of French politics aided Eisenhower in breaking the deadlocked negotiations. The French elections of June, 1951, had been followed by the usual Cabinet crisis and negotiations were in the hands of caretaker civil servants, not Cabinet members. Chief among these civil servants were Jean Monnet and Hervé Alphand. Now, under the twin pressures of Eisenhower and Bruce, the French negotiators consented to a radical revision of the carefully qualified original Pleven Plan. The French negotiators now agreed that equality meant that Germans should have units just as large as French Army units (called "groupements" to avoid the ugly word "divisions," which the French Assembly would not countenance), and that from the moment of the ratification of the treaty, all units —French, Belgian, German, Italian, Dutch—should come under the same international control. Eisenhower's soldier staff at SHAPE then hammered out the military structure of the new compact—its divisional sizes and tables of organization, its air and armor complements, its command staff. Bruce's brilliant civilian staff hammered through the political structure of the compact—the nature of sovereign assembly and authority, of ministerial control and supervision, of budget and taxes. In Germany, the American High Commission subjected the government of Konrad Adenauer to the same kind of pressure. No opposition was encountered in Italy, always enthusiastic for any kind of European Union; the Belgians and Dutch governments protested feebly at the draft compact, which cut so much out of their authority over their own citizens, but these were small states and they were steam-rollered.

It would be pleasant to write that the making of Europe has come upon her people like the sun after a storm, that they have danced in the streets, raised flags to their housetops, held their babies up to see the faces of the bold men who proposed this revolution.

But it is not so. Perhaps no event in history has been accepted so cautiously by those who wished it most. It has been accepted as men accept surgery performed on their bodies, not out of joy, but because they feel it necessary and can see no way, honestly, to escape it.

Only rarely in my traveling in Europe have I heard people bring up the subject of Union outside of those capitals where politicians congregate.

Once, when I was in Germany, I visited the University of Heidelberg and stayed to chat with the officers of the student council. Of the four student officers, three had been soldiers in the Wehrmacht during the war. They were clean-cut, attractive young men and one of them still limped from his war wound. They were, all of them, disillusioned with politics and shrugged at the parties that the new Germany had thrown up. One of them volunteered he would never fight again for anything, not even to free East Germany from the Russians.

I asked him, "Isn't there anything you want to do in Germany, any purpose you think is important?" He said, after long thought, "Yes, Europe. I think there must be a Europe. These little countries are old-fashioned. Europe is something to work for." "But why," I asked, "why are you so enthusiastic, why don't other Europeans talk like that?"

They thought for a while and one of them said, "I was an officer in the war. I fought from Normandy to Budapest, I was in France and in Poland. Germans are the only people who have ever seen how this continent can work when it is all one. And it can work. We know what it can do. It must work."

I have heard occasional businessmen talk like this too. One was an American. He had come to Europe to manufacture ball-point pens when the ball-point pen seemed the greatest invention in writing since the stylus. He moaned about doing business in Europe: "Did you every try to do business in nine currencies and make them balance in dollars? I have Finnish marks, German marks and Danish marks. I have French francs, Belgian francs and Swiss francs. I'm bankrupt in one currency, even in another and rich in several others, and they're all blocked and I can't balance them off. You go crazy trying to figure out whether a profit in a blocked currency is really a profit, or is it a loss, and what does a loss in a free currency mean?" I asked him why he didn't quit. But he wouldn't quit. "You can do things in Europe you can't do even in America. The ball-point pen was a flop in America; it was no good, no one researched it or engineered it. But in Europe I have nine factories, with nine kinds of engineers and nine kinds of brains working on it. The pens I make here are better than any I make in America, and it'll be better yet. No one can touch the Finnish know-how in plastics; we're putting in Finnish plastic extrusion machines in all our plants. The Dutch know all about inks. The French are magnificent on styling; they know more about anodizing aluminum in any shade or color than anybody else in the world. The French figure out the most ingenious machines for making parts; then I give them to the Germans who make the machines sturdy and simple. My chief shop practice engineer in France is a girl from Israel; my chief research engineer is a German; the physical research on the nature of inks and vacuum is being done for me at the University of Leyden in Holland. When you put these brains together, nothing in the United States can touch the pool. If I could make this Europe work, the sky'd be the limit."

The most ardent advocates of European Union that I have found in Europe have been politicians. Politicians are usually men of more than average intelligence trying to do what their voters want them to do, and most of them are frustrated almost to despair by the compromises they must make between logic and popular passion. In the past three years in Europe, scores of politicians have climbed aboard the bandwagon of European Union for the two reasons which make it most promising: they think they can clean up some of the nastiest technical frustrations of their trade, and they believe they can win votes by so doing.

One Belgian parliamentarian who has long sat in both the embryo and active organs of the new Europe put it this way: "What makes politics at home isn't going to make politics in Europe. In all our countries religion is terribly important. It binds together inside every Catholic party in Europe, both leftists and conservatives, simply because they are Catholics. It forces together conservatives and Socialists just because they are non-Catholics. But when you come to talk about Europe, you leave religion at home—that's a matter of state politics; let the states argue about Catholic schools or free schools. In Europe people can sort themselves out of different lines. Spaak and Dehousse who are both Socialists in Belgium find their best allies in the European Assembly in people like Brentano and Teitgen who are Catholics at home in Germany and France. It's too early to see how it will work out, but if Europe is made, it will have new politics and the old parties will have new labels. Maybe we can even get at new problems and settle them in new ways."

At present, three concrete projects of Union are under examination by the Europeans. One is the Schuman Plan, already binding and in operation. The second is the European Army, already signed but awaiting ratification. The third is the European Constitution, already drafted but not yet signed. Each is another face of the same concept and the same urge.

In each, the same six nations—France, Germany, Italy, Belgium, Holland, Luxembourg—have compacted their unity. In each of these compacts, the six have agreed to remove from the power of their individual governments certain sovereign powers and transfer them to a supranational Authority which, henceforth, shall exercise them without obstacle or hindrance as the Federal Government of America exercises the powers granted it. Each compact sets up an Executive Authority to act for Europe as a whole, subordinates it to an Assembly of the people of Europe and regulates it with an independent High Court.

At present, each of the linked enterprises stands at a different stage of maturity or conception.

The Community of Coal and Steel, embodiment of the Schuman Plan, is already in operation. Its laws and taxes are binding on 160,000,000 diverse peoples who have never, since the time of Caesar, known the same laws. It moves solidly forward, but very slowly, simply because not even the men who conceived it had previously imagined how crusted and stiff were the arteries of Europe with the controls and obstructions packed into them by generations of national rivalry and abuse. Like doctors operating on a patient for a mild surgery, the High Authority of the Schuman Plan has found the patient upon examination to be just as gravely ill as the most pessimistic forecast. None of the simple plans have proven quite as easy to put in practice as early prediction supposed. To give every European industry fair and equal rates on the Continent's railroads has meant ploughing through national rate systems thick as encyclopedias to ferret out each particular device each nation used to cheat, gouge, extort and impede the traffic of a competitor. The stripping of tariff barriers has suddenly threatened old coal mining villages in Belgium and antiquated cartel-protected plants in central France with the competition of more modern and efficient producers. Can they be allowed to collapse overnight, can their citizens be thrown out of work without giving a three or five year transition period? To wipe out cartels means that they must first be investigated—a long, probing, delicate process. And what does one do when one finds, as one does, that in southern Germany one coal cartel has supplied all the coal at its own fixed price for fifty years and that there exists now in the entire area not one independent coal merchant whose competition can be revived, or through whom the consumer can be offered a fair chance at the market?

Yet the magnitude of the task has not discouraged the High Authority of the Schuman Plan. In a Europe rotted by cynicism and trembling in indecision, a visit to Luxembourg where the Coal-Steel Community has made its first headquarters is, even to the most jaded political tourist, something of inspiration. Here in Luxembourg are men who have passed both the dream and the plan stage and who are excited by their own action. Luxembourg is where a High Authority of nine men—Germans and Frenchmen, Italians and Belgians, Dutchmen and Luxembourgers—all sit around one table talking to one purpose under the chieftainship of Jean Monnet who has ceased to be French and has become European. Luxembourg is where officials of the Community casually make appointments at six o'clock in the morning because that is when they begin work, where a onetime French railway chief and a onetime German railway chief jointly explain to a visitor with loud laughter how their respective railroads once tried to cheat each other. Luxembourg is a place where the measure of entirely new problems is found; the simple problem of language is enormously complicated as the Community requires one-quarter of its staff simply for translation and interpretation. But the once-feared problem of taxes to support the Authority proves as simple as counting on an abacus board. The industries of six countries have begun without a murmur to pay their dues—at the rate of $50,000,000 a year—to their new master, which promises to use the taxes to reinvest in and make fruitful their industries.

The progress of the second enterprise of European Union, the Defense Community and European Army, is more difficult to read. It was conceived in peace for an imminent war which has not happened. On paper it is a most elaborate and detailed document. Each of the governments of the contemplated Union has already signed and sworn to support it. But for many reasons their ratification hangs fire. Unlike the Schuman Plan which dealt with such simple quantities as coal and steel, the European Army scheme deals with the complex organization of men in armies, to be trained and to die. It has become too complex in detail for ordinary people to understand its critical essence, and thus the politicians who support it have difficulty rallying popular support.

On paper the European Army sets up a Continental Defense Force which shall consist of 40 standing divisions—14 French, 12 German, 11 Italian, and 3 from the Low Countries. They are to be so mixed together that no corps will consist only of troops of one nationality. Its men are to wear one uniform, have one flag. Men will be commanded by officers of their own nationality only up to division level. From division level up, officers will be scrambled in nationality, and the supreme staff will be responsible to no individual nation but to the Community of Europe. The High Commission that commands this Army will preside over a government controlling a tax system and budget large enough to maintain the Army, establishing international military academies for training its officers, procuring and producing the arms and equipment of this European Army wherever in Europe the facilities, the steel and the ingenuity offer the best buy.

Many things have gone wrong with the timetables and schedules of this Army, nor are the soldiers of SHAPE any closer to seeing German troops in arms than they were three years ago. There are many reasons for this. The urgency of peril is over, in largest part because of SHAPE's own military achievement which makes German soldiers far less necessary now than they seemed in the Korean crisis, and in lesser measure because of Russia's apparent disinclination since Stalin's death to seek a test of arms. Again, the changing world has affected French and German attitudes deeply. The Germans, seeing the change in Russian attitude, wonder whether the unity of their country might not be speeded more by negotiation with Russia than by that gesture of defiance toward Russia which is involved in the Defense Community. The French, drained by their war in Asia, suddenly conscious of the burden of their African Empire, wonder whether the strain of the overseas lands may not reduce their strength and contribution in the Defense Community so greatly as to make it inevitably a Community under the leadership of German generals.

No serious criticism exists anywhere in the six countries powerful enough to undo the Community of Coal and Steel. Doubt and second thought pucker everywhere at the prospect of the Defense Community.

The third project of European Union is called, technically, the European Political Community (EPC) but is more generally spoken of as "the Constitution." The Constitution is perhaps the most exciting of all three efforts so far made to bring the dream of Europe home to its people. Alone of the three projects, it proposes to draw its charter powers not from the governments of the compact but by direct elections from the people of these countries in their homes.

Like the European Army, it bears the markings of American fashioning. Dwight D. Eisenhower from his headquarters at SHAPE was the first man publicly to invite the Europeans to make a Constitution of Union, and the first official governmental invitation to Europe to write such a constitution was issued in Washington in the fall of 1952. Unlike the European Army, however, these American markings are superficial, for the Constitution was conceived and fought through by European leaders in devoted, creative enterprise all through the winter of 1952-1953, to meet their own needs.

These needs, fundamentally, were to create a sovereign political authority to pull together not only the Coal-Steel Community and the European Army but all the other projects and schemes that pullulate in European minds today. Moreover, all these projects, to thrive, must sink taproots not into parliaments but into the people themselves. The Constitution of Europe, as drafted and presented to the people of Europe by 55 legislators sent from their respective national parliaments, provides, therefore, for organs capable of infinite expansion, yet deriving their powers directly from free popular vote. A European Executive Authority will be chosen by the President of Europe as his Cabinet. This President will, himself, be chosen by the vote of the two legislative chambers of Europe. The upper chamber will be a Senate of 87 members, selected by the various national parliaments. The lower chamber of 238 members will, like the American House of Representatives, represent not the states but the people, who will vote directly for men of their choice. A High Court consisting of the men already chosen as the common High Court of the Schuman Plan and the Defense Community will be its supreme judicial authority. A Council of National Ministers, one for the Cabinet of each country in the compact, will be the transmission belt bearing the directives of the European Executive back to their national governments and interposing, with limited rights of veto, over actions of Europe that go too far.

On paper the Constitution of Europe adopted by the Constitutional Convention and presented to the governments of Western Europe in March of 1953 at Strasbourg is a cumbersome, intricate document with little of the spare simplicity of the document that made America a Union of States. Better constitutions might have been drafted by half a dozen theorists in the privacy of their libraries and studies. The significant strength of the Constitution is that it was drafted by practicing politicians who wished to produce not a perfect document but a document adequate for the problem, yet loose enough to permit them to go back and campaign before their voters and win.

The intense opposition to the Constitution—and it is deep even among great advocates of European Union—rises from the very fact that its authors are so grimly determined to carry it to popular judgment and that their chances of winning approval, if they can get it to a popular vote, are even.

Those who seek the Union of Europe but oppose this draft Constitution of Strasbourg advance two chief arguments against it.

The first is that England is absent. The English in their withdrawal from Europe and their insistence on association without participation have exerted a powerful force even in the councils from which they are absent. Without England, say many continental advocates of European Union, the six-nation Europe of the Constitution becomes a "little Europe"; it becomes a Europe in which Germany is the strongest and dominant partner; it becomes a Europe in which the Protestant voice is submerged by an overwhelming Catholic majority. Such a Community, they say, divides Europe into two halves rather than uniting it.

Rather than an efficient and small Europe, their second argument runs, it is better to have a looser, more inefficient Europe, organized in a series of interlocking yet overlapping functional communities. There might be several interlocking Europes—an agricultural Europe that included Denmark and England plus the unifying six; a defense Europe from which the English would abstain; a cultural Europe in which all would join; a transport Europe in which even the Swiss might join.

To the observer who follows the progress of European Union day by day, its pace seems discouragingly slow. Its champions encourage each other, in their serious moods, by saying that it was nine years before the American Articles of Confederation were fused into the American Constitution; in a jocular mood, they tell each other that it requires eighteen months of pregnancy to produce a baby elephant and "Europe" is something more massive and difficult to make than a baby elephant.

Nothing, however, in this correspondent's memory measures the progress of the movement more vividly than the faces and moods of two contrasting scenes I witnessed, separated by only two years.

The first was in Paris in the spring of 1951, when the final documents of the Schuman Plan were presented for signing in the Salon de l'Horloge of the French Foreign Office. After having traveled through the winding tunnels of technical diplomacy, it lay embossed in parchment, awaiting the signatures of the famous men who sat around the table. First Konrad Adenauer signed, stiff, erect, unsmiling. Next Robert Schuman signed—a man grown and shaped under the same tongue and same flag as Adenauer in the long-forgotten days when the Kaiser's Reich seemed the most durable strength in Europe. Then Count Carlo Sforza of Italy signed—his last important diplomatic act before his death. Count Carlo Sforza had begun his diplomatic career in the turn-of-the-century years when the young Sforza might win renown because the senile Emperor Franz-Josef at a court ball in Vienna had actually stopped and flatteringly inquired of him, *in Italian*, whether he liked the weather. Sforza had been a distinguished diplomat ever since. No public audience watched the signing of the EDC, except for the little secretaries of the Quai who peeped out shyly from behind the red velvet curtains to stare at the great men. Thereafter, everyone repaired to the reception hall to sip champagne and wonder what it was that had happened. Treaties had been made and signed in this fashion for hundreds of years.

The second scene was in Strasbourg in March of 1953, in the hall of the House of Europe, as the Constitution of Europe was finally brought to vote before the Constitutional Convention. The Assembly Hall and its galleries bristled with vitality. A German delegate looked up and said, "My God, do you know who those people in the galleries are? They're my constituents; it costs 12 marks for the bus ride here, and 12 marks to stay here for a day, and they lose a day's pay. This is serious!" An automatic translation system spewed out the arguments over the Constitution simultaneously in English, French, German, Italian and Dutch. The delegates spilled over into the sun-drenched lobbies bargaining, cajoling, explaining. No ministers of government, no man who had known Europe before the First World War raised his voice. New men, snuffing power in the prospect of a new forum, dominated the floor. They had made a constitution and they planned to fight for it. Their Europe was to be made not by diplomats but by people. As they met, the cabled dispatches bore the tidings of Stalin's death, and they were angry that the news of death overwhelmed the news of the birth they were trying to bring about in the border town on the Rhine. By a vote of 55 to 0 (with five abstentions) they passed their Constitution and in the morning they woke to find the greater news from Russia had squeezed their action into a paragraph.

"Do you know what Louis XVI wrote in his diary the day the people stormed the Bastille on July 14?" asked one of the constitution-makers. "He wrote 'rien'—nothing. But something had begun and it was the French Revolution. So they say we have done nothing here. But it has begun. We will take it to the people and they will make the revolution."

XIII

the basin of freedom

In politics, those things we cannot see are always more important than those we can. This is because the most stubborn and important facts are ideas that exist in people's minds and not the way those ideas express themselves in guns and concrete, buildings and roads. This is why the biggest political fact in the Western world is the most difficult to describe.

The name of this idea is a dull alphabetical label, NATO, an addition of four initials which stand for the North Atlantic Treaty Organization.

Much of NATO is, to be sure, hard, tactile and visible, showing itself in a thousand faces. Just six miles outside of Paris the western speedway of St. Cloud throws off a dark ribbon of cobblestone that deposits you before a gray building called SHAPE, outside which snap the flags of fourteen nations in brilliant reds, golds, blues, whites, greens. This is a part of NATO. But NATO is also six noncoms in the early hours of the morning, monitoring spitting radios and clicking teletype machines in one room that centralizes a web of invisible lines that make the Atlantic Basin, from Washington to Istanbul, from the North Cape to Sicily, one net of instant communication. NATO is an airfield in northern France with the pilots of six nations scrambling into the air, flying French, British, American jets, listening to the command of an Englishman who takes orders from a Belgian who is under control of an American, and all getting up to combat height within two minutes to attack the imaginary enemy. It is also a white, hushed building on a hill above the Seine, carpeted with thick brown felt where permanent delegates of 14 nations, supported by an international staff of 150 economists, soldiers and diplomats sit in constant session, totting up the plans and powers of 365,000,000 people.

NATO is the Reception Hall of the Elysée Palace with the red and blue uniformed chamber orchestra of the Garde Republicaine playing Mozart under the glistening chandeliers beneath Gobelin tapestries, while all the great men of the West—Edens and Schumans, Plevens and de Gasperis, Ridgways, Alexanders, Achesons, Harrimans, Wilsons, Butlers—stalk about sipping champagne and nibbling petits fours from the flower-burdened buffet tables. But it is also the wind-swept bridge of an American aircraft carrier operating at night in the North Sea with a polyglot screen of foreign destroyers in front of it; the admiral orders the screen to close up in combat pattern ahead of him, and on the radarscope he can see the luminous pips turn slowly and fall precisely into combat pattern. "And," says the admiral later, "do you know it wasn't until morning that I could look out and tell what nationality they were, but they were all right there in place during the night."

NATO is all this—but these are only its outer faces. At its heart NATO is an idea, an idea which has taken years to flesh out into the imposing fact of its present dominance in world politics. This idea is that somehow, in a way no one can quite describe, there grew up about the Atlantic Basin a civilization which is like no other in the world. In this civilization the individual man and liberty are the measure of political value. Together the people on both sides of this great ocean (less than a sixth of the population of the world) makes a community in the greatest sense, bred out of traditions, religions and technology that none of the other major civilizations of the world share. It has taken centuries of internecine bloodshed to make them realize that they are one. Not until now, when desperately challenged by other counterattacking civilizations, have the men who live around the Atlantic realized that they must band themselves together to defend, each people with its lives and substance, the lives and substance of every other member. It is an alliance like no other in history, for at its base lie no objectives of spoil or conquest. All the rest of the globe may be bargained over, but NATO itself was not erected for bargaining. It was erected for defense of the heartland of freedom and a heritage which only too late was realized to be common property. It is within NATO that America finally came of age in world affairs, pledging herself for the first time, by a revolutionary act of statesmanship, to sacrifice men and treasure not at her own will and timing but whenever any member of the Community of the Atlantic should be wantonly attacked.

Like all great ideas, the vision of NATO did not come full blown to a single prophet, contemplating the world in solitude from his mountain cave. It grew out of the minds of many men, burdened by responsibility in a period of trouble. But since its story must start with a time, a place and a name, the moment when the concept was first uttered can be fixed on the evening of December 16, 1947, in the flat of Ernest Bevin, England's Foreign Minister, at 22 Carlton Terrace, London.

The sixth meeting of the Council of Foreign Ministers had just ended. Mr. Molotov had that afternoon said NO in a hundred different ways to the ministers of the West, covered them with scorn and abuse for the last time, and left.

On that day, the great wartime alliance which destroyed fascism had finally come to its end. That evening, Ernest Bevin invited the Secretary of State of the United States, General George C. Marshall, to a quiet dinner at his home—just the two of them. Bevin had an idea. He had become convinced that at no time in the future could anybody look forward to a day when the Russians would deal in any other terms but force. He was convinced that there was only one way for the West to survive. The Western Powers had to work out some sort of union that would put Western Europe together and then back it with the military strength of the United States and Canada. Later, Bevin had the word-smiths of the Foreign Office work out the idea in a polished diplomatic phrase calling for such a "mobilization of energy and spiritual forces as would inspire confidence and energy within and respect elsewhere." But in the beginning it was a simple idea, the kind of idea that comes to a shrewd, hard man who has been organizing for thirty years of his life. Ernie was a union man; he had got off his seat on a two-horse dray thirty-seven years before to organize the transport workers of Bristol, and had been organizing ever since—dockers, truckers, warehousemen, unions, parties, congresses. When things got tough you organized. Ernie was a genius at organization and had organized the biggest single labor union in the entire world in his lifetime. Now that he was Foreign Secretary, the way out of a problem still seemed to be in organization.

Marshall liked Bevin's idea. But, he warned Bevin, he was in no position to do anything about it right away. He had his hands full pushing the Marshall Plan through Congress; Congress was in no mood to offer blood and manpower at the same time as money. But go ahead with organizing Western Europe, Marshall said to Bevin, and we'll see what we can do to help in Washington. On the boat trip back to New York, Marshall tried the idea out on several of his aides as well as his Republican advisor, John Foster Dulles. By the time they got off the boat in New York, Dulles, too, thought the idea was a good one. By New Year's Day in Washington, at the seasonal rounds of eggnog and highballs, the idea had begun to circulate: the British had proposed a new kind of alliance, a complete break with American tradition, one whereby America pledged itself to a permanent military alliance guaranteeing the safety of the western half of the European peninsula. Most people at the State Department liked the idea—that is, if Congress could be persuaded to buy it.

Congress was in a particularly propitious mood early in 1948. The Republican oracle on foreign affairs, Senator Arthur Vandenberg, had just spent a year recasting the Monroe Doctrine to meet the needs of this century. At first glance there seemed little connection between the Monroe Doctrine and the proposed European Alliance. But, one hundred years before, the Monroe Doctrine had proclaimed America's intention of defending the entire Western Hemisphere against outside attack. The changing values of a postwar world had made it necessary to rephrase this lordly pronunciamento in more democratic form, and after several years of negotiation, by the end of 1947, Pan-American defense had been set up as a cooperative enterprise of equal partners. This was a substantial achievement, and Senator Vandenberg who, as the chairman of the Senate's Foreign Relations Committee, had largely captained it was rightly proud. Therefore, when Secretary of State Marshall explained Bevin's idea to Senator Vandenberg, Vandenberg replied immediately that it was a very good idea. It seemed a logical and complementary regional agreement to the one he had just masterminded with South America.

It took only fifteen months to produce a finished definition of the Atlantic Pact—troublesome, intricate months disturbed by

Communist aggression abroad and the quadrennial fury of an American presidential campaign at home. In Europe, Bevin went ahead to organize with remarkable swiftness the association of France, England and the Benelux powers in a treaty signed at Brussels in the spring of 1948 and known, at that time, as Western Union. By April he had finished his job and, growling by cable to Marshall, he demanded: Where were the Americans? The Brussels pact, said Bevin, was a delusion in its very military posture if the United States did not mean to back it up by force. Other European voices were added to the cables from London. The Communists had just seized Czechoslovakia. What would the Americans do, cabled Foreign Minister Bidault from Paris, if the Russians were to march tomorrow? What would the Americans do, cabled Prime Minister Spaak from Brussels? Stalin sent a menacing note to Norway, demanding morsels of her land— Would America back them up in refusal? cabled the Norwegians.

But Washington was where the burden of decision lay, and in Washington matters could but move slowly. The making of any treaty is a complicated process requiring the nicest attention to detail, the most careful wooing of the political support that must ultimately approve it, the most skilful cultivation of public opinion by well-timed speeches, well-planted stories, well-planned leaks to the proper pundits. Moreover, this was an especially complicated treaty, raising many new questions. The practical heart of the matter would have to be America's guarantee to come to the aid of any power in the Community attacked by an aggressor. This required clearance with the soldiers of the Pentagon. The Pentagon said the treaty had to be made broad enough to provide for global retaliation against the enemy, anywhere, with any means, instead of a constricting contract which permitted America to meet the enemy's attack only at such point as the enemy might choose to attack. There was an even knottier constitutional problem: only the President and the Congress of the United States have the right to declare war. By the Constitution, no treaty can be written that commits America to battle unless the people through their Congress assent. Finally, there was a problem of practical politics: 1948 was a presidential election year and no group of generals or State Department civil servants felt bold enough to write so profound a change into American life until the people should have chosen their new leadership.

From the spring of 1948 down to the beginning of 1949, committees revolved about committees in Washington, as all the various layers of interest, American and global, were consulted. State met with Pentagon to elaborate a draft of the American point of view; Marshall and Lovett sat with Vandenberg and Connally; Vandenberg and Connally pushed an empowering resolution through the Senate; State Department negotiators met with the Ambassadors of Britain, Canada, France and the three Benelux countries to bridge the gap between European and American opinion. By January all the proper formulas had been correctly phrased, including the key formula which bound all powers to a declaration that:

". . . an armed attack against one or more of them . . . shall be considered an attack against them all, and consequently they agree that . . . each of them . . . will assist the Party or Parties so attacked by taking forthwith . . . such action as it deems necessary, including the use of armed force, to restore and maintain the security of the North Atlantic area."

With this, the definition of the Treaty was complete. There remained the final task of inviting in the flanking powers of the Atlantic Basin, those lesser states necessary to guard the long sea lanes between both halves of the Free World. Norway, Portugal, Iceland, Italy and Denmark all received invitations and accepted. Ireland and Sweden were invited but declined. Two years later, two more states were added, Greece and Turkey. But, on April 3, 1949, twelve nations signed the North Atlantic Treaty in Washington, and for the first time in history, the peoples of the Atlantic recognized their kinship and pledged themselves to its common defense.

The central problem of the Atlantic Alliance is a hard physical job that involves killing and fighting. It is to prevent, by force, the Russians from breaking through the political line drawn across Central Europe to occupy and annihilate the countries west of it. This is a problem of map and terrain, of men, of materials, and of spirit.

The map divides its advantages in Europe about equally between the Atlantic Alliance and the Russians. The area of Russian Occupation in Europe is a huge, almost trapezoid protrusion into the west from the homeland—about 650 miles from the borders of Russia itself to the Elbe, and up to a thousand miles wide from north to south. As a buffer belt, it is one of the most stupendous defenses in depth ever acquired by any nation's diplomacy.

Nonetheless, it has its weaknesses. All along its southern frontier from the Swiss Alps to the Black Sea it is ringed by mountains occupied by hostile peoples. It has no outlet to the sea except Albania, which on the outbreak of war could be pinched off in a matter of days by Western police action. This long southern flank is rendered doubly vulnerable because within these Russian lines and under various Communist flags live millions of people who would betray communism and the Russians to come over to the West at the first military opportunity.

It is the western frontier of this protrusion into Europe that is the warhead of the Russian torpedo. Here the Russians sprawl across Germany from the Alps to the North Sea on 550 miles of front. Here are massed their best troops. These troops are, at one point, only 90 miles from the Rhine line; they are only 40 miles from the city of Hamburg, the most important western port of entry into Central Europe. They are closer to Paris than Minneapolis is to Chicago. From their positions the map invites them out of Germany in two directions. The map invites them first, across Germany's flat northern plains and strategic autobahns, toward the Low Countries. This is the route that every raider from the East has taken on the charge into France, since Attila the Hun first led his horsemen to the Marne. Farther south, the map also invites them on another axis down several traditional corridors through the central German hills, directly across the narrow waist of Hesse, which Americans defend today, to the Rhine. From the advanced Russian lines to the Rhine crossings is an easy four-hour drive.

To offset these terrain advantages, geography has also set several obstacles for the Russians. The first is the Rhine river, a deep, swift-flowing stream that can be defended brilliantly by troops well dug in and prepared to die. More importantly, the Russians are penalized by sheer distance. If they struck forward out of their German lines, they would be operating over 800 miles from their main base of industry and support, through thousands of villages of hostile peoples, across narrow communications. The logistics of a Russian offensive in Western Europe are immensely difficult.

We have no idea of how the Russians view their huge military problem. With the Soviets, secrecy is a source of strength in itself. The mystery with which they shroud the substance of their military strength not only protects that strength but brings a bonus of exaggerated and distorted fear to the hearts of their enemy. At SHAPE, the military headquarters of West European defense, they tell a story about a man whom we shall call the Red-Pencil Colonel. Until recently, the Red-Pencil Colonel masterminded a desk in the Intelligence Section where, day after day, arrive intelligence reports on the Soviets from most of the military and secret service agencies of the Atlantic Powers. This raw data usually arrives in a jumble of encouraging and discouraging news items, mixed without evaluation. The Red-Pencil Colonel would read these reports slowly and thoughtfully and then carefully underline with his red pencil each item that reflected some new growth of Soviet strength, some ominous change, some new spurt in military technique. The reports that passed out of his desk, after his scrutiny, thus screamed in red underlinings of Soviet strength and power, while, by contrast, Soviet weakness and blunders escaped the eyes' attention.

Reading reports so prepared—both in secrecy and for publication—the Western world has the tendency to see every Red Army soldier as ten feet high, every Russian general as a genius, and every Russian division as a crack armored force. This is not so. This frame of mind is, moreover, very dangerous, for even without exaggeration the Russians are so powerful a military force that it is just barely possible to manage them without wrecking our entire peacetime lives. To amplify their real strength with fear can be as crippling as to underrate it with complacency.

If we cannot guess, for we do not know, what Russian strategic thinking is, we do know that their strength is measurable in crude but substantial form and we know their major resources and weaknesses. In the simplest military terms, we know that Russian strength lies not in immediate impact force but in the tremendous war reserves of a domestic life, permanently policed, permanently organized, permanently geared for swift conversion to war. Our difficulty lies not in countering their present hitting power but in doing so without wrecking our own social systems by the kind of permanent mobilization in which the Russians live. We know Russian weaknesses too: militarily, their chief problem is transportation, or the delivery of their fighting forces in time to the line of combat. Politically, further, we know that they count among their forces thousands of men who hate their system and its leadership. The Russian soldiers, in the last war, proved, at times, the bravest fighters and, at other times, the quickest deserters and surrenderers.

All the facts that this writer has been able to learn about the Red Army in the past five years can be summarized in a few pages. The Russians have in uniform at present about 3,900,000 men, of whom about 2,500,000 are ground forces. This is about half the troops now in the uniforms of the Atlantic Alliance. To this limited Russian force-in-being must be added over a million satellite troops in Eastern Europe of very doubtful value, plus the foot soldiers of China's Red Army in Asia. But all these depend for guidance, morale and arms on the Soviet system itself, and to counter these the West may call on the Yugoslavs and Japanese in time of trouble.

The ground forces of the Soviet Union are organized, so far as is known to Western intelligence agencies, into some 175 combat divisions and 40 or 50 specialist divisions (chiefly artillery and antiaircraft). There seems to have been little change in the global size of this force over the past five years. Most of these divisions run to between 10,000 and 11,000 men when activated, while the cavalry and antiaircraft divisions among them call for as few as 5,000 men. At present, the home divisions within Russia seem to be substantially below strength and only the frontier divisions in Germany and the Far East stand at full strength.

These Russian divisions have a fantastic amount of real estate to guard—one-fifth of the earth's land surface. In Europe alone they must be prepared to overrun or repel Allied forces on an arc of 5,000 miles from the White Sea in the sub-Arctic, down through the Baltic, at the front in Germany, down along the long line of the Balkans and in the Caucasus. In addition, other troops must stand guard over the restive Moslems in Central Asia, while yet more must man the ramparts of the Far East against any combined Japanese-American threat to Siberia. The vast manpower of the Russian General Staff is never poised, therefore, at any one specific objective on its long frontier but must be deployed carefully and skilfully, ten divisions here, five divisions there, another cluster in yet another geographical area in patterns which are highly secret.

Of all the dispositions made by the Russian General Staff, none is more dangerous to the West than the concentration which called the North Atlantic Alliance into being—the twenty-two Red Army combat divisions stationed with their ten artillery and ack-ack support divisions in Eastern Germany, readily available for a push on the home countries of the Community. This formidable force of 300,000 men is the most highly mechanized of all Russian formations and its equipment, being the best craftsmanship of Russian arsenals, is very good indeed. The disposition of this force follows very closely the suggestion of the map. Two striking armies of four divisions each are stationed close to the warhead in two revealing pockets. The Third Shock Army sits near Magdeburg, deployed as if to cut across the North German plains on the rush to France and the Low Countries; it faces the troops of England and the Low Countries. The Russian Eighth Guards Army sits near Weimar, behind the glowering Thuringian ridges, cocked to sweep across the open basin of Lower Franconia or down the Fulda Gap. Their objective in time of war would be Frankfurt and the Rhine crossings, and here the slender waist of Germany must be defended by American and French troops. Behind these two hammer fists at the front are the other four armies of Russian occupation, deployed near the meshing points of the great autobahn which give them easy flexibility in pouring their forces down either avenue of attack as opportunity develops. Behind these, in turn, lie some eight other Russian divisions guarding communications in Poland (two), Austria (four) and Rumania (two). Supporting this force, in turn, are the troops of the satellites and the deep reserves of the Soviet homeland.

If this force could seize Western Europe, it could extinguish liberty forever in its homelands, more than double the Soviet Union's industrial capacity and reduce America to a garrison state beyond the Atlantic.

In 1948, while the Soviets were attempting to strangle Berlin by blockade and while the protocols of the North Atlantic Treaty were being worded in Washington, the shadow of this Soviet force darkened all of Europe.

In those days, the Red Army in Central Europe might quite literally have marched out of its garrison dormitories in Germany and in a fortnight have taken all of Western Europe; it would have met no more than token resistance and very little of that. Western defense forces in Germany consisted of something under 200,000 badly organized men. Two British divisions armed with wartime Churchill tanks already obsolete, and supported by an archaeological collection of decrepit trucks and transports, guarded the North. Three very weak French divisions, some of them armed with old Sherman tanks that had been bought as scrap from Belgian junk dealers after the war, held the center. In the South, the equivalent of two American divisions, deployed and trained to police Germans rather than fight Russians, were scattered and lost over three hundred miles of front. The lines of communication of both British and American troops ran south out of Bremen and Hamburg, so closely parallel to the front that a Russian raid might have scissored them in forty-eight hours, leaving them isolated from supply.

Behind this fragile crust of strength, the reserves of the Western world consisted of a possible Belgian division in Belgium, one possible British division in England and six battalions of combat ready troops in the United States one full month away. The French could muster as their contribution to the strategic reserve but two understrength divisions, one of whose regiments employed as armor old German Tiger tanks for which spare parts were no longer available. That was all. Except for London, no city in Western Europe boasted even the most primitive air defense—all Paris was guarded by two antiaircraft batteries. The United States Air Force in Europe consisted of two combat wings; the French Air Force boasted 30 Vampire jets (already obsolete) and several squadrons of old propeller-pushed World War II pursuits. Russian fighting strength in Europe outweighed Western fighting strength by more than three to one. "All the Russians need to get to the Channel," observed one American military statesman at the time, "is shoes."

To counter this enemy strength, the West had but one weapon —the Strategic Air Force of the United States, laden with atomic bombs. During the years of crisis, the sole deterrent to Soviet impulse was the vast investment of free minds and free energy in the exploration of the deadliest of sciences. But already the Russians were at work creating their own Strategic Air Force and fashioning their own bombs.

This is now history. The politics of the entire world have changed because all this is like a remembered nightmare. Billions of dollars, hundreds of thousands of men, incalculable thought and effort have been invested by the Atlantic Community to create one new fact, among the half-dozen most important facts in the world today. This fact is as simple as it is important: in Central Europe today, the power balance has shifted from the Russians to the Atlantic forces.

Stripped of words and propaganda, the Atlantic effort in Europe has reached the point where, in Germany, along those dark ridges and thin streams where our patrols pass Russian patrols in the dark, we can mass a heavier weight of armor and men than the Russians. At the critical German front, we can mass 500,000 men against the Russians' 300,000. Two hundred million West Europeans no longer go to sleep nightly in the knowledge that tomorrow the Russians could rumble through their streets.

Our line of battle in the critical central area counts six American divisions, four and two-thirds British divisions, five and one-third French divisions, three Belgian divisions, one Dutch division, two-thirds of a Danish division, plus another division of odds and ends. This force is backed by another fifteen divisions in various states of readiness. South of the Alpine turntable are nine Italian divisions braced by the equivalent of a division and a half of British and American troops ready to bottle up the mountain passes from Austria to Trieste. Beyond that, down around the Mediterranean, is the Yugoslav Army loosely tied to our strategy, plus eleven Greek and twelve Turkish divisions under coordinate command. By the end of 1953, at their present rate of progress, the North Atlantic countries will be able to provide their common command with almost one hundred divisions ready or mobilizable in thirty days.

It should be said immediately that the word "division" is the fool's gold of the amateur strategist, and the generals who command the forces of the Atlantic Alliance wince whenever anyone attempts to count their divisions. "Division" is a word that may mean anything from America's magnificent Big Red One, at the very fringe of hostile contact and perhaps the finest self-contained fighting force in the world, to the two French divisions freshly formed in 1952 with barely thirty per cent of their effectives and the Greek and Turkish divisions hardly stronger than regimental combat teams. The fighting value of every unit varies widely, depending on all the treacherously complicated factors of supply, training equipment, leadership, morale and reserves of ammunition. It is, therefore, vital to note that though the increase in calculable division strength in the past two years has been more than substantial, fighting strength has grown even faster in the immeasurable improvement of all the many other factors that go to make a fighting army.

The Atlantic armies are based and in position. No longer are the troops scattered in hopeless garrisons, helter-skelter through Germany. They are poised on a known line, with presited positions and deployment areas, with avenues of attack and withdrawal surveyed, engineered and zeroed in. No longer must American supplies move down the dangerously vulnerable north-south routes from the North Sea to Bavaria. They are beginning now to enter by the safe ports of the Bay of Biscay, deep in the French rear, and then move horizontally across France to Germany over an enormous American communications system that deposits supplies in massive, awesome dumps all through the Rhineland and Germany's Black Forest. British supplies, similarly, follow protected channels from east to west across Belgium and the Low Countries to the North German plain. The generals can now face front with their rear protected.

The Atlantic armies are now, moreover, armed and equipped. Four million tons of American military supplies, plus 503 planes and 82 warships, had arrived in Europe between the beginning of NATO, in the spring of 1949, and January of 1953—enough to make of every army in Europe (except the English who equip their own soldiers) a fighting composite of American hardware and native flesh. Europeans in NATO complain that the biggest single failure in the military plans of SHAPE is the lag in delivery of American arms, the slow crawl of production and delivery which still leaves nine billion dollars' worth of arms appropriated for foreign military aid tangled in procurement and production. But, though American shipment has not completely met American promise, what has actually arrived has already changed the character of the Atlantic forces from pulp to armies. America's divisions in Europe are the best equipped of American history, bristling with guns and spearheaded by the new automatic-sighting M47 tanks that handle like kiddy-cars at the touch of a joy stick. The French no longer operate wartime Shermans but M46's equipped with ninety-millimeter guns. The British have replaced their wartime Churchills with new Centurions, their ancient desert ordnance with the newest trucks. Belgians, Italians, Dutch, Norwegians, Turks, Greeks all inch slowly forward to planned goals as they pick up American arms landed on their wharves.

The Atlantic armies are, finally, commanded. NATO need only be contrasted with the puny Anglo-French Alliance of 1939, which was expected to stop Hitler, to show how much has been learned. The Anglo-French Alliance of 1939 envisaged the delivery of a single packaged product on the shores of France after the outbreak of war, this package to consist of six British expeditionary divisions wrapped in military cellophane, lacking any basic supply, support or maintenance system. NATO has never talked in terms of such packages; its purpose from the beginning has been to arm an entire community, with all its territory, to make it bristle with present guns and present reserves, centrally commanded in peace as in war. A single command looks at an area of operation quite differently from the way a coalition staff looks at it. It sees all its member countries as one single apron for the deployment of its planes and fields; thus, one new NATO field is being finished each week in this year, 1953, in Western Europe. By early 1954, over 100 of the 158 fields needed by SHAPE in Western Europe will be operational, and the squadrons of eight different nations will use them under a command that can flick their planes north, south, west or east instantaneously. Invisible channels of sound already lace the air: Norway is linked by NATO's own cable and high-frequency circuits to Aberdeen in Scotland; submarine cables of NATO crisscross from France and

Italy under the sea to Africa; Paris is in voice communication with Air Control at Fontainebleau; a score of VHF circuits link both these centers of command with Metz and forward combat posts; Lyons is linked by NATO lines with Chambéry for defense of the Alpine turns.

Under the Standing Group of NATO, which sits in Washington, operate the field commands. Two of these commands are naval—SACLANT, whose headquarters at Norfolk, Virginia, is charged with the defense of the sea-lanes between Europe and the American continent, and CHANNEL command, a smaller counterpart, which protects the sea-lanes between Britain and the Continent. The great field command, of course, is SHAPE, the business front of the Community, that controls all forces on the mainland of Europe. SHAPE's subordinate Northern Command (the weakest link in the structure) defends the Scandinavians and patrols the Kattegat out of which Russian submarines must pass to penetrate the Atlantic. The Central Command of SHAPE holds the German front with two Group armies, one Franco-American in the South, and the other British-Low Countries in the North. Each of these Group armies, moreover, is provided with its own tactical air force. A Southern Command is responsible for Italy's Alps and patrols the Mediterranean. Attacked today, the men who sit in the clean gray SHAPE headquarters in Marly Forest outside Paris could dissolve their offices overnight, slip away to secret underground war headquarters, and exercise operational control over troops stretched out on a 5,000-mile arc of contact with the enemy.

SHAPE's generals would not welcome the challenge of war at any time, but if it came now it would throw into mournful, almost disastrous, relief half a dozen weaknesses about which SHAPE's generals have ululated long and unsuccessfully to their civilian superiors.

The first of these weaknesses in the still-unfinished structure of Western defense lies in the air. Air power in the strategy of SHAPE is critical, for SHAPE is not geared to attack; it is built for defense. It must wait until the Russians move before it can hit back and when it hits it must strike at the weakest point in Russia's strategy—her communications. Western Europe is safe behind SHAPE's guard only so long as the Russian homeland reserve cannot be delivered in overwhelming numbers against it. One German military estimate—and the German knowledge of Russian fighting is deep and extensive—is that to deliver another sixty divisions in sixty days to the central front, the Russians must have from six to eight crossings over the Oder and Theisse Rivers. To give our ground troops a fair chance to recoil in good order before the first Russian shock while our own reserves gather, our Air Forces must be able to slice and keep slicing these Russian communications wherever, as at marshaling yards and river crossings, they are vulnerable. This our Air Forces cannot do at the present moment. They lack, flatly, anywhere near adequate numbers of planes and men. Superlative progress has been made in international coordination of command, of language, of scrambling of squadrons and flights. All that can be done to organize men and build fields has been pressed. But, in the rush to build ground strength and divisional cadres, planes and the pilots to fly them have been neglected. By the end of 1953 SHAPE's tactical air force will still be far from its goal of 4,000 planes (although most will be modern jets), which is the minimum requirement. But against this we know the Russians can mobilize up to 8,000 planes (of which half are probably jets) out of their 20,000. To be really safe, SHAPE's generals feel they must have at least 5,000 planes, and unless this canopy is provided in good time, our troops would have to fight outnumbered in the sky.

The second of SHAPE's command weaknesses is political. SHAPE is a community command, unlike a Russian command which can dispose of satellite divisions across the map as expendables. A hybrid of many tongues and men, SHAPE must rely on cooperation as much as on the imperative to do its will. Yet this is difficult because high command falls most naturally to those with experience, and except for the British and Americans, none of the NATO partners can name a single general who has commanded a full field army in battle. Inevitably, Americans and Britons outweigh all other partners in key positions of control, arousing resentment among all the non-English-speaking powers. SHAPE is, therefore, constantly forced to seek not simply the best officers in the best posts but also the proper admixture of nationals to harmonize wounded pride with military efficiency. SHAPE works at the problem; progress has been slow but encouraging. SHAPE has established its own NATO Defense College to train international officers, for, in the words of SHAPE's brilliant commander, General Alfred Gruenther, "There are only two kinds of wars–Indian wars and coalition wars. All wars of the future are coalition wars and we have to learn how to fight them." But until time and experience train men of the right kind, SHAPE's command problems must remain plagued by pride, personality and national prejudice.

A third weakness and a vital one is summed up in the one tedious word "supply." In the face of a full Soviet assault our Atlantic troops might be able to fight for two weeks or a month, might be able to withdraw and then hold the Rhine for six weeks, but then they would run out of fuel, ammunition, guns and troops. When NATO's Permanent Council thinks of the day-to-day problems of fighting a war it thinks primarily in terms of reserves –of oil and shells, of syringes and carburetors, of manpower that can be phased into the line on D day plus three, D day plus ten, D day plus thirty, D day plus ninety. For it knows that the Russians, thanks to their perpetual state of civil and military mobilization, have all such reserves stacked up hip-deep and rolling in the interior of their police state.

The supply problem leads directly to the last of SHAPE's big worries–"flexibility in the field." In its emergency early years, SHAPE's job was to tack together, in bits and pieces, whatever manpower it could scour up to form a crust of opposition at the front, called the "couverture." The emergency job is done, and SHAPE's task now is to fuse these parts into one new flexible force. An army's purpose is not to sit still but to move as a fluid constellation of impact and firepower, instantly responsive to one central direction. In specific terms, it means that American troops must be ready to move overnight up to a threatened French sector, or that French troops must, if necessary, be raced toward the Belgian frontier. When such troops move, intermingling and separating as direction dictates, they must know they will receive the same kind of support, the same type of artillery fire, find ready the ordnance shops and supply depots that can keep their weapons and tanks firing, find proper medical and hospital services to care for their wounded. The generals, whatever their uniforms, agree on these things. But the roots of each nation's army go deep into generations of national tradition; parliaments and cabinets must assent whenever any national army is wrenched about to fit a new pattern, whenever any change in equipment for the sake of standardization requires a revision in the nation's industry. Generals know that troops must train in swift movement and that base installations must be built to permit this movement. But each simple move involves complex national sovereignty and budgets. Who pays for the housing, feeding and fueling of such national troops on the march? Who pays for the farmer's cow killed or the village bridge weakened—the maneuvering troops, or the nation that plays host to them?

The balance between strength and weakness, between accomplishment and short-fall is debated feverishly in all the lobbies of SHAPE and NATO. It is pointed to with pride, or pointed to with alarm, depending on who the audience and who the speaker.

Yet when all is said, the stupendous fact of real power cannot be obscured: the Russians could not now take us, as they could have in 1948, with the garrison they man in Eastern Germany. If the Russians should wish to attack they must mobilize all the forces of the homeland for their effort. War in Central Europe is no longer an adventure for them, it is a desperate gamble. At the point of contact, the Atlantic Powers marshal more and better hitting power than is immediately available to the Soviet Union.

The operative word here is "immediately," and it accounts for the contradictions in all public accounts of NATO's work. No officer at SHAPE deludes himself into thinking that SHAPE's forces could resist, without swift reinforcement, an all-out onslaught of the Soviets. Our shock troops in Europe are more numerous than the enemy's, but if the Russians mobilized for war, the SHAPE command could only survive if our mobilization were as swift and massive as theirs. It is this that makes the Western generals behave so frequently like schizophrenics. They have, on the one hand, the natural human itch for praise for work well done. But, on the other hand, they know that if they pause for praise, parliaments and peoples will relax instantly, slash budgets, strip down taxes—before the necessary planes and pilots are supplied, before the war reserves are in warehouses, before the almost-finished creation of their devotion receives its capping, final increment of strength. Their duty then, as they see it, is to moan rather than boast, to exhort rather than comfort and to flog reluctant civilians along the path of duty, however great the strain and unwilling the flesh.

It is here that the problems of NATO leave the desks of generals and come before that civilian judgment called statesmanship. For, although generals behave in their tradition of duty when they urge ever greater effort, civilian statesmen know that complete security against the Russians can never be possible unless the Atlantic Community is willing to force its citizens into the same strait jacket of discipline and drugged effort that the Soviet state imposes on its citizens. Somewhere along the way historic judgments must be made: not only how much the Western way of life can be permanently burdened by arms without crushing it to extinction, but also where these arms should be gathered, which of the many danger points in our life has greater priority on them, and how such strategic advantages as our arms have brought us in Europe shall be capitalized.

The Russians, too, are burdened by just such problems, for their resources of war are even smaller than ours; Russian resources appear greater only because they are multiplied by internal terror. While we have been deploying and strengthening in Western Europe, the Russians have been faced with a major decision. Their problem has been whether or not to attempt to preserve their 1948 superiority over us, whether the cost of the effort be worth the probable result. The response of the Russians has presented, indeed, a fact almost as significant as our own growth to strength in Central Europe. The Russians have not budged. They maintain today in Eastern Germany the same twenty-two divisions they maintained in 1952, in 1951, in 1950, in 1949, in 1948, all the while our strength has been trebling. They have, it is true, re-equipped their forces as have we with fresher weapons from Soviet arsenals. They have expanded the number of runways in Eastern Europe and lengthened them to take care of new jets. They have borne down on organizing the satellite armies. And, most of all, they have concentrated on the communications net, the transfer points of their mixed-gauge railways, the motorization of their armies to cut down on the delivery time necessary to bring home divisions to bear on the central front. But basically the Soviets have stood pat.

Their decision comes out of no sweet desire for peace; nor can it possibly be to the liking of the Russian generals on the German front, who, like any generals, must have howled like wolves to the Kremlin for increase. It can only have been a central political decision taken in Moscow which recognized that in the frame of the Cold War the Atlantic Powers were pressing an irresistible advantage. The Soviet Union could not prevent this Atlantic success without stripping other enterprises more vital to it elsewhere —enterprises of domestic expansion at home, or military expansion as in Korea. Faced with the fact of Atlantic dominance in Central Europe and the crude but effective community organization of the Atlantic states, the Russians have thus been forced to shift tactics. Since they cannot shake Europe and the Alliance apart by force or the threat of force, they must now attempt to seduce it into disunion or magnetize it apart by politics and economic war.

It is here, as the Russians try to mount a new and different response to the Alliance, that the problems of the next chapter in the Community's history begins. Even while the soldiers are laboring to rivet together the final structure of their achievement, their civilian masters must begin to wrestle with the problems attendant on their success. And it is here, as the soldiers say at SHAPE, that the problem moves "downtown."

"Downtown," as the officers at SHAPE use the word, means the cream-colored annex to the Palais de Chaillot, sitting in its green park overlooking the Seine River in downtown Paris. Here are housed the 150 senior civilians who form the Permanent Secretariat which supports the Permanent Council of the North Atlantic Treaty Organization. "Downtown" is, however, much more than this corps of international civil servants; "downtown" is the symbol of the political authority to which, in our kind of system, the soldiers must remain forever subordinate. The soldiers' problems are stubborn and difficult and, if war comes, are transcendent. But the problems of the civilians who must guide NATO are even more difficult and, if peace is to persist, even more important. The slow growth of NATO from its idiot infancy to the beginning of common sense, along with all its hope of maturity, can be traced in the effort of the civilians who direct it to grapple with its two chief political problems: how to understand each other and how to understand their soldiers.

The problem of mutual understanding in any alliance is as old as the first memories of history. One scholar among NATO chieftains likes to begin the story of its troubles with the phrase "Once upon a time" and continue with an account of the Confederacy of Delos. Two thousand years ago, the free and democratic states of Greek civilization, linked by a common culture and religion, but separated by the then vast distances of the Aegean Sea, found themselves menaced by an Oriental dictatorship, the despotism of Persia. To defend themselves against the menace they bound themselves into a league of free nations called the Confederacy of Delos. The politics that wrecked the Confederacy of Delos are as vivid today as when the archons of the city-states wrestled and debated them as live issues. For it became immediately apparent that there was a fundamental imbalance in the Confederacy. Its mainspring and leader was the great democracy of Athens; its lesser members were the Greek city-states of Ionia, no less proud, but infinitely weaker and living cheek-by-jowl with the enemy on the frontier of Persian power. Between the Athenians and the Ionians there was no clear area of understanding except that both were in peril. They could not agree on how supreme commanders should be appointed, how contributions should be made to the common treasury, or on the measurement of the Persian peril. Its members argued whether Athens, which contributed two hundred ships to the Confederacy, should have only the same single vote as the tiny states which contributed but one. Athens insisted that it was her decision alone whether the little states might trade with the Persian enemy, or whether neutral states should be blockaded for such trade. The lesser states argued that the success of the Confederacy lessened the peril and thus its burdens might be reduced; Athens argued that only constant exertion and effort kept the Persian peril contained. The Confederacy of Delos died, finally, when the weight of Athens pressed its lesser allies down to the servile position of puppets. After that, Athens and the little Greek states alike decayed to impotence to be finally swallowed, not by the Persians whom they feared, but by unknown and unexpected enemies from other quarters.

Since the day of its foundation, the North Atlantic Community has been acting as if it were a rehearsal of the Confederacy of Delos in modern dress, America cast as Athens and the European states as the Ionians. The thread which runs through all the meetings of the Community's great senior bodies is the struggle over how its members shall share the burdens which all know to be necessary but none know how to apportion. Each decision taken by civilians to meet their soldiers' measure of the peril reaches back to the roots of their domestic politics, for they require that young men be conscripted, that exhausting taxes be levied, that disturbing controls be slapped on at every level of industrial life. When the governments divide in the Atlantic Council, they divide because each common burden weighs with different force in different member countries. When they divide, they usually divide in a complex system of strains which sets the United States and Canada, who are rich and strong, against the Europeans, who are poor and weak. This built-in rift in the Community is infinitely difficult to settle because justice and common sense are so equally divided in debate.

The European case is, in essence, that while both Europeans and Americans are commonly pledged to defend liberty, it is folly to defend liberty by crushing the European citizen under such a weight of armor as to make him believe that liberty is not worth defending. Europeans argue that America is rich, unscarred by previous wars, and therefore best able to support the defense against peril. They argue that America can produce 12,000 airplanes and 12,000 tanks a year all the while throwing off refrigerators, chrome-plated autos and a million new homes for the comfort of its citizens. But when the British switch to arms, it means less toys for her children, less metallic exports to pay for the food she must import from abroad. When Americans spend fifteen per cent of their national income on arms, there is enough left so that ordinary Americans may eat steak once a week, go on vacation and buy a new suit twice a year. But when France tries to spend twelve per cent of her national income she must pare away at the living flesh of medical care, old-age pensions and schools, or bury the twelve per cent in the even more wicked device of inflation. What use are arms in the hands of men too disaffected to fight? ask the French.

The American reply is, in essence, that America has two alternative strategies which it can adopt. One is a strategy of trans-Atlantic Alliance to shelter the whole domain of the free world. The other is to go it alone, defending her continent by transpolar bombing to keep the Russians at long range. She adopted the strategy of the Atlantic at the request of the Europeans, who live in the reach of Russian guns. America has been the quickest and firmest of all powers in meeting its commitments to NATO, has summoned her people to enormous exertions. She insists she has the right to demand an equivalent effort of her Allies abroad. To which the Europeans always reply that what appears to be equivalent effort to Americans is always a greater proportionate strain in countries like their own which are so much weaker.

This problem of how the great burdens should be shared has always, inevitably, twined itself with NATO's second problem—how to deal with the soldiers. It is the soldier's duty to impress on his civilian government the exact military measure of the enemy and how much is needed in troops, organization and hardware to counter it. But when the civilians study the soldiers' requests, they must know what the soldiers are talking about—whether it is the enemy's immediate capacity, total capacity, or apparent intentions. Before the civilians agree, they must know how the burden assumed will bear on the economy and politics of each country involved. The story of NATO, on its political side, has been the slow groping process by which its members have tried to come to grips with each other and with the soldiers at the same time.

NATO began in the spring of 1949 in a total fog in which there twirled in absolute confusion a number of imposing committees that circulated like roadshows between Paris, London, Washington. In this fog, lesser committees of soldiers, known as Regional Planning Groups, measured off the various sectors of defense, assigned them, north, south and central. Each little committee assumed that all the might of the Red Army would come to bear on its sector alone, and so calculating, they all made their requests for troops. When added together their demands reached the total of 307 divisions for Europe alone, or something like three times the Allied strength at the height of World War II. Meanwhile, the committees of Finance Ministers, Foreign Ministers and Defense Ministers who are the governing bodies of the Atlantic Community had continued in their blithe assumption that the American war surplus stocks would be sufficient to arm the entire defense effort, with perhaps an extra injection of five billion dollars of American aid to prod the project ahead. NATO's first shock came when the confrontation of civilians and military showed that the gap between the soldiers' demand and civilian provision was of the order of 200 billion dollars. Ever since, the story of NATO, year by year, has been the slow whittling down of the soldiers' estimates of divisions needed for Western defense from 307 to 96 to 70 to 60, and the subordination of their estimates to what the Community can afford to pay.

The present common-sense approach of NATO to its complicated problems was not conceived at any single meeting, at any single conference, by any single decision. A series of jolts propelled NATO from its early madness of irresponsible committees into an organization which now, however primitive, points to the way ahead.

The first series of jolts came to a climax at the Brussels conference of NATO in December of 1950 when, in the first panic of the Korean War, as American troops were flung back in disorder by China's Communist armies, it was recognized finally that committees could not conduct battles. It was then that all the Regional Planning Groups were abolished, that a single military headquarters, SHAPE, was set up with a chain of command over all Atlantic troops on the Continent, that the target of effort was boiled down from 307 divisions to 96 and General Dwight D. Eisenhower, a flesh and blood individual, was named SACEUR, or Supreme Allied Commander Europe.

The second series of jolts climaxed in the Lisbon conference of NATO, early in 1952. Until then, the leadership of NATO had lain in the hands of its soldiers, and chiefly in the magic personality of Dwight D. Eisenhower, with no civilian authority strong enough or wise enough to summon the soldiers to account. At Lisbon, finally, the soldiers were forced to answer to a body of civilians why they wanted the troops they said they needed and to yield to the civilians the decision as to how quickly how much of their request could be met.

At Lisbon, the governments gathered in NATO established a Permanent Council of the North Atlantic Treaty. This Council of fourteen civilians was then housed in Paris to sit in permanent session, supervising the work of the soldiers while constantly communicating with their governments on day-to-day adjustments and problems that rose in the great Alliance.

The Lisbon conference did not so much abolish the end goal of 96 divisions in Western Europe as postpone that goal. The civilians pledged themselves to raise 50 divisions in the following year and agreed to decide future targets only when current targets had been met. (This figure has since been raised, cautiously, in 1953 to a target of 56 ready divisions in Western Europe.) At Lisbon, finally, the old concept of a Soviet timetable of attack and war was set aside. The favorite American date of the year of peril –1954–was abandoned. Instead, implicitly, the conferees recognized that perhaps never would there be a showdown year with the Russians, that the Atlantic world was entering into a long period of balancing of power with the Communist world and that success or failure would rest on a long-term test of wisdom and equilibrium.

Now, at last, in the year 1953, the Atlantic Community has come to recognize military goals as fluid, changing objectives. For the spring of 1953 marked not only the maturing of SHAPE as a military field command, but also the maturing of two developments long cultivated by the West, yet, until now, too visionary to enter into the hard calculation of combat.

The one is technical–it is our entrance into that era which one of our most eminent American generals has called the era of "atomic plenty." The swift and secret attack by American scientists simultaneously on the problems of nuclear field weapons and of the amazingly accurate NIKE guided missiles came to success only in the fall of 1952. The impact of this success on SHAPE thinking has been profound but is, as yet, immeasurable. Today American generals estimate that three medium bombers could dump the same devastation on a given front as required 2,700 bombers in the breakthrough of Saint Lô in 1944. At SHAPE, all plans and requirements–for field forces, reserves, buildup, composition of tactical air force—are being freshly restudied for the change that must be wrought in them by the addition of these new resources.

The second development which has shaken all SHAPE's previous military calculations is political. This is the startling uprising of the Berlin workers in June of 1953. The Red Army of Occupation in East Germany reacted to the uprising with extraordinary technical efficiency, moving three full divisions into Berlin within twenty-four hours, a feat wringing respect out of professional soldiers no matter what their uniform. But this enormous drain upon an occupation force of only twenty-two divisions, by an unorganized and unsupported uprising of unarmed workers, has revealed a paralyzing weakness at the base of Russian strength. Hitherto, it has been assumed at SHAPE that the Red Army's divisions faced forward, while the policing of Germans in the rear could be handled adequately by the *Volks Polizei* and *Bereitschaften* of the Communist East German government. It is now obvious that the East German government cannot guarantee the security of the Red Army's rear, and that the Red Army's twenty-two divisions in Germany (as its eight divisions in the satellites) are insufficient to fight forward and police their rear at the same time. For the first time SHAPE can consider defense strategy in terms of a forward counteroffensive, with support ready and available behind the enemy's lines.

Politically, we live still in what may be called the post-Lisbon transitional era of the Atlantic Community. Twice each year this Community sends its leaders to gather in Paris for the meeting of the North Atlantic—three ministers of state from each of the fourteen members plus planeload after planeload of accompanying experts. Motorcycle escorts screech through Paris as the beflagged limousines purr up the rise to the Palais de Chaillot. The hotels of Paris bristle with strange uniforms as the Military Committee of the Alliance gathers to present the Council with its observations; two-star and three-star generals flick in and out of the Committee rooms bearing bulging brief cases full of top-secret data, dancing attendance like office boys on the yet more imposing four- and five-star generals who will present their thinking to the civilian chieftains sent by the people. For three or four days the ministers sit together studying the report of their military committee, examining the account books of Western Defense, scrutinizing the progress in the field, prying at each other's wills and resistance as they decide what to do next.

Yet these meetings are not nearly as important as the method and understructure of the organization they top. The full council meetings of the great ministers are called only to review and settle the problems that have been refined for them by the Permanent Council, which, with the 150-man corps of international civil servants of NATO's Permanent Secretariat, has sat in year-round supervision and interrogation of parliaments, congresses and soldiers alike. Each summer the soldier staffs of NATO, both at SHAPE and in Washington, start their preparation of next year's military targets—what new airfields they need next, what pilot training programs are required, what divisions must be activated, what support troops must be trained. Simultaneously, NATO's Secretariat has prepared for each member government a questionnaire several inches thick, pressing it for details of performance toward last year's targets, its proposals for expansion and contribution in the coming year, its suggestions for broad NATO development. When all these questionnaires are in, the Secretariat of NATO assembles an over-all picture giving the sum of military effort of all fourteen powers, their weaknesses, their failures in the previous twelve months, their proposed global effort for the coming period. When this civilian compilation has been completed and placed beside the military requirements set by the soldiers at SHAPE, the inevitable gap between military demand and civilian response is apparent, and the ministers of the Atlantic Council have a clear problem to wrestle with.

If this were the only function of the Secretariat they would, of course, be no more than a group of military bookkeepers. But there is much more to their operation. Lightly, almost imperceptibly, NATO's Secretariat has cast an international restraining authority over each nation's sovereign impulses. Long before the ministers gather for political adjustment of their differences, the Secretariat, acting for the Community, has summoned individual powers to account. It has examined the books of a small Scandinavian power and thanked it for its promised increase of one division next year, but persuaded it that, militarily, the Community would prefer to see the increase of strength come not in a divisional formation but in the specialist, supporting troops which SHAPE's generals need for flexibility of action. Long before the soldiers at SHAPE have clearly traced the problems of 1954 and 1955, the Secretariat will have singled out such a problem, say, as spare parts, and pointed out that in another three years, when American deliveries of new equipment to the Alliance cease, the Alliance will break down unless the Europeans, now, create the industries to supply needed spare parts for the American tanks, guns, planes and radar. Simultaneously they point out that this burden of maintenance, added to current military obligations, will by 1955, at the present rate of military growth, equal the outer maximum which economists say Europe can sustain. And what then?

The shadow authority of NATO's Secretariat extends even over the United States, gently intruding in American affairs in a way that only Congress ever exercised before. In September of 1952, for example, the United States replied to NATO's questioning with a 250-page document reporting all our military secrets with the exception of atomic energy and strategic bombing policy. For eleven days, NATO's experts pondered American replies, analyzed them, clarified them by queries to American technicians. Then, still unsatisfied, the Secretariat summoned the Permanent Atlantic Council delegates of the United States to the Palais de Chaillot to answer some twenty points which it considered obscure or confusing.

In the Council room of NATO's headquarters four long tables, covered with the usual green baize cloth, were arranged in a square. At one side sat the American delegates like witnesses in a witness box. Facing them was the secretarial staff of NATO. To their left a table was reserved for other delegates from other nations, for in NATO any nation has the right to sit in judgment on the policy of any other. For the two interrogations of the Americans in 1952, French, British, Italians, Canadians, Danes and Norwegians sent examiners. Then came the questions:

"You say," asked one examiner, "that the United States expects the Korean War to be over by July 1, 1953. Why?"

"You say," asked another expert, "that the United States plans to spend so-and-so much as its contribution to the infrastructure of pipelines, airbases, communications demanded by SHAPE. Do you plan to appropriate it as a separate item or are you going to reduce the foreign aid program pledged to us individually by that amount?"

"We asked you," demanded another, "to tell us just how many divisions you have in America available for duty in Europe in time of war and you replied 'zero.' What does that mean? Does that mean you are going to use the home reserve of American troops independently or that we can expect to have them at SHAPE's command on request?"

"How about the answer to that minesweeper question?" asks another. "We asked how many minesweepers America would turn over in a crisis to clear the access channels to Europe and you said 'zero.' Does that mean you will operate them independently or that you really have none?"

"How about America's measures to control inflation?" asked little Denmark, and was completely dissatisfied with the answer of the giant's spokesman.

To Americans fresh out of home such questions seem like violent intrusions on pride, for no one but American Congressmen have ever had the right to summon the American government to account. Yet NATO's control over America is the gentlest exercised over any government, for all governments must submit to this examination and most are treated more harshly. Only America, when pressed, can infrequently refuse to answer. Only America can consistently hold out, if she wishes, against the infrequent 13-to-1 vote in Council and make it stick. Sometimes the British can resist a 13-to-1 Council vote and occasionally the French, too, dare outface the Alliance. But no smaller power can do else but give in to a 13-to-1 adverse vote; for them NATO is more than a community; it is a new kind of government.

For five years, in Paris, the Communists have cast around for words to smear the effort of the Western world to organize itself. Each word has been chosen by the Communists in an effort to pack the phrase with contempt. Western Europe has been called *les pays colonisés*, or *les pays marshallisés*; the Communists' adversaries have been denounced as "the americanized press," or the "americanized governments"; the process has been deftly ridiculed by calling it the "coca-colonization" of European civilization. Recently, at last, even the Communist press has been wrenched about to use a new word we have forced on it—the word "Atlantic." The policy of the West is now called "the Atlantic policy." This, in a fundamental sense, is a victory, for now communism recognizes a new field of force, a new, if primitive, source of political energy.

It would be pleasant if NATO could relax now with this force in being and its dearly purchased triumph of military equilibrium in Europe. Yet the Atlantic Community is only at the beginning of a new chapter, probably even more difficult than the old. For it is only by comparing NATO, the governing body of the Atlantic world, with its adversary, the government of the Communist world, that its weaknesses become apparent.

The Russian dictatorship possesses the matchless advantage of being able to deal with an entire family of problems at the same time. The same Politburo decision that ordains an army-in-being ordains the factories and resources to provision it; ordains swift turns between peace offensive and malevolence; balances arms, propaganda and resources, between Europe and the Orient, between politics and arms, with a silent shifting of gears. The Russians, globally and politically, are mechanically flexible.

What cramps the Atlantic Powers is lack of flexibility. When the Atlantic Community acts, fourteen different powers must agree at the same time to a common decision. When a startling peril confronts them as did the crises of 1948 and 1950, they can call into being the mighty array of military force that SHAPE now commands. But as each new problem arises in the long balancing contest between the Soviet and the Western world, a new travail must be endured as the fourteen nations attempt to strike a common attitude.

Today, NATO is frozen about the decisions of 1948 and 1950. These decisions rightly saw the Atlantic Basin as the centerpiece in world strategy and moved to secure it; since then, the Atlantic Community has rigidly dedicated itself to the creation and equipment of military divisions in Western Europe. Its success has stimulated new Russian political tactics, for the Russians react politically as well as strategically; yet NATO, living in its post-Lisbon state, is prepared to cope with none of them.

New problems tumble one upon the other in a cascade that no one is yet prepared to sort out. There are the geographical and political problems of Asia and Germany. The central position of power in the Atlantic is secure, but meanwhile in Asia, in Korea, in Indo-China, in Malaya, the Communists have mounted a vast flanking operation. There can be no strong and healthy France in Europe so long as she is mired and sickened by the infection of war in Indo-China; there can be little even-tempered consideration of policy in America, so long as men die in Korea.

Germany is as difficult a problem as Asia—great as have been its sins, as troublesome as its Occupation has been, its very health has contributed to the revival of Western power. Germany trembles half in, half out, of the Atlantic Community, unable to decide whether, ultimately, to throw its weight with the Community or stand aloof. The larger Atlantic Community cannot be healthy until its leaders have decided on a common attitude to Germany.

The struggle of ideas is equally beyond NATO's present power. NATO possesses body, limbs, organs—but no soul. It keeps books but raises no fresh flags or banners. Its propaganda staff consists of forty-one people (including clerical staff) busy filing press clippings or recording the progress of arms for the world's journals; its entire budget for molding opinion and explaining itself to the world is a trivial $60,000 a year, or one-fifth of the cost of a jet plane. Even more sadly, one must record that no multiplication of budget or personnel would do NATO's public information service any good, for there exists in NATO no central core of thinkers, turning over the ideas of freedom to refresh its dynamic. No serious body of analysis studies the Russians and the Communists in any but military terms, and nothing in NATO provides people with the living image of the free, expanding, fluid society which it is the armies' purpose to guard.

It is here, in political direction, that NATO is sadly wanting. Each nation cautiously shares in NATO a tiny portion of its secret intelligence on the Russians, and the ultimate product is a fuzzy blur in which the enemy's purposes are never seen clearly, and our own purpose frays as a result. British and Americans divide in NATO on the measure of the menace—is it over or is it increasing? Has it ceased to be military and become political, or is it an ever-growing military peril? Americans and French divide violently—do the Russians now plan to upset the economic world in which we live, precipitating us into cycles of depressions, while increasing their own welfare, comfort and economic capacity, as the French hold? Or is their purpose to build and build and build simply to erect a military machine that can crush freedom in one blow, as the Americans hold? All these theses cannot be correct, but if either the British or French or American thesis is the right one, then the Community must take a radical new reading of its purposes in the next few years. Yet it is not prepared to do so, it fumbles while it should decide.

The Atlantic is an area in which people live who are set apart from all other peoples by one underlying concept—that of the free man, his body free from arbitrary arrest, free from arbitrary tax, free to speak, free to gather, free to think. It is this civilization, challenged from within and without, that its member states have joined to protect. Yet they have not even arrived at the definition of their common enmities. Are other peoples with different concepts of life enemies because they are different, or enemies because they are organized by Russian control for potential assault on our homes? Is China an enemy because she is Communist, or is she an enemy because she has become the instrument of Russian diplomacy? Is the civilization of the Middle East dangerous because it wishes to change its relation to the Atlantic Community, or because it flirts with Russian purpose? There are many communities in this coagulating world, only one of which is sworn to destroy Atlantic civilization, the Russian. There are the civilizations of the Moslems, of the Dark Africans, of the Chinese, of the Indians, of Southeast Asians. Toward each, in the new diplomacy of great communities of men, our civilization must have an attitude. Yet NATO is still too confined to consider them.

There remains then a final set of problems: the attitude of NATO's peoples to each other. NATO's vigor has risen from a military threat, and its directors have rigidly limited their deeds to the legal words of the compact. Therefore, when such a disaster as the floods of the Lowlands desolate the homes of a member country, each member reacts individually shipping sandbags, clothes, medicines to the stricken land, but the great executive machine of the Community, NATO, lies inert, unable to think or act swiftly enough for any other purpose but war. Again, though the European members of NATO recognize that the first upward surge of their recovery is over and that a chill stagnation of industrial expansion has succeeded it, NATO can do nothing. Though NATO was built to erect a barrier behind which the welfare of each nation would increase in peace and safety, it cannot find the authority to examine what next step must be taken to increase that welfare.

The Atlantic Community has, in short, won its first victory—it has created that field of power that finally inspires as Ernest Bevin once hoped "confidence . . . within and respect elsewhere." But this has been a negative victory—it has been a victory of defense, a triumph of resistance. Wars are not won by defense, nor are souls won by men who are simply "against." With the equilibrium of 1953, NATO has arrived only at the end of the beginning. The tasks that knock for admittance to discussion are those of creation, of imagination, of going forward. It is what comes next that counts.

XIV

communism--the challenge

Americans are so frightened by the evil in communism that they fail to see that the greatest danger is not the evil but the attraction in it. Only Americans live in a society in which communism can seduce no healthy mind. Most of our senior Allies and the myriad-man countries who live outside our Alliance are made of people who stand transfixed by fear of communism and its sinister charm at the same time.

The magic appeal in the Communist faith is simple. It is the belief that pure logic applied to human affairs is enough to change the world and cure it of all its human miseries. It is buttressed by the belief that the processes of history are governed by certain "scientific" laws, which automatically guarantee the triumph of communism when the situation is ripe, if only its protestants have the courage to strike and act.

This simple credo carries an almost irresistible attraction to two kinds of people everywhere in the world: first, to small coteries of able and ambitious young men hungry for the ecstasy of leadership, and, secondly, to larger masses of miserable ignorant people who have just begun to hope.

To both these schools of converts, the fatal flaw in the Communist faith is neither apparent nor important. This fatal flaw is embedded in the nature of human beings whenever they gather politically. Human beings tend to be illogical. The logic of which communism boasts is never certain, therefore, of success in any political operation unless simultaneously it imposes so rigid a discipline as to make ordinary people mere bodies in the sequence of their masters' planning. Logic cannot succeed if its premises are to be shaken over and over again by vagrant human emotions allowed freely to express themselves in all their passion and frailty.

Any political organization which sets out to be totally logical thus calls for total discipline; total discipline inevitably requires police, and police bring terror.

But the weakness of communism lies less in the calculated immorality of terror than in the inevitable internal appetite of the discipline. The discipline feeds on itself; it shrinks the area of discussion and decision into ever narrower, ever tighter, ever more cramped circles. Fewer and fewer men have less and less access to the raw facts which are necessary for wise judgment. The discipline they control and impose inevitably sneaks back to weaken them, to blind or deafen them into stupidity and error.

To those who come to communism out of ambition or out of misguided intelligence, this flaw is not immediately apparent. Each of this type of convert cherishes the illusion until too late that the ever-shrinking circle of discipline will leave him safe at its center of creative leadership, rather than crushed and tortured as discipline contracts about his own soft human body. To the second category of converts, those who come to it out of hunger and ignorance, this flaw in communism (even if it could be explained to them) seems unimportant. They have always been excluded from decision and control over their own lives. Communism promises them simply "more"; they are ready to believe. The hungrier and more ignorant they are, the more difficult it is to explain to them that their own hopes and welfare are directly dependent on the freedom of creative minds, with which they are unfamiliar, to think independently of all discipline.

To the Western world, so challenged by communism, this flaw in the adversary presents a grotesque problem. Communism's prison-logical system of human organization grows in strength decade by decade even as its leadership becomes less and less capable of wise and sensible decision. For all its dynamism and strength, the Communist world falls into blunders with increasing frequency, blunders which are only rectified by great wrenchings of policy that shake the world with disaster. To deal with communism, one must recognize both its strength and its blunders clearly.

Communist strength today is radiant with power at two levels. It possesses, in Russia, a base of physical force adorned with every instrument of compulsion and combat, still in flood tide of expansion, carried on by the momentum of those warped geniuses who made the Russian revolution. It also possesses, still, the fire and power of a missionary faith, seducing men's minds everywhere with the simplicity of its logic. Its achievements and physical strength within its Russian base marry with its evangelical kinetic outside Russia to give it the sweep and appearance of an irresistible tide. Yet, by its own internal laws, as its area of control and success spreads, its discipline must become ever tighter and ever more constricting. And this process, extending and deepening, not only on the periphery of satellite and associate states, but ever more ruthlessly at the center in Moscow, has already begun to addle the thinking, fuddle the judgment, provoke the unrest, and produce those inevitable blunders which give the Western world its opportunities.

Such an event as the death of Stalin, by shaking the superstructure of discipline, by admitting for a brief moment the clash of several opinions and the consequent opportunity for a slightly larger area of discussion at the summit, has given the Communist machinery of politics a momentary opportunity to review some of its errors. But, unless communism ceases to be communism, the process of discipline calls for a new tightening of control, a new struggle to apply the logic of a single man to a world of dark and uncertain phenomena.

There are both opportunity and danger in the momentary situation, but before one can take comfort from these opportunities, one must first measure how great have been the triumphs of communism and how forbidding is their portent.

The place to begin this examination is, of course, Russia. This is because the most remarkable Communist success since the war has taken place not in China, nor Eastern Europe, but in Russia itself.

One stark fact protrudes like a monument through the fog of secrecy and propaganda with which the Russians surround every restless stirring in their system. Ostrich-like, the Western world has consistently refused to face this fact squarely. This fact is the stupendous industrial and technical progress of the Soviet Union since the war. Never in the entire history of the Russian people have they known a swifter period of industrial achievement or a longer unbroken movement forward than that since the year 1945.

Since the war, Soviet industry has grown in heft at a rate never equaled in any other society. Since 1945 the Russians have almost doubled their prewar production of coal (up from 166 million tons a year to 301 million tons), their production of steel (up from 18 million tons to 34 million tons), of oil (up from 31 million tons to 47 million tons) and nearly tripled their production of electric power (from 48 billion kilowatt-hours to 116 billion kilowatt-hours). This increase, it should be stressed, is the increase only as measured against the best Russian records of the prewar years—which means that the actual increase has been much greater because before the Russians could reach these peaks, they had to repair war devastation greater than that of any other nation except Germany.

Russian basic industry still measures at only one-third, roughly, the size of American basic industry, producing a third of our steel, a sixth of our oil, a fourth of our kilowatt-hours, three-fifths of our coal. It is the trend, however, that is disconcerting; only seven years ago these proportions read one-fifth of our steel, less than a tenth of our oil, less than a fifth of our electricity, less than a third of our coal. Since then, our industrial base has expanded as never before in our history; yet the Russians have narrowed the gap, not only relatively, but in a few cases absolutely. If we project the growth curves of our industry and Soviet industry, assuming there will be no great depression, there seems little danger that the Russians will overtake us in this generation. But our grandchildren may have to face the disconcerting possibility that in the world of tomorrow, Russia could be the world's prime industrial power and America the second.

This perspective is ominous. But set against the pattern of life in Western Europe, it is more ominous still. Western Europe—France, Italy, Germany, England and the Low Countries—is a population bloc of 207 million people; this is the same as that of the Soviet Union. At present the Soviet Union produces half as much coal (301 million tons against 530 million tons), three-fifths as much steel (34 million tons against 51 million tons), half as much electricity (116 billion kilowatt-hours against 196 billion kilowatt-hours) as Western Europe. Although a great gap still exists between the two, the drama arises from the spectacular stride and rhythm of Russian production. Since the war, Western Europe has progressed at a pace swifter than at any time since just before World War I. But Russian efforts make West European progress seem puny. The British, for example, are the greatest coal-producing power of Western Europe; they have not yet recovered their prewar level of production. After seven years of desperate effort they have now set as the target of their effort, to be reached over a period of twelve years, an increase of 20 million tons annually. Since 1950, in a single two-year period, the Russians have increased their coal production by a total of 40 million tons annually. The great steel-making powers of Western Europe—England, France, Benelux and Germany—with all the aid and prodding of the Marshall Plan have succeeded in adding only eight million tons of new steel capacity to their economy since the war. The Russians alone have added more than twice that amount of capacity and plan almost to double their present total by the end of this decade. If Russia's industrial planning goals are met—and, in view of the record, there is little reason to believe they will not be—by 1960 she will have pulled abreast of West Europe in basic industrial production.

Up until now in the political rivalry of communism and freedom, freedom has been sold in Western Europe not only as a good in itself but as a more fruitful way of acquiring the comforts of life. For thirty-five years the contagion of communism has been limited in Europe by the knowledge that the Russian worker lives at a sub-barbarian standard of life. While the gap between Russian and West European standards of life is still huge, the possibility, although not the certainty, exists that within another fifteen to twenty years the masters of the Soviet world can, if they wish, close this gap. When and if the closing of this gap becomes apparent in material goods, the politics of Europe will change as a tide changes; if comparative poverty becomes the price of freedom, freedom will fight from defense positions.

To Americans, the growth of Russian industry seems laden with many threatening prospects—the prospect of an enormous increase in military strength and power; the prospect of vast Russian patronage of the backward world by the production and political sale of capital goods in which Russia specializes and which the backward world needs so much; the prospect of commercial dumping in world markets to cause the prices of grain, of gold, of timber, of rubber, of raw materials to fluctuate wildly. The West Europeans, too, see all these prospects, but one other worries them more. It is that the Russians will sluice their vast productive increases into a proportionate increase in the consumption goods available to ordinary citizens, and that having done this, they will lift the Iron Curtain to amplify the appeal of communism to the workers of stagnant or slowly expanding West European lands.

In the fall of 1952, shortly after the announcement of the current Russian Five Year Plan, the French government asked several of its economists to draw up some statistical comparisons between French and Russian standards of life, as they appeared likely in the last year of the plan, 1955. By 1955, said the answering report, the Soviet Union will be abreast, in per capita averages, of French production. Each Soviet citizen will enjoy, statistically, 1,384 kilograms of coal as against 1,250 for the Frenchman. He will have only 206 kilograms of steel as against 232 kilograms for the Frenchman, but after deducting twenty-five per cent from the French steel total for exports to pay for France's vital imports, the Russians will enjoy more steel per capita, too. In 1955, France will still retain a lead in electricity—at least 850 kilowatt-hours, possibly more, per head as against 756 kilowatt-hours per head in the Soviet Union.

The report made even more striking comparisons for those fruits of industry that actually reach the citizen and affect his unthinking politics. By 1955, it appears, the average Russian will have, statistically, at his disposal twice as much grain as the average Frenchman (870 kilograms against 350), twice as many potatoes (600 kilograms against 300), more fish (13 kilos a year against 9.5), more table fats (17 kilos against 14), more cotton cloth (28 yards against 16), as many shoes (three pairs every two years). He will still have less sugar (20 kilos a year against the Frenchman's 26), and far less meat (24 kilos against 47 kilos). By as early as 1955 or 1956, was the prediction, Russia might, if her masters politically wanted to, offer her citizenry standards of living roughly equal to those of the French.

Let it be said at once that most other economists consider such calculations outrageously gloomy. Such calculations assume that Russia's agricultural planning targets will be met—and Russian planning almost always breaks down in agriculture. Such calculations also leave out of account not only the quality of produce but also such essentials as fruits, vegetables, hospital care, vacations, milk and those thousand-and-one unplanned service comforts that go to make what we in the West consider a decent standard of living. Moreover, even though Russia by all calculations will pull abreast of Western Europe in basic industry by 1960, and assuming the profit goes to the citizens instead of to the war machine, the effort to convert this basic industry into a consumer industry will have to be prodigious. In any advanced Western country like America, England or France, far more people are involved in processing the basic goods of industry than in creating them, and far more subtle skills are involved. Russia is geared to produce generators and dams, not fractional horsepower motors for Mixmasters, record players and vacuum cleaners. Russia is geared to produce steel for guns and tanks, not for houses and canned foods. Russia is geared to produce crude textiles in enormous quantities to be sold by the yard to peasant women willing to cut and sew them; she is not yet geared for the vaster effort of ready-made clothes.

Yet the argument of just how far off the French survey is in its judgment of the intersection year is a narrow one. If, as most economists believe, it cannot possibly come before 1960, it is certainly possible that standards of living in Russia may overtake standards of living in such countries as France or Italy by 1970. After 1960 it will be only a matter of political decision on the part of Russia's masters as to just when, and in what way, they take advantage of their economic strength—whether to pour it into a stepped-up military effort to overawe the West, whether to pour it into buccaneering to wreck the world market, or whether to pour it into comfort goods for ordinary people to disrupt the politics of Western Europe by contagion of demonstration. And it is precisely here, in all likelihood, that the major problems of Russian foreign policy lock with the central internal struggle now going on in Moscow.

Of all those areas which Russian secrecy guards, none is more jealously sheltered than the inner area of decision-making where personalities, ambitions, rivalries and emotions clash in just this kind of problem. Like subterranean monsters, Russia's masters grapple with each other in the deep, beyond the range of sight, and only an occasional stinking bubble breaking to the surface tells us that a struggle is going on at all. Because our own political thinking is almost hypnotized by the clash of personalities, and we lack any such information from Russia at all, we are thus reduced to primitive fascination with detail—the counting of place and position of leadership as the members of the Politburo line up on Lenin's tomb in the Red Square, an examination of the lines in the suet-like folds of Malenkov's face, the remembered rudeness of a Stalin to a Molotov in the presence of a stranger.

This fascination with secrets at the summit is pointless, for here all our instruments of intelligence fail. Moreover, it is dangerous because it diverts our attention from the great peripheral areas of Russian life where social pressures accumulate. Eventually, these pressures do lock in the Kremlin's darkness, but at their birth, at the grass roots of life, no censorship can conceal them. And these forces are so broad, all-embracing and profound that even Russian documents must reveal, along with the great facts of economic triumph and recovery, the complementary facts of an internal political struggle, developed and incubated by this economic progress.

This internal struggle does not seem to be so much a struggle of personalities—viz. Malenkov versus Bulganin versus Molotov—although the clash of personal ambition must be important. Nor is it even a struggle of rival organs of power—viz. army against state against secret police against party. In its coarsest form, the struggle seems to be one of generations. On the one side are ranged several decades of Soviet leadership cut off by a dividing line of age near the forty-year mark. On the other an inchoate, confused, but potent body of men, ranging down from the forty-year mark, press up against this old leadership. The issue, as expressed in party speeches, is one of doctrinal orthodoxy, of hard-shell primitives against younger, questioning revisionists. Even in the cannibal morality of central Russian politics, issues are important; but when issues are joined in Russia, not only policy is at stake, but the lives of the men who divide over them. The issue at stake within the Soviet Union seems to be, basically, how and what the Soviet people shall do with their growing power and resources.

The chief body of evidence for this assumption comes from the proceedings of the last full-dress gathering of Russian leadership, the Communist Party Congress of 1952. One need only match this last Communist Congress in Moscow against its predecessors to see how sharply age and change is working in Soviet society.

The Russian revolution was made by young men. Lenin, at the age of forty-seven, directed the entire apparatus of revolt. But Lenin was the old man. His chief lieutenants were Stalin, thirty-eight, who created the machinery of secret police and terror, and Leon Trotsky, forty, who forged the Red Army out of nothing. Molotov was but a stripling youth of twenty-seven, yet already old enough to be noticed by Lenin as a coming man. The early Congresses of both party and state in the first decade of Soviet existence were dominated by men who, in American cities, would be considered the Junior-Chamber-of-Commerce age group. The last Communist Congress in which all these revolutionary fathers participated, in 1924, was an assembly of men eighty-two per cent of whom were less than forty years old.

Since then, the party has slowly changed. As it matured under the various Five-Year Plans and as its leaders grew older, the percentage of the young under forty dropped until it was only seventy per cent. But the great purges of 1934 and 1936 butchered off those aging revolutionary founders who were Stalin's contemporaries and rivals. Stalin packed the party with his own hand-picked young men, and by the 1939 Congress the percentage of young men under forty was up to eighty-one per cent again. This generation of Stalin's boys has remained in power from 1934 until today—longer than any other governing group in power in the modern world, longer even than the New Dealers, who were their contemporaries, held power in Washington. The change in the profile of Soviet leadership as this group has slowly aged is traced in the records of the Communist Congress of 1952. Only twenty-three per cent of the delegates to the last Party Congress were under forty. Never before in the prewar party had the middle-aged made up more than a third of the delegates, but at the last Congress they were three-quarters of the Assembly.

Nor is this monopoly on power by one homogeneous age group the only characteristic revealed by the last Congress. Until the outbreak of the war against Germany, the Communists had stressed, not only theoretically, but in actual practice, the working-class and peasant origins of their party leadership. Thus, proudly, they recorded that in 1924, sixty-three per cent of their delegates were of working-class origin; in 1927, seventy-one per cent; in 1930, again seventy-one per cent; in 1934, sixty per cent. Then, abruptly, just before the war, such social backgrounds were dropped from the records. Instead, the Russians now describe background only in terms of education. Today, as the record of 1952 shows, sixty per cent of the top leaders of Communist Russia, gathered in their Congress, have received a college education and another twenty-five per cent have had a secondary education sufficient to classify them as intelligentsia. In their own Marxist terms, the men of the Communist Congress of 1952 were a far more "bourgeois" body than either the British Parliament or the French Assembly, possibly even more "bourgeois" than the United States Congress. Of the 709 delegates to the Communist Congress, no less than 282 were graduate engineers, another 68 were agricultural engineers, 98 were teachers or professors, 18 were economists, 11 were doctors, seven were lawyers.

The profile of the new Communist leadership that emerges is quite different from that of the rough, hard-bitten, earthy men who brought the revolution to power under the cruel and brilliant leadership of a handful of intellectuals. What emerges is the outline of a group of men, predominantly middle-aged, who entered into power after Stalin had wiped out the founding revolutionary fathers in the purges of 1934 and who have clung to power ever since. If one substitutes the term "businessman" for the Russian word "engineer" or "economist," what emerges is a governing class dominated by the Russian counterpart of the Western businessman-producer. They are men engaged in building a materialistic society in which the critical values are success and production, in which no labor unions exist to restrain them and in which government and police are their tools and hand-servants. It is not at all surprising to find that the most conspicuous name cast up after the death of Stalin should be a representative of this group, Georgi Malenkov, a man of fifty-one, trained as an engineer by the revolution, summoned to power by Stalin after the 1934 purge. Nor that the new ten-man Politburo should include about the same proportion of businessmen-engineers-producers as President Eisenhower's Cabinet.

Though the political values of these men are different in the most barbarian way from those of Western businessmen, it is almost impossible not to be amused by how closely their cultural values resemble those of our Victorian forefathers and how much they scorn all those forms of art and spirit which in the West are usually associated with the Left and revolution. Like the dynamic, grasping Victorian man of affairs, Russian men of affairs frown on "fancy" and "arty" experiments. In their music they like clear melodies, not modern dissonances or harmonies—woe to the composer who fails to soothe their tired minds with sweet, familiar song. In their art they spit contempt on all those forms of modern experimental design and color which they call "bourgeois formalism." They like pictures that tell stories. Though Picasso may be the pride and joy of the French Communist party, Russian artists know well that their art cannot range beyond the homiletic paintings of the school of Sir Edwin Landseer on the one hand, or the poster-craft of Madison Avenue advertising on the other. In short, the leaders of the Russian Communist party are Philistines and what they dislike is subversive.

Like the Victorians again, these men have easily acquired a taste for the privileges of luxury and comfort that go with aristocracy. Since communism is now a full generation old it has had time to develop a system of élite complete with special privileges, that runs with monotonous repetition from end to end of their supposedly classless world. This correspondent first noticed the pattern in the primitive wartime capital of Chinese communism at Yenan which, even in its then egalitarian state, already provided the leaders with the cleanest and neatest caves, the best food, the warmest clothes. It had even learned how to divide the pitifully tiny supply of milk so that babies of important people would not go without. The pattern has repeated itself, ever since, in every Communist capital I have been able to visit. In Belgrade, in 1949, the élite lived in the once-fashionable streets of the Dedinje district, with its gardened mansions, shopped at special stores where special luxuries were available at special prices. In Budapest, in 1948, the élite lived in the fancy suburban houses across the river in Pest, where once the bourgeoisie played in comfort, while along the luxury row of Warczi Ucze, the leather-makers, glove-makers, custom tailors seemed still to be doing a thriving business though no ordinary worker could afford to shop there on his salary. At the Leipzig fair, in 1950, the chief international trading mart of the Communist world, the booths glowed with wares offered for the aristocracy of communism—gleaming, brass-fitted pleasure speedboats, superb crystalline glassware, ornate ostentatious Zis convertibles sent from Russia, as luxurious and chrome-bright as American Cadillacs.

Those who have visited Moscow—this correspondent has not—report that the entire system of special privilege reaches an apex there. To Moscow are shipped the Czech ornaments, the Chinese silks, the Hungarian telephones that Russian trade extorts from its satellites; the first seasonal consignments of Israeli oranges are speeded to Moscow from Odessa by plane. For the generation in command, the spoils of success include chauffeured automobiles, modern apartments, servants, television sets. The salary after taxes of a plant manager runs between ten and twenty times the salary of his workers. The rewards may not be opulent in themselves, no more perhaps than a $20,000 salary might be in the United States. But set against the everlasting squalor of the people who provide the rewards, in a supposedly classless society, the differences are staggering. And, when one reaches the very upper levels of Soviet consumption—the inner circle of the party or the peak stars of movies, letters and ballet—there consumption reaches a level that few of the heavily taxed wealthy of the Western world can any longer enjoy.

Greed and ambition work on individuals in Russia in the same way they work outside Russia. Edward Crankshaw, the great British student of Russian affairs, offers for examination several quotations from a recent and very popular play in Moscow called *Beketov's Career*. Beketov, the villain, is an engineer in a provincial factory trying to sabotage production so that the plant director might be dismissed and Beketov step into his shoes. Beketov explains it all to his wife.

"Think, Masha, in a year or two if all goes well, we shall get to Moscow . . . Moscow, Masha, Moscow. . . . I might, who knows, become a department head . . . not so bad, Masha, not so bad . . . and then, why not, a deputy minister! Think, Masha—

a flat on the Gorky street, a private villa on the outskirts somewhere outside by the reservoir. . . . And you, Masha, with your beauty will dazzle the world. . . . I can see us together at a great reception. . . . I stand a little apart and feast my eyes on you, surrounded by ministers and vice-admirals. If I close my eyes I can see you now . . . you are wearing a long velvet dress the color of a ripe cherry. You have golden bracelets, glittering on your wrists. And here, Masha, just a little above your heart burns a diamond rose."

The play was not written to criticize Beketov's ambitions; flats on the Gorky street, villas in the country, velvet gowns, golden bracelets, diamond roses are all accepted as normal for those who succeed in Russia. What the play attacked was simply the villainous methods by which Beketov hoped to reap these normal rewards.

Russian leadership at the top—conservative in taste, dictatorial by training, increasingly accustomed to comfort—does not want to be disturbed from below. Yet, increasingly, one senses in Russian statements and Russian press comment that a disturbance grows. It was the last Russian Communist Congress in 1952 which traced the silhouette of the disturbance most clearly. The disturbance rose not from a political group but from an entire generation whose sin seemed to be a simple human desire to share some of the wealth they had laboriously produced. This generation, it appeared, though brought up under the discipline of police terror, still itched with human desires and wants that challenged the leaders who wanted to continue to propel Russia to further power by a logical direction of their unslackening exertion.

The clearest description of this generation comes from the major political event of the Congress—the long, philosophical monograph of Stalin, his last legacy to his party. Most of the old mythical enemies had disappeared from Stalin's speech; there was no longer any denunciation, as in by-gone years, of "Right deviationism" or "Left deviationism," of Trotsky, or Bukharin, or the White Guards. Instead, Stalin's target of denunciation was squarely and simply a faceless group of men described as "certain comrades" and then precisely defined as the young people who had grown up under the Soviet system. It is these, said Stalin, who, having known only "the colossal attainments of the Soviet power," feel that the state should now share with them the long-promised wealth of communism. It is these "certain comrades" who advance the perilous idea that capitalism in the West has changed its nature and become "progressive." It is the young who believe that capitalist states may actually have begun to content themselves with "average profit" and that thus one may hope to avoid war. All these mistakes were denounced by Stalin not only as error but as sin. The capitalists are still hell-bent not only on "average profit" and "super-profit" but on "maximum profit," said Stalin. It is not possible to permit the people now, at this moment, to taste the produce of the machinery they have so sweated for—communism is still a long way off. It is not possible, said Stalin, to relax and permit the peasants of Russia to trade and exchange on the free market, as is their irrepressible desire. The free market must be wiped out. It is not possible to let the millions of peasant families finally organized in collectives begin to think that their collective land belongs to them, even in a collective sense. The land belongs to the state.

It is impossible to strain out of the obscurity of Stalin's speeches a precise profile of the tension—whether it was a pressure within the party of younger leaders for more power as well as more spoils for themselves personally, or whether it was a pressure from the people outside seeking relaxation, expressing their pressures through junior members in the party. Yet, in the words of succeeding speakers, it seemed a multiplication of both.

The second major pronouncement of the Communist Congress was the speech of Georgi Malenkov, the present Premier. Malenkov's speech had all the earmarks of a document drawn up in haste, by a man covering his own uncertainties, substituting facts and generalities for specific analysis. Malenkov did not attack the "young" as such. Picking up the Stalin line, he seemed to be wrestling less with a conspiracy within the party against the state than with the erosion of the party by human nature. His recurrent theme of the softening and slackening of the party is tasseled with phrases like "rottenness," "decomposition and putrefaction," "morbid diseases." The party, as described by Malenkov, is infected with people using party position for personal profit, individuals personally corrupt or simply pursuing careers. Succeeding speakers echoed Malenkov. Where Malenkov had hauled the corruption of the party in Ulianovsk to light, Krushchev followed to expose the corruption of the party in Rostov. Mgeladze described with horror a situation in Georgia all too familiar to American politics—the party machinery was becoming simply a cloak for old mountain clans, whose cliques and families were packing the best positions and dominating local affairs.

The chief action of the Congress was another tightening of the discipline, which had been tightening consistently for thirty years and which was, nevertheless, now challenged once more. The party laws had previously given one member "the right" to spy on another; now espionage of each member upon another was made "a duty." Dangerously, each subordinate was made responsible for reporting on the sins, errors and weaknesses of his superiors as if no man anywhere in the state could be trusted; simultaneously the masses were urged to denounce the cadres. Finally, the senior machinery of the party was reorganized, its Politburo, Central Committee and Secretariat all devalued and reshuffled.

The acts of the Congress were perhaps the last major architecture of state drafted by Stalin. They laid the base for a new and ruthless defense of the old orthodoxies, the foundation for a new series of purges which seemed to be only beginning when death abruptly erased the power of the aged dictator in March, 1953.

What has happened since Stalin's death is too fresh for sober judgment and may take years to be fully understood. In the confusion of his succession, however, one fact already stands out with striking sharpness—it is how great and contrary must have been the pressures playing within the Russian state even under his direction and bloody discipline. Within less than twenty-four hours after his death, the detailed reorganization of party and state he had ordained the previous October was dismantled. Within another month even the machinery of terror had been disgraced and its freshest victims, previously caught in a senile impulse of anti-Semitism, released. Within the next three months a whole series of measures were ordained to relax the discipline of state—intellectual, economic and political—and appease the pressures from below. In the same period a new façade was erected for Soviet foreign policy, behind which even its fundamental strategy seems in the process of changing.

No one knows who is responsible for these decisions. All that can be assumed from the outer episodes of Russian evolution since Stalin's death is that the struggle over policy continues not only among individual leaders but among the rival organs of power (or combinations of power) they control. The swift triumph of Malenkov over Beria; the curious appeal of the victorious group to, and their use of, the municipal Moscow Soviet; the careful insistence of the victors on the collective nature of their leadership and repudiation of any personal ambition or virtue mark only the first round in a struggle that promises to be long drawn out. All that is known is that the remaining contestants for power are drawn from a generation of middle-aged men pressed from beneath by that generation of the young first described by Stalin in the fall of 1952. Whatever rivalries now simmer in the Kremlin will probably, therefore, end with the victory of the man or men who can most successfully mobilize from beneath the support and the energy of the younger generation. It was thus that Stalin, twenty years ago, mobilized their generation when young to wipe out their elders, his contemporaries.

Externally and internally, therefore, the new leaders may find that their needs coincide. On the Communist borders of Europe no mobilization of force can recapture the military superiority of yesterday when Western rearmament had not yet won its present dominance in Central Europe. A relaxation of Soviet military pressure might seduce apart the coalition that the policy of Stalin created against Russia; it might even plunge the coalition into a spiral of depression. Internally, too, such a relaxation is politically wise, for the ultimate victor in the political struggle will probably be the one who can give the under-generation its first taste of comfort.

To re-establish leadership and reimpose unquestioning discipline takes time. During this period, for an indefinite number of months or years, the Western world may find itself face to face with a more relaxed Russia than for many years. This relaxation offers both opportunity and danger. It is an opportunity to solve specific East-West disputes by dealing with men in the Kremlin who, for their own purposes, need peace abroad for a time. It is a danger if the Western world accepts the relaxation without counteraction, letting itself go slack at home, both socially and militarily. For if the Western world cannot organize its economic and political resources for another and vaster push forward, the Russians, as their economy and welfare expands, may win politically what they can no longer win militarily.

However much the political struggle within Russia may mollify the manners of Russia in the outer world, there is nothing that promises any withering of that essential Communist faith which considers us a world in decay and pledges the faithful to seek our doom. Whatever tactical evolution it goes through, Russian foreign policy is unlikely ever to diverge from that purpose which has held firm ever since 1945—to disturb, divide or disrupt any effort of the Western world to brace itself for the challenge of tomorrow.

It is important, therefore, to look coldly at the techniques and record of this foreign policy since the war. Western amateurs of politics have frequently held that the postwar epoch has been marked by a series of brilliant, Stalinist master-moves which have designed the sweeping expansion of communism over the globe. But if one breaks Russian foreign policy down, area by area, it becomes immediately clear that neither brilliance nor foresight was involved, and that Russia, rather than having made the most of the opportunity offered it, has made the least. If one divides the areas of Russian operation into Eastern Europe, the Far East and Western Europe, one can see clearly how little wisdom or Russian direction contributed to the triumphs which so menace us.

The record of Communist triumph usually begins with Eastern Europe, the first area in time and geography to be added to the Communist world outside of Russia.

Eastern Europe is a collection of eight states in which live one hundred million people of odd races and tongues who, since the beginning of history, have lived in fear of and under attack between the explosive forces of Germany and Russia. From the moment the Western world was forced to join Russia in alliance against Hitler, the West's ultimate victory was mortgaged by the geography of war to yield the one hundred million people of Eastern Europe to the Russians. They lay on the way from Moscow to Berlin, and, if victory was to be won, they would have to fall to the Red Army, which they did. Nothing could prevent it.

The postwar politics of Eastern Europe began when the Russians proceeded to organize this purely military conquest. In 1945 it might have yielded them either an enormous increment of political-military strength, or remained mere satellite real estate. It has remained real estate.

Out of the lands of Eastern Europe, the Russians have won: a buffer belt of great technical military importance which at its narrowest is two hundred miles deep; an increment of industry that adds some thirty per cent to their industrial strength but which burdens them with fifty per cent more population; and, finally, between sixty-five and seventy divisions of puppet satellite troops, whom they must equip and who are offset by the defection of Tito's army.

No conquering army could have failed of these targets; even the Japanese, in their organization of Occupied China during the war, did better. What the Russians failed to do, as they might have done, was to make of these lands a basin of political infection for all the West European nations facing them, to make of their people, not bitterly hateful puppets, but allies, at least as reliable as those American diplomacy has created in the Atlantic Basin. By presenting the most repellent of all political wares in the show window that fronts on Western Europe, the Russians urged millions of Europeans back to acquiescent loyalty to their own sick systems. By pressing savage industrialization programs on their satellites, the Russians have reduced their economies to misery and prodded them to hopeless revolt. Everywhere in Western Europe, Communist agents and zealots now must sell communism on the basis of abstract Communist theology, while in every slum in which they chant their message, some moody refugee from Communist Hungary, East Germany, Poland or Rumania can testify to the brutality of its actual practice.

The blunder was, of course, inherent in the fatal flaw of communism—its need to impose discipline. For the Russians did not enter these lands entirely unloved; nor did they find stony soil in which to plant their gospel.

No episode returns to my memory of Eastern Europe with greater clarity than an incident of a visit I made to Hungary in

1948. For the Hungarians, 1948 was the Indian summer of their recovery. Men had recuperated from their war wounds, the women were gay, the fiddlers loud, the night clubs thronged, and, most important of all, the first good postwar harvest had been gathered in. That fall the Russians chose to begin both the collectivization of the land and the purges. Two Communist escort-interpreters drove me out into the country to visit one of these new collective farms.

We arrived at the farm late in the evening, and the old chairman of the collective greeted us with a big bottle of vodka, a plate of red peppers and salt, and a hearty welcome. I wanted a picture of exactly how they had made the "revolution" in that village.

The old man started at the very beginning, with the land. The land had belonged to the manor lord. The peasants had lived in the ramshackle muddy *U*-shaped stable compound, where pigs wallowed in the mud, geese cackled and farm animals evacuated. It had been that way as long as they could remember. Then Marshal Tolbukhin's Red Army drove through, pushing the Germans before them, and established its headquarters a few miles away. It was only a few days after Tolbukhin had set up camp that Ber Julio returned one day from a visit to headquarters.

At this point I interrupted and asked, "Who was Ber Julio?"

"Ber Julio?" said the old man. "You don't know Ber Julio? Ber Julio was the man who made the revolution here."

"But who was he?" I asked.

"Oh, he was one of us," said the old man. "Ber Julio was always interested in politics; he was even a member of the Small Peasants Party before the war. He was a fine man, was Ber Julio, with big black eyes and a wonderful, beautiful black mustache. How he liked to talk! He was always talking. He came back that day from Tolbukhin's headquarters and called us all together, right here. He got up on a table and he said, 'Comrades, this is the greatest day of our lives. Now the land belongs to us and we are going to divide it!' Everybody was there, the men, the women, the children; some of the women even brought their chickens along so they shouldn't be stolen, and some men carried their pigs, too. Ber Julio sat in the courtyard on a chair in front of the table; there was a red-check table cloth on the table, and he told us just how we were supposed to divide the land, how we should make a list of families who needed land and then how we should measure."

I interrupted again for the story seemed a gay one, and I wanted more detail. "Well, where is Ber Julio now? Let's call him here and have Ber Julio tell us exactly how they divided the land."

At this a hush fell over the table, swiftly broken by a clatter of excited and angry Hungarian in which Ber Julio's name was repeated over and over.

"What's the matter?" I asked the interpreter. "What's going on?"

Nothing was the matter, said the interpreter, nothing. Ber Julio just wasn't here today. But where was he, I persisted, where could I find him and talk to him. At this there came more Hungarian, equally excited, and finally the interpreter turned and said, in white embarrassment, "It's difficult to talk to Ber Julio—he's been arrested."

My face must have shown astonishment, for again a flow of angry Hungarian burbled around the table, this time directed against the interpreter. The man flustered, paled, expostulated in Hungarian to the others and then turned to me and said sharply, dropping a black curtain over the conversation, "Ber Julio is not important. You have asked to see collective farms. Let us tell you about the collective farm and the houses we are building."

Ber Julio, thus, had been arrested within three years of the time he brought the "revolution" to his village from Marshal Tolbukhin's headquarters. How many hundreds of thousands of other Ber Julioes have been arrested in the years since then, no one can count. Since 1948 police budgets have jumped in every state in Eastern Europe from an increase of fifty per cent in Bulgaria to an increase of four hundred per cent in Poland, where it equals two-thirds of the military budget. Estimates of those imprisoned or exiled to forced places of residence range up to a million. Western attention has been fascinated by the phenomenon of the self-cannibalizing coalitions which the Russians set up as government in all the Eastern European states. Each of these coalitions was first devoured from within by those who controlled the apparatus of Communist discipline, and then the discipline, in turn, devoured and murdered the Communists themselves, until now the entire original leadership of the Czech, Bulgarian, Rumanian, Hungarian, and Albanian Communist parties is gone, and that of the Polish has been severely punished. But the names of the sincere men, innocent dupes, shabby careerists and merciless vendettists selected by the hangmen at the top run only to hundreds; it is at the base, where Ber Julioes in countless thousands have disappeared, that the Russians have thrown away a loyalty they might have had.

If this thrusting-away of all normal native sources of friendship was the most serious general blunder imposed on the Russians by their mechanical compulsion to discipline, the sharpest single defeat it brought was the loss of the Yugoslav state.

Since the breach between Russia and Yugoslavia, scores of Yugoslav officials from Tito down have offered fragments of the story. Yugoslav editors complained about the insistence by Russian news agencies that they print dull Russian copy instead of hot Yugoslav copy; Yugoslav trading agencies told how Russia forced on Yugoslavia shoddy and faulty equipment at prices two and three times world market prices; Yugoslav planners described Russia's insistence on acquiring Yugoslav natural resources and key communications on terms that would shame the most reactionary imperialist oil company. But none of these tales is as illuminating as the original Tito-Moscow correspondence which opened the breach.

The issue was joined, squarely, on none of these lesser matters but simply on discipline. Only after almost three weeks of wriggling defensive correspondence could Tito bring himself to make his first countercharge. "If you were to ask us," wrote Tito to Stalin, "if there were anything with which we were not satisfied on your part, then we would openly say that there are many reasons why we are dissatisfied. What are these reasons? It is impossible to mention all the reasons in this letter, but we will mention a few. First, we regard it as improper for the agents of the Soviet intelligence service to recruit in our country, which is going toward socialism, our citizens for their intelligence service." What Tito was trying to escape, precisely, was the tightening of the circle of discipline about him, as his own party had tightened it about so many others.

By contrast, the most amazing thing in all the Russian letters was not their insistence that all satellites should submit to Russian discipline (said Stalin in reply, ". . . It is only natural for Soviet workers to talk with Yugoslav citizens, to ask them questions and to gain information, etc."), but how this discipline and the narrow channels of its intelligence blinded them. For the ultimate Russian judgment was that their final appeal to the Yugoslav people to overthrow Tito and destroy him would be successful. Blinded by their own misleading information, they lost.

What is equally important–from their experience with Tito the Russians learned but little. The heresies for which Tito was blasted out of the Cominform–excessive nationalism, opposition to collectivization, conciliation of rural "kulaks," suspicion of Russian trading motives–were denounced as sin in 1948. Only in 1953 did the Russians begin to realize that Tito, not their own intelligence net, had been correct in political appreciation of Eastern Europe.

From 1948, after the breach with Tito, the Russians proceeded, in Eastern Europe, to impose the most rigid programs of heavy industrialization while simultaneously exhausting the satellite economies either by reparations (as in Rumania, East Germany and Hungary) or by outright trade thievery (as in Czechoslovakia and Poland).

All this was very logical by the theory of Communist industry. Statistically, the results read beautifully as satellite after satellite wrote new records in steel production, electricity production and coal mining. But in human terms the adventure added up to a series of blunders which were not evident through the layers of their own misinformation until the spring of 1953. For the greater the effort invested in mills, mines and equipment, the less effort remained to provide ordinary people with food, clothing and shelter, until finally the resentment of hungry, tortured people who could not eat statistics vented itself in the disturbances of the spring and summer of 1953.

Beginning in the early winter of 1952–1953, with the recrudescence of guerrilla resistance in Poland (quiet since 1948), spreading in May with the rioting in Czechoslovakia, bursting out uncontrollably in Poland and East Germany in June and July, the fermenting resistance forced a total revision of Russian policy of occupation by midsummer.

Nothing is more eloquent, perhaps, of both Russian shortsightedness and Russian cynicism than the experience of Matyas Rakosi, puppet dictator of Hungary. Having extorted, in May of 1953, a spurious ninety-eight per cent vote of support for his dictatorship, Rakosi took off for Moscow to parade his triumph before his masters. From this trip he returned to find himself, six weeks after his electoral triumph, removed from office, stripped of honor and dignity, and all his policies repudiated. Whereupon his successor puppets proclaimed the imminent liquidation of collectives, repudiated the heavy industry program, amnestied thousands of "kulaks" and enemies of the regime—exactly as Tito did three years earlier.

The Russians in Eastern Europe, in short, have gained no more than the minimum advantage mortgaged to them in advance by war. This minimum advantage they have squandered by terror and ruthlessness, to make of their prize one of the greatest handicaps communism in the West must overcome today, and one of the more promising opportunities for Western counterthrust in the future. There, where the Red Army and police are most firmly in control, they are politically least potent, and communism least challenging.

The Communist victory in China, too, is usually regarded as a magnificent triumph of Stalinist leadership, the greatest single burst of Russian expansion since Yermak Timofayevitch brought his horsemen to water in the Amur in 1581.

Centuries hence it will probably be seen differently, for the historian of the future will be able to set it against its proper background of time. This background of time begins with the extraordinary nineteenth century, during which the states of Western Europe succeeded, in less than one hundred years, in bringing Asia, Africa and, in fact, the whole world, with its many tongues and traditions, into single submission to Atlantic civilization. To the historian, the unique quality of this expansion will be quite apparent; so will the fact that withdrawal by the Atlantic Powers from these areas was inevitable under the stress of geography and the nature of human beings. It was quite impossible, he will realize, that the Chinese could remain forever placid as foreign gunboats patrolled their rivers, foreign troops quartered in their chief cities, foreign officials ran their postal systems, foreigners directed their universities, set their customs and collected their taxes, while Chinese sat by humiliated and excluded.

Revolt was inherent in this situation. But the historian will also see how this natural revolt coincided with another revolt almost perfectly tailored to fit the Communist faith. In Asia, the Communist faith finds people sharply divided into numberless hordes of ignorant and hungry, a thin layer of time-descended, antique village gentry who govern and a tiny few who possess modern learning and education. To the hungry and the ambitious, communism offers opportunity which, in those eyes that have never seen liberty, seems fresh and golden. For the able young men it offers jobs, careers, achievement. To the hungry, communism offers no less than they had before and perhaps more. Communism kills, tortures, executes and mangles in Asia, but the hungry have always known this at the hands of their governments. To counter the hungry hordes and the ruthlessly ambitious young men there exists no solid middle class as in Europe, nor even a substantially prosperous working class that has tasted liberty. There exists, as a counter to both, only the millennial old layer of village gentry who have forever controlled law and order in those gatherings of huts which stretch endlessly across the horizon of Asia, village touching village as far as the eye can see.

The Russians did not invent this situation in China; they came upon it ready-made and only after thirty years of error did they finally succeed in profiting by it. The revolt in China grew from the impact of Communist faith upon a rotting society, not by the discipline or control of Russia.

The Chinese Communist party, as it stands today, is, indeed, the result of a conflict with Russian leadership. The Russians, like the Atlantic Powers, experimented for years with a succession of warlord adventurers who seemed to them, momentarily, to represent the tide of change. It was the Russians, not the Americans, who first created Chiang Kai-shek as a man of fame, giving him the captaincy of the early Nationalist Armies and an honorary Vice-Presidency in the Comintern. The original Communist party of China, organized in the early 1920's by the Russians, perished in 1927 when Stalin ordered it to obey Chiang Kai-shek and Chiang Kai-shek annihilated it. Stalin discarded Chiang Kai-shek only after Chiang had first discarded him. What was left of the Chinese

Communist party after this disaster was then ordered by Moscow to concentrate its activity in the large cities of China's coast to agitate among the workers of dock, mill and factory.

By this time, however, many Chinese Communists had become embittered by the mechanical way in which adventurers sent from Russia disposed of their lives and destinies. A minority faction of the Chinese Communists, therefore, split with the docile majority of the party and declared, with prescient shrewdness, that China's revolutionary future lay in the villages of the hungry peasant population; the enemy's weakness lay in the weak and crumbling landlord-gentry, not the tiny but modern, urban middle class which might resist. This faction was excoriated, anathematized and cast into outer darkness by international communism long before the word Titoism had been invented. But it survived, while the original, official Communist party of Russia was hacked to death in the streets of the cities by Chiang's police.

This splinter-party not only survived; it became the progenitor of Asia's revolution, and its leader, Mao Tse-tung, is now the master of China and the men of his choice and early companionship are Red China's overlords.

Neither in original concept nor in military aid did Mao's movement owe anything to the Russians. Not until six years after the breach year of 1927, when Mao's riflemen had carved a Communist Republic in South China out of tens of millions of peasants, did the Comintern in forgiveness come to its support with espionage, arms and advice. But this advice proved as disastrous as the earliest Russian advice to the Chinese Communists, for it led to a premature attempt by Mao's hit-and-run guerrillas to go over to positional warfare. When, as a result of this advice, Mao's guerrillas were driven out in 1934–1935 in the foot-retreat from South to North China known as the Long March, Mao turned in fury on the chief military advisor sent from Moscow and placed him under arrest, in which captive condition he remained for six years until he could take flight back to Moscow.

The strain between the Chinese and Russian brands of communism, which began at the moment of Mao's seizure of Asian leadership in 1927, persisted through every verifiable turning of this association down to the final sealing of the Russo-Chinese Alliance in 1950. Through this discord, it should be noted, Russian analysis persisted in an underestimate of Chinese Communist strength and power as gross as was Chiang Kai-shek's.

This underestimate shows most clearly in the Yalta agreements, perhaps the most misunderstood of all modern historic documents. By the Yalta agreements, Americans and Russians made the coldest kind of bargain, snipping off slivers of China's living domain, with American consent, to hand to Russian imperialism. It was a deal that had only one possible interpretation. By recognizing America's power to dismember China, Russia implicitly recognized America's mastery over and sphere of interest in all the rest of China (much as they probably hoped, by the same bargain, that America recognized Russian suzerainty in Eastern Europe). Those who refused to recognize the deal were the Chinese Communists.

The underestimate shows again in the looting of Manchuria. When the Russians rushed into Manchuria in the last week of war, they stripped it of its industrial vitals as savagely as they attempted to strip Eastern Germany. Removing machinery and equipment valued by the Chinese at $2,000,000,000 (by the Americans at $800,000,000), the Russians left industrial Manchuria a smoking wasteland, its factories a wilderness of empty sockets. It is difficult to conceive that Russia, if she had believed that China would soon fall under her leadership, would have ravaged a base which might have speeded China's regeneration by a decade.

The underestimate shows again in the last reliable report of Russian-Chinese Communist clash supplied by British sources in that critical year of the Asian War, 1948. In July, 1948, the Chinese Communists called a supreme military conference in southern Hopei to debate and decide the prospect that lay before them. Manchuria was about to fall; Chinese Communist troops were already far south of the Great Wall, poised to strike at Chiang's scattered troops in the central valleys. The Russian military delegates this time advised caution. They declared it was too soon to strike, that Chiang was still too powerful to be overthrown without three or four more years of guerrilla operation. Against this view, Chou En-lai, now China's Premier, took the floor to insist that now was indeed the time—one final push and all would fall. Chou's party listened to Chou, not the Russians, and fourteen months later all China floated the red banners.

It was only then, after a generation of fumbling, that the Russians found their opportunity. They had, in all likelihood, delayed the triumph of the Chinese Communists by a full decade. But however late they formally recognized the power of Communist China (Russia recognized her only three months before the British government), they found in the new situation an opportunity almost impossible to fluff. The new Chinese revolution had come to power with fanatic hatred of all things American, resulting from America's prolonged and bungled intervention in China's civil war. All the Russians had to do was to keep the hatred boiling.

Moreover, the very nature of Chinese Communist leadership called for just the kind of operation that Russia was now able to mount. Mao and his brethren within China had been remarkable social engineers, coldly efficient organizers of manpower, gifted with a political understanding of their own country of which other Communist parties, slaves to Muscovite direction, were barren. Yet in the outer world of the twentieth century, where different tools and techniques from any known in peasant China are employed, the Chinese Communists were almost amateurs. No group of leaders had ever been more swiftly whirled out of total ignorance and destitution to command so powerful a force. Until his 1950 visit to Moscow, Mao Tse-tung had never been outside of China and had spent most of the previous quarter-century in hill villages among the most primitive of his countrymen. Chou En-lai and Chu Teh, his two most prominent deputies, had both spent only the briefest student years in Western Europe twenty-five years before, to which Chou had added a several months' convalescent stay in Russia during the Sino-Japanese War. Only four years before their intervention in the Korean War, all of them had been forced to trudge in sandaled feet, as refugees, from their cave capital at Yenan before Chiang Kai-shek's advancing armies. And now they led the most powerful community in Asia. Russia needed only to warp their untutored minds and cultivate their natural suspicions to use them for her purposes in the outer world.

Russia's championing of China in the United Nations and the outer world is ordained thus not only by Communist brotherhood but by essential imperial policy, too. For if Russia makes herself the only middleman between China and the West, all Chinese thinking can be distorted and twisted to Russian purpose. Within this isolation it is possible to drench not only the public Chinese press but the inner understanding of her leadership with Tass reports, Russian diplomatic reports, Russian espionage reports. To keep China mentally isolated from the West until the mechanical discipline of Moscow can manacle, physically, the organization of Chinese communism is vital for Russia. And war in Korea, for the Russians, must have offered not one but two virtues. Not only has it drained Western strength month after month, but more than that, it has kept China dependent on Russian aid and thus on Russian diplomacy.

The expansion of communism in the Far East is thus not the triumph of Russian calculation, but the triumph of Communist faith in an overripe social situation in which the West let itself be trapped on the losing side.

Here again the immediate perspective is one of hope and danger. For if the internal logic of communism demands ever greater, ever tighter discipline, Russian instruments of discipline must be at work as they are everywhere in the world of communism, squeezing, prying, grasping at the central machinery of Chinese communist control. Yet no advantage can be taken of that fact so long as the Chinese are isolated and must be fueled, armed and munitioned by the Soviets. It is unnatural to believe that a man like Mao, who so often proved himself right when Stalin was wrong, should now at the zenith of his power suddenly adopt the cloak of humility in the presence of Stalin's successors. Yet there is little chance of any breach between Peking and Moscow until Mao, himself, feeling his strength, conscious of Russian ambition and blunder, finds an opportunity to think for himself.

The burden this imposes on the West is emotionally staggering. It has already required war, bloodshed and sacrifice of our youth, month after month, in an attempt to convince Chinese communism that it has stupidly called into being superior and hostile force. And the truce we have won in Korea—whether offered on Mao's own initiative or suggested by the Russians—is meaningless unless it is linked to greater strategy. This strategy requires only that when the war is finished we must turn quickly and shrewdly, our wounds still aching, with sorrow in ten thousand homes, to offer Mao Tse-tung an exit out of the Russian world into a larger and freer one where he can make his own decisions and act in his own interest.

It is, however, in the third and last area of Russian enterprise abroad—Western Europe—that the contradiction between communism's stultifying mechanical discipline and the kinetic, expansive power of its faith shows clearest. In Western Europe, communism, stripped of its police garments of secrecy, operates open to our examination. And it is probably in France that the imposing resources of communism are most clearly wasted by political stupidity.

The French Communist party is the most valuable piece of property Russia owns within the Atlantic world. In many ways it is a frightening thing. It is not a band of wild-eyed, ranting street radicals, nor a convocation of visionaries, nor yet a parcel of chivied and harassed clerks. It is a solid, powerful organization whose leaders are not hunted little men but powerful administrators, endowed, as all members of the Communist élite, with their substantial luxuries—automobiles, bodyguards, chauffeurs, villas in the suburbs, good food and great prestige. Under different names, the party owns impressive blocks of Paris and provincial real estate. It is the greatest publishing enterprise in all France, owning and controlling more daily newspapers (sixteen) than any other publishing group, and distributing half a dozen of the nation's largest weekly magazines. It directs a dozen-odd training schools over the country, specializing in all techniques from control of labor unions to the tactics of street battle in a riot. It has a paid, internal, full-time bureaucratic staff of 14,000 functionaries who are as devoted to the preservation of these jobs and their livelihood as desk men anywhere. Beyond that it knows that within and without its own paid staff, it can command a core of hard men, the so-called "durs," who number perhaps 10,000 zealots ready to go out and die in the streets at its command.

Moreover, it is a fighting organization. Year by year, since the early fluid days of Liberation, the Communists have perfected the tactics of riot and street-bloodshed until they are as elaborate as any field manual produced for the United States Army. Commando squads are drilled and trained by Communists in every major city of France; they have mobilization procedures which gather zealots at collection points in industrial slums and factory districts and commit them to action in converging columns on any given point. Their tactics are refined down to the precise selection of riot areas (usually, in Paris, a large subway intersection is chosen, for subway exits and entrances make the best sally ports and escape vents); their street weapons are perfected to the point where Communist pikestaffs—spike-studded staves—are fixed at a length ten inches longer than a policeman's club.

Probably no other Communist party in the world has carried the theoretical study of insurrection and street violence to the same degree as the French Communists. But what one technique can achieve, another technique can counter, and in the past five years, the French police system has elaborated a drill-and-routine system for meeting street violence which beats anything the Communists can oppose.

Yet what cripples the Communists most in their riots is not only this police system but even more the political blindness with which their own discipline directs Communist force. Violence is a technique which, in the theory of insurrection, can succeed only when it is supported by vast masses of ordinary people who fall in behind it. And here, at this juncture of political acumen and mechanical tactic, the French Communist party finds itself manacled by Russian discipline.

The most remarkable demonstration of political stupidity by French Communists was the mechanically successful riot called to protest the arrival of General Ridgway in Paris on May 27, 1952. The Communist rioters were given as their street-slogans the lies of American germ warfare in Korea, and Ridgway was labeled the Germ-Killer. The zealots marched into the streets, did brilliantly and were beaten. The rest of Paris stood apart from the riots, calm and unruffled.

The stupidity of the Communists, from a political-insurrectionary point of view, lay in the choice and timing of their issues. On the very day that the Communists summoned the miserable slum-denizens of Paris to riot against Ridgway, a choice issue had just been offered to them on which hundreds of thousands of Parisians might have joined them in the streets. That day was the day on which the pacts of the European Army were signed at the Quai d'Orsay, and a French government agreed to German rearmament. Given the age-long hatred of Frenchmen for Germans, given the remembered cruelty of yesterday's Occupation, uncountable numbers of Frenchmen would have backed the Communists in bloody protest. But much as they might have wished, the discipline of international communism deprived French Communists of this explosive opportunity. Only a month before the riots, the Russians had diametrically reversed their previous policy and called on the world to permit a German National Army again. Since Russia was now in favor of a German National Army, French Communists had to be, too. And so they had to go into the streets on an issue that was a lie and could find no support except from their zealots. They shed blood and were beaten at a moment when, had they been free to choose their own policy, they might have brought down a French Cabinet.

This political isolation is the greatest problem of the French party today. For, like the Russians, the French Communists have concentrated on organization, technique and discipline to the exclusion of new political thinking. The party is not permitted the initiative of imagination which is so necessary to make a fresh appeal. Thus, it rests on its base, grows fossilized, moves only mechanically, improves only technically. It retains hard, operational control of the greatest labor union federation in France, but this federation, the CGT, has fallen from 6,000,000 dues-payers in 1946 to 1,500,000 today. The party still retains probably half a million card-holders out of a postwar high of a million. But even these card-holders no longer come willingly to party headquarters to pick up their cards each year; instead the zealots must go from house to house to woo laggard members, inviting dubious backsliders to cell headquarters for a party of cakes and wine, at which cards are slipped into their hands with great ceremony. Although the party is still the largest publishing enterprise in France, the circulation of its chief official daily, *L'Humanité*, has fallen from a postwar high of 600,000 readers to 175,000.

Communism in France is stagnant; it has nothing new to say; it earns no new members. How then is it possible that this fossil force can still, in any election in France, earn twenty-five per cent of the votes of free and intelligent Frenchmen? How is it that in the spring of 1953 the Communists could win enough votes to give them the mayoralties of hundreds and hundreds of villages, towns and cities in the most libertarian of European nations?

The answer brings us to the irreducible core resources of communism. The resources are not embodied in guns and tanks, in organizations or pikestaffs. They lie in the permanent opportunity that such countries as France, Italy and Greece offer to any revolutionary party as it was offered in China. The sickening social rot in these countries, the filthy, tumid slums of the poor made even uglier by the extravagance and luxury of the rich, have created in the course of a century a class of men who are permanently disaffected from Western European society. One-fourth of France, one-third of Italy, has no confidence that the democratic process, liberty, reason, Church or God will give their children good food, good schools, good clothes, sunlit rooms. The metropolitan area of Paris—an urban agglomeration of 5,000,000 people—has built, *in the eight years since Liberation*, only 3,500 low-cost housing units, while the minimum estimate of need in the area is for 20,000 such units every single year. In the city of Paris, for the past three years, one out of the city's twenty wards (arrondissements) has accounted for half of all new housing built; this arrondissement is Passy, where live the rich, the comfortable, the fat who can afford to purchase space in the clean, new, privately financed buildings going up. But in those arrondissements which are unofficially called workers' quarters, eighty-two per cent of the housing is over ninety years old, built before the American Civil War. In these arrondissements, where the majority of Parisians live, it is believed that as many houses have been condemned as inhabitable or collapsed of decay as have been built since the war; the city government refuses even to divulge such figures of decay and condemnation out of shame. The estimated hundred thousand young couples in Paris who have no home of their own, and no hope of getting one, expect nothing from anybody. The health charts of Paris trace inescapable patterns; if one superimposes the charts of distribution of tuberculosis, malnutrition and overcrowding in Paris' electoral wards over any political map of the city, these wards where misery is highest coincide precisely with the wards the Communists carry.

Over a period of twenty years, the French Communists have wriggled their way into the leadership of the disinherited. But these legions of hopeless men are not of their creation; they have, in France, much deeper roots. From grandfather to father to son, French workers hand down tales of a century of rioting and clash with the cops. The *flic* is the natural enemy of the worker in a hundred industrial slums across France; he has been the enemy since the Paris Commune of 1870 and probably longer than that. Such men have heard from their fathers, who have heard from their fathers, how lampposts can be torn down and cobblestones torn up to make barricades to stop a police rush. This mass of one-quarter of a nation which, for a hundred and eighty years, has been ever in pursuit of a revolution and been ever denied its fruits, has now fallen under Communist leadership, much as a medieval fiefdom might be seized by a strange, rude baron when its rightful legatees were too weak to defend it.

The Communists may stand isolated as they do now in French politics not only from the nation as a whole, but from the submerged quarter of the population too. Workers no longer pay dues to the party with the same regularity; they may refuse to strike on political issues in Russia's interest which cost them a day's pay; hundreds of thousands of them have stopped buying the Communist papers. But when voting day comes, they trudge to the polls and vote Communist because it is the party of the slums, the party all the *gars* vote for. They may loathe and despise individual party leaders and party thugs. But no other party offers the single thing they want most: to kick the system apart, to turn it over, to change it. They may read in their papers that other workers in Poland, Czechoslovakia or East Germany riot bloodily against communism-in-power as a new system of exploitation—but they do not believe it. Among such men, the missionary impact of Communist faith meets little resistance; they may or may not know that the change communism brings will deprive them of liberty. But that does not matter to them yet; their muscles, anger and devotion are ready to be mobilized by anyone who offers change.

As they won Eastern Europe by the automatic fortune of victory, and won China by the subterranean working of the native Asian revolt, so the Communists have inherited these people in Western Europe in a game of no-contest. What is remarkable is that Russian leadership has been able to turn these resources to so little profit. In part this failure has been due to the active, positive wisdom of the Atlantic Powers in the Atlantic theater of operations. But in equal part it is probably due to the manner in which the logic of Communist discipline committed Communist policy, until now, into the hands of Joseph Stalin.

Now that Stalin is dead, it is possible to see his role in events more clearly. In his time, the world lived in the presence of an authentic genius. But it was a genius of hideous malevolence, and it is one of the paradoxes of man's chronicle that the Marxist faith which sprang from total repudiation of the individual's value and importance should finally become slave, as no other faith in history, to one sole personality and that personality, Joseph Stalin.

What was positive about Stalin's genius were his qualities as executive and administrator, first recognized by another diabolical genius, Lenin. It was Lenin who discovered that he possessed in Stalin, among the scores of noncommissioned officers of Bolshevism, a man who commanded gifts of organization granted to few men in any era, and it was under Lenin that Stalin was first permitted to organize a party, a secret police, a state and a machine.

Only after Lenin's death, however, did the talents of Stalin come to full fruit as he proceeded to captain that stupendous development of Soviet resources which still, even in our hostile eyes, must evoke awe. The Stalin reflected through the fragments of gossip of scores of men who have met and talked with him is a man whose mind grasped facts and sorted them out with the impersonal efficiency of a calculating machine. Over and over again, foreign visitors reported with astonishment the range of his factual knowledge—on steel production in America, on meat production in Argentina, on bauxite development in Bosnia. Stalin's fascination with and mastery over the supreme elements of industrial management are now celebrated forever in the steel mills, coal mines, planes, guns and concentration camps that he caused to be erected over the vast, seemingly measureless expanse of Russia.

This genius of organization, however, had severe limitations. Like most executive types, Stalin's weakness lay in policy making. As long as Lenin lived in vigor and was braced by the other coruscating Bolsheviks of the early revolution, Stalin was used as the hard, merciless executive arm. But he was excluded from the higher circles of policy-making and decision from the weeks of insurrection in 1917, in which Stalin consistently misjudged the political situation, to the season when Lenin himself was brought low by paralysis and death.

Lenin himself guessed wrong in his belief that organization was a mechanical thing which could safely be entrusted to Stalin. Organization has a life of its own, a dynamic rhythm and greed that forever seeks to tighten, to expand, to perfect. And it was in the expansion of the organization of communism that Stalin, its master, moved slowly out into the world of policy-making, where his errors were written into the bloody sorrow of our generations and concealed only by the fantastic myth-making machinery the organization threw up to protect his prestige.

Perhaps no statesman of any time has a record of so many miscalculations, of such magnitude, over so long a period of time as Joseph Stalin. Through them all runs a single thread, a single element of error. They were all political, not organizational, mistakes, and all showed themselves wherever Stalin came in contact with the outer world. Wherever his police and administrative machinery could impose discipline and control, the success of this untaught mountaineer was uncanny. Where he made his errors was always in the judgment of the free impulse of human beings, of how they might react, how they might express themselves beyond the areas of his police control. Trapped by its own machine, his thinking was suffocated by the incense of his slaves.

Stalin's errors of judgment run from his first intervention in Russian foreign policy—the misjudged Bolshevik invasion of Stalin's native Georgia in 1921—through every major turning where the changing world posed a new problem for the Russian state. Stalin erred, first, in China when, but for his insistence on supporting Chiang Kai-shek, who betrayed him, the Communists might then have taken over the Chinese revolution in 1926 and 1927. Over the advice of all the older Bolsheviks whom he had by then humiliated, Stalin insisted that the Chinese Communists commit themselves to Chiang's leadership. The Comintern was still so directing Chinese Communists, even after Chiang had already begun to execute them in Shanghai.

Europe was closer home than China, but here, too, the dictator's inability to judge the movement of politics beyond his apparatus of control brought disaster. Germany was the chief scene of Stalin's mistakes in Europe. The first of these were the instructions of Stalin to the German Communists through the late nineteen twenties and early thirties which made them de facto Allies of the Nazis in wrecking the structure of the Weimar Republic. If Communist preparation for Fascist triumph in Germany sprang from Stalinist ignorance, his next mistake in Germany sprang from sheer duplicity, also ignorant. This was the Nazi-Soviet Pact of 1939, an incredible misreading of the mind of the Nazi élite, which brought to Russia the worst war in her violent history.

Such mistakes show themselves at almost any point beyond Russian borders where a particular Stalinist judgment can be isolated and analyzed. It shows over an arc of the world stretching from Sinkiang (where Stalin chose and was betrayed by a murderous little warlord called Sheng Shih-tsai) as far as Yugoslavia (where Stalin continued to believe that the royalist partisans of Mihajlovic were the true instruments of Soviet wartime purpose long after Tito's Communist partisans had exposed their treachery and absorbed or wiped them out).

All these previous blunders, except the Nazi-Soviet Pact, were, however, reduced to nothing by his misjudgment of the world since 1945. In 1945, Stalin stood victorious in Europe and Asia, allied to the United States in friendship. He possessed the gratitude and respect of the power most able to help the ravaged Soviet Union, a power which, by equal token, was the only possible threat to his regime. And then, completely misreading the instinct of America and the free world, he threw this friendship away in that stupid sequence of events and behavior which has made of the American people the greatest enemy of the Soviet world. By his own actions, he summoned up the united hate of the most powerful nation in the world.

Throughout his career, Stalin displayed to the world only one consistent political tactic, the constant refinement of a single instinct—to divide, by slyness, suspicion and treachery, any group of enemies who formed against him. His entire pilgrimage through politics, from the first record of Bolshevism triumphant, is marked by the same pursuit of association, division, isolation and destruction of his enemies. And though the highways of modern history were strewn with the bones of his victims, Stalin never ceased to invite his enemies to walk first down the road of alliance and friendship before splitting and murdering them. Nor, until the

Atlantic Community shook loose from his embrace, had any man or state taken the hand of Stalin in partnership and survived except as slave.

There is an almost monolithic purity in the way Stalin refined the same tactic over and over again—the tactic of the sly, suspicious peasant moving from man to man in the village, whispering, gossiping, seducing, smiling, as he turns each man against his brother, now by threat, now by promise, now by temporary partnership in crime. To destroy his first great rival, Trotsky, Stalin split away from him his most eminent contemporaries in the Politburo, Zinoviev and Kamenev. Having isolated Trotsky (later to murder him) with their help, he sought new allies to destroy Zinoviev and Kamenev. Having isolated Zinoviev and Kamenev (later to murder them) with the aid of Bukharin and Rykov, he proceeded to devour Bukharin and Rykov. Finally, after having killed all rival Russian leadership in cold blood, he turned his talents to broader scenes.

It was in the outside world that this peasant cunning failed, for it could work only in a state where suspicion and intrigue are magnified and controlled by prisons and police discipline. Successfully, Stalin wrote his Nazi-Soviet pact to divide the capitalist countries of the West against each other—only to find himself one of the greatest victims of his maneuver. Diabolically, he tried to incite Bulgarians against Yugoslavs to divide their potential strength in his new postwar empire of Eastern Europe. Cunningly, his agents tried to divide the Politburo of Yugoslavia against itself from within—and Stalin lost Yugoslavia. Even at the very end, in his last pronouncement to the Communist Congress in Moscow in 1952, he described his world strategy in the same old terms—the eventual breaking off of Germany and Japan from the "regime of the United States," the eventual hope that capitalist England and capitalist France would "be forced to tear themselves out from the embraces of the United States and enter into conflict with them."

But by then it was too late. The world had caught on to his style at last and was organized to resist. At this point, Joseph Stalin died.

The legacy Stalin left the world of communism is twofold. It consists, first, of the mighty expanding base of Russian power, a state whose strength multiplied faster under Stalin's lash than any previous society in history. It consists, secondly, of the political missionary faith of communism, much weaker, though still potent, than when he took leadership after Lenin. Everywhere this faith fell under Stalin's police discipline it withered or crystallized into a God-cult, but wherever it could operate freely, as in China, it showed itself still explosive and kinetic.

Dimly, the Atlantic world has recognized the twofold nature of the challenge and has attempted to cope with both. It met the challenge of Russian power with magnificent audacity in time of danger and, by its great Alliance, threw up that shield of power which shelters it now in Europe. But the necessary effort to meet the challenge of Russian power was organized so quickly, in such emergency, that it disrupted entirely the first, groping efforts of the Atlantic world to answer, with the Marshall Plan, the deep illnesses and sicknesses of Western Europe which make it so vulnerable to the Communist faith.

It is here, now, in this chapter of history, that the new masters of Russia must be reviewing the Atlantic Alliance as it lies before them. It must be obvious to them, as it should be to us, that Russia has gone as far as force will carry her, and that where the pressure on us is still alive, it is carried primarily by the missionary faith, not by armies. If now the outer world can be lulled or soothed into stagnation, with all its social tumors and cancers still poisoning its health, the faith may succeed where the armies and intrigue failed. If the Atlantic world conceives of its challenge simply as a challenge at arms and now relaxes with its temporary advantage, while the Soviet Union continues in its broad and disciplined expansion, its very success at home may regenerate the withered faith abroad. But it can do so only if the Atlantic world sits still—which is the problem all the free states of the great basin face, and America, its leader, most of all.

XV

America abroad

The first American Embassy I ever visited hugged the side of a hill above the Yangtze, thousands of miles away from Europe, in the now-forbidden city of Chungking, in China.

It was almost fifteen years ago when I first climbed that hill, before either America or Europe had been caught in the Second World War. The only war going on then was the war between the Chinese and the Japanese and this was a war I could watch in comfort from the embassy balcony. One climbed the slime-covered stairs in the cliff of the south bank of the Yangtze, squeezed through the hot alleys, and came out finally on the crown of an umber ridge where sat our embassy. From its gardens and balcony, looking down on the gray city across the river below, one might watch what was happening as from an imperial box in a Roman amphitheater.

All through that summer of 1939, the Japanese Air Force bombed Chungking, and from the embassy we could watch the planes coming in formation and see the bombs dropping. Then, after an interval, we could hear the *crump-crump-thud* as the salvos boomed from the red flame and black smoke rising in the city. But we were safe. We were safe because the American flag flew over the embassy and the flag was protection. We could look down from our heights into the yellow Yangtze and see our gunboat, the *Tutuila*, lying bare and white in the current, deserted by every other craft. The *Tutuila* was safe in mid-stream because she, too, bore the canopy of a huge American flag. We were all safe, sitting there drinking Martinis on the rim of death, because we were Americans.

I remember sitting on the embassy porch one day with some of our military service attachés, and one Marine officer said, after the daily spectacle was over, that, by God, Japanese bombing was sure ragged and some day they were going to drop one short or over and it would land square on the embassy whether it was meant to or not, and then there'd be an incident. He said if we were smart we'd move the embassy from this hill to the second range back inland where if the Japs hit us it wouldn't be a mistake, they would mean it. Somebody else said, No, we couldn't do that because how the hell would the Chinese get all the way over there to talk to us, and that's what we were supposed to be doing, talking to them.

At which the Marine officer turned and said, "Look, what we've got, they need. If they want it badly enough, they'll come to see us no matter where we put the embassy."

Almost a century of American diplomacy lay embodied in that wisdom, and none of us then knew how, even at that moment, that diplomacy was changing under our eyes. Down in the city, even under the bombings, lived six other Americans with whom our government had, ostensibly, no concern. Two economists advised the Chinese on the causes and cure of inflation, the first in an almost numberless procession of American economists who have been advising the world ever since on the causes and cures of inflation. Then there was a sturdy, happy engineer called Dan Myers, who knew all about machinery and its maintenance; he was industrial purchasing advisor to the Chinese government. William Langhorne Bond, who, through twenty years of civil and international war, created the first modern airline on the continent of Asia, was the fourth. The fifth was Colonel Claire Chennault, United States Army, retired, private advisor to the Chinese Air Forces on the tactics, training and employment of military pursuits. The sixth was a balding, middle-aged little fellow with the attractive and happy garrulousness of a country storekeeper. He purported to be a merchant of skins and hides and was the first secret American agent I ever met. His special skill was in cracking Japanese radio codes, and our government had lent him to the Chinese government to work on their intercepts of Japanese messages. He was an extremely witty man, but had been exiled by whatever embryonic secret services we then had to Chungking, because of his talkativeness. At that time, we were not yet at war with Japan and therefore the embassy and all the embassy officials studiously ignored him, for, although half the gossipy town knew all about him, his mission was supposed to be ultrasecret. When old "Osborne"—which was the name he used—talked of his boyhood in an Indiana town, in the sunlit days of the early century, or told the adventures of his bearded grandfather who was a Union veteran and the town drunk, it seemed wonderfully adventurous to all of us that he should now be here in the mysterious Orient cracking Japanese radio codes for Chiang Kai-shek.

These men had all been invited to Chungking by the Chinese government because the Chinese sensed intuitively that there was somehow locked in the minds of such men part of the magic which had made America great, magic which these men could transplant. These men had no collective name; in those days they were just "advisors"; there were just six of them, and the United States government washed its hands of them completely.

In the years since then I have watched this original corporal's guard of American individuals grow and grow, swell and swell, by scores, hundreds and thousands across the face of the earth into one of the most elaborate and amazing tools any diplomacy has ever known. The older Foreign Service officers and diplomats of the State Department have been all but submerged in the tide. Even before Pearl Harbor, the American government had begun to deposit on the steps of the Chungking embassy American technicians with diplomatic passports, who were in no way different from the private advisors who had come before. But they were agents now of official purpose and their missions—to reorganize trucking on the Burma Road, or teach Chinese peasants how to inseminate cows artificially with bamboo rods, or how to refine vegetable oil—were now official missions. In the fifteen years since then, such men have grown to legions. Some represent the United States government, some act for American private enterprise, but they seem almost interchangeable as they go about their tasks—reorganizing coalpits in Belgium, mines in the Congo, fishponds in Indonesia, blast furnaces in Lorraine, malaria control in Sardinia. Each man in his own sincere, tedious or inspired fashion has brought some fragment of the American secret with him. Yet no foreign government and no other society has been able to put these fragments together as America does; none has succeeded in capturing the mystery of the American way.

The American Embassy in Paris today is as different from the old embassy in China as imagination can conceive. In the year 1952, the American Embassy in Paris was responsible for 2,500 American officials and employees in the Paris area, who, with their wives and children, made an overseas community of 7,500 Americans, all involved somehow in American policy in Europe. Of these 2,500, only 129 were Foreign Service officers of the State Department, and of these, only 31 were permanent career diplomats trained to speak for the United States abroad. The others were experts on labor relations, on social security, on inflation, on trade and payments, on communism, on atomic energy, on biology, on radio, on press, on films, on aviation, on artillery, on radar, on oil. They were clerks, stenographers, administrators and technicians who maintained the instantaneous teletype and voice circuits that linked the Paris embassy not only to Washington but to nine other capitals across Europe. In a single month the telegraphists in the embassy basement might transmit as many as 4,000,000 words of information to the United States government in Washington (the equivalent of two and a half volumes of the *Encyclopaedia Britannica*) and might receive half that many words in incoming reply from all over the globe. To shelter its multifarious activities the United States government had become a major owner of Paris real estate, owning no less than seven large office buildings, seven private residences for dignitaries, plus a warehouse on a suburban island crammed with 15,000,000 dollars' worth of stockpiled equipment—stationery, desks, chairs, typewriters, teletype machines, filing cabinets, adding machines, trucks, radio equipment and projection equipment.

In the years since the end of the war, the American "expert" has become in the outer world as much a stock character as was the British traveler of the nineteenth century, or as 2,000 years ago the Roman centurion must have been in conquered Greece. Americans flood around the world as scholars, engineers, soldiers, economists and craftsmen, displaying the arcane skills and wisdoms of their civilization. They come to lecture in European universities on their latest publishable findings in nuclear theory, and they come as security agents to scrutinize and train other peoples in the prevention of leakage of nuclear knowledge. The American government recruits labor organizers who exhort European unions to organize; it recruits businessmen who exhort European businessmen to compete. Garment cutters of the Amalgamated Clothing Workers come to show French clothing workers how Americans cut clothes. Private emissaries come to show Belgians how to dig coal, to teach Italians how natural gas is drilled and capped, to teach Englishmen how to operate modern refineries, to show Indians how to use the plough. The vast phrase "technical assistance" by which they are grouped only dimly sums up their meaning in the nations where they go. When one reads the list of requests for American "technical assistance" as they pile up at the State Department, at the MSA, in the U.N., or at UNESCO, one has the impression of distant governments gathering in council late at night by smoky lamplight, scratching out a Sears-Roebuck order form for two microbiologists, one public-health expert, two agronomists, one deep-sea fishing expert and a sheet-steel man, as if such men were interchangeable parts created by some mysterious social machinery which, when installed in their country, would generate the same mysterious energy as it does in the United States.

Strangers are fascinated by these Americans. Where a generation ago people laughed at the British servant of empire traveling through desert or jungle carrying his tin washtub and dinner jacket, they now regard Americans with astonishment. Americans bring with them not the tin washtub and dinner jacket but a composite of all the villages and towns they left behind in America—to create wherever they rest their own villages-in-exile. Thus there is an American community life in Paris, in London, in Athens, in Rome, in Bonn and all the outposts of American dispersion in Europe, the Middle East and Asia. At their PX's, supported by the sprawling United States Army around the globe, they may buy in special overseas American money everything the hometown American department store sells from Kleenex, to Klim, to Kiddicraft toys. In the large communities, the PX provides special laundries to do American washing and garages commissioned to maintain American automobiles at American prices. In Germany and various other outposts, the community provides first-run, fresh Hollywood movies, and all across Europe an American radio net provides the canned programs that Americans enjoy at home. At the American office buildings, at the American snack bars, at the

PX, the community newsstands offer the nourishment of American thinking—either the *Stars and Stripes* or the *New York Herald Tribune* of even date, or the overseas edition of the *New York Times* twelve hours later. Americans of the dispersion vibrate on home wave-lengths. *Time* and *Newsweek* are available in overseas editions on the same day they are available back home. *The Saturday Evening Post*, the *Ladies' Home Journal*, the *Atlantic* and *Harper's*, *True Story*, *Saga*, *Argosy*, *True Detective*, *True Crime* and *Real Western* follow only a few days after they appear in Odessa, Texas.

The members of this community are frequently maligned people, for they appear in the daily dispatches only when it is noted that they can buy cigarettes at ten cents a package, whiskey at $1.75 a bottle, that they get a full month's vacation every year, two months' home leave every two years, housing allowances and special tax-free gasoline. Yet they are, by and large, clean-cut, honest, hard-working people, very American—indeed, in Paris, the personnel officer of the Marshall Plan refused to hire any American who wore a beard, not specifying whether beards were un-American or unhygienic, insisting only that Americans abroad had to have "face validity." These Americans cling to the homey seasonal celebrations. For Christmas and Thanksgiving the Post Exchanges go into contortions of ingenuity to bring turkey, cranberry sauce, plum pudding and all the trimmings up to the counters in time and in quantity for the holiday yearning. The Fourth of July is the major community event when the Ambassador, or High Commissioner, or commanding general usually invites all the permanent members of the dispersion to a reception. Indeed, one of the best measures of the explosive growth of the community abroad is the Fourth of July celebration. In Paris, the embassy's reception, a garden party, on the morning of the Fourth demands a full eight months of the Ambassador's meager annual entertainment allotment just for the fruit punch, Coca-Cola and thin sandwiches he must provide to the Americans who now live in Paris or happen to be passing through.

These Americans, with a few, loud, inevitable exceptions, are what would be called at home "nice people." They are, as a group, exceptionally honest people; since the war they have distributed some 27 billion dollars in Europe, yet no scandal has been exposed remotely comparable to those which have rocked Washington and our great cities in recent years. Most of them have come overseas earnestly wanting to help. They bear skill and wisdom which they freely offer to share. Moreover, the foreign nations where they dwell have sought and even begged that they be sent.

Yet, when all is said, they are, in varying degrees, hated, disliked, mistrusted, or accepted in either humiliation or restraint by the peoples of other countries. Where they have done their best work, they are, at most, respected. But nowhere are they met with that simple fondness and liking, that reflex friendly smile which greeted Americans abroad fifteen years ago. Though the strangers know they need Americans, they accept them out of reason and logic, not with any outwelling of that old and once-famous "reservoir of good will" we had around the globe. The days when an American newspaperman could travel through Central Asia and come to a mud town and find the school children lined up waving banners saying *Welcome Traveling American Journalist* are just a memory.

Why?

To answer the question one must withdraw a bit and set these new American emissaries against the long history of America's infiltration into the world.

The penetration of American mores, habits and cultures began almost half a century ago, long before the *Reader's Digest* became (as it is today) in its English, French, Spanish and Scandinavian editions either the largest or second largest monthly magazine of its type in England, France, Spain or Scandinavia. The influence of America began to seep into Europe about the turn of the century, at an unnoticed subterranean level at a time when the high avenues of culture seemed one-way streets bearing European knowledge of medicine, mathematics, science, art and letters in a contradictory flow into America. It was about then, at the turn of the century, that German children began to dress up as cowboys and Indians with feathered headdresses made in Nürnberg to celebrate Fasching while French children dressed as cowboys and Indians to celebrate Mardi Gras; it was about then that "My Old Kentucky Home" and "Way Down Upon the Swanee River" came to be among the best-known songs in Holland, about then that British newspapers began to use their front pages, as American papers do, for news and not for advertising.

The tide of American cultural penetration has risen ever since, flowing on decade by decade, invading European kitchens with Pyrex and Scotch tape, spreading Coca-Cola in nine different languages from Oslo to Casablanca, pocking the Canebière in Marseille with pinball alleys, jukeboxes and nickel slot-machines.

Hollywood's role, since the First World War, has been incalculable. In town after town, city after city, all through Western Europe, Hollywood, month after month, draws more customers to see the dreams it throws on the screen than any body of native movie-makers. Hollywood has filled average Europeans with the same dreams as average Americans—of the penthouse, of shiny convertibles, of well-furnished homes; it has filled their nightmares with the same symbols of the smoking pistol, the ominous ringing of the telephone, the stab of violence puncturing the course of life.

Where legend, commerce and Hollywood had pioneered, the United States Army occupied. The war threw 3,500,000 Americans down inside Europe. It made American techniques standard in auto maintenance, in airport direction, in water sanitation. The United States Armed Forces Network, blanketing the air with jazz and broadcasts, had for a while the largest listening audience in Europe and has probably taught more Continentals the use of idiomatic English than all the schoolhouses in the Continent. The war left behind too many legacies to count; it left behind hundreds of thousands of tons of cast-off army clothing which clothed European men for years, and it also left behind hundreds of tons of American X-ray equipment, which changed the practices and techniques of European doctors in every hospital that had use of them. The American armies of occupation have carried on where the armies of the war left off—teaching Germans and Frenchmen to make and serve hamburgers and hot dogs American style, inducing English mothers to dress their children in the same kind of snowsuits that the children of American airmen in the neighboring air bases wear in winter.

The war, in a completely different way, created a void in Europe's letters and publishing as great as the void in Europe's economics. Into this void rushed American magazines and books, while American news agencies inundated European newspapers with their instantaneous copy from around the world. American columnists were and are syndicated and quoted in Europe as Pertinax, Geneviève Tabouis and the "leaders" of the *Times* of London were rarely quoted in their greatest days. This penetration of letters not only ranges from texts on steam engineering and polymerization of long-chain molecules through Hemingway, Faulkner and Mickey Spillane, but right down to the level of the first lip-moving child reader. The only censorship law in libertarian French journalism is one that gives the Ministry of Justice power to supervise the imitation-American comic books that have flourished in France since the American Army passed through. I once called on the supervisor of comic books at the Ministry of Justice and he led me through his files—stack after stack of *Sioux Boy*, or *Texas Jack*, or *Les Aventures de Richard Casey*, cover after cover with the American images of the slouching cowboy, the negligeed woman, the space ship. He insisted I record that France was against censorship, that censorship was wicked, but "we must protect our children, we have the right to protect their minds."

Thus, long before the host of new American experts descended on Europe, the Europeans had felt American culture pressing itself on their minds. They knew what was happening; many resented it; but the changes were irresistible and were being absorbed by Europeans at their own rate and digested into their own systems by their own metabolism. The new postwar diplomacy of America brought change to Europe in another, different form; it brought men who insisted that Europeans rewrite their tax laws, who insisted that European troops be trained so, armed thus, and deployed yet a third way; it brought proconsuls who could, in many of the continental countries, by a twist of the screw, break or unbreak any of the governments they dealt with. The Americans of the new dispersion were like nothing ever seen before in diplomacy; their mission was no longer limited to reporting, defining and communicating; their mission now was to transform and influence strange peoples. But no one, least of all the Americans, knew what kind of change it was that America sought.

Perhaps the most instructive adventure in honest bewilderment during the long American intervention in Europe was the productivity drive of the Marshall Plan. Productivity is a mother-word that covers one of the more exciting areas of economics—just how much a given worker with a given set of tools will turn out in a day. Fifty years ago at the turn of the century, American and European workers turned out roughly the same amount of product a day and standards of living in the two civilizations were roughly the same. Today, with variations for different industries, an American worker will produce anywhere from three to five times as much as his European counterpart.

Productivity was always one of the Marshall Plan's key words. But it became overwhelmingly important when the Korean War forced the Atlantic world into its rearmament effort. Economists pointed out that America with 150,000,000 people turned out about $300,000,000,000 worth of goods a year, whereas Marshall-Plan Europe with 260,000,000 people then turned out only about $150,000,000,000 worth of goods. But if Europeans could produce as efficiently as Americans, they would have been producing $450,000,000,000 worth of goods. Thus, ran the reasoning, if we can goose up European productivity, there will be an increase large enough to meet increased military and civilian needs at the same time. In the fall of 1950, therefore, the Plan charged ahead with the productivity program. In the next two years, one thousand American experts came to Europe to show how it was done. No less than ten thousand European specialists in production were sent to America by the Plan to see for themselves how it was done. And yet, no spurt took place, no sudden rise in wealth, nothing but the slow creeping advance that had been going on since the war.

By that time, Americans in Europe began to peel away various clichés that had blinded them. People had said that Europe could not produce because she lacked a mass market; yet American shoe manufacturers pointed out that England, Germany, France and Italy each had between 40,000,000 and 50,000,000 people and no American shoemaker makes shoes for that big a single market. The experts threw away the easy answer that Americans were just different, for the men who worked in American auto plants, coal mines, clothing shops were descended from recent European stock—Scots, Irish, Poles, Germans, Italians. It was true that the quality and quantity of American resources were matchless—coal seams five feet thick, the world's best wheat fields, adjacent to the world's best cotton fields, adjacent to the world's best oil fields were all linked together by one of nature's most extensive internal waterway systems. But, though this gave America a decided advantage, it was not enough to explain the spread that tripled American productivity. Europeans complained that they had suffered devastating inflation and two ravaging wars, but none had been as badly ravaged as the Soviet Union. And there lay the ugliest fact of all, as unforgettable as an aching tooth, that the Soviet Union was increasing her productivity far faster than Western Europe.

After much exercise at the problem, Europeans, too, began to discard old clichés. The French invented a word for the most offensive of their cliché-coiners. They called them the "N'y-a-que's." A "N'y-a-que" was a specialist who came back from America mouthing the phrase "*Il n'y a que faire*" which meant "All we have to do." According to these men, all that had to be done was to install forklifts, or pipe Muzak into the plant cafeteria, or design a new materials-flow system. But after listening to a long train of returning "N'y-a-que's" report their discovery of the American secret, the French finally decided there was no particular little secret that was the clue to the big secret. The main clue was there for everyone to see and every visitor reported it—Americans just worked differently, there was an indefinable spirit that made Americans work harder, more efficiently, better, more together. It was the spirit that was the clue.

There was another thing Europeans learned upon their investigations which surprised them no less than the Americans to whom they reported. It was that Americans possessed no ingenious device, or machine, or shop practice which their own best engineering minds had not already thought of; many of the finest American processes and machines had, in fact, been invented in Europe. Indeed, most returning European engineers could state, honestly, that there was usually one plant in their own country's industry that was equal to the finest America could offer. The difference was that in America the best technique was usually standard all through the country, while in Europe the best technique was exceptional and was applied as a splendid oddity in an industry that as a whole was archaic.

The best answers of all came from the American experts in the productivity drive, most of whom were practicing American businessmen and good Republicans. Over and over they singled out for condemnation two facts:

First, they denounced the fossilization of European industry. The general dictum at the end of any swing through a European industry would go like this: "They've got the boards of these plants loaded up with marquises and counts, and all of them are tied together in one big combine. They're so god-damned cartelized they wouldn't know *how* to go out and get business even if it was there. They buy from one cartel and they sell to another, and you can't shake them loose because they don't want to be shaken loose because they can always turn a profit in the same old-fashioned way because their cartel protects them no matter what."

Second, they were appalled by the waste of labor in European plants. "If I wasted labor," said one of the Americans, "the way these people waste labor, I'd be bankrupt in a week. They don't know how to use men at all; they pay them dog's wages, and to tell the truth they aren't worth more than that for the kind of work they put out. They've got three men doing every job I use one man for back home."

None of these American business experts ever worded the burden of his findings in terms of theory, but what they meant, most simply, was that the changes through which America had lived since the turn of the century had never happened in Europe. As Americans, they had either advocated or denounced all the reforms which had been shoved down the bitterly protesting throats of entrenched privilege in America over the decades and could not explain them to Europeans. But, finally, they had come to accept as completely normal the American industrial-commercial system created fifty years ago by the wave of turn-of-the-century trust busting which had rescued American industry from the fossilization of European cartels. They had even accepted the overwhelming development of American labor unions which has made American labor the most expensive single ingredient of production. Honed to a fine-cutting edge by the grindstone of competition, held rigidly in place by the demands of monolithic unions, the American businessman had developed something he calls the science of "management." But, in trying to sell management in

Europe, he found it unsalable because the pressures that had incubated management in America were lacking.

The productivity drive, launched with such fanfare in the fall of 1950, was already dead by the beginning of 1952. By then, a few Americans had begun to realize what it was they were really trying to do; they were trying to shake Europe up, remold her, reshape her drives and purposes. They were not merely trying to peddle techniques as they had originally believed and as the Europeans still believed; they were trying to instill in Europe something of the spirit which had remade America, and remakes her again, every generation. But by then the original leverage of the Marshall Plan in European life was gone, for we were no longer giving out chunks of four or five billion dollars a year; what we were giving was less than what our strategy demanded Europe contribute to the common defense. To bring about the changes we sought would have required a completely new American program conceived with the same vigor and the same resources as the original Marshall Plan. For what we wanted, fundamentally, was a revolution.

It is only a rare American who realizes that in his lifetime he has lived through such a series of changes in American life that amount to a peaceful revolution as stirring in its way as the Russian or Chinese revolution. And even rarer is the American who realizes that this revolutionary essence in our life is, or must become, the chief arm of our foreign policy to meet that revolutionary faith which is the chief arm of Russian foreign policy.

American purpose overseas is quite simple—to achieve peace and security. But in the chief area necessary for American security—Western Europe—the fiber of life has rotted and weakened so that it can resist the Communist message only with difficulty. Vaguely, and with some success, we have tried to help or compel the European governments to give their citizens those comforts and benefits of everyday life which Americans at home increasingly enjoy. But this has been done usually in terms of specifics—of financial advice, military equipment and training, engineering and techniques. Yet all these specifics and techniques are only the visible end-product of a generation of social upheaval and experiment in American life which, when it is not duplicated in Europe, causes our techniques to fall on barren ground.

Most Americans accept the faith of America wordlessly, for they live by it. America is, at its heart, the fluid society. It is the restless, unceasing desire of Americans that opportunity remain forever open, that society never lock in layers and classes of fixed privilege and fixed entry.

This has always been the faith of America. But this generation of Americans has kept its rendezvous with destiny by keeping opportunity open even through the growth, complexity and concentration of twentieth century science, industry and communications. Americans have done so in myriad interlocking experiments with their system—by the stabilization of the cycle that once made farming a gamble and not a way of life, by the powerful intrusion of labor unions on American production and society, by government fostering of research, science and education, by the spread of arts in every form all across their continental expanse; by the leveling brutality of their income tax, by the constant application of research and invention to the ever-expanding industrial capacity of a nation which has doubled its heft in thirty years, by new roads, new schools, new systems of social security. None of these changes were achieved easily; most were torn out of the country in fury and contention. But all have flowed from the inner spirit which holds that people must remain fluid, that society must remain open, that no group or groups must be able permanently to cling to yesterday's privileges in society because it profits by them and fears what comes next. It is this faith in the opportunity of tomorrow, more than anything else, which has kept America from any infection of communism. And it is this faith, totally lacking in some countries of Europe or unable to express itself effectively in others, which we have been trying, without realizing, to spread in Europe by the injection of techniques and "expertise."

The contrast between the Russian and American expansion in the modern world is one of direct opposites. The Russians sell an idea, above all their idea of the revolution and the logical state. Then, having penetrated with their idea, they follow to consolidate with their techniques, cold, brutal and bloody. But Americans bring their techniques first, the logistics and mechanics of their system, and they leave its mothering, begetting idea to follow naturally behind.

Over and over for the past fifteen years I have watched strangers studying American ways, as if by dismantling an American combustion charger they could learn how to make themselves as warm as Americans. And over and over I have seen Americans trying to show them how the combustion charger works without explaining that the trick is not in how the metal parts of the combustion charger fit together but how the combustion charger is used socially, and to whose benefit. In every possible different context, I have watched puritan and conservative Americans thus transformed by their efforts abroad into radical symbols of disturbance.

A classic example was the experience of General Joseph Stilwell in China. The government of Chiang Kai-shek wanted guns and planes and wanted only to learn how to use the guns and planes. But Stilwell insisted that they must learn to fight, which is quite different from learning how to shoot a gun or fly a plane. Learning to fight, he said, meant that Chinese officers must stop selling their soldiers' ration for private profit, that soldiers must not be kicked, beaten or have their ears cropped, that they must be well fed and clothed, that their leaders must be brave and daring. This was the important thing in fighting. He could not get the idea across, and thus Chiang's armies, for all their guns, could not fight.

Our experience in Europe has not been quite as dramatic, for no democratic government in Western Europe is remotely comparable in mentality to the medieval Chinese Nationalists. Yet, even in Europe, an American, behaving true to American standards, finds himself a radical. The last chief of the Marshall Plan in France was a tall, blue-eyed Bostonian—Republican and rather conservative—named Henry Parkman, whose duties required him to deal with a French Cabinet including three different shades of Socialists. His final months in Paris were scarred by a continuing wrangle with the French government, and the substance of that wrangle was public housing. It was the conservative American who kept insisting that the French government must use some of the Marshall Plan financing to push decent housing for its slum-sheltered Communist-voting citizens, while the French, all the while paying lip service to their progressive party names, wriggled and dodged to avoid the obligation.

Like all peoples, the Europeans hate being disturbed by outside forces except as they themselves invite these forces and transmute them into native political doctrine. But caught thus and eroded by the long-rising tide of American mass culture while suddenly pushed about to specific action by American spokesmen on mission, Europeans have felt somehow suffocated, trapped and helpless. The less able such countries have been to resist American pressure, as in France and Italy, the greater the number of those who hate us. The better able they were to resist, as in England and Belgium, the greater the number of those who still respect us.

What has baffled Europeans is that they see their need for America; they see the techniques of America; but the purpose and inner essence of American society finds no expression in American policy abroad.

The British, perhaps, show the result of this experience more clearly than any other Europeans because, first, they are the closest kin to Americans in language, tradition and institutions, and, secondly, because they have been subject less than any other nation in Europe to the invasion of American experts or the pushing around of American advisors. Yet, even so, the British like all other Europeans have seen the magic of America purely through its techniques; they have been hypnotized by forklifts in American factories, by automatic looms in weaving mills, by American shop practice in cadence, layout and hand tools. When either British Socialists or British Tories discuss educational reform in Britain—which is long overdue—they protest immediately that they have no intention of "Americanizing" education. "American education" is a mocking term among British intellectuals. They know American education as Hollywood shows it with drum majorettes twirling the baton, the football team charging out onto the gridiron from under the stadium, the fur coats, flags and coeds dancing in technicolor. Or they see it as refracted into a distorted image of terror by Congressional investigators and supercharged patriots. But only a few technical specialists and odd Americanophiles are aware of the larger purpose, of the tradition, the extent, the promise of the vast American system of public schools, universities, scholarships, accessibility, research. Yet, nevertheless, while sneering at American education and all its ways, Britons recognize that, still, there is something important in it. It is the selective nature of this recognition that is illuminating. Out of the whole battery of American educational experience, British educators are nearly unanimous in selecting two, and only two, schools to be imitated in the overhauling of British learning. These are the Massachusetts Institute of Technology and the California Institute of Technology. The impact of the postwar years has convinced them that in technology, only in technology, is buried the essential American message.

Europeans have, over the past five years, submitted to incessant prying, pushing and prodding by Americans. They try desperately to placate such Americans by agreeing to create a payments union that can link their currencies, to equip a division and place it as directed under American command, to stimulate the production of one commodity or embargo trade in another.

But every minute they do so they sense a smoldering, unexpressed indignity working within them, because America still keeps asking for more and remains forever unsatisfied. Europeans cannot recognize, for Americans never explain, that what America seeks is not simply technical innovation but something else. What America seeks are changes in spirit and society, of revolutionary profundity, that will meet the challenge of the black revolutions of this century. For where change has been imposed by dictate, as in the American Occupation of Germany, or brought about by native power, as in Turkey and Britain, the fiber of resistance to the challenge is healthiest. Where it has misfired, or crawled too slowly, as in France and Italy, it is weakest.

In theory, the burden of bringing America's influence to bear on the world should fall upon the Foreign Service of the State Department. These professional diplomats-by-career stand to the new recruits of the American community abroad as regular army officers stand to civilians recruited for war emergency. Out of approximately 15,000 Americans employed by the government in Europe, only 260 are men who have been trained professionally and chosen officially as permanent career Foreign Service officers to speak for the United States abroad. Theoretically, they should be in command, applying the policy of the elected Congress and directing the new machinery of experts and reserve recruits in its application.

Actually, nothing could be more remote from the truth, and few fragments of current affairs tell better of the built-in handicaps of United States foreign policy than what has happened to the once-proud Foreign Service of America in the years since the war.

The Foreign Service officers of the United States are recruited much as army officers. There are, at present, 1,496 such officers scattered around the globe. In taking their oath of office as young men, they accept a life and career that may send them scuttling from the jungles of Africa to the arid wastes of the Middle East, to the ricelands of Asia. Service in Paris may alternate with service in Léopoldville, Aden, Santiago de Chile, Calcutta, Trondheim or Melbourne. When they move, they move with wives and children, who grow up far from home in strange languages, subject to strange diseases and the neuroses of homelessness. All this they accepted with their oath of office; their job is to observe, to understand and to report accurately and coldly to the United States wherever they are ordered to go. There is no wealth to be gained in this career, certainly not enough to make up for two years in the malarial wastes of Accra, the steaming, fetid streets of Calcutta, the prison confinement of Moscow. At the end of his career, a Class I officer may earn $12,500 a year which is reduced to very little by the extra expenses of his position and constant travel. When he retires, if he has served well, he expects only two things —a pension, and a certain amount of dignity and honor because he has served the Republic well.

Today, it may be flatly stated that few men who serve the United States do so with less honor, less respect, or less reciprocal loyalty from their fellow citizens. In the decade in which the foreign affairs of America have become the most important problem in politics, the officers of the Foreign Service have become the favorite whipping boys of public debate. Variously described to the public as homosexuals, cookie-pushers, or just plain bunglers, they have been most publicized as that branch of the American government most infiltrated by Communist agents—this despite the fact that not one verifiable Communist or fellow traveler has yet been turned up in investigation of the Foreign Service.

To someone who, as this correspondent, has watched them for fifteen years in all the capitals that stretch between Peking and

Paris, no picture could be more ridiculous, or more directly at variance with the truth. In these years I have come across not one homosexual in the Foreign Service of the United States; I have found some fools and bunglers, but no more, proportionately, than in the United States Army or the United States Congress. Most of the Foreign Service officers I have known have been honest, competent people in whom has been rooted a conservatism of instinct so deep and so unyielding that their chief weakness as an instrument of the American purpose has been a stodginess and lack of imagination the very opposite of the radicalism falsely imputed to them.

In the years since the war, under attack, the native caution and conservatism of these men—with a few brave exceptions—has deepened until now it has reached a level of timidity which gives the American people a Foreign Service of eunuchs. Not only has the long attack almost completely demoralized them in their daily routine, and reduced their influence and impact on foreign powers with whom they must deal, but it has done so during that period when world affairs have forced every foreign ally to look to these men for daily guidance in American policy.

The beating the Foreign Service has taken is not, of course, accidental. It flows from the nature of the turbulent world in which America must live. For thirty years two of the major problems of American foreign policy were states and societies in boiling change—Russia and China. The Foreign Service, back in the pre-Roosevelt days of a Republican State Department, therefore, began to train among its younger officers specialists in the particularly intricate problems of those countries. Since both these countries were moving at a furious pace to ends no man could see, the specialists so recruited were among the more brilliant and venturesome young men who entered the Foreign Service twenty years ago. Both in Russia and China, these men achieved such eminence as scholars and communicants of the strange cultures they lived in that they evoked the jealousy of the foreign offices of every other nation dealing with China and Russia. In China, as a matter of fact, the Russians were so impressed with the China Language Service program of the American State Department that in 1943, in mid-war, they began to imitate it.

In both Russia and China, events then proceeded to pose problems for Americans which are among the most tragic and difficult of our history. In the long debate on our attitude to these countries, the reports and attitudes of the Foreign Service officers have since been published, aired, investigated and disputed, not for what they were—clinical professional reports on the progress of a disease—but in order to determine how much the reports themselves were infected with the disease. It was as if Americans, tortured and frantic with the growth of a cancer they could not arrest, turned with savage blindness to wreak their vengeance on the doctors who had failed to cure it.

What has happened to the China Service officers of the Foreign Service has been an object lesson to every other career diplomat, whether a junior aspirant or the father of a family waiting for his pension and retirement.

The basic burden of the reporting of the China Service in the critical years was that, in the inevitable clash between the Chinese Communists and Chiang Kai-shek, Chiang would be the loser. This correctness in judgment has resulted, however, not in honor either collectively or individually to the China Service. China has gone Communist. In some fashion the men of the China Service were held responsible. The China Service, therefore, no longer exists. Of the twenty-two officers who joined it before the beginning of World War II, there were in 1952 only two still used by the State Department in Washington—both had had the luck not to be in China during the war, or anywhere near the center of Chinese politics previously. Most of the rest were still serving the American government, but not in Formosa, Japan, Central Intelligence or anywhere else where their intimate knowledge of a China with whom we were desperately at war in Korea might be useful. They were scattered all around the globe. One with twenty-five years' duty in China was in Vancouver; another with twenty-two years' duty in China was in Athens; another with eighteen years' duty in China was in Guayaquil. At the moment of writing this book in Europe, all the postwar chiefs of the China desk of the State Department who have not been dismissed are stationed in London, in Paris, in Bonn, or in Rome—and are pleased with their obscurity. But while America pondered the meaning of each Chinese Communist gesture and statement in the truce talks of Korea, the men who for years had been assigned to observation of Chinese Communist leadership, and who had brilliantly succeeded in entering their inner councils during the war, were completely ignored at a time when their advice was needed most.

The Russian experts of the Foreign Service have suffered nothing like the indignity of the China experts. But the frigid official farewell to their most distinguished chief, George Kennan, when he was allowed to depart from the service, the humiliation and vituperation visited upon Charles Bohlen before his confirmation as Ambassador to Moscow only underscored what many Foreign Service officers have always believed: that it is dangerous to write seriously, or clearly, about an explosive subject. The cautious officer now feels that each report should be drafted so that no matter what Congressional committee reads it ten years hence, or what public controversy is aroused in later post-mortem of affairs, the report should be virgin of any strong, hence dangerous, opinion.

One of the most able of the political appointees added to the diplomatic service since the war was chatting with me once about a Foreign Service officer whom we shall call Lew, and who served as his deputy in the small but not unimportant country where they were stationed. I had known the Foreign Service officer many years before in Asia as a particularly forthright and perceptive man. His chief asked me, "You're a friend of Lew's, aren't you?"

I said, "Yes."

"Well, I can't make him out," was the reply. "He writes perfectly brilliant reports on the situation, all the facts are in, but somehow he never says what we should do, and I never know what he really thinks."

I mentioned the conversation to Lew and Lew laughed, dug me in the ribs, and said, "We've learned, haven't we?"

In one Central European country I met a young man of twenty-six who had just joined the Foreign Service, and he held me fascinated for an hour with his description of a new and dangerous situation I had not heard of before. I remarked that I certainly hoped the State Department knew about it. "Well," said the young man, "my chief is So-and-So." Here he mentioned the name of a fine professional diplomat who had been attacked in Congress and the press quite frequently over the years. "I like old So-and-So, and I think he's wonderful. But I don't want to write this in my report to him. They'll probably keep on investigating him for years, and when they go through his files at the Department, if my name is at the bottom of a report addressed to him on a subject like this, they'll link my name with his. That won't do any good so I'm not putting this on paper. I'll tell him when I see him next time."

During the course of the past seven years the candor and thus the value of the professional Foreign Service officer of the State Department has been reduced almost to the vanishing point. It has been reduced, moreover, at a time when, as we have seen, American influence was creating in the Americans-in-dispersion in the community of exiles and experts one of the most promising and elaborate new diplomatic instruments ever devised. It has been reduced at a moment when, as we have seen, the boldest and most revolutionary approaches are needed in Europe and the world to accomplish America's purpose of revitalized societies. But boldness is now the rarest of qualities in professional American diplomacy, for to be wrong is dangerous, and to be both wrong and out of step with Congress is disastrous.

The boldness which has, occasionally, broken through the timidity of the State Department since the war is almost never the kind of professional boldness which we expect of our generals in time of war. It is the boldness of the gifted amateur, of the man whose entire career is not at stake if a trenchant memorandum he writes now is published ten years later for hostile scrutiny. Thus, the boldest of American enterprises in Europe—its push toward European Union—owes nothing at all to the professionals in the State Department. Its two godfathers were General Dwight D. Eisenhower, invulnerable in his prestige to Congressional sniping, and David K. E. Bruce, American Ambassador to France. But Bruce was not a State Department professional; he was a Virginia gentleman, who had acquired considerable fortune in private business as well as much political judgment as a member of the legislatures first of Maryland and later of Virginia. Bruce entered upon his stewardship of the American Embassy in Paris with the wise and simple belief that because America was the kind of country it was, and because he was America's Ambassador, things should happen, American influence should be felt, actively, in creating the kind of world Americans sought. Of Bruce's two chief lieutenants in the diplomatic push that rammed through the Schuman Plan and brought the European Army and Constitution as far as they have come, one was a young Treasury official similarly invulnerable to the hazards of a diplomatic career. The other was a brilliant twenty-nine-year-old Foreign Service officer whose friends thought him too young and devoted to his mission to realize how far he was sticking his neck out.

At any mention of the European Army, one can arouse among the professionals of the Foreign Service the best informed and most intense discussion both pro and con of whether the Bruce captaincy of European Union was wise or not. But, although no one has seen their recent dispatches, it is quite safe to bet that only the rarest few have gone beyond the coldest reporting of fact, injecting neither misgivings nor enthusiasm into their accounts. No Congressional committee ten years hence will be able to charge the great majority of them with strong opinion one way or another; their dispatches are neutral. They have found it best only to list the facts, not weigh them, which is what the American taxpayer paid to train them to do.

What has cramped the State Department's professional diplomats, baffled our allies and reduced the usefulness of our wandering experts and proconsuls is something peculiar to the new diplomacy of the twentieth century which Americans at home only vaguely understand.

The new diplomacy which America practices is a multiplication of two things—of the orthodox instruments of power on the one hand, by the dynamic social ideas which beget them on the other hand. In this newer diplomacy, the older tools and servants of foreign policy are, whether they wish to be or not, bent to the service of an expanding, penetrating system of political ideas. The pressures that America exercises, fundamentally, on Europe are not pressures for specific gains or objects (although they always shape up this way in negotiation) but the pressures of a home community continuously overflowing and spilling with radiant, change-making energy.

In America, therefore, the true source of foreign policy is neither the President, nor the Pentagon, nor, least of all, the State Department. It is the people themselves, expressing their voice through Congress. While the President, the Pentagon or even the

State Department may be allowed to advise Congress or act in a critical emergency, in the last analysis it is Congress, day-in, day-out, that decides how American influence overseas shall be cast.

It must not be thought that the Congress of the United States is a distant comptroller of events at long range. In these days of twelve-hour transatlantic flights and easy Congressional junkets, Congress is just around the corner from Europe. In the first seven weeks after the Congressional recess of 1951, no less than 150 Congressmen visited Paris either on committee, junket, vacation or sharpshooting. During one period in December of that year, the Paris Embassy was warden to fifty Congressmen in the same week.

Before these Congressmen all the world trembles. Both foreign dignitaries and Americans-in-dispersion abroad look forward to these visitations in somewhat the way villagers of medieval Europe must have received their seigneurial lords—in a mixture of tongue-tied dread and hushed servility. At Paris, every visiting Congressman is met at his plane, his room is booked, he is supplied with French francs, given a map of Paris and an information kit. As soon as he arrives, he is provided with his PX card entitling him, too, to ten cent cigarettes, cheap liquor and gasoline coupons. If a Congressman wishes to pick up a few souvenirs for family or constituents, the embassy lends him one or two young ladies to help him hunt perfumes, parasols or costume jewelry. If necessary it will shop for him independently whether he wants a shrunken Indian head, an African drum or a Toulouse-Lautrec lithograph. If he is lonesome, the embassy has several chaste and comely young secretaries who know Parisian theaters and night spots and will accompany him of an evening. In case of emergency, when a rare Congressman, strained by his exertions, relaxes too jovially with unaccustomed French wines, the embassy has at hand several stalwart young Army officers to accompany him on the night rounds so that no chance encounter on the Place Pigalle results in hurt to the Congressman or affront to the dignity of the United States.

Whether present in the flesh or not, Congress is master. No paper is prepared in any outpost, and no proposal is ever received from any intelligent foreign chancery without forethought of how it will sound when translated to Congress. Long before Congress has reconvened in January, the overseas branches of American operation are already preparing "presentation" hearings. In some outposts overseas personnel rehearse mock scenes before Congress, with amateur staff actors playing the role of Congressman Taber or Congressman Reed or Senator McCarran to dream up the nastiest possible questions. Some Congressional committees, not content with the formal presentations, keep permanent men overseas checking on American operations. The Swiss government on one occasion arrested as a spy one of Senator McCarthy's agents who was alleged to have made an abortive attempt to trap an American diplomat in an indiscretion.

Everyone who does business with America knows that Congress is the true source of American decision. Some foreign powers now bypass both State Department and President in order to make their appeal directly to Congress. Though none has gone so far as the Chinese Nationalists or Franco's Spain, most of our major allies keep men in Washington whose job is chiefly to lobby and to entertain American Congressmen. The emotions of individual Congressmen can result in a hundred million dollars more or less for their strained budgets; they must be cultivated.

Given the freshness with which the American Congress has come to the scenes of world action, its record of statesmanship is imposing. The two most positive expressions of American dynamism—the Marshall Plan and the North Atlantic Pact—were both expressions of Congressional determination and understanding. Congress' instant support of the two swift emergency gestures of the Executive—the Truman Doctrine and the intervention in Korea—were, again, illuminated with wisdom.

Yet it is from Congress, too, that the greatest weaknesses of American policy abroad spring. For where Congress is strong is in the forthright act, the clear response to a clear issue clearly presented. Usually, it acts correctly. But where Congress creates weakness is, paradoxically, where it should be strongest—in the expression of American philosophy of which it is the embodiment. And in the multiplication factor of modern diplomacy—which multiplies the instruments of diplomacy by the social pressures behind them—Congress frequently comes close to crippling American purpose overseas.

Congress has been at war for some eight years with the executive leadership of the Presidency. For some fifteen years before that it was led, frequently over its bitter protest, through a program of social reform which many of its members, to this day, accept in practice but denounce in theory. In its surveillance and suspicion of the Executive overseas, it now insists that the Executive conduct itself in a way that will satisfy a range of Congressional opinion that can only be satisfied by the blandest generalities. The instruments of American diplomacy overseas are hobbled by their fear that an experiment may arouse Congressional vituperation, and that a blunder, honestly made, may become the subject of Congressional inquisition. They must, in dealing with aliens, limit themselves to the hard, specific demands of strategy that can be justified before Congress; they cannot—unless they are led by rare men like Bruce—incubate or underwrite any of the changes, social, industrial, political or educational which might fortify the naked techniques they offer instead. A Soviet Embassy is a seat of political infection; its political agents operate in intimate touch with and influence not just Communist parliamentarians but local revolutionaries and revolutionary parties. No American would urge that his embassy abroad engage in agitation and manipulation of political passions as the Russians do. Yet, even within the limits of decency, most American Embassies appear dumb and stuttering. An American Embassy cannot urge on or explain to other peoples just how American society is shaken up and reshaken each generation because the Congress of the United States finds such philosophy controversial. It can sell America only by pictures of white New England churches, which are safe; or with forklifts and cat-crackers, which are neutral; or lure Europeans with the "smell of frying bacon," which must substitute for the American message.

It is not only this split between Congress and Executive which weakens policy. American policy is weakened even more by the behavior of Congress—or rather Congressmen, as individuals—at home where Congressmen consider their action unlinked to the broader struggle going on in the world. No amount of carefully orchestrated American propaganda can hide from other peoples what Americans do at home; no censorship shelters American politics in their little follies. Yet these little follies, however small, when amplified and rebroadcast abroad speak louder than the Voice of America. When a Congressman like Senator Joseph McCarthy suggests that the most important American Ambassador abroad be given a lie-detector test, or when, by threat of Congressional investigation, he wrings an accord from a Greek ship owner, or when he sends two youths, entirely untrained in foreign affairs, hunting through Europe on a ten-day trip to discover subversion among men on the firing line against communism—his impact on European thinking and American foreign policy is greater than any Ambassador in its service.

Always, at every turn, the men directing policy overseas return to worry about Congress. It may be an economist who says, "We spent five years trying to get Europeans to export more to America and when finally the Danes started to sell cheese in America, Congress slapped a quota on them. Now how can I go back and explain to the Danes that Congress had a hassle over oleomargarine, and because they repealed the oleo tax the Wisconsin dairy people got hurt; so in order to sweeten things up, they promised to give the Wisconsin Congressmen a better break on cheese, which is why we had to choke off foreign cheese. Or how can you explain that sort of thing to people who make Sheffield cutlery in England? Or garlic growers in Italy?"

It may be an American public-information specialist who says, "You can't substitute propaganda for the kind of things America used to mean to the world. They used to think of us as a big, happy country. Americans always had this saucy attitude to life and the Europeans loved it. But now we act scared, we act nervous. No amount of propaganda can make us attractive."

Whoever speaks, of whatever facet of American policy, his theme is the same—that no action taken overseas has a fraction of the importance of the behavior of Americans at home, among themselves, as they speak through their Congress.

No sudden change has followed the replacement of one administration by another in the command of American foreign policy. In Europe the drive for Union that Dwight Eisenhower sponsored as general is being pursued with the same vigor (albeit in greater difficulty) under his Presidency. The gradual slowdown of the rearmament program which had begun at the Lisbon Conference in 1952, under Churchillian influence, has continued through the spring of 1953 in Paris with the approval of the new American Secretary of State. The slow conviction that America must open its gates to European trade, first recognized in the declining days of the old administration, has been hardened under the new—and runs into the same Congressional opposition.

What has changed, however, and changed fundamentally, is the opportunity. The death of Stalin, the first tactical tentatives of the new Russian leadership have changed the rivalry of the West and communism from the rigid contest at arms—in which we are so close to overtaking them—to the more hopeful, yet more difficult, contest of political judgment and shrewdness. To maneuver, American policy needs a complete flexibility, for it must be fast, shrewd, cold and imaginative. It needs, first, an Executive unblinded by its own propaganda, endowed with wisdom, courage and boldness. But it needs, beyond that, a Congress willing to let its Executive lead where it cannot go itself and a Congress self-disciplined enough not to destroy, by its domestic behavior, the spirit that supports its actions overseas. It is not too much to say that the future of the world lies less in the struggle within the Kremlin than in the struggle within the American Congress.

XVI

decision at Washington

One day in Paris the scholarly Ambassador of a very minor power told me a story.

He had collected the White Papers, Blue Books, Yellow Books, Orange Books and all the published notes and dispatches of the diplomacy that had led to the First German War in the summer of 1914. He had wanted to trace, day by day, the negotiations of the last six weeks before that great accident. For the First World War, he insisted, was an accident that might have been avoided, while all the horrors that have since followed have flowed inevitably from that accident as flame from fire. The Ambassador had been, therefore, naturally disappointed in studying the clocked and dated cables that went Vienna-Belgrade, Belgrade-St. Petersburg, Berlin-Vienna, Vienna-Paris, Paris-London, London-Berlin to find that, even with a generation of hindsight, he could not pick out the man or the decision or any precise moment-of-no-return when the war might have been stopped before it was triggered off.

But he found something equally exciting. It was an omission. For, if his researches were correct, said he, in all the published cables of foreign ministers, sovereigns, ambassadors and chancellors not a single European diplomat had mentioned the United States, speculated on its strength, or wondered about its attitude. Not only that—none of the published records of those last twilight weeks recorded the intervention, remonstrance, or initiative of any American emissary in the six great capitals to assert the will of America in the century which she was to dominate.

The Ambassador told this story in a moment of exasperation, adding, "But that was only thirty-five years ago! And now—now we cannot plan, we cannot think, we cannot breathe without asking first, before anything else, what will America do? What does America want? What can we do about them?"

The Ambassador was not unfriendly. He represented, indeed, one of those nations on whose automatic support America instinctively counts. What exasperated him was that he and his country were no longer fundamentally independent. They had been dragged by this century's events into an association that made them, willy-nilly, members of a community from which they dared not break and in which leadership was irrevocably American.

It is with similar exasperation that Americans sometimes look out on the world. They are annoyed like the Ambassador because they can no longer act independently and dare not break from the community they lead. They are upset because they cannot face, alone, a world of ever larger social-and-power agglomerations. Powerful as America is, she cannot ignore the fact that decisions are no longer made by single nations; decisions are made by a diplomacy of communities of nations, in action and in contest with other communities.

Let us look at these communities.

The two major blocs of power in the world are the Atlantic and Russian-satellite blocs. But beyond these are other sharply defined communities—the Moslem Community of nations with particular problems and aspirations of its own, the Latin-American Community, the Africans, only now emerging into an awareness of their own kinship, the community of peoples called India, called Southeast Asia, the Japanese, and the Chinese.

At this writing, America is no longer at war with the Chinese but is still greatly threatened by the Russians. It can count on the support only of the Atlantic Community and the Latin-American Community. All other civilizations and communities hang in the balance, in various degrees of disturbance and ferment, between ourselves and the adversary.

The simple listing of community names suggests the strategy imposed on the Atlantic world.

Defensively, it is to preserve and strengthen the unity of our community and defend it from Russia's effort of disruption.

Offensively, it is to swing the communities-in-between firmly to our side and then, ultimately, go on to divide the adversary's community from within and leave him isolated.

For Americans, in this strategy, Europe is the key.

It is the defense key because it gives us a line of resistance that starts 3,500 miles east of Staten Island and multiplies our military strength with powerful allies.

It is the offensive key because Europe is an association of powers who still wield far greater influence than ourselves in the changing civilizations of Africa, Southeast Asia and the Middle East, whom we hope to swing to our side.

The defense approach to strategy requires, above all, that Europe be kept content within the Atlantic Community, immune to the seduction and intrigue of Russian diplomacy. This brings us, therefore, to the two current problems of Europe which press like twin nightmares on the day-to-day operation of American diplomacy across the Atlantic.

The first of these is the recurrent economic stagnation of Western Europe; the second is the German problem.

The first complication—Europe's economic stagnation—is the most inviting area of vulnerability to Russian attack. Nothing is more eloquent of Russian thinking than the stability of their garrison strength in Central Europe since the war. It is questionable, looking back, that the Red Army's garrison divisions were ever deployed for attack at a preconceived date. It is more likely that they represented an insurance policy, a guarantee in the Russian mind that if an accident happened they would be able to strike swiftly and mop up easily, or, at any rate, jump off with an advantage while their home reserves rolled in for a second and finishing blow.

The NATO effort to purchase a counterinsurance policy was as necessary in our counterstrategy as was the Russian garrison in theirs. But this effort has been so costly and the emotion needed to force it on the taxpayer so intense that it has diverted the United States from the original interrupted purpose of American intervention in Europe in 1947, which was the Marshall Plan whose goal was originally set as the reorganization of European economic life. It is usually forgotten that the Marshall Plan expired in quiet, halfway through, as we have seen, without ever having finished its tasks.

Western Europe thus lies vulnerable today not so much to Russian military aggression as to Russian political-economic aggression. At this writing, the Organization of European Economic Cooperation reports that production in Western Europe, after rising ten per cent a year from 1948 through 1951, has been stationary since the beginning of 1952 and is sustained chiefly by the American boom and the domestic arms effort which is so unpopular politically.

Although the full political impact of a rising standard of living in Russia may be twenty years away—or even further—Russia's growth has given her powers of economic disruption which are immediate. Though Russia's masters may be unable to give their growing population for many years much more than their present meager pantry supplies, they may find it quite profitable politically to dump wheat on the world market, selling it cheaply to England, Germany or the other major European importers, at once, to cut them away from America. Though millions of ordinary Russians do not even dream of driving their own automobiles, Russia's masters may well buy up oil they do not need. They may find it profitable to take Persian oil at the Persian Gulf in their own tankers, swapping it for cheap textiles or capital equipment, in order to break the Anglo-American petroleum control of the Middle East. Other raids in the world market are equally possible. They would be disturbing in any situation, but in a Europe that marks time, socially and economically, as it does today, these raids could be devastating.

The second problem within Europe—Germany—is diplomatically even more perplexing than economic stagnation.

Since 1947, all American diplomacy in Europe has been erected on the assumption that Germany was permanently split and that Western Germany could thus be brought to mesh its strength in a greater dynamic West European Union. The rigid counterdiplomacy of Joseph Stalin made this assumption valid and permitted us what success we have so far won. But it now lies in the power of Stalin's successors to undo our diplomacy by undoing his. Should they offer to give up Eastern Germany on condition that Western Germany repudiate association with the West through

European Union, they might be able to undo all our work overnight.

This prospect of a Russian offer on Eastern Germany haunts our statesmen. But what is usually ignored is how deeply intertwined this problem is with the problems of Europe's economic health. The Germans, whether split or united, will probably swing to the power bloc that offers them the greatest opportunity to thrive and earn a living. Germany's amazing recovery has taken place in the post-Korean boom, when both devastated Germany and the entire world clamored for hard goods. But the Germans have not yet been forced to face a buyer's market, or meet the competition of the more efficient heavy industries of England and the United States. The slight downturn of 1949 in world trade found the Ruhr eager and avid to sell and trade its goods with the Russian world; a major depression might twist all German commercial aspirations in that direction. The Germans are a people not yet naturally and traditionally convinced of democratic values; while many Germans cherish freedom, many would willingly sacrifice it for other benefits. Behind the dignified façade of the Bonn government these contrary impulses clash. The problem of the division of Germany is technically manageable as long as the Western world is booming, for Germany reunited, no matter what compact is signed on paper, will gravitate to the most inviting and most vigorous of the rival blocs. In a depressed Europe and a depressed world, however, Germany, even staked down by our half-million troops, will be tugged politically and emotionally away from us.

If these twin problems—Germany and economic stagnation—are intertwined, certain strategic measures are obviously necessary to meet them at once.

The first is so necessary even from a domestic point of view that it needs no laboring. It is that our economy be so managed, at whatever cost, that no nineteen-thirty-style depression recur. A depression of this depth is the only thing absolutely certain to rip apart the entire structure of resistance to a Communist-dominated world.

The next is the encouragement of a system of trade which lets Europeans both trade in our markets and share in the resources of the trading world which at the moment is dominated by America.

It is impossible to keep Western European industries from exchanging what they produce with the Soviet world if they cannot squeeze through the tariff barriers of the United States to earn the dollars they need to buy our goods.

Yet, again, a third measure is the support of the movement toward European Union. This movement is important not so much because the German troops it promises may be useful militarily, but because it is the only authentic structural change yet proposed that may rock West Europe off dead center.

European Union, it should be stressed, is not an iron-clad guarantee of dynamic forward motion; it is only the opportunity. The use Europeans make of the opportunity depends mostly on them.

But the United States can help. It can help, technically, by underwriting on the American capital market the investment loans of the Schuman Plan already adequately underwritten by its High Authority, or it can help by tax concessions to American investors in such foreign bonds as are deemed in the national interest. It can help, even now, with money. Though the first enthusiasm for the Marshall Plan is over, the United States will be appropriating billions for foreign aid for years to come. At the moment, this aid is rigidly linked to military purpose. Yet if Congress would permit, once more, a flexible approach so that the sum might be used either for military or civilian aid, we might be able with far less money to do more good. For now, with the experience of the Marshall Plan behind us, we know where the bottlenecks are which must be smashed, where the Communist political strongholds are, what the argument is about, and we could earmark our grants, politically, not for relief, or for budget-balancing, but for specific social and structural reforms.

If these are the burdens on American policy, burdens equally grave lie upon Europe. For the Europeans are as responsible for the present peak of strain in the Atlantic Community as are the Americans.

Europeans have a tendency all too human to blame all their ills and failures on American leadership, as if the perils and problems which America crudely forces them to grapple with were of American confection, not the ugly face of reality. Sometimes their petulance has the same ring as that of a sensitive adolescent forced by a coarse parent to do his ugly, unpleasant, but necessary homework.

Much can be overlooked—even the European attitude toward the Korean War. Though nothing in postwar history, except the Marshall Plan, more swiftly raised American prestige in European eyes than our defense of Korea, no other American action was more swiftly transformed into a source of emotional criticism of America. Many Europeans look on the American effort in Korea as a twentieth-century reproduction of the Northwest Frontier between India and Afghanistan—a far-off frontier, held on a skirmish line between civilization and barbarism, which can be manned for decades with adventure-seeking regular officers and the sodden outcasts of industrial unemployment. For them, MIG Alley is the equivalent of the Khyber Pass. Although European soldiers fought on the front lines in Korea, no European appreciates the extent of American involvement, nor does he grasp the fact that thousands of Americans, drafted from the age of eighteen, fought daily in defense of a land which was not theirs, that the United States was strained emotionally and physically by a major war, and the dead returned with each ship from the Orient. Europeans focus generally, in their thinking, on the ugly phenomena the Korean War produced in American domestic politics, or on the exaggerated military burdens which American emotion demanded of them.

American diplomacy can—and must—overlook this attitude if the Community is to survive; it must overlook many other European failings and faults.

What American diplomacy cannot overlook, what it must hold Europeans primarily responsible for, is to provide the initiative and will to make of their own resources a new life. If the chief burden of America's diplomacy in Europe is to aid Europe toward the expanding, fluid society, the chief duty of the Europeans in this strategy is to make themselves healthy, to tear down what is ancient, or has become useless with age, and go forward to make opportunity for each of their individuals.

This is the essential drama of Europe, for there is fire in the ashes of the old civilization. America can fan it to flame or smother it, but the flame cannot be fed from America, it must blaze from its own sources.

The offensive approach to world strategy begins in Europe, too.

The offensive approach must start with what is held—the Atlantic Community and the Latin-American Community—and go on to acquire the friendship and support of the other communities that lie between ourselves and the Russians.

In most of these in-between communities, the Atlantic Community relies for immediate negotiation and bargaining on Frenchmen, Britons and Belgians, who are or have been established abroad in positions of power, or are about to withdraw from them.

Neither we nor the Europeans have ever as foreigners thoroughly understood these in-between civilizations.

These neutral blocs are usually included in the phrase "Free World" which is both misleading and dangerous. Almost all the people in these other blocs, steeped in poverty, hunger and disease, deprived of education and decision, are incapable of thinking informedly about the twentieth-century world, or of choosing their own governments. Anyone who thinks that world problems (which baffle even the educated West) can be wisely decided by the free vote of illiterate and superstitious peasants whose horizons reach no farther than the village well is the victim of self-delusion. Governments are imposed on these people and they persist and succeed, perish and disappear only as they draw loyalty and give opportunity to the ambitious few with the acquiescence of the hungry many. To millions in these countries, communism masquerades as true progress. The people of these countries seek chiefly that the governments imposed on them appear to be governments of their own, not governments of alien white men, and that these governments bring some tiny visible advantages to their daily life. Among such people, communism can take hold—but only if we, by ignoring reality, permit it.

Much of Western political thinking is irrelevant for the in-between countries. Freedom, as it developed in the West, was a unique growth that went hand in hand for two centuries with the development of science and industry. Most of the peoples of the backward world in their lust to create a modern technology are willing to skip freedom, in order more quickly to have the technologies that freedom fostered. Freedom may develop among them later, as it works down from the top to an increasingly educated, increasingly well-fed citizenry. But for this generation, freedom, as we conceive it, does not weigh too heavily in their choice. What they want is to be governed efficiently by men of their own tongue and training and led, however slowly, toward some of the wonders of modern civilization of which village gossip whispers.

The problem in the in-between communities is, therefore, one of transfer of power, a transfer of power from the hands of Atlantic government to the hands of efficient native leadership, followed by such astute maneuvering as will make these native leaders see that there is more to be gained by friendship with the Atlantic world than friendship with Russia. Such a transfer has taken place effectively in both India and Japan. It is being bungled in the Middle East and large regions of Africa.

Basic strategy must be to keep India and Japan with us, to soothe and smooth the transfer in the Middle East, Africa and Southeast Asia, and then, finally, come to grips with China in a political-economic effort to magnetize her away from Russia where her national interests diverge from those of Moscow.

This strategy, imposed on us by the world, must shape the tactical approach to each concrete problem.

To begin with, there are two wars in Asia to be settled, of which one, the Korean, now that the truce has been signed, approaches at this writing the stage of final negotiation.

The second, in Indo-China, will be far more difficult to settle. Examined coldly, it must be at once apparent that a healthy France in Europe is of far greater importance to the Atlantic Community than a sickly, sullen France bled white by war in Asia. If, then, France desires, as the majority of the French Assembly seems now to desire, to negotiate directly with the Communists in Indo-China, or if it means that Indo-China must be split in two as most countries on the Communist border are, then it is to our interest that this be done. For what we may lose territorially in Indo-China, we will gain in Europe by creating a France better able to lead the drive to European Union she launched.

Moreover, an Indo-China settlement permits us to move closer to another strategic objective in Asia. It not only liquidates a colonial domain repulsive to the Southeast Asian communities but brings about a general peace. And only peace in that area will permit the natural strains between China and Russia—encouraged by us—to reassert themselves.

Nor, if we know what we are doing, is the German problem, though the most difficult in Europe, entirely bleak.

Our interest in Germany is first to encourage her internal democracy over a period of years, and next to incorporate her strength in a European Union which she cannot dominate by brute force.

But, while it is still necessary that German social and industrial strength be geared into a broad, expanding European Union, it is, in our present position of military strength, no longer immediately urgent that German troops be armed and put on the line at once. We have advanced swiftly toward both objectives of German rearmament and European Union in the past years. We are therefore in an enormously powerful position to wring Russian consent to the more important goal, European Union, at the expense of the latter, German arms.

Moreover, the entire context of international affairs strengthens our bargaining hand. For the Russians, it is clear, are under greater strain internally and in their fermenting satellites than we might have hoped for several years ago. Never since the war have the Russians expressed such eagerness to sit down and talk with the West as in this year of tidal decision, 1953. It was to wring this respect and attitude from the Russians that all American diplomacy in Europe was so ably conceived five years ago.

So thoroughly have the Russians lost in Central Europe that it now appears they are willing to offer settlement on a basis which is almost as great a gamble for them as for us—the neutralization of a reunited Germany as a buffer between the East and West. Such a settlement, however, achieves none of the vital purposes of American diplomacy, for it again opens the opportunity for Germans and Russians to connive and concert together as they have done so often in the past. Our diplomacy has won a position in Europe strong enough to repudiate such a settlement, while simultaneously trading little for much in the interlocking of interests between East and West.

What appears to worry the Russians, fundamentally, is the specter of an armed Germany as spearhead of an Atlantic coalition. By postponing the arming of Germans, or yielding on it altogether, we can exact an enormous price. We can exact, in the first instance, the reunification of Germany by free elections which is necessary to bring the Germans wholeheartedly into European Union. We can advance, and possibly ultimately get, the next proposal on our program which is the promise of free elections in Czechoslovakia, the only people of democratic tradition in Communist grip.

The yielding on the rearmament of Germany may to many Americans seem a huge concession. It does, indeed, require the most skilful adjustment of our diplomacy so that the Constitution of Europe and the other organs of European Union do not falter or collapse because the European Army is allowed to lapse. But a reunited Germany, bound in social and industrial union with the rest of West Europe, under the surveillance of England and America, is a far more valuable quantity than a split Germany, with twelve divisions, trying to bargain her way out of our embrace by a separate understanding with the Russians.

There are tactical and interim solutions to almost every problem on the map of Europe. But only provided we realize that this struggle is to be a long one; that peace is not to be had by one climactic settlement but rather by a myriad of small ones, made and revised from year to year; and that no rigid military posture or investment in arms is adequate in itself.

American diplomacy comes to the world's stirring politics bearing two traditions that have confused and contradicted each other from the beginning of our country's history.

One is the tradition of the crusade, and the other the tradition of the deal.

It is the crusade we usually learn about in our history books—the brave words of "Unconditional Surrender," of "Fifty-four Forty or Fight," of "Freedom of the Seas," "Millions for Defense, Not One Cent for Tribute." The deals are less often honored. Yet it was a deal with a ruthless dictator that added the Mississippi Valley to the original revolutionary states, even as that dictator prepared to wipe out liberty in Europe. It was a deal that stretched the northern border of our country to the Pacific along the forty-eighth parallel although the nation had screamed "Fifty-Four Forty or Fight." It was a deal which settled the most unfortunate war in our history, in 1815, when three of the best poker-players of Congress sat down to undo the war the "War Hawks of Congress" had screamed into being. Only after the death of Abraham Lincoln and the seizure of power by the Congressional zealots of Reconstruction did victory, total and unchallenged, complete and uncompromising, become the major attitude of American diplomacy in the world. And only the ever-swelling power of America in a world that could not stay her made this attitude possible.

Today, America stands more perilously poised than ever between the alternatives of the crusade and the deal, at a time when our power is, for the first time in a century, limited by powerful enemies. The alternatives of crusade and deal reach deep into American domestic politics, too, for they aggravate the sputtering institutional rivalry between our Congress and our Presidential leadership. Since, in the emotional language of American politics, "crusade" is a far more appealing word than "deal," by corollary, the Congress of the United States has always been in favor of the crusade, while the President and his Executive officers have been forced, whatever their profession of faith, over and over again into the deal.

Of the crusade as a foreign policy little need be said. Its strategy is clear. It means war with Russia at the earliest opportunity. But its implications are obscure. All crusades, from the first adventures that bore that name, have begun at home, venting their wrath on victims closest at hand who may be real, fancied or completely innocent objects of suspicion. The crusade must then prepare the instruments of attack at a cost incalculably higher than the present huge burdens of defense and seek the opportunity to strike. It must strike not knowing whether it will carry allies with it on the strike or not. Under whatever name the crusade masquerades, "Rollback," "Liberation" or "preventive attack," it cannot be had cheaply. We might eventually win, but our cities would, in the process, become rubble heaps, our children die and our entire economic life collapse.

The alternative, the deal, seems superficially to carry immortal shame—the tolerance of the evil of communism.

Yet the deal need not smell. It is only shameful if it is approached naively, or in the spirit of friendship to be pledged with the enemy. If it is sought, however, on the only terms that the adversary might consider—as an interim solution in a long-range struggle until a new relation of force-dominance gives one or the other of us permanent advantage—it can be both shrewd and advantageous. For the Russians believe, by their inflexible mythology, that we are a world doomed to rot from within, while we know we are not. For them, in their thinking, time, relaxation and stagnation are certain to erode us into impotence. Yet we, by our thinking, know that the power not only to survive but to thrive and build a better world lies in our hands. By their thinking, the other communities that lie between the Atlantic and themselves must eventually fall, by their laws of history, into the world of communism. But, if we are wise enough, we can make this dogma as false as their dogma of the classless society. Their rigid laws of history and politics see no vigor left in our philosophy of liberty—which makes them that much more vulnerable, at every contact, to penetration by the acids of our free culture and thought. Our philosophy even when engaged in crusade must brook the constant internal penetration of their ideas and their faith. Their philosophy cannot be penetrated by our ideas and faith except by prolonged contact and the education of negotiation. The deal—made of the myriad little deals—is the easiest way of exposing them to the seepage of questions and perplexing alternatives which ultimately, we hope, will erode their system of politics, at home and abroad, into impotence.

Starting off from these assumptions, each adversary believing he will outwit the other, we can make slow adjustments, wisely, carefully, successfully, provided we do so under certain conditions of thinking and practice.

The first should be the realization that at no given date will it be ever possible to arrive at any one settlement of all the issues between ourselves and communism in Russia. What separates us is so vast, so many-sided, so difficult even to phrase in common terms that never can there be, in the future, a great peace conference after which all is sweetness and light. The deals to be made are little deals, separate, individual adjustments at points of greatest mutual irritation. The last time a war of conflicting faiths rolled over Europe in the seventeenth century it took thirty years of a butchery which reduced Central Europe in places to cannibalism before men arrived at a tolerance of what they felt were each other's abominations. Only then, without ever having settled the issues on which they went to war, did the antagonists abandon their crusading and resign themselves to adjustments on a day-to-day basis, permitting each ruler domestically to impose his religion on his own people in his own way. The issues of faith between ourselves and the Russians can never be settled; only external irritations can be adjusted. But they are important.

The second condition is that a program of arms be continuously maintained throughout the long process of bargaining, a program that does not jerk from impotent slackness to intolerable economic burden imposed by emergencies. Without such a base in arms, the adversary might find victory so cheap and tempting as to make impossible any reasonable adjustment.

Yet another condition is that America accept the fact that the chief vulnerability of the Atlantic Community now lies within—socially, politically, economically. To armor this vulnerability our allies must be urged and helped to change as we have changed in this half-century. Not all these changes will be in America's image, and many will be the subject of bitterest controversy both where they occur and within our Congress. Yet our allies must change if they are to go forward. The corollary of this approach is that if the burden of arms becomes too heavy for them to bear, we must not force them to carry so much that the burdens will crush the necessary social changes we seek.

A fourth condition is that American leadership, acting within the broad purposes laid down by Congress, be free to do so without impossible daily Congressional interference. For what the Executive must do is not only to think clearly and vigorously; it must adjust this thinking to match the maneuvers of the adversary, of the communities-in-between and of the allies we already hold within our community. It cannot make these adjustments if, at the same time, it must conduct an equally burdensome strategy of compromise and foreign relations with its own Congress.

There is a last requisite which is the most important. It is that America remain, or recapture, the image of freedom and the promise of prosperity. For, whenever the edges of liberty are nibbled in America, or whenever Americans fumble at home in their progress to a better and more vigorous life, millions of people trembling between rival attractions are shaken loose into Russian hands. No maneuver of the enemy in the long period of negotiations that may now be likely could hurt America in the outside world as much as political squalor or economic chaos in the homeland.

Which is why, now, for the first time in fifteen years the story of America's security lies chiefly at home. And why this correspondent, after fifteen years of following that story abroad, is coming home.

Le Lavandou, July, 1953

index

Soviet Dominated Europe
ICELAND
SCOTLAND
Edinburgh
EIRE
Dublin
GREAT BRITAIN
London
NETH
BELGIUM
Brussels
LUX
SEINE R.
Paris
LOIRE R.
RHINE R.
FRANCE
RHONE R.
GARONNE R.
PORTUGAL
Lisbon
Madrid
SPAIN